Successful, Low-Cost Direct Marketing Methods

**A Handbook of Highly Effective Marketing
and Direct Marketing Methods.**

~ Premises ~

· Money is not the criteria for the successful launch of a new product.
· Everything you need to know to bring your product to the attention of a
national marketplace is included in this book.
· This entire campaign may be created by writing less than
20 pages of material
· While this book is written in what seemingly is a very casual,
conversational style, it is actually heavily referenced and the level of
information quite deep. It took me 25 years to learn this, you are much
more fortunate. You can learn this in a few nights of easy reading...
· This book is a complete marketing plan.

BOOKS
THEY'RE EVERYTHING
YOU'VE EVER IMAGINED...
AND MORE!

DANIELLE ADAMS
PUBLISHING COMPANY

Cover Design: Chris Sandoval, Sandoval Graphics

Successful Low Cost Direct Marketing Methods
by Jeffrey Dobkin

Published by
— The Danielle Adams Publishing Company—
Box 100
Merion Station, PA 19066
Telephone 610/642-1000
Fax 610/642-6832

ISBN # 0-9642879-6-X 2495
Library of Congress Catalog Card Number: CIP 95-79826

Reference: Marketing, Direct Marketing, New Product Marketing, Sales,
Small Business; Product Development; Inventing, Brand Marketing
Lead Generation

~ ATTENTION ~
Schools, Clubs, Organizations, Business Associations, Book
Wholesalers, Distributors, Resellers, and all interested parties; Contact
the publisher for information on quantity discounts. Any person with an
idea, inventor, entrepreneur or small business owner should read this
book BEFORE paying for an ad, or mailing a sales letter.

Printed and Bound in the United States of America
— Printed on Acid Free Paper —

Successful, Low-Cost Direct Marketing Methods

~ By Master Copywriter ~

Jeffrey Dobkin

DEDICATED TO
~ PATRICIA R. DOBKIN ~
Who remains ageless.
As beautiful and radiant as the day we met.
She still knows how to make me smile,
I still know how to make her laugh.

To our three children,
~ Danielle · Adam · Nicole ~
They are the center of my universe...
and will be forever.

To my brothers and best friends,
~ Dean and Robert Dobkin ~
Our parents would be happy and proud of us all.

To the people of the Armed Forces.
Thank you for keeping us safe and ensuring
our Freedom.

To all who have tried.
Whether you have succeeded or failed,
I salute you for trying.

And to those who have tried and failed,
and have had the courage to try again.
You are my real heroes.

BOOKS

THEY'RE EVERYTHING
YOU'VE EVER IMAGINED...
AND MORE!

tm

DANIELLE ADAMS
PUBLISHING COMPANY

— In Appreciation —

To the following persons and firms, whose faith in my ability never faltered,
and whose trust has kept my business and myself alive and healthy. Thank you.

~ To The Entrepreneurs ~

And Small Business Owners Of America

They have risked everything for the chance to follow their dream.

It is through their dedication and hard work
America is the Heartbeat and Soul of Innovation.

~ Ellen Thompson ~

Serial Entrepreneur

www.247advisor.com

Ellen has been instrumental in creating my website, for which a simple
"Thank you" doesn't even come close to expressing my true appreciation.
Her realistic outlook on the success (and failure) in business is both refreshing
and encouraging. A true entrepreneur and a good and trusted friend.

~ Gil Sandoval ~

Sandoval Printing

9 Minnetonka Road

Hi-Nella, NJ 08083

856/435-7320

Printing and Graphics. I've known, done business with,
and trusted Gil and his family for the past 38 years.
Thanks, Gil, for continual great service, and highest quality of friendship.
And to Chris Sandoval: For his patience in having me as a demanding client and
his awesome creation of the cover of this book.

~ Robert and Jan Chevalier ~

Robert is the CFO of Corporate Facilities, Inc. a Philadelphia contract furniture
dealer specializing in Knoll Office Furniture. But it's his eagerness to be fair in all
his business - and his life - that has attracted and retained so many loyal
customers and friends. It's his and his wife Jan's graciousness that has made me
feel so comfortable on the many trips we have been on together. Thanks Bob and
Jan. Patte and I appreciate all you have done to make us feel at home when we are
with you, anywhere in the world.

Section I • Getting Results From Free Press

The Danielle Adams Publishing Company
Box 100, Merion Station PA 19066

Section II • Direct Mail

In Direct Mail Your Success May Be Just 42¢ Away

Other Elements of a Direct Mail Package

Lists: The Most Important Element in Any Mailing

The Danielle Adams Publishing Company
Box 100, Merion Station PA 19066

The Catalog Campaign - How to Get Your Product in Catalogs

Section III • Marketing Through Magazines

The Danielle Adams Publishing Company
Box 100, Merion Station PA 19066

Section IV • Ads

Types of Headlines

The Danielle Adams Publishing Company
Box 100, Merion Station PA 19066

Section V • The Ultimate Campaign

A Technique to Delay Brain Death in Heart Attack Victims.

Go on — save someone's life... read this chapter!

Target the Catalog Industry!

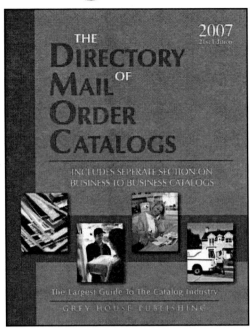

THE DIRECTORY OF MAIL ORDER CATALOGS 2007 21st Edition

INCLUDES SEPARATE SECTION ON BUSINESS TO BUSINESS CATALOGS

The Largest Guide To The Catalog Industry

GREY HOUSE PUBLISHING

Published since 1981, the **Directory of Mail Order Catalogs** is the premier source of information on the mail order catalog industry. It is the source that business professionals and librarians have come to rely on for the thousands of catalog companies in the US.

New for 2007, *The Directory of Mail Order Catalogs* has been combined with its companion volume, *The Directory of Business to Business Catalogs*, to offer all 13,000 catalog companies in one easy-to-use volume.

➤ Section I: Consumer Catalogs, covers over 9,000 consumer catalog companies in 44 different product chapters from Animals to Toys & Games.

➤ Section II: Business to Business Catalogs, details 5,000 business catalogs, everything from computers to laboratory supplies, building construction and much more.

Listings contain detailed contact information including mailing address, phone & fax numbers, web sites, e-mail addresses and key contacts along with important business details such as product descriptions, employee size, years in business, sales volume, catalog size, number of catalogs mailed and more.

Three indexes are included for easy access to information: Catalog & Company Name Index, Geographic Index and Product Index.

The Directory of Mail Order Catalogs, now with its expanded business to business catalogs, is the largest and most comprehensive resource covering this billion-dollar industry. It is the standard in its field. This important resource is a useful tool for entrepreneurs searching for catalogs to pick up their product, vendors looking to expand their customer base in the catalog industry, market researchers, small businesses investigating new supply vendors, along with the library patron who is exploring the available catalogs in their areas of interest.

This is a godsend for those looking for information." –Reference Book Review
"The organization, scope and continuous updating and revision of this work ensures its place as a standard reference." –ARBA

Pub. Date: December 2006 13,000 listings; 1,300 pages Softcover ISBN 1-59237-156-6, $350

Grey House Publishing
PO Box 860 ✦ 185 Millerton Road Millerton, NY 12546
(800) 562-2139 ✦ (518) 789-8700 ✦ FAX (518) 789-0556
www.greyhouse.com ✦ e-mail: books@greyhouse.com

Successful Low Cost Direct Marketing Methods

A Handbook of Highly Effective Marketing and Direct Marketing Methods

If you have an idea or product to market, you've come to the right book. This manual is magic. This book shows you step by step one of the most effective ways to market a product with little money. No experience is necessary. And no selling phone calls are needed - ever.

New ways to immediately start marketing are discussed in depth. A how-to guide makes your marketing and advertising more effective. The book is rich with ideas presented with exceptional clarity, in an easy to understand and easy to use fashion.

Unique campaigns are presented with explicit directions on how to adapt them to your own products. Where to discover new markets, and how to explore them. How to enhance your own current campaigns and make them work harder.

Discover procedures for exploring new markets; learn the rules for increasing response, including the reasons behind them. It's quite simple, really. If you have product, you can begin marketing it right now. Instructions are all included in this reference text. If this sounds like your dream I assure you it can be your reality. This book shows you how to achieve it - step by step. Anyone can do it.

Every product has an inventor. Just look around - everything you see was at one point a thought, a glimmer in a person's imagination. Some people worked hard and long to get their product or ideas to the marketplace, some had assistance and expertise from people who have done it. Some people hit a home run the first time they stepped up to the plate. Through these pages I've tried to increase your batting average, and make sure you're on the scoreboard as soon as possible, at the least cost.

Money is not the determining factor of the successful marketing of a product. If it was, Euro Disney and New Coke would be knee deep in profits. You just need a product or idea, a plan easy enough to implement so you will, and some perseverance. Throughout the book I have outlined in a clear and precise manner exactly what to do, and what steps to follow.

Don't let your early sales attempts be misdirected. Don't follow the path of so many who plan for failure: calling a dozen or so firms, then when no one buys their product, they give up. Having counseled many individual entrepreneurs, start-up firms, young firms, and small, medium and large businesses, I understand completely how devastating a few early sales rejections can be. It's very tough talking to people on the phone and having them say "no" to your sales pitch time after time - to a product you invented, are developing or marketing.

Ask any sales person - you've got to knock on a lot of doors to make a sale. For every "Yes" you may get a hundred "No thank you's." Sounds pretty dismal, doesn't it? Or does it? One positive response out of a hundred sounds like a winner to me. Kindly remember, a 1% response rate in direct mail marketing may be all you need to become very rich, very fast.

This book is based upon my founding principle of Multiple Exposure Marketing. It concentrates on finding qualified prospects through both established and nontraditional direct marketing strategies. Following up by a planned sequence of multiple exposures to your best prospects. All without a single selling phone call.

The Danielle Adams Publishing Company
Box 100, Merion Station PA 19066

Through skillfully planned marketing as demonstrated in this reference manual, your customers will raise their hand and come to you. I accept the fact there are thousands of people who aren't interested in your product. Fine. They won't call. There will be thousands of people who definitely will be interested in your product. And they will call. This is the way the campaigns in this book are designed. Use the step-by-step techniques to initiate the campaigns, and interested customers will step forward.

The enclosed method of marketing doesn't use any telephone selling. From the privacy of your own home or office you can initiate entire campaigns without a single phone call. So in case you have call reluctance, don't like the phone, or fear call rejection and getting the "no's" most salesmen get paid to hear, you won't hear any. Non-selling telephone campaigns are included for those who don't mind telephone work.

When you market a product, there are only a few moves you can make that are the most effective, the most profitable. Fortunately, with their correct selection they can be very, very effective. They are the basis of every marketing program I have ever written. Here they are.

~ Overview ~

Getting Results from Free Press

Generating publicity: Publicity is not just for the rich; the media responds to any well planned and executed campaign. What is it? How do you get it? How do you generate it? The specifics: how to get maximum free press coverage - and get written-up in as many magazines as you would like.

A press campaign is simple to understand. A press release is a short description of your product typed on a sheet of plain paper or letterhead. It is sent with a photo of your product to editors of newspapers and magazines. When published, it appears as a short story written by the publication, plus the photo.

The statement "everyone loves new products" includes newspaper and magazine editors. I don't know of any who don't welcome a well presented new idea or product. The pages of some publications are comprised of as much as 80% press material.

By reading this book, your chance of sending a publication a press release and having them publish it is unusually good: maybe 80%. If you'd like to see your idea or product write-up printed in a magazine - for free - the press release is the vehicle to do it, and the chapter on consistently getting free press is the way to go about it.

From the free write-up you receive, you're likely to get a few orders, plus lots of leads and inquiries: people expressing interest in buying your product or service, or at least receiving more information. Depending on the type of inquiry you receive, you'll respond with a direct mail package to entice them to buy. If you follow the outline of the press release plan, you can get multiple free write-ups, and get more inquiries than you ever thought possible at almost no cost. The direct mail chapter then shows you how to prepare effective mailings to these inquirers.

The beauty of a press release: the only cost is the sheet of paper it's written on, the photo, the envelope and the postage to send it. Unlike an ad that you write, design, typeset, lay out, and purchase magazine space for, a press release is run for free.

Bad news: Since the write-up from a press release in a magazine is free, as you can imagine lots of individuals and firms send press releases. Good news: Surprisingly this can work in your favor. Most press releases are not to the specifications the editors would like, and because of this are unsuitable for publication.

The Danielle Adams Publishing Company
Box 100, Merion Station PA 19066

When following the guidelines in this book for submitting press releases, your press release has the same opportunity for review and publishing as one sent by General Motors. If properly prepared and sent with a nice letter, your chances of having it published in the magazine may be even greater. Yes, even if you work from your home or a small office. I can't tell you how many brilliant new businesses have started this same way. Everyone likes new ideas, and most innovative ideas come from entrepreneurs and smaller companies.

> Writing press releases • Writing style • Design and layout • Photo Releases • Rules for correct presentation • Why follow these rules? • Targeting the releases to the correct editor • The editorial selection process • How to increase your chances of having your release printed • Actual campaign to have the best possible chance of getting it printed in your top 12 favored magazines • How to write an effective release, one that won't have the benefits edited out • Timing • Marketing campaigns using only free press • Submitting press releases • Getting maximum exposure • Writing benefit oriented releases to maximize response. Don't risk writing or sending a press release until you read this chapter of specific instruction and insights.

Direct Mail

The longest, most in-depth chapter in the book to market a product or service.

Direct mail enhances all other marketing campaigns. It's also the lowest cost way to enter most markets. Costs for direct mail campaigns can be well under a dollar to reach each of your very best prospects, on a one-to-one personal level, several times. You can aim an entire campaign with precision, with virtually no wasted advertising expense.

What are the important parts of a direct mail campaign? Which elements work the hardest inside your mailing package? Which parts of the package do you really need? And which ones don't you need when confined with a tight budget constraint? The results may surprise you: a simple series of letters may be the key to selling your biggest accounts. No fancy brochures may be necessary. Just the precise aim of a very targeted campaign of a series of letters. If you can write a letter, you can be successful in direct mail. If you can't, you can learn how to from this book. Or you can copy the model letters in this book and use them. Letters are included to help you market your product to catalogs, to your largest accounts, and to your biggest potential customers.

> Effective campaigns on a limited budget using almost no money • Letters as direct mail vehicles • Copy for letters and flyers • The creative package • The offer • Pricing your product • Tricks of the trade • Limited time offers • Lift notes • Setting shipping and handling fees • Increasing order size • Envelope teaser copy - getting your package opened or thrown out? It's up to you • Informational data sheets • Long copy vs. short copy • Lists - specifications, selection of lists for you to mail to, how to sell your own list • Catalog campaign, how to get your product in catalogs, where to find catalogs in the specific markets you select • How to submit your product for the best chance to have it included in a catalog.

Marketing

What the heck is marketing, anyhow? If you're not sure what exactly marketing is, you're not alone. The shortest definition I can think of runs just five words, marketing means "Selling to a defined group." Sales means selling to anyone. When you narrow your selling effort down to a targeted audience, that's marketing.

In a broader based business meaning, marketing includes everything you do to sell the product, and get it to the purchaser. So it includes pricing, packaging, distribution, advertising, press releases - everything. In the marketing chapter, we'll discuss marketing in the sense of finding the people who want or need your product. This is direct marketing, as addressed in this book.

Once you have defined who the people are that want or need your product, the marketing chapter shows how to find them. We'll find groups of prospects who are the most likely to become purchasers.

Let's take an example. If you have a product that water skiing enthusiasts will love, the marketing chapter will show you in clear and direct terms, an easy way to find water skiers, instructors, boat owners, water ski shops and marinas. Let's not stop there - let's find people who rent slips for their boats, jet ski owners & licensed boat captains. Obtain names of competitors in water ski events, and find people who have boat licenses. Let's compile ship supply store owners, and property owners with boat docks. You'll find campaigns to get your product into water ski catalogs, power boat accessory catalogs, and see if mailings to their recent purchasers will pay off. This is just to start.

Here's an unusual statement. (You might want to check this out right now to see if this really can be done.) Without any experience, using the methods outlined, it's possible to find all the people in your specific target markets in a single evening. Then the next day create a press release and send it to all the magazines in their target markets. Don't believe this can be done? Check it out - you have the book in your hands.

If you have a product that sheet metal workers will buy, or football players need, or florists can use - all these groups are easy to find, following the step by step instructions included. Any group you can define you can find.

I've taken a lot of marketing classes, read tons of books on marketing, and have counseled many clients on marketing. I've even presented classes on marketing. What I've learned is that everyone has their own ideas about how to market - and I can't argue with any way that makes you money, as long as it's within the realm of legality and good taste. In this book there are methods that will work for you, and there are strategies that will supplement and enhance your own marketing methods. They're plentiful. Complement your own style with these programs. And make your own selling method work even harder with the principles found on these pages.

Use this book to enhance your current campaigns to become additionally successful. Discover more ways to find new prospects, low cost ways to enter new markets, and increase your client base inexpensively.

If you have a product, this book shows you - step by step - how to find the people who are most likely to purchase your product, then several methods of how to reach these groups at an exceptionally low cost.

Marketing Through Magazines

Magazines give you wide reach to a market, but no depth. Ads give you big numbers of possible readers, but the very format sometimes makes a harder hitting sales tool (such as a direct mail piece) necessary to give prospects a more in-depth sales pitch. But to reach the numbers, the magazines are a great start.

Once you have identified your audience, you'll learn how to find all the different magazines serving those industries in the Marketing Through Magazines chapter. How to use the magazine reference books for this purpose, and the advantages of each are shown. You'll see which manuals to use where, and how to use them more efficiently. Searching for your markets will be narrowed down to about an evening at the library; it will be time well spent.

The Danielle Adams Publishing Company
Box 100, Merion Station PA 19066

This is the chapter that shows you how to do all your marketing in one evening, and how to execute the complete press release campaign the following day. In addition, you'll find the specifics of negotiating with the magazines for a good rate, and good ad position. This placement strategy is simple, and the rules follow logic and common sense. What to say, and exactly when to say it, will help even the first time buyer of magazine space sound like a professional. Finally, how to pinpoint the magazines in which you'd like your ads to appear - out of the sea of magazines serving your markets. It's easy once you follow these procedures and tips.

Marketing Through Magazines shows you specifically what easy-to-use reference tools are available in any library - to quickly learn the marketing function.

> How to define your Markets: figure out who you are going to sell to and where they are • Where and how to reach them • Easiest to use marketing reference tools, and the characteristics of each • How to use marketing references most effectively the first time you see them • Additional services they provide • Defining your markets • Pick your most likely target audience from potential markets • Primary, secondary, and tertiary markets • Different industries serving each of your markets • Specific magazines that address your target industries • Assessing each industry • Assessing the magazines serving those industries • Tightening the list of markets and magazines when you are getting serious • Good advertising and press months • Bad months to advertise • How and when to negotiate for ad space costs and position • Don't miss the one evening marketing plan • The execution of the entire PR plan the following day • How to analyze the magazines serving each market

Ads

The logical progression from a successful press release campaign is to start looking at magazines for the placement of an ad. Find the magazine that has the very best chance for your success. Generate some sales from the ad directly, then send direct mail literature (from the direct mail chapter) to people who have inquired, which will generate additional sales.

How to create an ad that generates the maximum response is easier than you think - whether you do this yourself or give it to an ad agency. Either way, how to achieve better direct response effectiveness is addressed in depth. Make sure your ad will absolutely positively be the most effective it can be.

> Making the ad yourself • Ad size considerations • Ad design • Rough and tight comprehensives, final mechanical • Writing the headline • Writing the body copy • Finalizing your ad • Most important part of an ad • Marketing with free gifts and premiums • Qualifying the respondents • Setting Response Parameters • Qualifications of each type of response • Qualifying the response you want to receive • Generating the response you are looking for • Lead generation vs. Direct orders • Make sure your ad will be 1. Effectively written - to receive the most response 2. Placed in the best possible magazine 3. Run in the most effective month; that 4. Ad space is purchased at the maximum discount you can get 5. Appears in the best position in the magazine

Plus: How to find a good agency. Some agencies are like boats - they are large holes into which you endlessly throw money. Some have never had a campaign for a client that made money for anyone besides the agency. They all look good up front. This is how you pick one out correctly, the first time.

The Ultimate Campaign

Using what you have learned in the other chapters, you are encouraged to create a winning sales campaign aimed at your best markets and your 100 (or 1,000) best prospects. As incredible as it sounds, is how incredible this campaign works. All you need is your idea or product, and to follow this step-by-step plan for an excellent marketing campaign.

You'll be able to introduce any product to any industry, to any marketplace nationally. Conduct a comprehensive multi-industry marketing campaign that addresses both a media campaign and multiple contacts to your 100 best and largest prospects. Note that there are NO TELEPHONE SALES PHONE CALLS used in this campaign. Wage an unusual print campaign based on my own proven marketing methods; use the same materials in any industry or market; sign on new inquirers into the same program at any time. It's a formatted, systematic program that can be expanded or reduced according to your needs.

There are hundreds of different ways to sell or market products. I have presented an easy to follow step-by-step method of finding and reaching people who need your products, then producing meaningful sales. It's a formula you can duplicate and use over and over to repeat your success with every new product and idea.

Ideas are presented for your immediate use. Implement campaigns to get new customers and increase your depth of exposure in your current markets. Then add new markets you've resisted entering because of the unusually high market entry costs. Get more customers and reorders. Get more and more catalog houses offer your product, so you can sit back and get checks in the mail. I've seen it happen to clients, and it can happen to you.

Learn hundreds of tips, tricks, and inside information about marketing that are presented in a clear, easy to understand style of writing. Step by step instructions on how to be effective in bringing a new product to market. Read this book in a few nights of enjoyable reading. Read it again and again for the wealth of information. Keep it as a valuable resource in marketing.

You don't need anything to start but an idea, a product, or a service, and the desire to make it happen. Call if I can be of any help: 610/642-1000 rings on my desk.

Please drop me a note if you like–or dislike–this book, or have any criticism or suggestions. It's only through your feedback that I can make the next edition better and more effective. I hope you enjoy this marketing reference tool and make good use of these marketing and direct marketing techniques. Feel free to write me (jeff@dobkin.com) anytime with questions or comments.

Written for

Those who don't know how to market products.
Those who know how to market products but would like
    to learn more effective ways.
The Inventor and the Entrepreneur.
The small firm with a product but little money to invest.
The medium size businesses with sales up to $40 million.
Corporate fallout who now look to market their own products.
Home based business owners. Owners of second income businesses.
Anyone who would like to get it right, the first time.
Anyone who has ever had an idea and said
    "This is a great idea, I could market this and make millions!"

    Well... here's how...

BOOKS
THEY'RE EVERYTHING
YOU'VE EVER IMAGINED...
AND MORE!

DANIELLE ADAMS
PUBLISHING COMPANY

~ Getting Results from Free Press ~

The press release is the lowest-cost, most valuable tool you can use in any marketing campaign. It's possible to run an entire marketing campaign on just press releases. This chapter discusses how to prepare a press release campaign. What exactly is a press release? How to write a higher quality release. An analysis of the secret selection process used by editors to choose which releases they publish. How to submit your release with the greatest possible chance of having it published.

Overview: PR as a Tool—the Press Release

The most effective you can be in marketing or advertising for the least amount of money is to use the press in your favor. Using the information in this chapter to create a press release, you can get a free write-up about your product or service in a multitude of trade magazines, consumer publications, and newspapers. It's easy, and it's really free.

A press release is a one- or two-page document that contains a brief write-up about your product or business. When sent to the editor of a magazine and successfully published, it appears as a short article that looks as if it was written by the magazine.

The press release—also called a "news release" or "publicity release"—is the starting point of every public relations (PR) campaign. The most basic tool of any public relations agency, a well-prepared release can generate thousands of inquiries and sales for the cost of a photo, a few sheets of paper, and postage. New product introductions, business announcements, and newsworthy items may be brought to the attention of an entire industry or a segment of the population by sending press releases to editors of magazines and newspapers.   This free publicity is yours for the asking, or at least for submitting a well-written release that conforms in style and content to an editor's expectations.

Press releases are written in a brief, newspaper style of writing. They contain hard factual or descriptive information about your product without much fluff—but if you're careful, you can sneak in a few benefits. A press release is not an ad, and glowing adverbs and adjectives cheering the product on with compliments are usually not welcome—and not included—if the news brief is published in a magazine or newspaper.

News of community events, business news, photo releases, press stories, and new product press releases that are written well are usually welcomed by the press, although they are not always published. Everyone likes new products, and the people of the press are no exception. They know their readers like to see something new, or hear about a different angle or approach to an older product.

In this chapter we will mainly discuss product press releases. Product releases are the staple of new product marketing. They are exceptionally

The Danielle Adams Publishing Company
Box 100, Merion Station PA 19066

low in cost to produce, and are published in magazines and newspapers for free. Writing a press release is easy; this chapter describes exactly how to write one step by step. At the end of the chapter, resources are shown where you can have your release written for you (if needed) either free, or at very little charge.

Because you are going to write the release tailored to your market, some preliminary knowledge about your audience is necessary before you start writing any press release or publicity campaign. Is your market high-tech? Are there special words or phrases you need to include? Is your release information general or specific? Should your language be simple, for a consumer audience, or technical?   Are you sending releases to consumer publications, trade publications, or both?

Your release should be written specifically to your audience. Consider which industries you are targeting to receive your press releases, and think carefully about which industry publications in which you want this free publicity to appear. Tailor your press release to the editors and readers of these magazines and journals.

Your *marketing universe* is defined as all the people who possibly need, want, or will buy your product. This universe is broken down into smaller market segments or niches. Over the next several chapters you'll be compiling a list of magazines that serve the different market segments. From the reference lists of magazines, you'll select the best publications that reach your target markets, and send press releases about your product to them. You'll also learn to focus on particular publications in those markets for a more targeted publicity campaign, or for possible ad placement. It's easy, and we'll go step by step. So even if you've never done anything like this before, the instructions will be clear. In fact, it might take longer to read the instructions in this book than to create the release and send it.

Ads can be very expensive to make up, and there is usually a substantial cost for each placement. A press release is written once, sent to a wide range of magazines, and printed for free. It's the shotgun approach. If you'd like to see a short descriptive article about your product published in a magazine for free, you'd send the editor a press release. Let's take a brief look at the media and at the specifics of writing a press release. In the marketing chapter you'll learn in detail how to find and select the correct magazines to send the release.

Trade Magazines Welcome Your Press Releases

Magazines are broken down into two distinct categories: trade publications and consumer publications. There are thousands of magazines that go to consumers, but if you think that's a lot, you should see the list of trade publications that go to all the different industries. Even seemingly small industries like "spray painting" and "bicycle retailing" have four or five trade journals dedicated to them. The larger the industry, the more magazines that serve it. If you think the industry where you work is boring, or the magazines your spouse reads are uninteresting, you have never read an article in the lawncare industry called "10 Points on Increasing Your Lawn Mower Sales" or "The Five Big Types of Peat Moss."

Of all the industries I have ever researched, the medical profession, by far, has the most trade journals. Including research journals, physician specialty journals, sub-specialty publications, and new products magazines, members of the medical profession are targeted by well over 3,000 magazines each month. It's a big money industry—physicians make a lot of money, hospitals make a lot of money, and the pharmaceutical companies make really big money. All this money supports a lot of advertising, so journals abound.

Most industries are smaller, and an average small-to-medium-sized industry like metal finishing or baking is served by about a dozen trade publications. Logic prevails, and the bigger industries—or the richer markets—are served by more trade publications. Medium sized industries like the pet industry or motorcycle industry are served by 20 to 40 magazines. Larger industries are served by up to 1,000 magazines. Fortunately for marketing purposes these classifications are broken down into smaller identifiable niche markets of specialities and subspecialities.

As a result, the trade press of these smaller industries is usually hungry for news, new products, and fresh ideas by way of press releases.

Since the smaller industrial markets are less rich, they are often neglected by some of the big marketers. As a result, the trade press of these smaller industries is usually hungry for news, new products, and fresh ideas by way of press releases. The chances of having your release printed in these markets is pretty darn good. It's usually in the trade publications serving the small industrial communities that your products and ideas stand the best chance of being featured in print through a new product release.

Reaching Consumer and Trade Publications

Having your publicity release published in consumer magazines is much harder than in industrial publications. Consumer publications are targeted by more companies to receive releases, and they certainly get inundated with free publicity requests from the bigger firms. If you've got a lot of perseverance you can usually get your release into the trade publications, but the consumer magazine people need more pampering. Their numbers tell you why. A medium size trade journal will do well serving 15,000 to 50,000 people. Circulation for a consumer magazine may be 10 times that—and still be on the small side. Consumer publications can have press runs up to 3, 5, 7 million, and more. Every marketer likes the big numbers the consumer publications have.

A Consumer Press Release Campaign Example

Several years ago I ran a campaign for a small firm selling wood-splitting wedges. We budgeted about $1,000 for a small publicity campaign, mostly to the consumer side of the home products market, but also to a few of the trade magazines. Most of those fees were for market research, phone calls, writing the release, and sending the release and letters. You could perform this campaign yourself and it would cost under $100. Let's take a look at this press release campaign, then at how it applies to your products.

First, we defined our markets and our audience. Consumer markets were (1) people who own wood-burning stoves and (2) people who have fireplaces. Both of these groups of people were likely to be homeowners. Next we identified our main target trade industries: wood-burning stove wholesalers and retailers, and fireplace accessory shops. We compiled a press list of which trade and consumer magazines serving these markets were to get releases. (Finding the publications serving any industry is easy, and is explained in detail in the *Marketing Through Magazines* chapter.)

From our magazine press list, we prioritized the top three publications in each of our markets. For a successful PR campaign we wanted a write-up in each of them. Then we noted the next dozen or so secondary publications we'd really like to be written up in. Then a group of about 30 of the next best publications. Finally, there were about 50 more magazines where we thought that if we received a write-up it would be nice, but if we didn't, we'd still enjoy waffles for breakfast the next morning. In all, there were about 100 magazines on our release list.

Preparing for a Phone Campaign

I wrote a short synopsis of what I was going to say to each editor, then called the top three. With this prepared presentation in front of me, I gave my general pitch: the meat and potatoes of the press release in a capsule version. I also gave an example, and a pertinent story that wouldn't fit well in the letter or the release. I was well prepared to make the call, and the whole presentation to each editor took only about two minutes.

A nice way to present yourself to the editor is to ask, "Are you the person I should send this release to?"

If you decide to make calls to editors, I've found that a nice way to present yourself to the editor is to ask, "Are you the person I should send this release to?" This sets up the nature of the call as being, "Can you help me?" which is a pretty friendly platform to work from.

If the editor was friendly and sounded unhurried, I gave him the one- minute spiel I had outlined in my notes. If he was curt or sounded busy, I told him I would send the release, briefly mentioned the product that was being introduced (so he would recognize it when he saw the release, and remember he got a call about it), and thanked him for his time.

Later that day I sent a telegram to the top three editors thanking them for receiving my call and for their interest in the product—even if there wasn't any.

The next day the top three magazine editors received an overnight letter alerting them that the president of the firm I was working with had been advised of their interest in our product, and that samples would be arriving shortly. It sounded as if a big firm had hired me. Truth is, the firm had only one part-time employee besides the president (owner) who manufactured the splitting wedges in his basement tool shop.

The following day, the editors received a two-page letter reiterating what I had told them on the phone, the press release, a photo, and a brochure of the product. I also informed them that several samples were being shipped to them under separate cover. Consumer magazines received the consumer release showing the retail price and our toll-free ordering number, and industrial magazines received a release slanted toward the wholesale trade.

We shipped editors about a half-dozen product samples with a nice note asking them and their staff to test out the product in field conditions. They received the samples the third or fourth day after the initial call. We also included a note saying that a dozen more free samples were available if they returned the card we included. To make it easy for them, we pre-typed their name on the card and included a postage-paid self-addressed envelope. This insurance was cheap: each product cost the firm only about three dollars to manufacture. If an editor requested the samples, we felt a write-up of our product was assured.

This was our primary campaign, and what we lacked in money we made up for in hard work: personalizing as many elements as we could, pre-addressing the order card for samples, etc. We showed them our diligence by creating a well-thought-out campaign. We let them know that we cared, and that we would be a good firm with which to work. It was evident that a lot of personal effort went into each package the top editors received.

The 9 secondary publications got everything in the initial campaign but the phone call. The 30 tertiary publishers got the letter, the release, the photo, and a card to get a few samples. The next 50 got the letter, the release, and the photo along with a post card (not pre-typed) for one free sample. "Yes! Send me a free sample!" our cards said. Sure enough, only the people who took us up on our free sample offer gave us a write-up.

You Can Achieve These Results, Too

We received a full 1/3-page write-up in one of the top three magazines. Our release was published in the new product section of another—which was a real hot spot for the magazine. The release was picked up and published by a dozen other magazines in both the consumer and industrial markets.

The Danielle Adams Publishing Company
Box 100, Merion Station PA 19066

In some consumer markets, your chance to get published in the bigger magazines is about the same as shaking hands with the Pope—it can be accomplished, but only with great effort and sometimes a great deal of expense.

If my client had purchased ad space equivalent to the number of lines of coverage we received, it would have cost about $10,000. In the consumer magazine that gave us a 1/3-page write-up, ad space sold for about $12,000 a page. My client sold over $8,000 worth of products from that single write-up alone. You can do as well (or better) with your own press release.

We were successful because we ran a good, tight campaign with creative thought, structure, and effort behind it. In addition, we offered a quality product. But sometimes even a good product and a strong campaign are not enough. Some select industries and the industry publications that serve them are inundated with releases. In some consumer markets, your chance to get published in the bigger magazines is about the same as shaking hands with the Pope—it can be accomplished, but only with great effort and sometimes a great deal of expense.

As hard as it is to generate publicity in some of the bigger, richer magazines, that's how easy it is in some of the smaller publications. I recommend targeting smaller markets and smaller circulation publications to begin with—you have a terrific chance of seeing your release printed the very first time you send one. There are thousands of small publications that will be pleased to receive your release and more than happy to publish it—you just need to ask the right way.

Defining the Product Release

Of all the different kinds of press releases—such as those announcing new store openings, community events, public appearances, news, business news, and personnel promotions—the ones we'll focus on are about products. This book is mostly about product marketing, although a good deal of what is written may be applied to marketing a service. You can use this information whether you are marketing to consumer or industrial markets, and the techniques are effective whether you send releases to newspapers or magazines.

Product releases are one- or two-page documents, typewritten and double spaced, that contain a description of your product. You send one to an editor along with a black-and-white photo (or color transparency, if the magazine warrants it) of the product. About 95 percent of press releases are only one page in length, and I recommend you limit most of your releases to one page. However, there are feature releases that run longer and are more in-depth. Feature releases can run as a story and are more common in newspapers, which publish a volume of such information on a daily basis. Feature stories work well in some sections—like travel and auto.

Some types of releases don't contain photos, but most product releases do. The photo you include is important because it instantly represents your products and firm with a visual graphic. For a photo to be usable, it must be clean, sharp, and in focus. Product photos are best in black and white in a 5" x 7" or 8" x 10" format. Use a glossy photo, with enough room surrounding the actual product in the photograph to allow the magazine to crop or cut the photo to size. This allows the photo to fit into the editor's available space requirement, which may be vertical or horizontal. The better the fit, the more likely to be published.

Ads vs. Press Releases

There's a big difference between an ad and a press release. In an ad, you say anything you want, use any type of photo or illustration, create a border—or no border—and have it look exactly as you wish. When you send it to the publication, you are guaranteed to be in the issue of the magazine you select. You also have to buy the space in the magazine; you pay for the ad to appear. Ever see a nine-square-inch piece of paper worth about $2,000? If you placed an ad you probably did. You can pretty much put anything within the realm of legality and good taste in your ad, and some magazines don't even care about that. The magazine publishes it, and sometimes you get a terrific response that covers its cost. Those are the ads you see running time and time again, year after year.

A release is submitted to a magazine. Just the word "submit" should tell you something: Press releases are considered editorial material and reflect the writing style of the magazine. The editor publishes the release in the magazine's own typeface, and the writing conforms to the style of its other columns. When published, your release appears to have been written by the magazine.

In politics, and in the movie and music industries, releases about people or events are the norm—the people are the product. The most common type of release in the rest of the world is the product release. If you have a product to market, the traditional product release is a basic marketing tool. For our own purposes, the biggest difference between an ad and a press release is that the release is published in a magazine for FREE. And since it's printed as editorial it has excellent credibility.

Depending on the type of release (news brief, product release, business expansion, personnel change, promotion, or new owner), press releases usually appear in a section of the magazine with other releases of the same category. Most trade magazines have a special new-product section where the photo is printed, directly followed by the write-up (sometimes called the "blurb" or "edit" by industry personnel) you have submitted. When selected for publication, if your copy wasn't written in the magazine's editorial style, it will be edited and tailored to the magazine's format. Why do you think they call them editors?

Recognizing a Published Release

You can probably recognize a release when you see it. It looks like a one- , two-, or three-paragraph article about a person, place, or thing. Feature releases are longer and run as a story. Releases are always printed in the magazine's own typestyle and are usually accompanied by a photo. Lots of times when you see a short article in the newspaper and ask yourself, "Why the heck did they write about that?" It's a press release.

To see examples of press releases you only have to turn to the entertainment section of any newspaper. Outside of reviews, probably about 90 percent to 95 percent of the stories printed on these pages are press releases or feature stories, written by public relations firms or press agents. These can be stories about rock groups, movies, screen personalities, or new album releases. The PR pump in the entertainment industry is voluminous. This industry lives on PR.

> # In newspapers— except for the first few pages—probably about 20% or 30% of the stories are generated from press releases or press feature articles.

Take another example. When you see a model of a car written up in the newspaper, do you think the paper sent a reporter and photographer to the car showroom to write about that particular vehicle? No. The automobile manufacturer sent the photo and news brief to the car editor, who ran it as a short story. In newspapers—except for the first few page—probably about 20 percent or 30 percent of the stories are generated from press releases or press feature articles. In some publications, up to 80 percent of the stories are releases. Feature articles are simply manufactured stories, sent to publishers and run as features.

Your Chances of Being Published

Let's talk percentages for a minute. My firm marketed identification tags to the pet industry. The pet trade magazine press was always hungry for new products and usually welcomed our product releases. The chance of our firm getting a product photo and write-up into print was approximately 80 percent for each publication.

Why was this? Well, we were known to the industry. The pet market was the primary industry where most of the products we manufactured were sold. Another reason was that we weren't submitting releases all the time, so when we did send one, it was particularly newsworthy and had a higher value as a submission to the editor. Publications like to print material from a number of new firms. This shows their readers that they cover news, events, and products from a wide variety of sources.

But take a different industry, like the car industry. The big guns in the automotive industry, those who purchase most of the pages of advertising, are the automobile manufacturers. Between new car models and the new accessories being introduced every year, they always have something new. I wouldn't be surprised if an editor for an automotive magazine receives about a dozen new product releases from EACH car manufacturer EACH MONTH. Of course, they can't print them all or they'd sound like a house publication or an ad for that manufacturer. But they have to print some. They can't ignore their advertisers—the manufacturers are the major sponsors of the magazines. They purchase the bulk of the publication ad space as well as sponsor the major industry events. You can imagine the volume of releases editors get from these giant firms. Then there are accessory manufacturers, hard parts manufacturers, and aftermarket part companies of every sort. They all send releases, every month.

It is always easy to tell when the car manufacturers want to get a new vehicle written up by the consumer media. First, they schedule a news conference in, say, Hawaii. They send all the top editors plane tickets and complimentary hotel room reservations. When the editors land in

Hawaii, they get the new car the company wants to introduce—the one the editors are going to write about. The editors then have the chance to "demo" the brand- new car for the three days they are there. The actual news conference (complete with a press kit that includes 8" x 10" glossy photos, press releases, and feature articles already written for the editors and ready to run) is held on the last evening, right before the big dinner at the nice hotel. The really nice dinner, at the really nice hotel. Get the idea?

But don't get depressed or discouraged. There's room for free write-ups for those of us on limited budgets, and room for those with no budget, too. Here's how to get your press release published.

How To Write a Press Release That Gets Published

Lesson 1. Stick to the traditionally accepted format. The closer you can stay to the professionally accepted format, the better your chances of getting into print. Start with a blank sheet of white paper, or use your letterhead. The parts of the release are the header, the headline, and the body copy.

Header

The header contains information about the release that is not part of the actual product news. This includes the release date; the name of the person who wrote the release; the name of a contact person, with a phone number, for additional information; and a release number. I like to include a company name and phone number, although some of my colleagues would argue this point. All of this information appears on the right-hand side of the page, with one piece of information per line for easy referencing by the editor. This also creates a white space on the left of the page, where an editor can make notes and mark instructions.

Above the header, print "Press Release" in big letters across the top of the page. If you are typing on a typewriter and you have boldface, this is the time to use it. If you have only one style of type on your typewriter, type "PRESS RELEASE" in capital letters by itself on the top left of the page, with all the other header information on the right—this will make it stand out. A banner heading of "PRESS RELEASE" will allow the editors to put it in that big pile on their desk, or in that special drawer with all the other releases, or do whatever they do with them. But at least they'll do it without having to squint and wonder what the heck that particular piece of paper is. So give them a break. Let them know what it is right up front.

The Danielle Adams Publishing Company
Box 100, Merion Station PA 19066

— FOR IMMEDIATE RELEASE —

DM Methods/Small Business 2/8
More Information - Jeffrey Dobkin (President) at
Danielle Adams Publishing · 610/642-1000
jeff@dobkin.com · No Kill Date!

Header

New Book Helps Small Businesses Market Products

Successful Low Cost Direct Marketing Methods is a step-by-step low cost action plan for marketing a product nationally without phone calls. Readers can learn the insider secrets of direct marketing in a few evenings of enjoyable reading. Information-rich text and examples are crammed into a 2 lb., easy-to-follow marketing tool and reference book.

Biggest benefit in headline.

"Anyone can market a product nationally, working just by themselves, from their home or small office," says the author, Jeff Dobkin, who spent over two years researching and writing the reference data. The methods in the book provide in-depth direct marketing techniques to increase the effectiveness - AND lower the cost - of any PR, marketing, direct marketing, or advertising campaign for new or existing programs.

Benefit.
Benefit.

"A few evenings with this book will change the way you market products, forever—I promise you. You'll never, ever even consider going back to your old style of marketing again," says Dobkin. A 100% satisfaction guarantee is offered with every copy, and Mr. Dobkin reminisces, "Yep, I got one back, I think it was last year, sometime."

Guarantee.

The book is written to make it easy for anyone to bring a product to market including inventors and corporate entrepreneurs, home-office businesses, and owners of small businesses with up to about 20 employees. It's a review course for big business owners. The heavily referenced book is also for the professional marketer looking for innovative and new low-cost marketing techniques. *Direct Marketing Strategies* provides a firm foundation in marketing - with plenty of examples - then offers advanced techniques in traditional and non-traditional marketing methods.

Establish additional need.

Among the unusual marketing techniques discussed are how to do all your marketing in a single evening, and how to complete your entire publicity campaign the following day - even working by yourself. No brochure? You don't need one to use Jeff Dobkin's unusual marketing techniques. The last chapter is an easy-to-follow national marketing plan.

Benefit.

Benefit repeated.

This book is almost 400 pages of information-rich reading in Mr. Dobkin's breezy, conversational style of writing, filled with inside secrets and practical direct marketing methods. "You've never learned this stuff in college. It's lean and concise marketing information," says Dobkin. "You know the boring historical part you always skipped over in your college textbooks? I left that part out."

Complete ordering information.

Successful Low Cost Direct Marketing Methods (ISBN:09642879-6-X) is available for $24.95 + $4 shipping from the Danielle Adams Publishing, Box 100-Dept ____ Merion Station, PA 19066. Phone 610-642-1000, 800-234-IDEA. Visit www.dobkin.com. Publisher guarantees satisfaction.

###

Ordering Info ### indicates end of release.

PRESS RELEASE

For Release: EMS —11/08— No Kill Date
Additional Information: Jeff Dobkin, President
The Danielle Adams Mail Order Company
610/642-1000

Disaster Emergency I.D. Tags Keep Kids Safe

Instant Write-On™ Identification Tags can instantly help locate a lost, confused, or injured child's parents, friends, or group. Once completed with medical information, emergency identification tags can save a child's life in a medical emergency.

Hurricanes in Florida, earthquakes in San Francisco, mudslides in L.A., floods in Georgia - natural disasters instantly create emergency conditions for millions of children. While no one can fully prepare for a full-scale disaster, Danielle Adams Instant Write-On™ I.D. Tags equip EMS teams to better handle large-scale upsetting forces that may involve reuniting lost children and parents - with a low-cost, easy-to-use child identification system.

Instant Write-On™ Tags will accept emergency information written with any pen. The child's name, parents' names, phone numbers, any medical conditions, or the building where the child is staying can be written on the specially prepared plastic. The tags are folded and latched closed, keeping the information clean, safe, and securely locked inside. Tags lace onto a child's shoes or sneakers in a <u>closed and locked</u> position - **for the child's safety, the name and address are completely concealed**; the tag itself remains *highly* *visible* to provide emergency information fast.

In non-emergency times, the I.D. tags make great low-cost giveaways for traveling children. Knowing a home address in Chicago won't help if a child gets lost while staying in another city. Parents can write a local address on the tag - if a traveling child is lost or injured, they are always carrying a local phone number. Private labeling identification tag with your group name, a sponsor's name, or both printed on each tag is available.

Wholesale cost is under $39 per hundred, including private label. Free samples are available on letterhead requests. Please write to Danielle Adams Mail Order Company, Inc., P.O. Box 100 Dept ___, Merion Station, PA 19066. Call 610/642-1000 or toll free 800-234-IDEA for more information.

###

A recommended alternative: Instead of the big "Press Release" heading, type "FOR IMMEDIATE RELEASE," if it is, in large letters or boldface. This will also alert the editor that it's a press release. At the same time, it tells the editor it's OK to run the release right away, in the issue he is working on RIGHT NOW. So if there is an editorial space to fill in the issue on their desk, your release has a good chance of being included.

If you have a future date for a new product introduction, and you want all the press releases to appear in all publications at the same time, write the specific date you'd like the release published: "FOR RELEASE JANUARY '08," or whatever date you'd like. Editors recognize this and will usually honor your wishes. For best results, 95 percent of your releases should be "FOR IMMEDIATE RELEASE."

Type your name in the header, preceded by the words "For Additional Information Contact," so if editors need more information, it will be easy for them to find an immediate resource to call. Include your phone number, start date (or today's date), and kill date—the date after which you no longer want them to run your release. For example, if your release is about an event, the kill date would be the day after it is held. If the release can run anytime, specify "No Kill Date." Having this information presented concisely makes it look like you send a lot of releases. A tight press release format makes you look like a big company, and big companies are always sending lots of releases. This makes you look more reputable and builds your credibility.

Give each publicity release a number in the header so you or the editor can identify it from other releases. You can make it up, like I do. Everyone has their own system, and mine has been working well for my firm and my clients for many years. If editors call you and have a question, they can refer to the release number, and you'll immediately know which release they're talking about. The release number I assign is the month and year, and the first characters of the industry, then C for consumer publications or T for trade magazines. So a release number for a new camera strap we are marketing to consumers may look like this: "Release number 11/8PC," where 11 = Nov, and 8 = 2008), P = Photo Industry, and C = Consumer publication. If you are marketing several products to one industry, you may simply precede the release number by the product name: "Camera Strap Release 11/8PC."

Writing the Headline and Body Copy

Write a brief, catchy headline describing your product. This can be your product name plus your biggest benefit, brief description, or biggest selling feature. A good headline tells the story. For example: "New spark plug reduces emissions." Or "Oversized tennis racket reduces tennis elbow." If the editors don't like this heading, it's easy for them to change it, and they probably will. No problem. So unlike an ad, while the headline is important, there is a strong chance it will be changed.

The traditional style of writing any release is in a brief newspaper format. Answer the questions of who, what, when, and where—and if you can say it in a short form; how and why.

The body copy of the release then keeps to the facts, like a newspaper story—even when writing for magazines. Like traditional newspaper stories, press releases are written in what's called an inverted pyramid style—the biggest facts and most important elements are first, and the rest of the paragraph supports or explains the first facts with less important information. Still smaller details follow. For example: "Car crash kills two. The expressway was tied up for hours today when a crash occurred at ten in the morning...." The entire release is written in this inverted pyramid style—with all the important elements shown first. This can definitely work to your advantage.

The Benefits-First Release

Here's another option. This is the Jeff Dobkin press release, and I call it the Benefits-First Release. Naturally, it's benefit-rich, because in direct marketing, it's the benefits that sells products. Begin your release by mentioning the product briefly, then immediately follow this with the biggest one or two benefits it offers readers. This is not traditional, and you may elect to stay in a more traditional inverted pyramid format. But I've had pretty good success with this, as long as the writing is brief and it sounds like news.

Remember, the reader only buys the product to gain the benefits. So while the "benefit-first" format and style are not typical for press releases, if printed, they will definitely increase your response. I recommend this type of release to professionals and to people who are familiar with press releases— and have had success in having them published.

Specifically, here's how it works. A brief mention of the product and benefits early in the lead paragraph of the release usually gets printed. "A new (product name) providing/offering (benefit, benefit, benefit) is now available from...." For example, "A new oversized tennis racket that reduces tennis elbow, offers more power, and allows greater ball control is now available from...." The formula is: "New product offers benefit, benefit, benefit...." Since the release moves quickly into something that sounds like a product description, the release and the benefits are usually kept intact.

The next lines show the product in use: "Beginners and people with incorrect swings now strike the ball more naturally." Then show where: "in practice, regular play, and tournaments." The formula for this is: "Applications are 'who or what use, use, use'; in 'type, type, type' of usage." In these few lines you have shown <u>what</u> the product is, its <u>benefits</u>, <u>how</u> it's used, <u>why</u>, and <u>where</u>. The rest of the release continues traditionally, returning to the newspaper format describing the features of the product: "All new composite material is used...."

_____

The selection process is simple, fast, and brutal—and very unforgiving of mistakes or poor work.

_____

The inverted pyramid style allows the editor an easy and fast way to edit, by starting at the bottom. This holds true for all releases and is the traditional way a busy editor trims each release down to a size that will fit the allotted space in his magazine. Since the most important information is found at the top of the story, the editor knows anything cut from the bottom of a correctly structured release won't be missed nearly as much. If your important elements are at the bottom, there is a greater chance they will be edited out. In the Benefit-First type of release, since the benefits are presented in the first sentence or two of the release, chances are better than 95 percent they won't be cut.

Whatever style of writing you select for your release, if it sounds too much like an ad or if the body of the release is poorly written, unlike a poor headline, it will take too much time for a busy editor to completely rewrite. So it won't get rewritten. It'll get tossed out. The selection process is simple, fast, and brutal—and very unforgiving of mistakes or poor work.

For the best results, if you are writing a release and want to get it published in a particular magazine, read some of the other releases in the magazine and copy the magazine's particular style of writing. Write directly to the audience of the magazine. Editors are flattered by people who take the time to know their magazine and direct their energies specifically to it.

Next, double space the body copy of the release.

Why do you double space, and do you have to? The releases are reviewed by an editor, who goes over them with a red pen and strikes out anything that does not conform to the format of the magazine section where it will be printed. He also takes out the extraneous parts that make the release sound like a sales pitch or ad. He then writes instructions to the production department, marks brief changes, and makes other changes in wording inside the double spacing and in the margins. So leave big margins, too. Anything you can do to make the editor's job easier and faster gets your release closer to being published.

At the end of the release, the very last component of your body copy should be your company name, address, and phone number. After your street address, put the word "Dept. ____" with an underscored line after it. The magazine editors will insert their publication's initials in this block when they publish your release, so when you get inquiries you'll know from which publication they came.

Releases traditionally end with the number sign typed three times (###) and centered on the page. You can also type three asterisks (***);

either set of marks will signal the end of the release. Busy editors will appreciate this—it is a courtesy, not to mention standard format.

If your release runs over one page, do not break a paragraph in the middle—end the first page at the end of the last full paragraph, type "MORE" at the bottom right of the page so editors will know to look for another page (if there isn't one, they'll know it's missing), and start the next page with a fresh paragraph.

Include a Photo

It's best to include a black-and-white 5" x 7" or 8" x 10" glossy finish photo, unfolded, so note: the envelope you'll need for mailing photo releases is larger than a standard number 10. If there is a crease or fold in the photo, it won't be usable since the crease will show up when printed.

The correct way to identify a photo—and your release photos should always be identified—is to take a shipping label or file folder label, write the product name and your company name and phone number on it, then stick it on the back of the photo. Or take a piece of tape, write your product name and company identification on it, and tape it to the back of the photo.

If you write directly on the back of the photo, chances are the pen or pencil pressure will push into the emulsion side (front) of the photo and scar the picture. This scar will show up when the photo is printed, making the photo unusable to the magazine.

Don't use paper clips or staples to attach the photo to anything, because they also may scar the photo. Use a photo mailer or include a piece of chipboard to stiffen the envelope so the photo doesn't bend in transit. If it's not obvious which end of your product is up, write "TOP" in very small letters in the top white photo margin. If an editor doesn't know which side is up, he won't guess—he'll simply use another firm's release.

Clear, sharp, professional photos are best. If no one will have any idea of what size your product is, you should include a size reference in your photo (if tiny, include a dime; if slightly larger, a hand or ruler; if larger still—a person). If people are included, action shots are best. Keep the people in the photo large. More than likely, the photo will be reduced when published, and if the people are too small they won't look good. All in all, an action shot of your product in use is best. Send a photo <u>with</u> each release (not separately). Photos are never returned, so don't ask. If you need it, have a duplicate made before sending it. Electronic photos are now and accepted - and excellent - way to go and you can send them on disk.

Timing the Release of Your Material

The timing of your release is very important. Keep in mind it usually takes about <u>three or four months' lead time for your release to show up</u> in any magazine. This is the average lead time for both ads and press releases to appear; magazines run that far in advance with their printing and production schedules. Larger publications can take a month or two longer, so allow for this time in your campaign. News magazines (*Time, Newsweek*) take shorter lead times, as the information printed in them must be more current. Call for specifics; each publication is different. Don't send a release any more than six months in advance of the print date. It'll get lost or filed (and don't ask where).

While you're impatiently waiting for magazines to run your release, get your releases ready to send to newspapers. Newspapers need only a few days to print your story, less if necessary, since they are a source of much more immediate information. Most papers prefer to receive releases about two weeks in advance of the date the story should run. This gives them a chance to schedule it in, or fill an open slot if a current news story breaks off or requires less coverage. Some papers prefer to get releases even closer to the publishing date, so they're fresher. In that case, the chances of your release being close at hand on the publication date will be greater. Other newspapers deal with everything on an immediate basis, and don't know what to do with anything that is dated more than two weeks in the future.

If you want all the publicity to be published at the same time, get your newspaper releases ready now, even though you won't be sending them for a couple of months. But now is the time to do a little preplanning, so when the time comes to send them—in two and a half months—all you have to do is drop them in the mail.

The Secret Editorial Selection Process—You Are the Editor

To put all those rules into perspective, let's take a look at a press release from the other side of the desk. You are the editor. It was unusually cold and damp when you awoke this morning, but the building super doesn't put the heat on till October 1. Too bad you ran out of coffee over the weekend. Through bleary eyes you shower, dress, and get into your car still groggy and tired. As you drive to work it starts raining hard. You can't remember ever seeing such a heavy volume of cars on the expressway. Although you left 15 minutes early, you arrive at 9:15, an hour and fifteen minutes late. There are nine phone messages written in various hieroglyphics on scraps of paper on your desk. You can read only four of them.

So how do you, the editor, pick out releases? First, you look through them, and throw out all the ones that don't give you double spaces between the lines so you can comfortably make your corrections.

Sitting at your desk, you—the busy editor—look at the volume of press releases. Three days are left till the closing of your gala September Back-to-School issue. In a stack to your immediate right are about 80 releases. This stack, by the way, matches the 20 or so other stacks of paper sitting on your desk, marked for your "immediate attention" for the September issue. This happens every month, so you've learned to take it in stride by working 30-hour days till the issue goes to press.

So how do you, the editor, pick out releases? First, you look through them, and throw out all the ones that don't give you double spaces between the lines so you can comfortably make your corrections. This cuts the pile by about a third. It gets rid of the novices. (Now you can understand why your releases should be double spaced.)

As the editor, you trash all the releases that don't look good, figuring if the release doesn't look good, or if the photo isn't good, the literature your readers will receive—if any—will be of the same quality. This may reflect poorly on your magazine, so you throw them out. These first two steps take about a minute.

This brings us to Lesson 2: Submit neat, clean releases, double spaced, with good, sharp, in-focus photos.

Now you go back through the pile of about 40 releases, knowing you have room for about 8 in this issue. Each month, some people write with a ballpoint pen on the back of their photo exactly what the photo is, the release information, or their own version of *War and Peace.* So you, as the editor, check for writing on the back of the photos. You won't be able to print these without having the writing show through. They are unusable, and you toss them out, too. You see this mistake every month, time and time again.

The pictures with no identifying information such as manufacturer or product name could get imposed incorrectly in the production department, so you throw them out, too! Well, that was easy. If it were earlier in the month, you could now take a break. You'd go for a nice lunch, or for a beer. But things always back up around the closing dates, so now you have to keep working.

If there is a good industry match, the acceptable product releases are now reviewed for newness and timeliness, and evaluated for editorial consideration. Will the product be of interest to your readers? Does it look like a good product to introduce—well designed, well crafted? Are your readers going to be happy or disappointed if and when they get the literature, or if they order the product? If everything fits, the release advances to the next level.

Influences at the Publishing Office

There are two distinct sides of any magazine or newspaper publishing office—the editorial side and the advertising side. While the editorial side and the advertising side aren't supposed to mix, in reality some magazines strongly consider editorial support for current or potential advertisers. Did I say that politely enough?

While I'm sure you, as the editor, wouldn't be looking for that special mark left by someone in your firm indicating the writer of the release will be called to advertise in your magazine or increase his ad space, some editors and magazines do. But of course, you wouldn't be swayed, as some magazine editors would, by the publisher who just came into your office and gave you the credit report of a certain potential advertiser, along with a stern look and a press release of their product. Would you?

Some publications aren't very subtle, and the salesperson may call you when the magazine gets your release and say, "Geez, if you book an ad for October, I can get this release in September's issue!" My standard reply is, "Well...." I say in my best good-old-boy Southern accent, "I just wanted to test your magazine to see if it fits our market. If the release tests well, your magazine would be a strong contender for our ad budget. Of course, we won't know until the release is out for about a month, so please call back then and I'll let you know the exact draw." Space salespeople hate me. But they hate everyone who does this, so it's OK. Because everybody does this. Therefore, they hate everyone. And it's OK, because in turn, everyone hates salespeople.

Advertising space sales personnel may call you and say they deliver the audience you need, and their book is definitely for you. And that you should take out an ad—they're sure it will work for you. They're sure it'll work, but remember, it's your money. If it doesn't work, they aren't out the few hundred or few thousand dollars. I've never heard one yet say if it doesn't work, don't pay for the ad.

The most common use of a press release campaign is to supplement an advertising campaign. If you are running an ad schedule in a magazine, they will usually accept your press release for publication in the magazine. This is almost a guarantee, depending on your ad size and the publication. It is especially true of the trade press where the circulation figures are smaller. In the consumer press, it's not realistic to run a 1/12-page ad for $1,000 in *Esquire* magazine and expect a big write-up for your press release. But with a $1,000 ad in a trade journal like *Modern Vegetable Farmer,* you can be assured your release will run.

It's common for potential advertisers to ask to have press releases run to see if the magazine's audience and the product's market coincide. Although when you speak with a salesperson at a publishing company, I'm sure it's very annoying to them to hear yet another story of a "marketing test" at the magazine's expense. But there's truth in this line of thinking— if your release does well, you should consider an ad. By the same token, most magazines will definitely run your release if you take out an ad.

There are some win-win situations in running a release: if the draw is good and you make some sales, you may take out ad space and become a longtime advertiser. If your release is published and draws only an inquiry or two from the reader service card, an ad won't work much better. I've never known a press release to draw poorly while an ad works well in the same publication, no matter what a space salesperson says.

Depending on the write-up you get, a press release printed in a magazine is probably worth (in dollars) between the cost of a sixth of a page and a 1/3-page ad.

If you measure and track the response to a printed release carefully, you'll be able to tell, to a good degree, if an ad will pay off. Remember, the

The Danielle Adams Publishing Company
Box 100, Merion Station PA 19066

release is being printed as editorial. This gives you a tremendous amount of credibility —more so than with an ad. So you may have great success with a published press release, and poor performance with an ad. It can happen.

If the release does well, my feeling is an ad can work also. As long as you know your target audience is reading the magazine and needs or wants your product, and you've received a good, solid response to your release write-up, you should be able to make an ad work. Whether it's going to be profitable or not is another matter—that issue is product- and offer-specific. Variables such as product price, profit per unit, ad cost, number of responses to the ad, conversion of leads to sales, and so forth— must be addressed before you can figure out the true profitability of a product ad in a specific magazine.

Value of a Published Release

Depending on the write-up you get, a press release printed in a magazine is probably worth (in dollars) between the cost of a sixth of a page and a 1/3-page ad. So look at the costs of a sixth-page, a quarter-page, and a third-page ad in that publication—and try to determine if your response rate, lead generation, inquiries, and number of orders will be enough to cover the costs of any of these size ads. Don't worry about it now, but somewhere down the line you'll have to figure in profit. If it's close to being profitable, you should consider an ad schedule   Then, if your first few ads break even, as you gain consistency and the credibility that goes with a repeated ad, your sales will definitely go up. Then you can seriously start thinking about profit.

Back at Your Editor's Desk

So you go to the top of the stairs, and throw them all up in the air directly above your head. The eight that land on the top few stairs get in, and the rest that floated downward are trashed...

OK, so you're back at your editor's desk, with about 20 releases surviving. With no other possible way out, you read them. The ones needing the least rewriting make your job easier, and that slims the pile down to about 15 high-quality releases, usable without too much rewriting. But remember, this month you have room for only 8.

So you go to the top of the stairs, and throw them all up in the air directly above your head. The eight that land on the top few stairs get in, and the rest that floated downward are trashed, or saved for next month's consideration. That's why they call it editorial—because they all don't get in, and marketers have to submit to this "part hand picked" and "part random" selection process that dictates what runs and what doesn't.

What I mean by this is, no matter what you do, there is a great element of risk that your release just won't get in, no matter what you do. At the last moment you can get bumped for any reason, or no reason at all. You have to accept this as part of the mystique of the press release, as opposed to an ad which you purchase the space for, and which absolutely does run.

THE DANIELLE ADAMS PUBLISHING COMPANY

~ Office of the President ~
Box 100 ✰ Merion Station, PA 19066
610/642-1000 ✰ Fax 610/642-6832

A FREE COPY OF *UNCOMMON MARKETING TECHNIQUES*
HAS BEEN RESERVED IN YOUR NAME.

Dear Editor,

Would you like to help your readers and industry colleagues succeed? The formula for success is quite simple, you know:

1. poor marketing = poor sales = failure
2. effective marketing = increased sales = success

Simple, isn't it? If you'd like to help your readers get more sales, more easily, and at the same time lower their marketing costs, I can help.

My new book, *Uncommon Marketing Techniques,* presents no history, no theory, and no bs. I cut through the theory and give solid, practical information in an easy-to-understand, conversational style of writing. Meat and potatoes facts and phone numbers. Tips and techniques. Trade Secrets. Effective marketing methods presented in a fast delivery, no bs style.

My information-intense marketing and direct marketing articles are featured in over 60 magazines and tough business newspapers - including Direct Marketing Magazine, The Savant (SCORE) and ASBA TODAY (American Small Business Association.) Over 2,000,000 people are exposed to my articles on marketing.

Now, all the articles from my book are available for publishing in your magazine. Articles are **information-intense**, and jam-packed with useful marketing techniques. Chapters include:

- *How to Create a Winning Direct Mail Package*
- *How To Create Your Own Great Ad, or Get One You Like from an Ad Agency, the First Time*
- *The Pen Campaign - the BEST CAMPAIGN I'VE EVER WRITTEN!*
- *The 10 Worst Mistakes in Direct Mail*
- *Increase Your Ad Response 10 Times*
- *The 13 Fastest Ways to Get Business Right Now!*
- *A Simple Rule to Create the Best Headlines*
- *Getting Your Press Release Into Print*

You're welcome to a **FREE REVIEW COPY** of *Uncommon Marketing Techniques.* You see, I put my money where my mouth is - I invite you to take a look - to see (at our expense) just how beneficial *Uncommon Marketing Techniques* will be to your readers. Or take a look at our website: 12 articles are posted there.

Thank you so much for your consideration to feature these articles, a review, or to publish our press release. Please call right now - **610-642-1000** or fax us (610-642-6832) for articles on disk, or to receive this new book - free, with our compliments. Thanks.

Kindest regards,

Jeffrey Dobkin

Header

New product offers benefit

Benefit-First Style Release

Credibility

Features Benefits

Features Benefits

Use Benefit

Additional use

Complete ordering information in last paragraph.

~ *PRESS RELEASE* ~

Direct Marketing Strategies/Small Business 11/8
More Information - Jeffrey Dobkin (President) at
Danielle Adams Publishing: 610/642-1000
For Immediate Release - No Kill Date!

New Book Offers Marketing Tips and Techniques

You can learn thousands of tips, tricks, and techniques of low-cost marketing methods that are crammed into a fast-paced new book, *Jeffrey Dobkin's Direct Marketing Strategies*. Over 50 independent chapters present a jump-in-anywhere collection of explicit how-to marketing and direct marketing information, delivered in a Dobkin's easy-to-read, conversational style of writing.

This awesome book makes learning fast and interesting - with a nice touch of humor rarely found in such a dry topic as marketing. Over 2 million people read Dobkin's columns on small business marketing; now you can get a wealth of industry insights and direct marketing trade secrets revealed in his information-intense book.

Chapters include "Getting Your Press Release into Print," a guide to writing effective press releases that will explode your chance of getting free publicity in magazines and newspapers from 5% to 85%. Also, "Increase Your Advertising Response by 10 Times," "How To Create a Winning Direct Mail Package," and "How To Buy a Great Mailing List."

Other chapters include "The One-evening Marketing Plan" specific instructions on how to complete your marketing in a single evening, and finish your entire PR program the following day, Plus "How To Create Your Own Great Ad - or Get One You Like from an Agency, the First Time" (advertising agencies never tell you this!); "How To Write a Small Classified Ad"; "The Biggest Mistake Firms Make in Marketing (and How To Correct It in Your Firm!)"; "How To Find the Markets for Your Invention"; "How To Find a Product to Market"; "The Best Marketing Tips for Small Business"; and "The Fastest and Best Ways to Get Business Right Now."

This new, title is a great follow-up to Dobkin's other book - the most practical marketing tool, *Successful Low Cost Direct Marketing Methods*. In a similar way, *Jeffrey Dobkin's Direct Marketing Strategies* offers useful how-to help for entrepreneurs, home office pioneers, and owners of small and medium-sized businesses as well as large corporations. It contains plenty of traditional ways to market, along with fresh and innovative new marketing techniques, plus lots of samples and examples of campaigns. You never learned this stuff in college.

Each action-oriented chapter is filled with practical real-world marketing techniques in ready-to-use form. "I cut through the theoretical crap and bring readers usable information," says Dobkin. "It's high-density tips and techniques for low-cost marketing, in a fast-paced, rapid-fire format. With just enough humor to keep people reading - even about marketing."

Jeffrey Dobkin's Direct Marketing Strategies, $14.95 (+ $4 P&H), ISBN 0-9642879-8-6, available in finer bookstores nationwide; signed editions directly from the publisher: The Danielle Adams Publishing Company, Box 100, Merion Station, PA 19066 • 610/642-1000, Fax 610/642-6832. Satisfaction Always Guaranteed. Visit www.dobkin.com

###

But if you call the magazine and speak to the editor, your chance for free publicity may be as high as 80% or 90%, from just the one phone call.

There are good reasons to keep your releases as close to the standard format as possible. It shows you are a professional, the product is probably good, and the readers will be happy with you—and with the magazine, for giving your product and firm editorial support. It'll also get you to the top of the stairs. After that, it's up to gravity and the luck of the float to get your release in print.

Increasing Your Chances of Publication to 90 Percent

The chances of your release being published do in fact depend on one or two other factors that you have control over. Suppose you submit a release to a magazine that normally publishes 10 out of every 100 releases sent in. Your chance of getting the free publicity of a press release write-up is about 10 percent. But if you call the magazine and speak to the editor, your chance for free publicity may be as high as 80 percent or 90 percent, from just the one phone call.

The reason for this is that most PR agencies, ad agencies, and businesses that send lots of releases don't bother to call. They send so many, they just don't see it as practical to precede each release to an editor by a phone call. So while editors get tons of releases (a hazard of being an editor), they don't get many calls. Your call to them says a write-up in their magazine has great value and importance to you and your firm.

Some editors are pretty busy and won't take a call. Others are hard to reach, especially around the closing dates of their publications. But some are regular people just like you and me, and not only are they fun to talk with on the phone, they are knowledgeable about their industry, gracious, and helpful. If asked what they look for in a release, they'll explain, as well as tell you how to submit one. They'll also tell you if their market is good for you and your product, and any of hundreds of other helpful things.

If you submit a release after talking to them, there's a good chance you'll get special consideration, at least the first time around. When they get your release, they will usually go back and start from the beginning of the selection process—so your release still must conform: good headline, double spaced, newsy format, brief, good photo, and so forth. Some things never change; you need a good, quality release to be considered. But if your release passes these early tests, and makes it to the final stair selection process, it'll be set aside on the top stair. Voilà. You're in. Congratulations.

Getting Too Much Free Press

Free press is really easy to get when you submit correctly prepared releases. If you apply the techniques in this book, you will definitely get multiple write-ups. A word of warning: you can do yourself in by having too much published about your product at once. It's easy to get overwhelmed by the inquiries.

The casually interested, the literature seekers, and the "just curious" can be numerous. When you watch 10,000 leads settle on your desk in one month, it can become quite overwhelming. The tertiary markets can supply you with an overpowering amount of inquirers, none of whom may buy your product.

If you are attacking several mid-size markets with a press release campaign, you will constantly be faced with the decisions of which and how many magazine publishers to call. In the industrial markets—where ads and press releases usually result in leads, inquiries, and reader service card responses (as opposed to the immediate sales a consumer campaign will generate), there is a danger of generating an overload of unqualified leads by calling all 80 or so magazines that serve your marketing universe.

The Danielle Adams Publishing Company
Box 100, Merion Station PA 19066

So before you send releases, I'd recommend you initially call only a handful of the trade magazines and not go too deep right away unless you are prepared for all the publicity you will receive.

It's difficult to judge all the marketing material you'll need to have on hand to be able to send it in a timely manner. Soon you'll be familiar with both the front end of getting your publicity in print, and the back end of fulfilling literature requests. So if you're new to the game, take it easy up front.

Only you can decide which magazines and markets aren't quite perfect for you—and I'd let them wait till after the first go-around. Initially, make calls only to your stronger primary markets.

"I'll call every editor and sort it out later," may sound good up front, but it can be a downfall as sure as any other effort in the wrong direction. Of course, if you have lots of money, staff, and can track all those inquiries carefully—go ahead, make those calls.

With consumer magazines, press releases can lead to more direct sales. So your calls to editors on the edge of your markets may pay off without the flood of back and forth paperwork industrial sales always seem to create. Since consumer magazines need more encouragement to run your releases, and the chances of having a release run is smaller, a heavier call schedule to the consumer press may be more practical.

Whatever you do, take the time to make sure when you approach the marketplace en masse that all your materials are correct, written well, and presented well. When you mail just a few releases and there is a mistake, you'll find out with only a little egg on your face. When you send out all your releases at once to your entire market universe, if there's a mistake, everyone gets it. So be aware: with the bigger numbers comes the chance for bigger errors.

Also, make sure you are prepared for success. That doesn't mean you're ready to make money, it means you're ready to receive and handle a volume of inquiries, send literature, ship samples, and have the resources to handle the calls your publicity generates. If you are working out of your home at night on this project, who will answer the phone during the day? And will you be ready to send out a few thousand replies in response to the number of leads the magazine press can create rather quickly? Licking a few envelopes is no problem, but when you multiply that by a few thousand, your tongue can get mighty dry.

Should You Send a Letter with Your Release?

There are several different schools of thought on this, and lots of my industry colleagues will argue against it, but <u>I absolutely recommend sending a cover letter with a press release</u>. Many firms—including some of the big PR firms—don't practice this policy, and don't agree with them. Their theory is, why send a letter saying "Here's a release about our product," when the editor can see there's a release enclosed for himself. How true. Your letter shouldn't say "Here's a release about..."

If there is any doubt about your credibility, no editor in his or her right mind will run your release.

There are several reasons to accompany your press release with a letter. First, the letter supports the primary objective of having the release printed in the magazine by giving you additional credibility. Any literature you send, such as brochures, spec sheets, letterhead, and anything else printed with your name and firm and included with your release increases your credibility. This includes corporate literature and brochures for your other products, as well as literature for your release products.

Think about it. If you aren't known in the industry, what basis do editors have to allay their doubts? "Hmmm, will this firm represent itself well to my readers?" Or, "Will this firm answer all the requests with good follow-up, exciting literature, in a timely fashion?" Anything you can include that will produce the answer, "Yes, this is a good firm to work with," is

New Invention for the safety of children.

Ms. Debbie Ludwig
Editor
The Children Magazine
234 Fifth Avenue
New York, NY 10017

Dear Ms. Ludwig:

At the request of some of our larger clients who needed a volume of low cost emergency I.D. tags for kids, we invented a new plastic write-on identification. It was developed specifically for the safety of children. Private label is available and we offer that as a free service to larger purchasers.

Childcare information is written on the tag with <u>any</u> pen, then the tags are laced onto a child's shoes or sneakers in a closed and locked position. For the safety of the child, their name and address are completely concealed yet readily available for a healthcare provider.

Our new I.D. tags increase the safety of children who are traveling - by keeping a local emergency address and phone on the child at all times. Tags are low enough in cost a new I.D. may be used for each night of a child's vacation and still not be expensive. Our emergency traveling tags also work for pets, too.

We've written our release specifically in the editorial style of your magazine, and hope you will publish it in the "New Products for Children" column we enjoy reading in your magazine every month.

Thanks. Your consideration to publish our release is appreciated.

Kindest regards,

Jeffrey Dobkin
President

P.S. So that you can see how effective these emergency identification tags are for kids, I've included a box of 100 for your evaluation. If you need more, just send me the postage paid card enclosed and I'll be glad to send additional samples to your home or office.

~ *FOR IMMEDIATE RELEASE* ~

Release Plastic Tags - Pet11/8●
More Information - Contact: Jeffrey Dobkin (Owner)
The Danielle Adams Mail Order Company: 610/642-1C●
No Kill Da●

LOW COST "WRITE-ON!" IDENTIFICATION TAGS
INSTANTLY PROTECT KIDS FROM REMAINING LOST

Biggest benefit in headline.

Immediately shows benefit and need.

Plastic Write-On! I.D. Tags offer immediate safety to any child. Protects children when traveling, if a disaster strikes, or any other emergency.

Benefit.

Write child's name, address and telephone information on tag with any pen, then fold and latch closed - keeping the informati●

Benefit.

clean, concealed, and secure inside. I.D. tag is plastic and

Description.

impervious to rain, flood waters, heat or sun.

When traveling: Kids knowing their address and phone at home won't help if the child gets lost while you're vacationing in another city, state or country. With the Danielle Adams Instant Write-On! Tags, you can write the local address and phone where ●

Establish additional need.

your family is staying that night - if the child is lost or inju●

Use.

on the road there is always a local phone number on the child to call to insure his or her safe return. Cost of each I.D. tag is low enough that a new I.D. may be created for each night's locati● without great expense. For runners, too.

Benefit.

Great for pets, too: Also instantly provides additional safet● to any pet that has no means of local identification. Samples ar●

Benefit repeated.

5 for $2 and include a stamped self-addressed envelope. Retail price is $39.00 per box of one hundred, postpaid. New! From The

Complete ordering information.

Danielle Adams Mail Order Company, P.O. Box 100, Dept ____, Meri● Station PA 19066. Phone 610-642-1000. Visa/MasterCard. Private label available.

###

indicates end of release.

The Danielle Adams Mail Order Company
P.O. Box 100 • Merion Station, PA 19066
Telephone 610/642-1000 • 800-234-IDEA

worth sending. If there is any doubt about your credibility, no editor in his or her right mind will run your release. With so many perfectly credible firms, products, and releases sitting on their desks, why should they take a chance?

For any product or release editors publish in their magazine, a poor performance by the manufacturing firm is a bad reflection on them. This can be caused by the firm's not sending literature in a timely fashion, or producing a poor-quality product. It also occurs if literature is sent to the reader with misspellings, or if it's dirty or unsightly. So credibility is one factor that adds to the consideration of your release being published—and this can be enhanced in your letter.

Second, the letter is the place to make editors think kindly about you and more positively about your product. It shows the extra time you took, and the importance you attach to running your publicity release in their publication. This gives them additional reasons to publish your release. In your letter, you can show them you did your homework by knowing their name and the name of the column where you'd like your release to appear in their magazine. This is done by personalizing the salutation and naming the column in the letter. Little things like this count strongly when you write to editors. They can see they are not just one of the pack of magazine editors getting a release, and that being published in their journal has true value to you.

Also, editors can draw additional information from your letter and run it when they publish your release. You can address features or benefits that you wouldn't write about in the release, yet these may be facts an editor would like to bring to his readers' attention.

Finally, your letter can highlight the important information you'd like him to see, and tell him why it's important. Never say "Here's a release about..." That would be silly. But do spend some time on a high quality letter—as an effective pitching tool to get your press release published.

You Can Judge for Yourself

Suppose you, as the editor, had two similar, well-written press releases land on your desk at the same time. One came in without a letter—obviously from a professional PR firm. You know it was mailed to everyone in the industry— and will probably show up in all the other trade magazines just when it would show up in yours.

The other release you received was delivered with a personalized letter addressed specifically to you. It's from the owner or manager of a small firm. The letter says how appreciative the sender is of your consideration to publish his release—then specifically names the column. It goes on to say that he'll follow up each lead with diligence by sending a letter and a specification sheet within five days of the receipt of any inquiry. All calls are returned the same day. The sender has enjoyed reading your magazine over the years, and is proud to write the enclosed release specifically in the editorial style of your magazine. Which release would you choose?

How Often Should You Send Releases?

When your initial releases are published in magazines—three to five months after you've sent them—you'll learn the response from the different markets and their follow-up requirements. Then you can make an intelligent decision about how soon you'd like the next campaign to run.

> **If you can't stand waiting, my recommendation would be to send a second copy of your release about two months after the first one is sent.**

The earliest time to send a second release to a magazine that has published your first release would be four months from the date the first release appeared. This applies only to a release for the same product; each new product is treated separately, and you can send releases for brand-new products at any time. The consumer press takes a little more time to recover from printing your release—six months to a year. You can send releases sooner, but I doubt they will be published. Of course, it doesn't hurt to try. Or create a different release and photo and send that.

It may take you a few months to find out your anticipated editorial coverage didn't appear in their pages. You can send to these publications again immediately. It may take four to five months for you to figure out a magazine isn't going to run your release.

If you can't stand waiting, my recommendation would be to send a second copy of your release about two months after the first one is sent. The worst that will happen is your first release will already be in the magazine blue lines (in preparation of being printed) or already on press. In either event—not that an editor would want to—it will be too late to stop the press and remove your release from the print run. So while you have duplicated your effort, this insurance can't really hurt you. The package can be exactly the same as the one you previously mailed, but I recommend you change it slightly.

You can send a release to an editor every month or so, until you get tired of sending them or the editor gets tired of seeing them—and hopefully publishes one. Perseverance can pay off. Some of my clients have used this as an effective publicity technique, although it's not my favorite. This type of campaign keeps your release in front of the editor's face, although it is expensive. It also places your release in his hands several times—perhaps one of the times may be when he has an open page. On the down side, it can be annoying. Change the letter to make sure the editor reads it each time. If you are sending releases with this frequency, it's best to change the release also—or at least the headline—to keep it fresh and new.

At the point you know your release is not going to be published and you feel a particular magazine is a "must get in" magazine, I'd call the editor. Let him know a press release is being sent, and ask the editor (if you can get hold of him) if there is anything you can do to increase the likelihood of your release being published. You can casually mention your old release bit the dust when you sent it the first time (if you can do this in an exceptionally nice way) and ask if there is anything you can do to improve the way it was written or presented. Ask if he feels the product is right for his audience. Maybe there was a reason it wasn't published. Editors are usually a good lot overall, and perhaps they'll tell you the reason and you can correct it.

While the press people liked your material and product when they were newly presented to them, once they publish your release, they're not as likely to favor the same product release again. They will be out looking for new firms and new products, just as you found them originally. But in six months, with such a low cost to generate a release, you can try again. When you send another release this time, don't wait for the next few issues to appear to see if you're in one—send yet another release about six weeks later. And—if it's important that it appear again—still another six weeks after that. This will give the editors a few good looks at your product—and hopefully it'll make them feel that enough time has passed for your release to reappear.

If you do get published, new photography and copy with a different angle or approach will definitely help prompt an additional write-up. A new product innovation or a significant improvement in your current model can be sent sooner—in just three or four months. That's what it's all about: new and news.

Sending Product Samples

If your product is enjoyable, small, and needed by everyone (or at least by magazine people), you may wish to include a sample with your release. Everyone likes to receive packages. Editors—if for no other reason than the curiosity factor—will generally open packages first. (Don't you?) This will make your release and campaign stand out among the many releases they get, and increase your chances of getting published.

Sure, sending everyone samples sounds like a good idea, but when you send out 80 or 100 releases and want to include a sample in each, it can get very costly. The entire cost is up front. Between your product costs and the shipping costs, it can get mighty expensive to send a sample to everyone.

> ## Usually, if an editor elects the option to receive several samples, he is going to run your release—you can ship the product and start celebrating early.

When your product is large, or can be used only by a small, select group of people when it snows, don't bother to send it. But if it's of reasonable cost to do so, you may wish to include a post card or hand-typed note to the editor saying if he would like a free sample, simply "Send the card or letter back"—and include a stamped, self-addressed envelope. This touch of detail shows your thoughtfulness and courtesy, and further ensures good feelings about your firm. Your note should state you'll be pleased to ship one to them at their home or office. Home *or* office is important—give them this option.

Usually, if an editor elects the option to receive several samples, he is going to run your release—you can ship the product and start celebrating early. It wouldn't be nice for an editor to get samples as requested, then not publish your release—unless the product is really poor.

When you ship your product sample, and they print the release, you can send me a bottle of champagne. Because you just got several hundred— maybe several thousand—dollars' worth of publicity, and I only got the smallest percentage of the money you spent for this book.

The Danielle Adams Publishing Company
Box 100, Merion Station PA 19066

Exceptional Presentations

For the larger trade magazines and the consumer publications, you may wish to make a nicer presentation than just a letter, photo, and release. These huge multi-publishers are used to all the glitz and gifts of the big agency campaigns and their powerful PR machines. Since they play with bigger numbers, you've got to be more clever—or spend more money—to make your release stand out and command attention. I prefer to use more ingenuity. The editors of these publications get a staggering number of releases—way more than the small magazines. In addition, the editors are kept pretty busy with more important functions than press releases. Here, you are battling just to gain the editor's attention, as well as to create a favorable impression, and ask their consideration to publish your release.

For the larger-circulation magazines, you may wish to wrap your release in a nice presentation folder so it appears on the editor's desk as a "Press Kit." Ship it in a box via UPS so it doesn't come in with the morning mail. Or ship it Federal Express so it stands out with a personal delivery.

You can also send it with a related item so it gets noticed. A good example of this was given by my brother's firm, which manufactures and markets electronic semiconductors, whatever the heck they are. One of their products is referred to in the industry as a chopper. So when they released a new version of their chopper, the press kit they sent to the magazines included an ax. Imagine when the "New Chopper" announcement, with a real ax, landed at the electronics magazines' publishing offices! It must have caused quite a stir and made all the pencils fall out of the editors' pocket protectors, because the end result was the new product release was written up in just about every electronics magazine where the release was submitted.

While this campaign was expensive, it generated quite a lot of publicity, and in the end the write-ups were certainly worth much more in magazine coverage than the campaign cost in ax purchases and shipping.

Shipping 100 axes around the country can be frightfully expensive up front to a small firm. If you can tie your campaign to something less expensive to buy or lighter to ship, you can be just as effective. An example would be to buy some globes of the world that you blow up like a balloon and send one with the "World Release" of your product in a nice box. Or with your "World Class" product. Or for the United States introduction... well, you get the idea.

For even greater impact, you can blow up the globe and send it inflated in a large box, with your release, of course. It'll arrive in the big box, which always carries a big curiosity factor. After the grand opening of the big box, an editor will have the globe on his desk for a few days. Naturally everyone will ask him about it. Then he'll probably take it home and give it to his kids, who will destroy it in about half an hour. By that time it will have served its purpose: landing with high impact, and creating a favorable impression.

Since it's light, the shipping costs are far less than the cost of shipping an ax. The globe itself is inexpensive. Even if shipped flat, it still has impact— and you may consider comparing this to the world being flat without the discovery of your product. It may sound silly, but if it grabs the attention of a busy editor and elevates your product to the front of their desk—and gets you extra consideration for being ahead of the pack—it worked.

Keep in mind that the remaining ingredients in the package should be quality oriented. Don't just throw a balloon in an envelope and ask why the editor didn't publish your release. Perhaps the theme of "globe" should be enhanced with a map of the world to further the cause. Or tied into a photo of the world in the backdrop of your release photo, and supported by the copy in your release. There is no substitute for a well-written release— or for a quality product promotion that is presented with professionalism.

Can you tie in your product with a clever related item that will gain attention in a favorable way? Surely there are hundreds of products at the discount stores that can be tied in to your submission. A pencil sharpener for sharp ideas. A box of crayons for bright ideas—with a letterhead in crayon- style writing. (You can even hand write "Press Release" in crayon to carry out this theme.) Or a flashlight for bright ideas. These are just examples—can you think of a natural tie-in for your product?

When submitting a release in the summer, a water pistol is always a favorite of mine—to "trigger" a good response for your "sharp shooter" product. When it lands, you can be sure the first stop the editor will make after reading your release will be the water fountain to fill it up. I don't care how old the editor is—when he gets a water pistol from one of the "Big Guns" in the industry, he becomes a kid again as soon as it has water in it.

Promotions like these are more effective on the consumer magazine side, and with the smaller trade press magazines. Big business magazines are more serious about their releases, but they still respond well to quality promotions aimed at the working press.

The bottom line is to get the attention of the editor, then present your product and firm with a fresh, favorable image.

In the magazine industry—especially the larger magazines—anything that gets the favorable attention of one or more people on the editorial staff is certainly a plus. When we marketed "Fireman Alert!" signs to the pet industry, we sent a stack of a few hundred to each editor, with a release. When they landed on the editor's desk I'm sure they were passed around the office—and everyone on staff got to know us from these promotions.

Press releases are limited only by your imagination. You can submit a traditional release with just a photo, a release with photo and letter, or, if you feel comfortable with something bigger or a more clever campaign, those options are always there for you. The bottom line is to get the attention of the editor, then present your product and firm with a fresh, favorable image. The people of the press welcome new ideas and enjoy showcasing reputable firms, showing new goods, and alerting their readers about new services.

Editors strive to give their readers a good mix of products from both large and small companies. And it's the American Way to support the underdog, who may be small and new to marketing but offers the best he possibly can, and stands behind his product with pride and an unswerving dedication to the hard work it takes to make it a success. I don't know an editor in the world who won't strongly consider a press release he receives when these strengths show up in the package.

The Last Part of Any Campaign

One final word about free press. If you'd like to have a favorable review from the editors after your release is printed, and continue to have releases published, send the editor a thank-you letter. They hardly ever get them, and it sure can make them feel good.

Does your product make a nice gift without being overpowering or obnoxious? If you haven't already, after your release is published is a great time to send one. When a product sample arrives at this time on an editor's desk, it's no longer a bribe to publish a release, it's a genuine thank-you gift. If you have any doubts about whether you should send your product with the thank-you letter, don't. But include a post card filled out with the editor's name and address, and on the top line type "___ Yes! Please send me a free sample," and let him decide. But just as important as the sample is a plain, old-fashioned "Thank you so much for printing our release." It will ensure good press relations in the future, and your next release will get strong consideration also.

Getting Help with Writing Your Release

After you have thought about this entire campaign, if you feel you can't write a quality press release yourself, immediate help can be found as close as your local newspaper. There are always, always writers on staff at a newspaper office who will write a press release for you, usually at a pretty decent rate. Most writers at smaller papers look for additional assignments that pay cash, and they welcome the opportunity to supplement their income without long-term obligations.

Newspaper editors, staff writers, journalists, even college interns working at the paper's office will be familiar with writing press releases, since a good percentage of newspaper stories are generated by either product releases or news releases. Newspaper journalists are trained in writing in a newspaper style, so chances are they can knock out your release in an afternoon and be pretty close to perfect.

Colleges, especially ones with a strong journalism curriculum, can also be an excellent source of writing talent. Although this resource won't give you someone with the experience of a seasoned journalist, as a newspaper office will, you can get some pretty bright talent through schools. Some students will have excellent additional ideas for your story. Some will have tremendous writing skills. Most will work for very little charge.

If you have a little extra cash, public relations firms and advertising agencies also have writers on staff able to draft your release in just a day or two. One advantage of using an agency is that the release should be well polished when it comes back to you. The agency should not only write the story after a brief meeting with you, but also put it in its proper form and return you a typed sheet that is laid out correctly and ready to duplicate immediately and send. Agencies may also give you better direction on where to send your release, along with advice about the rest of the elements that should go in the media kit, like the letter, the photo, and any other literature you feel will get your release into print. This resource will be more expensive.

Summary

To summarize the outline of the perfect PR campaign: A well-written, one-page press release and quality photo, sent with a well-drafted letter—a personalized letter, if possible—to the editor, by name. In your letter requesting editorial consideration, specifically name the column or section of the magazine where you are seeking a write-up. The best release is one that is tailored to each specific magazine. (Obviously, if you are sending releases to many magazines, you can't do this for all of them.) Separate releases are written for consumer and trade press.

The Danielle Adams Publishing Company
Box 100, Merion Station PA 19066

Publicity is not just for the rich. The media responds favorably to a well-thought-out and well- executed plan.

Before sending the release, call editors of the top magazines you'd definitely like your release published in. Add more calls, if you have the time, patience, and inclination, to the lesser publications and secondary markets. Include a sample, if practical. Then a follow-up thank you letter if you get in— building the relationship for the next time you need free press and publicity.

Don't be afraid of running a press campaign. Publicity is not just for the rich. The media responds favorably to a well-thought-out and well-executed plan. Most types of media—perhaps newspapers more than magazines, because of the volume of the printed words they publish—rely heavily on releases and pre-written stories for a significant portion of their space. Some editors are always actively looking for new products and releases. New product magazines constantly search for the new. It's a symbiotic relationship, if cultivated correctly, and chances are your well-drafted press release, media announcement, news story, and publicity statement will be welcomed by the multitude of editors who will be happy to give your new product a chance and publish your release. Entrepreneurial success is a part of the American dream. While you may feel alone sometimes, there are lots of people who are willing to help. Just ask.

Summary: To Create a Press Release

1. On a blank sheet of paper, write who your audience will be, then write in a style your audience can comfortably read.
2. Type "FOR IMMEDIATE RELEASE" on the top of a blank page of white paper or on your letterhead.
3. On the right-hand side, type "For Additional Information Call," then your name and phone number.
4. Directly under this, type the release number—which can be the date and your product's initials, plus T for trade publication or C for consumer publication releases.
5. Write a catchy headline and type it in caps and center it. This should include your product, and make everyone want to read the rest of the release.
6. Double space the rest of the release, and use wide margins. Write your product description in a concise newspaper style of writing. Include what, where, when, and if possible, how and why. Include a few user benefits, if possible, but be brief. Do not make it sound like an ad or it won't be used.
7. Include the important parts of the information in the beginning; editors cut from the bottom.
8. Try to stay within one page in length. End with the marks ### or *** centered on the page.
9. If the release runs longer, type "MORE" on the bottom of the first page and continue with a new paragraph on a second sheet of paper.
10. Include a sharp 5" x 7" black-and-white photo of your product (preferably in use). Don't clip anything onto, or write on, the photo. Identify the photo by writing the product name, company name, and phone number on a piece of tape, then taping it to the photo.
11. Send release copy, photo, and "Thanks for publishing our release!" letter in one envelope to editor.
12. When the release is published, send editor a thank-you letter.

~ Direct Mail ~

Every piece of mail you send represents an opportunity for you to conduct additional business with a customer, prospect, or stranger. The advantage of direct mail is the precise aim you can take with your money. This chapter will show you how to create an effective mailing piece, select your best prospects, and send it to them. Direct mail can be the lowest-cost medium if you are aiming at a very select group or market that you can define and target. The letter you enclose is discussed in depth, as the most important element inside your mailing package. The list of people or companies you mail to is also described in detail, as it is the most important element of your direct mail campaign.

Notes...

The Danielle Adams Publishing Company
Box 100, Merion Station PA 19066

~ In Direct Mail, Your Success May Be Just 42¢ Away ~

In Washington, D.C., 2,200 people manage and guide the entire postal service organization through rain, sleet, snow, and hail. Around the country are five main regional offices (Windsor, CT; Philadelphia; Memphis; Chicago; and San Bruno, CA), each with a staff of 400 people, who manage the processing operations for an average of 110 million pieces of mail each night, six nights a week, every week—week in and week out.

Reporting to the five regional offices are 73 divisions, which are managed by the 96 Management Sectional Centers (MSCs). There are 264 smaller Sectional Center Facilities (SCFs), followed by nearly 40,000 post offices throughout the United States, served by over 745,000 career employees. Your direct mail package can get lost at any point in this chain. But... it usually doesn't.

Marketing through direct mail is proof that advertising works. You send out a direct mail package; if you did it right, in return you receive envelopes filled with orders and money. What could be better?

Common to all direct mail pieces are four distinct elements. First is the creative package of art and copy, referred to in the industry as simply "the creative." This is the letter copy, the brochure art and graphics, the direct mail package form and format, and the size and style of company or product literature. Next is the offer: what you are selling, what your reader receives, and how you are wrapping it to be sold. Third is the price. And last but certainly not least, is the list.

Of these four elements, the list is most important to the success of your entire mailing. The most important part inside your mailing package is the letter. If they mail to the right list, with the correct offer, at the right price, some direct mailers have success mailing only a letter in an envelope. You can, too.

Because of its significance, the letter will be discussed in great depth. In the second half of the chapter, the other elements of direct mail are reviewed and analyzed. If you can write a good letter, you can be successful in direct mail. If you can't write well, turn to the resources part of the chapter and use it to find someone who can. Mail the letter they write to potential customers, and be successful.

The Letter

Ever notice when you get a magazine subscription offer, a mailing from the Franklin Mint, a solicitation from Publishers Clearing House, or a mail piece from any of the thousands of giant direct mailers, there's always a piece of paper that looks like a letter in the package? There's a reason.

A letter is the most effective you can be in direct marketing for 42 cents.

A letter is the most effective tool you can use in direct marketing for 42 cents. Without a doubt, a letter is the most effective you can be in direct marketing at any price. It's also the most underrated and underused tool in anyone's marketing arsenal. It is without a doubt the most important piece inside your direct mail package. In fact, the letter can be used alone, without a brochure or company literature, and you can still get a decent response. When people get your mailing package, they look at the brochure, but they read the letter. A mailing can work—and work well—using just a letter. In direct mail, success may be just 42 cents away.

There are two very different, effective uses of letters. The first is in a commercial mailing to the general marketplace of prospect—consumers or businesses. Examples would be what you receive from Publishers Clearing House, and letters in magazine renewals. Commercial mailings must pay for themselves immediately. The other use is a more personalized letter campaign sent to a very limited number of recipients, such as 50 of your best customers or 100 of your best prospects. We'll look at the general mailings first, then move to the more focused, targeted letter campaigns. Many of the rules of writing letters apply to both situations. With smaller, more personalized mailings you can get more intimate: your focus and wording may be tighter, and your objectives may differ from generating an immediate order.

A letter is a funny vehicle. Make it look like it came off a regular typewriter, and even though you print a million copies, people still perceive it as a personal note from you to them. When I write a direct mail letter that goes to millions of people, it's a personal piece of correspondence direct from me to a few million people. How unusual. Wait, let me rephrase that: When I include a sheet of paper in a mailing that <u>looks like</u> a letter...

OK, let's start at the very beginning. In truth, a letter is really a personal communication you write to one or two people. When you send it to a few hundred, a few thousand, or a few million people, it's an advertisement. Specifically, what you see in most direct mail packages is a one-page, highly stylized ad, designed to look like a letter. Any arguments?

When you include a page in your mailing package that looks like a letter, people really perceive it as a letter. They read it as they would a letter, a personal piece of correspondence from you to them. No other medium can do this. When people receive a brochure, they know that many brochures were printed. When they see an ad on TV, they know it is broadcast to everyone. But a letter—that's a piece of personal correspondence—that's different. You can produce such a one-to-one piece of correspondence, too. It just has to look like a letter. It is the strongest, hardest-working part of the creative package you mail.

Since "the letter" is really a highly specific, stylized ad designed to look like a letter, to achieve maximum effectiveness in this special format, this part of your mailpiece really should look exactly like a letter. Sounds simple but some people forget. The more it looks like a traditional letter, the better it works. This means typewriter-style type, on a white or light-colored page, with a letterhead. Its effectiveness can be astounding if it is written well, of good design, and aimed with precision.

The letter is far more important than a brochure, and it can be effective if used just by itself. If you set it up right, keep it visually interesting, and use good copywriting skills and tricks, sending a letter by itself in an envelope can be a complete and effective direct mail package.

A letter is a self-portrait of the sender in a direct mail campaign.

Brochures can take any shape, form, or slant. But a direct mail letter has to conform to a very tight direct mail format to be effective. Since it's so specific, this format is easy to learn.

In direct mail, the letter is the medium, the ad, the literature, and the sales vehicle. It's all rolled into one or two pages. In a direct mail campaign, a letter is a self-portrait of the sender. If you can write and design a good letter, and aim it with precision, you can make sales. Companies and individuals will buy your products and use your services. No other skills are required.

Ground Rules

Here are the basic rules to follow—an instruction manual on how to write and design a good direct mail letter. When should you break these rules? Only when you can find concrete evidence from your own mailings that following the rules draws less response. But I wouldn't hold my breath waiting for this. These rules have been proven time and time again in billions of mailed packages. When your mailings reach upward of a million households or businesses, you can start experimenting with what works best for your own products. Until then, stick to the rules. By following this format, it's possible to mail a single letter about your product or service offer to potential customers and have great results. No brochure or other literature is necessary, although it can round out the package nicely. The letter <u>sells</u> with user benefits. The brochure <u>tells</u> the product features. A brochure also gives you added credibility.

Unless you are exceptionally long-winded like me, most commercial direct mail letters should be typed on a single side of a standard 8 1/2" x 11" sheet of paper, then folded <u>copy side out</u> to be seen as soon as the recipient opens the envelope. If it requires more than one page, it's least expensive to use the back of the sheet for the second side (although this

The Danielle Adams Publishing Company
Box 100, Merion Station PA 19066

never looks as good as two pages printed on the face only, its lower costs may justify this). It should still be folded with the first side facing out. Although more expensive, it's better to use two single sheets printed on the face only.

If the package requires even longer copy, my first choice is to use an 11" x 17" sheet folded in half, providing space for a four-page letter. This is also the most effective format for a three page letter, leaving the back of the last page blank. This allows for plenty of selling copy and plenty of white space around it, so it won't look too forbidding to read. Always frame your copy with lots of white space in a broad border. This "breathing area" makes it look more inviting and appear easier to read. Which brings up rule number 1: People must read your letter for it to be effective.

If you find your letter is slightly too long for one page, extend the right margin—perhaps five or eight spaces—and type to almost the paper's edge on the bottom. Before printing the final copy, reduce the letter by 5 percent or 10 percent on a quality photocopy machine. You can also ask a printer to shoot it down by having a photostat made to 90 percent or 95 percent of its original size (the same as reducing it 5 percent or 10 percent, but this is the way printers describe this reduction). This reduction will give your letter additional white space around the top and sides.

So if it looks like it's going to take a long time to read, it's just tossed in the pile to be read sometime between later and never, and eventually winds up getting thrown out.

The reduction will also yield one or two more words on each line, and an extra one-half to one inch, top to bottom (10 percent of 11 inches is 1.1 inches). At the same time, the type will be slightly smaller, and again, more inviting to read. I sometimes reduce the size of the type just to make it appear shorter and easier to read.

Most recipients are reluctant to admit, even to themselves, that they are going to sit and read a promotional letter for 10 or 15 minutes. So if it looks like it's going to take a long time to read, it's just tossed in the pile to be read sometime between later and never, and eventually winds up getting thrown out. Hence, rule number 2: It must look easy to read to get people to read it.

Keep the letter visually stimulating. Use visual tricks to gain and hold the reader's attention. Keep the reader from becoming bored by a visual wall of repetitive blocks of plain gray type. <u>Underline</u> one or two words, <u>or a short phrase</u>, in all but one or two of the paragraphs.

Bold type can be effective if used occasionally to call attention to important points like the **Toll Free Number** or **Free Shipping**. Use bold in one or two paragraphs. For words in a list, bold can be used more frequently.

Use all capital letters only once or twice on a page for a short phrase that really is an attractive benefit, such as "FREE OVERNIGHT SHIPPING." You can get an idea of how effective this is even in this typeset page. When presented in typewriter-style type in a letter, it pops off the page.

Don't get too cute or go crazy with all those slick type styles (called fonts) now available for computers. Use a typeface that makes your letter look like it was just typed on a typewriter. There are several versions of typewriter-style type, and I recommend these over having the letter typeset in an advertising-style typeface. The fonts Courier, made popular by the standard version of IBM typewriters, and American Typewriter, a typeface designed by the typehouse of ITC (must be set at a service bureau or typesetting house) are my favorites. Several other typefaces are OK, too; these are just my personal recommendations.

The size of the type in a letter should be determined by the amount of copy you have and the amount of space you allot to it. I usually set the typeface of American Typewriter at 9/11 (pronounced 9 on 11) which means the size of the type is 9 point (there are 72 points to the inch) on an 11 point leading. Leading (pronounced as if written "ledding") is the amount of space between lines.

The term "leading" is a carry-over from the days when all type was actually cast in a mixture of molten lead. Thin strips of lead were placed between the lines to increase the space—hence the name leading.

In those days, typesetters sat next to a vat of the molten lead mixture, and each character was actually cast in lead, just the way it had been done for centuries. The individual metal characters were stored in two wooden type trays called cases, each containing multiple compartments. Type was taken by hand from the two type cases, upper and lower, which gave rise to the designations uppercase and lowercase.

The compositor, or the person pulling the type, placed it in a small metal tray called a stick. The metal type was then locked in a "chase," and an ink roller was rolled over it, leaving ink on the characters' raised surfaces. Paper was then placed on the inked character surface, and the image of the characters was transferred onto the paper in ink. This was called "pulling a proof." Type was purchased by book printers and advertising agencies in a "galley," and assembled into its final form, called a "mechanical." Ah, the good old days. Boy, times sure have changed.

Courier is still my favorite typeface for letters. It is used 12/12 because it looks OK in a slightly larger size. It can be used 11/12, 11/11, and 10/11 if the copy is long, but the believability of "this just came off my typewriter" falls off fast if it is used too small. When reducing type to smaller proportions, it's best to use American Typewriter for commercial letters. It looks typeset, yet professional, and the result still looks like a letter.

```
This is a sample of Courier 9/10
This is a sample of Courier 9/10

This is a sample of Courier 10/12
This is a sample of Courier 10/12

This is a sample of Courier 12/12
This is a sample of Courier 12/12
```

If it gives a clean impression, you can just use your old typewriter—I used one for years. An IBM Selectric isn't a bad choice, either.

—— **POWERFUL** ——

Powerful Investment Company, 5432 Spruce Street, Philadelphia, PA 19103
~ Telephone 215-987-6543 ~

September 2008

Dear Investor:

Want an easy and safe way to instantly double your money?

My grandfather told this to me when I was nine: Fold it in half and put it in your pocket. It worked pretty well then. Times change.

Without sound investment management, you don't have investments, you just have savings... like leaving money in your back pocket.

We believe <u>your money should work hard for you</u>. If you have $2,500 to $50,000 or more to invest, please call me personally at 876-5432. I'll recommend a managed investment program that can work hard at making money for you right now.

Recommended investments are based on your present financial resources and your financial objectives and goals. They are designed specifically for you. We can work together to outline a plan to make you more money, faster. Your investments will <u>start making money for you right away</u>.

Please **call now** and I'll be happy to send you - **FREE** - our track record and current stock recommendations. We always make this GUARANTEE: No charge for investment advice unless it makes you money. The <u>initial consultation is FREE</u>.

Thank you for your consideration to do business with us. We are always as close as your phone. Please call anytime.

Sincerely,

Jeffrey Dobkin
Powerful Investment Company

P.S. CALL NOW to receive our current stock recommendations you can use in your portfolio right now — to start making money for you immediately. Call 876-5432, and please always feel free to ask for me personally. Thank you.

Letter Analysis and Notes for Investor Letter

ASSIGNMENT: One-page letter to investors to solicit their business.
TEASER COPY ON THE ENVELOPE READ:
"A SAFE AND EASY WAY TO
IMMEDIATELY DOUBLE YOUR MONEY.
DETAILS INSIDE..."
This letter is set in Courier type, 10/12.

Objective: Call. In its call to action to get the reader to pick up the phone, this letter requests a phone call from the reader FIVE TIMES!

Letter stresses benefit of "Make More Money NOW!" which is what both my client and I thought drove the market. I sell the immediate call very hard.

Between the teaser copy on the envelope and the first paragraph, we figured nearly 99% of the people receiving this letter opened it. We were right - the mailing was very successful.

Note every line ending is directed - each paragraph has a first line slightly shorter on the right- hand side than the rest of the paragraph. This doesn't happen by chance.

The FREE offer of his current stock recommendations was a strong premium, the client later told me. Many people called for this free premium and were eventually converted to continuing clients.

Above all, the letter must look attractive. It should have lots of white space, making it look easy to read, even if it isn't. The best way for me to show you some of the tricks for reducing the look of the amount of information in a letter is to include several examples. Eye-catching tricks to make the information look short, to attract attention to selected benefits, and to draw the reader into the letter are included as letter models and referenced throughout the book.

Eyeflow

The eyes of the reader look briefly at the letterhead, then glance at the salutation, read the first paragraph if it's short, and scan the letter, sometimes reading a short paragraph or what's underlined or in bold while drifting down to the signature. Then they start reading at the P.S.—So the P.S. is one of the most important parts of a direct mail letter. It gets read first, and sometimes again last. This is the best place to restate your offer and your most powerful benefit. Every direct mail letter should have a P.S. To verify this, just check your mailbox, and see what elements all the successful commercial mailers have on their page that looks like a letter.

THE DANIELLE ADAMS MAIL ORDER COMPANY
~ SATISFACTION ALWAYS GUARANTEED ~
Box 100 • Merion Station, PA 19066
Telephone 610/642-1000

```
* * * * * * * * * * * *
FREE SHIPPING
OF ALL ORDERS
* * * * * * * * * * * *
```

Dear Business Owner and Colleague:

   To check stock instantly... To find out about a new product... To get a quick price quote...

   Please call us **Toll Free: 800-234-IDEA**! Your call is always welcome! For over eight years Merion Station has been pleased to provide a fast, accurate product distribution service to all our friends in the small business field. Call us TOLL FREE and get:

   · Immediate delivery on most orders.
   · All orders processed within 24 hours!
      Rush orders shipped same day!
   · Complete stock of parts from 90 manufacturers!
   · All manufacturer's discounts applied automatically!
   · Return privileges to one convenient source.
   · Complimentary instructions with
      quantity orders.
   · "Set" packaging for re-sold products.
   · Proforma invoicing, your account is billed directly.

   But most important, call us and get friendly! Yes, call us and get friendly, helpful people - happy to save you time and money and reduce your paperwork. We are pleased to provide you with a complete selection of products from 90 manufacturers from one source, plus FREE SHIPPING AND HANDLING. And your call is always welcome!

                    Yours very truly,

                    Jeffrey Dobkin
                    President

P.S. What's new? Call us to make sure your name is added to our complimentary mailing list to get our newest **FREE CATALOG** with OVER 10,000 products. Call right now - 610/642-1000 and we'll rush you a FREE copy right away! Then we'll always keep you posted with What's New!

                              Please open...

Letter Analysis and Notes for Distributor Letter

ASSIGNMENT: One-page letter, front of four-page brochure to small business owners. SELF-MAILER, NO ENVELOPE. FRONT PAGE WAS DESIGNED TO LOOK LIKE A LETTER.

This letter is set in Courier type, 10/11.5; original was set in American Typewriter.

Objective: Call. Call or Call Now is stated SIX TIMES in the letter.

FREE is used as an incentive for ordering, free shipping, free mailing list.

The catalog was given away as a terrific free premium, although it was really only a traditional product listing catalog of books the firm carried. The letter and the rest of the brochure sold the service with a hard sell stressing immediate shipping, toll-free ordering, and rush order accommodation. Firm was positioning itself as a friendly, service-oriented distributor.

Before Writing Letter Copy

Know your audience. To whom, or to what market segment, is this letter being sent? Write your letter as if you are writing to an individual person. You should know as much about him, and his fellow recipients, as you possibly can. Are they old or young; executives, college graduates, or blue collar workers; rich or poor; housewives or working mothers? To a large degree, this will dictate the composition of the letter. When writing, keep your audience firmly in mind. Make sure every reader will understand what you are saying. When in doubt, keep it simple and keep words short.

Next, know your product or service. If possible, hold it, touch it, feel it. Is it better than the competition, and in what ways? Are there differences you can point out that make your product unique? Is it cheaper, bigger, smaller or more attractive? What are the advantages or innovations of your product that make it unique? What makes it better than the others in the field? What sets your product apart? Before writing anything, you should have a clear picture firmly in mind of both your audience and your product. Product differentiation will translate into user benefits.

As in a magazine advertisement, nothing is worse in a direct marketing letter than having no objective. As in an ad, the usual objective of a commercial direct mail package is to have the recipient respond in some way: by calling, sending in a card, sending an order, making an inquiry, and my favorite, sending money. These objectives are wrapped in an attractive package of clean graphics and tightly written copy, both focused closely on making an offer the recipient can't refuse.

OK, you can pick up your pen now. To start, write the objective of your letter in the upper right-hand corner of a blank page. What do you

Your Local Cable Company
1234 Third Street • Mytown, PA 19004
~ Telephone 215-876-5432 ~

September 2008

Dear Neighbor:

We can make you famous.

While the cost of buying time on commercial
television remains high, right now advertising on cable
is at an <u>incredibly low introductory price</u>.

You can now have the impact of a television ad, at a
cost less than radio. Sight, sound, and motion will make your
business message stand out and come alive. The low cost means
you'll be seen with a frequency all our subscribers are sure to
notice. You'll get more calls, and more customers will come
into your store after seeing your ad.

Of course, you'll only be famous in Philadelphia.
But, if you're looking for <u>repeat buyers who live close by</u>...
customers in your neighborhood... and upscale prospects in your
own targeted shopping area - give us a call. And take advantage
of becoming famous at our low introductory price.

Thank you - we're sure you'll be pleased with your ad
results: an IMMEDIATE INCREASE in customers. Please call now
for our <u>limited time</u> only introductory rate schedule.

Kindest regards,

Jeffrey Dobkin
for Local Cable

P.S. **Call now (876-5432)**—we'll be glad to send complete rate
information in today's mail. Hurry, our low rate guarantee is
for a short time only. Please call today.

Letter Analysis and Notes for Cable Letter

> ASSIGNMENT: One-page, one-side direct mail letter. The package also included a one-page data sheet to solicit new advertisers for local cable station.
> Teaser Copy on Envelope: "We Can Make You Famous."
> This letter is set in Courier type, 10/11; original was set in 12/12.
> Objective: Call. To fulfill this objective, the letter asks FOUR TIMES for the reader to call!
> Letter starts with continuation of teaser copy for an electric one-line opening paragraph.
> Benefit-heavy letter copy states results of advertising on cable.
> Hurry-up incentive states offer is for limited time only, call now.
> Presented two times in letter.
> All paragraphs have shortened first lines to make letter appear easier to read. All line endings are called in every letter I write. Note how short line endings are in second paragraph - this is the only way it looked OK. If I left "television" on the first line, the second line was very short, as "incredibly" wouldn't fit. When you run into problems like this, just do what looks best.

want your recipient to do? Call? Write? Send in the reply card? Ask for information? Request a sales call? Place an order? All copy will be drafted to fulfill the central theme of your objective, so write it at the top of the page so you don't lose sight.

Then take a blank sheet of paper and draw a line down the center. List your product's features on the left, and the benefits of each feature to the purchaser on the right. From this you are going to pick up and show the benefits in the letter.

Show the features in the brochure, flaunt the benefits in the letter, and sell the response hard. That is the secret of success in direct mail.

Dear Neighbor:

My name is Jeff Dobkin. My phone number is 876-5432.

I live at 5432 Gregory Way. I've lived at this address for over 15 years. I'm your neighbor. I care about this neighborhood.

That's why I'm writing to you. If you care about the preservation of our neighborhood, please vote for me, Jeff Dobkin, as your representative for the 5th Congressional District.

My goal as a public official: to focus government on a local level. And to give each person ready access to government. My door is always open to you, and you may call me at any time. Even in the evenings, at my home.

Although I am the Democratic candidate, I firmly believe appointments to government positions should be made on the basis of a person's merit, not party affiliation.

My office will serve as an open-door advocacy center for neighborhood groups - as well as for individual residents - in dealings with the government. I fully endorse responsible government management that is completely accessible to everyone.

I know this is unusual, and that you are not used to a government representative with this type of openness. But you have my commitment as your neighbor and friend: I will serve our community's best interests, and preserve the unity of our neighborhood.

Please think about the open-door policy I have outlined in this letter. When you vote, please pull the handle next to my name. And Democrat or Republican, please vote for me, Jeffrey Dobkin. Thank you. Call anytime, your call is always welcome.

Yours very truly,

Jeffrey Dobkin
Your Neighbor

P.S. Please come out on Nov. 5 and vote for your neighbor, Jeff Dobkin. Republican or Democrat, show your support for our freedom of choice, and our right to choose our own government. Thank you.

> "There is no Republican or Democratic way to manage local government. Our township and government are best served by representatives who are totally accessible, and responsive to the needs of our own community."
> Jeffrey Dobkin
> Oct. 5, 2007

The Danielle Adams Publishing Company
Box 100, Merion Station PA 19066

Letter Analysis and Notes for Political Letter

> ASSIGNMENT: Political letter for Democratic candidate in Republican county.
> Envelope copy just showed name and address in typewriter-style type in corner.
> This letter is set in Courier type, 9/11.
> Sidebar is set in Bookman Italic, 8/12.
> Objective: Vote for Jeff Dobkin - stated in the letter THREE TIMES! To ensure voters remember my name, it appears SIX times.
> Approach: Everyone likes what's best for their own neighborhood and their own community. This is stressed hard throughout the letter.
> Electric single-line opening paragraph: Almost no one gives a home phone number in a mass-mailed form letter. In reality, an extra incoming phone line is only about ten dollars a month - if you buy the cheapest service and make no calls. It is worth it - it only rings on political calls, and a message machine may be connected to it to avoid interruptions at dinner.
> In all paragraphs except the last, the top line is slightly shorter on the right-hand side. This makes for a better design - it appears easier to read, and less busy overall.
> What appears as a quote on the side of the letter is really just additional and harder selling copy. The whole letter is a quote from me; I wrote it. This is just a layout device to increase readership of this hard selling copy - by making it a quote and having it appear outside the letter body. It also saves the three lines it would take if it were to appear in the letter body.
> In the second paragraph, only one space is used after the first period so that "neighborhood" fits on that line.
> Three times in the letter, I mention "Republican or Democrat" to lessen the distinction.

Products contain features. A person buys the product to receive the benefits of its features. The benefits are the advantages the features bring to the user. No one cares if you can make your product light in weight. That's a product feature. The benefit to the reader is, no more lugging a heavy product back and forth. That's what you sell, because user benefits are the reason a person buys through direct mail.

The feature of a lifetime guarantee on a pocket knife offers the benefit that your knife is of the highest quality customers can get; it's one that they'll have forever. It will become their old friend... and it's the last one they'll ever need to buy. Those are the benefits of a lifetime guarantee. The feature of a 440 carbon steel blade has little meaning to a potential purchaser, but if you say it will hold a keen edge, only needs to be sharpened once every five years and will be sharp enough to shave with after a full year of hard use—those are the benefits that sell products through the mail. A product has features, but the benefits are what attract the customer to make a purchase. Show the features in the brochure, flaunt the benefits in the letter, and sell the response hard. That is the secret of success in direct mail.

~ **WXXX Radio** ~
123 Any Street, Anywhere, USA ~

*We don't accept advertising, or take
contributions from those who would give us a playlist.
But to stay non-commercial, we need your help.*

Our Promise: More music - lots of it! Less hype. Less repetition.
Knowledgeable DJs. Diverse music. And NO COMMERCIALS.

Dear Introductory Member:

Ever wonder why all commercial radio sounds the same?
And why WXXX can bring you <u>fresh new music</u> from fresh new artists?

We don't depend on large research companies in faraway cities
to tell us what to play in Mississippi. We look to our own listeners
and friends to tell us what they'd like to hear.

Commercial stations have an overriding need to deliver their
audience to their advertisers. As <u>commercial-free radio</u>, we don't depend
on large advertising dollars for our money. We're not trying to make a
big profit - <u>we just need to pay our bills</u>.

            If WXXX makes a difference in your life -
                · Opens your eyes to new and emerging artists
                · Keeps you informed of music on the cutting edge
                · Plays music you don't hear anywhere else
                · Sounds fresh and new - with NO COMMERCIALS -
        we have only you to turn to. Your support is needed now
        to help WXXX continue with our commercial-free broadcasting.

Thank you for your introductory membership. You're now invited
to join and enjoy all the benefits of a full WXXX membership. Be invited
to private parties. Get invitations to special events. Receive our newsletter
all year long - just bring your original contribution up to
$40, to become a full member.

Join and meet other members who share your love of music. Get
your own WXXX Membership Card: good for special backstage events and free passes.
If you value your music, just send in your added contribution to get FULL MEMBERSHIP
PRIVILEGES for an <u>entire year</u>. So you don't forget, please send today.

                    Thank you so much,

                    Jeffrey Dobkin
                    for Radio Station WXXX

P.S. Get our new "Inside WXXX" newsletter - FREE - all year long. Get a great-looking
T-shirt or a terrific coffee mug. Or win $500 worth of music; see the enclosed brochure
for details. And <u>please send in your membership donation today</u>. Thank you.

The Danielle Adams Publishing Company
Box 100, Merion Station PA 19066

Letter Analysis and Notes for Radio Letter

> ASSIGNMENT: Letter series to increase membership. This letter is to upgrade contributors to full membership.
> Objective: Send money - requested three times in letter.
> Letter is set in Courier type, 8/11 to fit this book. Original was 10/12 and the shortened paragraph was 9/10. Copy at top of letter is 8 point Bookman on a 10 point lead.
> From the fifth paragraph on, the letter is very benefit heavy - what you get when you donate.
> Note use of pre-salutation blocks of copy - for two reasons: it (1) separates this copy from body of the letter to make it stronger, and (2) makes the letter body shorter by presenting this in smaller type up at the top. If this was in the letter body, the letter would run over one page.
> Letter series got progressively harder selling as we continued to solicit funds.
> Again, all sentence endings are planned.

AIDA

Rules of direct marketing. There are four reasons for almost every sentence in your letter, and each sentence should be written to fulfill at least one of them. AIDA. First, <u>A</u>ttract attention. Are they looking where you want them to? Do you have their attention? Are you drawing your reader into your work? OK, move on to number two. Arouse <u>I</u>nterest. Without interest, your letter never gets read. It gets tossed out, or the page gets turned. Once you have their attention, do you hold it? Is your copy compelling, demanding to be read? Will even a friend read it in its entirety? Are you making it so your reader can't possibly put it down until it's finished?

Third, <u>D</u>irect that interest... to your product, the benefits, and the offer, and point to the response. Fourth, ask for <u>A</u>ction. This is where your objective takes shape, and you earn your copywriting money. Ask for action several times (your objective): Send today... just check the "Yes" box... send back the postage-paid... Be specific when you tell your customers what you want them to do. Don't be afraid to tell them more than once. Make sure every line in your letter fits one of these four categories.

OK, you can start writing.

Start with a Rough Draft

To get the copy of your letter as tight as you can, you must realize up front you are going to write several drafts, and probably have many revisions. So the first couple of drafts are naturally going to be rough. Why do you think they call it a rough draft? Be prepared for this, and just concentrate on getting thoughts, ideas, feelings, and style down on paper. As you refine and rewrite them, don't worry, they'll get tighter. In this initial session, you merely want to get a few pages of copywriting, notes, and your main ideas and biggest benefits down on paper. Everyone starts with a rough draft. Everyone.

Here's the best trick I have ever learned in writing copy: Go back and delete your first sentence.

Here's the best trick I have ever learned in writing copy: Go back and delete your first sentence. Simple, isn't it? This brings your copy into a fast start, and 99 percent of the time it works.

If you are having trouble starting, just write anything. Start anywhere. Put hand to pencil and paper, and write just about anything that comes into your head. Write to your spouse or grandmother about your product. Write a letter to your brother. Just to start the words flowing from your pen and the creative juices percolating. Then go back and strike out your first two or three sentences. Another nice trick. If you are really having a bad day, strike out your first paragraph. Once you start, you'll find it's easier to continue, and then you can change the focus of your writing to user benefits. The hardest part of copywriting, as in all jobs, is starting.

Write at length; include everything you feel is a purchaser's benefit. Keep writing. This is not the time to edit your writing; that will come later. Now is the time to get all those ideas on paper. Make notes and rough drafts. Include all ideas. You can be windy when you write, like I am. For a one-page final letter, write three or four pages, minimum. Write profusely.

Then take a break. You deserve it. Nice job. Do not edit or nix ideas or thoughts when you are writing—leave everything in. Everything you think— the good ideas, the bad ideas, even the silly stuff—write it all down, no matter how outrageous it may be. If you start editing, you will stop the idea flow and the session will be self-defeating. <u>Then, in a separate session, edit severely</u>.

After a few rewrites, get away from your work for a while and do other things. Then, after an hour or two (a day or two if you have the luxury of time), return. This grace period is <u>a necessary part</u> of the creative process so you can see your writing in a fresh light. When you get back to the letter you wrote, read it fast and mark it up on the fly. Note words or thoughts that seem out of place and awkward, and strike them out.

If you can't decide if a block of copy should stay or go, strike it out at this time. Remember, there isn't room for everything. And there's no room for guessing—if you have to guess if you should leave something in or not, take it out—or your reader won't be so kind. When they get to the awkward part, they'll throw the whole thing away. For every letter I write, I'll have written it, read it, rewritten it, and refined it so many times before the final draft, I just about have it memorized.

Stress benefits heavily. Benefit-centered copy works, and you should orient all your writing to your product's benefits. With the objective in the upper right-hand corner of your paper, compare every line you write to it. Does this line or sentence help the objective, while fulfilling one of the four reasons for each sentence? Will someone reading this line be more interested in your offer? Will they be more apt to fulfill the objective? Then edit severely again. Keep the copy interesting, tight, and crisp. Leave only your best stuff on the page. Finally, edit again. I say this from lots of experience.

Since we all see so much information, especially promotional material, you have only a few seconds to grab and hold the reader's attention. Then you have all the time in the world or until your copy gets uninteresting, whichever comes first, to keep the reader in your package. The moral of this story: Keep your letters as short as you can. Use an exciting and provocative opening sentence. Start with your biggest benefit first, then expand on that benefit. You may write at length, but then edit very severely.

The Danielle Adams Publishing Company
Box 100, Merion Station PA 19066

Successful Low Cost Direct Marketing Methods

2-Page Self-Promotion Letter • Set in Courier 12/
Sent to Direct Mailers who sent me solicitation
packages that could use improvement.

THE DANIELLE ADAMS PUBLISHING COMPANY

~ Office of the President ~
Box 100 ✶ Merion Station, PA 19066
610/642-1000 ✶ Fax 610/642-6832

GET A FREE ANALYSIS OF YOUR DIRECT MAIL PACKAGE
OVER THE PHONE. RIGHT NOW!
~ CALL TODAY: 610-642-1000 ~

Dear Fellow Direct Mailer:

This isn't really a letter.

A letter is a personal communication you write
to one or two people.

But when you send it to a few hundred, a few thousand,
or a million people, it's an advertisement. This is a highly
stylized ad designed to look like a letter.

What you are reading is an ad for my services. I admit it.
What you mailed to me wasn't a letter either. It just looked like
a letter. Same as this.

While you may not know me, you've probably seen my work.
For the past 25 years I've been writing direct mail for ad agencies,
mail order houses, catalogs, and direct response firms. My writing
skills bring in additional orders and money fast, for people who
market through the mail, just as you do.

> *Every piece of correspondence you send is an opportunity to*
> *conduct additional business with your reader. If your*
> *communications aren't bringing you every possible response*
> *they can, I can help you change all that forever.*

If you'd like to <u>get more inquiries</u>, <u>get more sales</u>,
and squeeze more profit out of each and every mailing you
send, just give me a call: 610/642-1000.

The reason I am writing you is I have received your mailing
package. If you're mailing a lot of these, I can increase your
response. While there are no guarantees, a 200% or 300%
increase is not unusual. 10 TIMES or 20 TIMES can also occur.

There's no secret to what I do.

Next page, please...

The direct mail package you sent me may receive a satisfying draw, but you can increase your response rate by staying within a tighter successful direct mail format.

That's what I'll do… bring your mailing package up to spec. <u>More people will read it</u>. <u>More people will call</u>. You'll get more response, faster; and you'll make more money, starting with your very next mailing. And every mailing thereafter.

As a direct mail copywriter, I'm quite used to pulling-in <u>well over my costs</u> in additional inquiries, increased orders, larger sales, and more profit for each of my clients.

> <u>To discover the sales you're missing from</u> <u>your mailings, please give me a call. I'm always</u> <u>as close as your phone. There is certainly no</u> <u>cost, no obligation.</u>

Just let me know you'd like to get more sales and better results from each of your mailings. Why don't you give me a call right now - I'm friendly, and I'm always glad to help. The analysis is free, but this free offer is only for a short time, so please call now.

Kindest regards,

Jeffrey Dobkin

~ GET INSTANT HELP, RIGHT NOW, FOR FREE ~

P.S. Need help fast? GET A FREE REVIEW of your mailing package over the phone. Comments, criticisms, & specific instructions to make your package <u>immediately draw more response!</u> <u>Get more sales and inquiries with your very next mailing</u>. Just call me right now: 610/642-1000.

"Biggest Benefit Happened" Theory

One of the best ways to write benefit-oriented copy, and to develop your envelope teaser copy, letter lead, letter introduction, and P.S. copy—not to mention the headline of your direct marketing ad—is to ask, "What is the biggest benefit of using this product?" In the answer lie your ad headline, envelope teaser copy, first sentence, and the lead paragraph of your letter.

> # Give it all you've got, first—while you have everyone's attention. What are you saving it for?

Ask, "What is the best result that can possibly happen when a person uses this product? What is the best result they can possibly achieve?" For example, if I were teaching a copywriting course, I might stress in the sales letter, "By the end of this class, the headline of the ad you are writing will pop out of your typewriter, and the rest of the ad will practically write itself." Picture the biggest benefit, the very best result that can possibly happen, and write it in the envelope teaser, headline, intro, letter, or P.S., or incorporate it into all of the above. This is the big bang; give it all you've got, first—while you have everyone's attention. What are you saving it for? Fire all your guns at once, and explode into your letter. Why take a chance and wait till you lose readers? Start out with the best, first.

Lead off with your biggest benefit in the first paragraph, then expound on it in the second paragraph. More people will see it when it's presented first. If it's buried somewhere in the back of the letter, most people won't get that far. Feature it where it will attract the most attention and create the most interest right away. Lead off with your best stuff. Arouse interest right from the start.

Letterhead and Letter Parts

We now know the letter is really a highly specific stylized ad or brochure designed to <u>look</u> like a letter. To further this impression, use a letterhead with your company logo, if you have one (your company name and address typeset at the top) or your own name and address (if you are marketing a product or service personally). You can use a single selling line incorporated into your letterhead to let readers know what you're about, or use your first line to convince them to buy your product or service or call you. Examples showing quality would be: "A Tradition of Excellence," "A Tradition of Quality," "World's Finest...." Examples of selling the call would be "Call us Toll-Free," or "Your Call Is Welcome At...."

Following the letterhead, it's best to show a date, even if it's just the month and year (i.e., September 2007). But if you think the mailing may be delayed, leave this off. Better to have no date than an old date. Better yet to plan ahead, but you didn't need me to tell you that. When planning your mailing, start with the date you'd like to have it in the mail and work backward. Keep in mind that everything except sex and bingo takes longer than it should.

Letter Introduction

Use the area directly under the letterhead (but before the salutation and body of the letter) to get in a short message that will not appear as part of the letter. Directly below the letterhead you may, at your discretion, have a couple of lines dedicated to the most important selling features, best offer, or benefits, or a few lines that create additional interest. Some mailers even leave off the letterhead of company name and address in favor of an early, heavier block of selling copy.

Information presented here should be brief and in shortened form. This copy is separate from the body of the letter, and the space should be used to arouse interest. A few major benefits set off with bullets can also be effective. A visual enhancement such as lines, stars, or dashes may also be used here. When information is boxed off at the top of the letter by these elements, this device, in direct mail terms, is called a Johnson box. It can entice the reader who doesn't really want to read the body copy of the letter with a capsule of what is being offered, or just the salient points or benefits.

The copy above the body of the letter can be set in any type style and any size type, since it's not really viewed as part of the body of the letter. It can almost be an ad in itself, but don't use a border, which will take away from the intended image of the page: *this is a letter.* Following this area comes the letter itself, in traditional form and format.

The Salutation

To introduce the letter, "Dear Reader" can be used. It's safe, but it's always my last choice. Because this is a personal medium, the closer you can get to the heart, the occupation, or the passion of the person, the better. If you're writing to physicians, use "Dear Doctor" or "Dear Physician"; to veterinarians, "Dear Animal Lover." If you're writing to businesspeople, "Dear Colleague" is one of my universal favorites. It has a wide application.

To a specialized audience, such as people who own or work in pharmacies, "Dear Pharmacist" is a good way to start. To people who work with wood, use "Dear Fellow Woodworker." Common sense prevails. Other favorites are "Dear Neighbor," "Dear Friend," or "Dear Enthusiast." Following this are similar general terms like "Dear Valued Customer" and "Dear Valued Patron." My very favorite idea to enhance all the general headings is to put "and Friend" after the greeting. Examples of this are "Dear Customer and Friend," or "Dear Neighbor and Friend." Don't take a chance with something too cute, which may turn people off or appear insincere. Stay with the basics.

Letter Body

An opening paragraph should be one, maybe two lines at most. A single line can be most electric.

The Danielle Adams Publishing Company
Box 100, Merion Station PA 19066

The copy should be written to your audience. If you are writing to consumers, it should be in a <u>very conversational tone</u>—like this book. The text should read as though you're speaking to someone, man to man, woman to woman, one on one. If your offer is to businesses, or more technical people, you can use bigger words. But for the best response, it still should be conversational in tone. I never recommend big words. Scientists and technical people are just people with different sets of skills who don't know how to dress (plaid shirt, plaid sport coat, plastic pocket pen protectors, yeesh!). In every English class I've ever taken, the instructor has always told me to increase my vocabulary, especially if I wanted to be a writer. That's probably why I went into direct mail—big words don't work. It's a good thing I never let my education get in the way of an effective mailpiece.

Make the first line short and compelling to read. Like this.

Here you can see the value of a line that stands alone. Since it's short and set apart, everyone will read it. The first line of the letter is the single most important line because it must interest the reader and convince him to continue reading. It's like the headline of an ad, which grabs the reader and demands that he read further. That's exactly what the first line in your letter should do. An opening paragraph should be one line, maybe two lines at most. A single line can be most electric. Arouse the interest of the reader. Draw him in. A single line is too short to pass up, and everyone does read it.

To start the eyeflow of the reader, indent the first line of all paragraphs five spaces. This also breaks up the monotony of squared-off visual blocks of copy. Set the paragraphs to rag right (ragged edge of type on the right-hand side) to further break up the look of the copy. Never justify the main body of the letter.

To make the letter look less forbidding, be faster to read, and have an easier eye flow, make the top line of each paragraph shorter on the right-hand side than the lines in the rest of the paragraph. This adds an attractive design element to each visual block of copy (paragraph) and encourages reading.

Most of the time this works, but occasionally it creates a bad break, poor choice of a line ending, or a widow. If it creates a bad result, poor copy flow, or an awkward sentence ending, forget it. Sometimes this added element of design just doesn't work, as you may want to keep a thought or phrase together. Since we are dealing with letters as both copy and art, notice and make a deliberate call on where each line breaks on the right-hand side of the letter.

As in any piece of art, each element of the design can enhance or detract from the response. The more elements you consciously think about and directly control, the less you leave to chance, the better the letter will work for you. This will also ensure your letter will be consistent. Always keep in mind you are not writing a letter, you are writing copy and inserting it into a piece of art. The objective of the art is to create a handsome and attractive design that makes the copy appear easy to read. The objective of the copy is to guide the reader through a set of benefits leading logically to a desire to order the product.

Limit paragraph length to seven lines or less. If a paragraph runs longer than seven lines, break it into two paragraphs. Artificially broken paragraphs are OK—this isn't English class, it's real life.

Stagger the paragraph lengths so they don't all look the same, keeping the copy visually fresh and interesting. The objective of varying the text block design of the letter is to make it look inviting. No one wants to read a wall of type where each paragraph looks exactly the same.

To further break up the copy and keep it visually interesting, in the center of the letter you can list bulleted information that will catch and hold the reader's attention. Bulleted copy:

- Directs eyeflow to this area
- Draws attention to the important parts
- Shows the strongest benefits
- Enhances the best offer
- Highlights the guarantee
- Pulls the eye to features you want readers to see
- Increases the response you want

If your heart is set on showing the features of your product, the best way to list them is in this brief, bulleted style.

Another visual trick in direct mail letters is to use a shortened paragraph:

> You may also use a shortened paragraph in the center of the page to direct the reader's eyes to the important points. Indent a paragraph on both sides with wide margins, and justify the type to further set it apart from the rest of the letter.

This paragraph can be of a smaller or different typeface. A paragraph like this provides additional visual interest. When used with a smaller typeface, it can also increase the amount of copy you can get on a single page without making it looking crammed or forbidding to read.

When you are writing the letter copy, keep in mind that what you're working on isn't really a traditional letter, and you can't dash it off in a few moments. It's two-thirds copy, and one-third art and design. If the letter is going to many recipients, it's worth the time and effort you're going to put into it. Unfortunately, all this time is spent up front. When I write a tight one-page letter, it takes me about five to eight hours from start to finish. Most of the time I even know what I'm doing, with umpteen years of experience specifically in direct mail writing, and thousands of hours of practice. Allow yourself more time and take it. You may spend up to a week on a one-page letter. That's OK, too. I still have difficult assignments for which it takes a week or more to write and design a single page. Some are more difficult than others.

Avoid starting any paragraph with the first-person singular "I." Remember, you are writing in terms of reader benefits and should be speaking in print in terms of "you." You should use "you" throughout the letter. Instead of writing "I will send you," you should be thinking in terms of "You will receive." Think about what your readers will get—and let them know.

If you want to grade your letter copy with a numerical grade, give yourself 10 points for every time you use the word "you" or "your," 20 points for each benefit you mention, 30 points for mentioning the best benefit, 5 points for each action word, and 10 points for each action or command word directed at your objective (<u>send</u> in the postage-paid card).

Add 25 points for each time you use the word "free." Deduct 50 points each time you use the word "I," and deduct 100 points if you use "I" to start a sentence at the beginning of a paragraph.

Long Copy vs. Short Copy, Which Really Works Better?

Which works best, long or short copy? Usually, in the long copy vs. short copy war, the shorter the copy, the better. Get in, show your product, sell the benefits, make the offer, ask for the response, sell the order form or the call hard, and get out. If they like it, they'll buy it; or at least they'll send in the card to remain on your mailing list.

Actually, in direct mail, long copy can work better. In direct mail, copy is king. If—and this is a big if—you can get potential customers to read all your copy, you stand a good chance of getting their business. This includes a 20-page sales letter. The longer they stay in your package, the better your chances of a sale. But long copy is not without a downside. The trick is getting people to read it. With every additional page, a certain percentage of your readers fall off.

The big downside of long copy is, if you miss your mark with long copy —especially in the beginning—your long piece of direct mail can be long gone well before anyone gets to the good part. If it's not perfectly written, a long piece gets thrown out as soon as the potential customer gets bored or decides that the offer (if he gets that far) is not for him. To be effective, it's got to be a really compelling, catchy, clever, and benefit-oriented piece. It needs timing and tempo, and variance in pace. It has to be read in its entirety, or at least long enough for the reader to see the benefits and have them stick, and the offer has to be attractive enough for him to make a decision.

If your offer is made too late in the package, if your user benefits didn't come on strong till the last page, or if your lead story line got too windy, you face the gravest danger in the direct mail industry: the wastebasket. In direct mail, more packages wind up in a wastebasket than meet any other fate. Like 98 percent.

You could offer free $100 bills on the last page of an eight-page letter, but if the first page or two aren't written well or aren't interesting, no one will send for them. In long copy that fails, your offer won't matter if it's buried in the last few pages—no one will get to it.

You have about five seconds to be so arresting your customers won't dare put your letter down.

If your mailing package is short and not quite right, you still have a chance for it to be looked over and read, have the offer be seen and understood, and generate a response. The brevity of the design will allow a reader to skim to all the important parts. But if your package is long and not quite right (poor design, visually forbidding to read, not interesting, not benefit-oriented, not compelling), your customer won't have the time or inclination to figure it out. You have about five seconds to be so arresting your customers won't dare put your letter down.

Because of this five-second rule, I recommend that no one but professionals or A+ writers use long copy. The danger is too great that your package will never get read. Just think about the time you received an eight-page letter, scanned a few lines, and then threw the whole thing out. Whatever it was they were selling, you didn't know, you never found out, and you didn't care enough to look for.

Some copywriters consistently come up with long letters and packages that work wonders, and so can you. You just have to be a natural writer, put 25 years into writing effective copy for direct mail, be exceptionally brilliant, and be having a good day. Other than that, your chances of having a big hit with a long-copy package in your first few mailings range from slim to none. So I don't recommend it for nonprofessional writers. Not the first time out, anyhow. Once you get a little experience, you can try longer letters in your direct mail packages, if you like.

The time needed to create a smooth, successful long-copy direct mailing piece is also enormous. These pieces take much longer to write than they do to read. A four-page letter may take me 30 to 40 hours to write, and five more hours to typeset and lay out; what would it take you? Eight pages take me over 60 hours to write. And I have read every copy "how to" column in every direct mail magazine I have ever received for the past 10 years. In contrast, a one- page letter can take me 5 to 10 hours to write, edit, and lay out. Some projects are more difficult than others, and take longer. Some, in which the client handed me a tight rough draft, are much faster to put into the final form.

Remember—the letter we are discussing isn't a letter you dash off to your grandmother. It's copywriting. And artwork. They are blended to a form that looks like a letter. The better your effort up front, the more responses you will receive when your package is mailed.

While the bulk of the success of a direct mail package may be attributed to the copy, other mailing parameters—the list, the offer, the price, and the product—are important to its success or failure, too. Of these, surely the wrong choice of list can make any package fail. But in direct mail, if you are mailing to a good list, copy is king.

Certain situations demand long copy. For example, if you have no brochure and your product or service needs a longer sell or deeper explanation than can fit on just a page or two, a long-copy letter may work well. Just remember: the letter is where you show the benefits. You can list the features in a bulleted fashion, but the letter copy is benefit-oriented. Make sure it's irresistible to read. If you have more to say than you can in a single letter—and no time or budget for a brochure—there is hope: create a spec sheet or data sheet as described in the chapter "The $500 Campaign." If your customers are worth it, two letters are more than twice as effective as one. Create both and mail them separately.

Another exception to the long-copy-means-death-to-your-mailing rule: when selling subscriptions to magazines or newsletters, a letter longer than one page usually works best. People want to feel the style of the newsletter, or get a taste of the magazine. In this instance, long copy sells.

If you have an extraordinary amount of customer benefits, instead of weaving them into a long letter, consider listing them using bulleted copy. A list format is usually tolerated better than paragraph-style copy for heavy selling of a large number of items. It will keep your copy from appearing overly long. If you can show the benefits in list form in an attractive way, there is another reward: bulleted lists have high readership in DM (Direct Mail) packages.

If you still believe you want to go out on a limb with your writing and use long copy, go ahead. If I haven't talked you out of it by now, I guess I won't. Take your best shot. Just make sure it's interesting. Make sure even your family and friends will demand to read all of it, and that if you left out a page, they'll call you and ask for it.

Although long copy can out-pull short copy, you have a smaller window of opportunity. There's a greater chance the message will get lost in the clutter.

The final verdict: Long copy can be most persuasive IF—and that's the big if—you can get recipients to read it. That's the real danger. Long copy gives you the opportunity to tell the whole story, give more user benefits, and offer more reasons to buy. If the writer is skillful, long copy definitely can be more effective. You simply have more time to entice your customers. You can paint a better, clearer picture. You can overcome every objection, and state every possible benefit. So, in answer to the question, "What works better, long or short copy?" the real answer is, long copy can work better. But the real question is, can *you* make it work better?

If a person reads only half of your copy, it didn't work. This is especially true if it's the first half, because the order form is usually in the second half. To be effective, someone has to read all of your lengthy dissertation until they get to the order form and order. Even if they just skim it, they still need to wind up at the order form and order. Although long copy can out-pull short copy, you have a <u>smaller window of opportunity</u>. There's a greater chance the message will get lost in the clutter. If this happens, customers won't struggle to find it, they'll just toss the whole piece out. So stick to the simple, direct-benefit sales approach in your letters. Keep your mailing pieces short, sweet, and to the point.

If you want to write at length, a brochure can be much longer than a letter. Make it as long as you like! Heck, most people won't read it anyhow. Only the people who are ready to make a big purchase read all the information they can get on a product. So long brochure copy is perfect for them. But most recipients will just look at the pictures. Of course, your competitors will read it, particularly to see if there are any weak spots or typos, which they will call to everyone's attention.

The P.S. Every Letter Should Have a P.S.

Short and crisp. Since everyone reads the P.S., it can be the most effective part of the letter.

A steadfast rule in direct mail: Tell your readers what you want them to do. Then tell them again. Then tell them again. Be specific. I call this the Rule of Three. Tell recipients three times what you want them to do. Ask them to respond. Make sure you let them know what specific action you want them to take. This is known as the call to action.

The P.S. should state, or restate, the call to action. It may also contain the offer again, or the biggest benefits, or your guarantees. It's the final opportunity to sell your product, kind of like the check-out aisle at the supermarket. It should be your most powerful, persuasive copy. It's also a widely read part of your letter.

I usually do not recommend repeating yourself word for word on the same page, but restating the response you are seeking in the P.S. is the exception. If you don't get a response to your mailing, nothing else matters— unless your objective is to lay groundwork for the next mailpiece. So I usually ask for a response in some form or another two times in the body of the letter, then again in the P.S.

If you offer fast shipping, say so here. Special pricing? Limited-time offer? Say it here. Then ask for the order again. Send in the card. Call right now, while you're thinking about it.

Always tell your readers what you want them to do. Then tell them again. Then tell them one more time. Be specific.

The P.S. is the synopsis of the offer and the response you are seeking in your best, most convincing wording. Short and crisp. Since everyone reads the P.S., it can be the most effective part of the letter. Whatever your objective is, it should be there in a terrifically attractive form. But if not, just say it again in plain English. Remember, without a response the package fails, so don't be afraid to ask for the response again. Every letter should have a P.S.

Conclusion/Letters

Now that you're heavily armed with directions and instructions, you can start writing. Initially it will seem awkward—first writing the objective, then the features, and then the benefits. Writing at length about the benefits, developing a short, electric opening. Breaking paragraphs artificially. Always stressing user benefits. But don't worry—as you send more and more letters, the process will become second nature. Like riding a bicycle, you'll lose the awkwardness of the practice runs over a very short period of time. And it will start to seem very natural, this new way to write letters—or at least the paper they call a letter that's enclosed in all the most effective direct mail packages.

When mailing letters, don't be afraid to test the waters by mailing a few to friends to get their opinion. Or test your letter to 50 or 100 of your potential customers. The formula for success in direct mail couldn't be simpler: if it works, keep mailing the same package in ever-increasing numbers. As long as you mail to the same list, the percentage of positive responses should be the same. Now that you've taken the long course on letter writing, let's move on to other parts of the puzzle that can make your package even more effective.

~ Other Elements of a Direct Mail Package ~

The Creative

The "creative" is another name for the copy and art, in whatever form they take. The purpose of good creative in a direct mail package follows a central theme: draw the maximum number of responses from the audience. The creative is a broad direct mail term for the approach and style, the art and graphics, the copy platform, and the format. It's the brochures, the photos, the illustrations, the letter, the envelope. It's a postcard, or a self-mailer. It's sincere or it's humorous. It can be a single letter, a letter and brochure, or a heavy package with a dozen different parts.

The creative is the style, the sizzle, and the steak. It's how it's written, and the design. Is it an emotional plea, or a logical and rational appeal? Is it written to appeal to the needs of popularity, wealth, comfort, beauty, acceptance, greed, advancement, independence, or any of the dozens of

The Danielle Adams Publishing Company
Box 100, Merion Station PA 19066

basic drives we humans have? You can take a shot at this yourself, or purchase it from ad agencies or professional direct mail copywriters and artists. It depends on your ability, your product, your budget, how many pieces you are sending, and the value of each response. It's simply called the creative, and it is the copy, the artistic style, and the slant of the mailer you send.

Package Format

The mailed piece can be in any form or format: from a single postcard, an 8-1/2" x 11" sheet folded in thirds, an 8-1/2" x 11" sheet folded in half, an 11" x 17" letter in an envelope, a brochure in an envelope, a self-mailer, up to the giant package you get from Publishers Clearing House complete with letter, reply envelope, post cards, sheets of magazine stamps, lift notes, stick-on parts, "place yes here" notes, reply cards and everything else under the sun. Next year they'll probably include a 2007 Ford Mustang engine in their package just to get you to buy a couple of magazines. All these involvement devices are just to get you to spend more time looking through their package (to find the sweepstakes coupon they hide). They know that the more time you spend flipping through all this stuff, the more likely you are to see something you like and order a magazine. It works. They've been doing it for many years, and you get a very similar package every time.

Your mailing package doesn't have to be that elaborate to be effective. You can mail only a letter (if it's well drafted) and get a good response. Response can be increased further, and often dramatically, if the mailing is personalized. The most common format is a letter and a brochure, plus the response vehicle: reply card or order envelope. The easier it is to order or respond, the more people will. You'll quickly discover that enclosing a reply card or envelope usually pays off. If you have no brochure, a letter and a specification sheet can work just fine.

Involvement Devices

An involvement device asks the reader to perform a specific action with one or more of the parts of the mailing package. This helps increase the response by overcoming reader inertia and starting the action process. While involvement devices (ordering stamps, "Place Yes Stamp Here," "Pull tab to open," "Place token in red slot to get your free gift") work for the big mailers, you don't have to spend a lot to make a nice offer and keep the reader involved. A small, simple, low-cost sheet of paper you include may say "Kindly include this note with your order and we'll extend an additional courtesy discount of 3% if received by January 12." Or include a gift certificate good until a certain date. Both are very effective. If the mailing is very small, type a line for an official signature on the certificate and sign each one.

Lift Note

The lift note got its name from lifting the response rates. It started as a small folded sheet of paper that usually said on the outside, "Read this if you have decided not to order." Inside, the copy started out with "Frankly, I'm puzzled." It was popular several years ago, an immediate success from the first time it was used. Lift notes started appearing in all direct mail packages until the technique was so overused, it became ineffective.

Occasionally I still see lift notes in direct mail packages. Surprisingly enough, <u>I recommend them for most mailings</u>. As an involvement device, they keep readers in the package a little longer, and whenever you do that they are more likely to order.

Lift notes can range in size anywhere from a quarter of a sheet of an 8-1/2" x 11" paper to one-sixth or even one-eighth of a page. They are usually printed, then folded in half with a teaser line on the outside to make you open it. Inside is a hard sell for the order or an additional pitch for your response. It's cheap insurance. The lift note usually has high readership, and if you show a strong benefit and a strong selling position for the response it can work wonders at little cost. Since they may be small and printed four or six up on a single sheet of paper, lift notes are usually quite low in cost. And like the theory "The longer you stay in a store the more likely you are to make a purchase," if the lift note keeps the reader in the package a little longer, the reader is more likely to purchase.

Sweeps

If you want to give yourself a real headache, try a sweepstakes. Sweepstakes are good vehicles—until you run into a problem with a legitimate complaint, or an irate customer who screams "Unfair!" It can create a mess and ill

The Danielle Adams Publishing Company
Box 100, Merion Station PA 19066

feelings from customers. With one winner and so many losers, I don't recommend them for small firms. There are many government rules and regulations surrounding sweepstakes offers, and if you trip over one you can land with your other foot in court. If you still feel a sweepstakes would enhance your mailing piece, go to the premium shows or contact a premium or ad specialty house (listings can be found in some of the marketing magazines) and let them set it up for you professionally.

Smaller Mailings

If you're mailing a couple of hundred pieces in a consumer campaign, you can try your hand at the writing and graphics yourself—just to test the waters. Usually it doesn't pay to spend a lot on professional art and copy for this kind of a limited test mailing. For only a little money, a good letter and specification sheet can be very effective.

But write mostly in a conversational tone, as if you are talking to someone.

Some people are natural direct mail writers; they just don't know it. All their lives, teachers have told them to use long words and write like James Michener. This doesn't work in a direct mail environment. Short words work. Never use a 50-cent word when a 5-cent word will do. Make sure you supercharge your first paragraph. End paragraphs suddenly.

Don't let good grammar stand in your way. Of course, don't make goofy mistakes that will make you look foolish, but you're not in an English contest, either. You can use "ain't" if it fits your copy style. You can sell with an emotional plea if you are fund-raising. But write mostly in a one-to-one conversational tone, as if you are talking to someone.

When each response is of tremendous value, even a small mailing may be an exception to the "try it yourself" rule. If the mailing of 200 pieces is to CEOs of the 200 largest automotive firms in the U.S. to interest them in a new type of geothermal spark plug you've just invented, the parameters change. Get some help. When even a single response is worth big money, it's worth it to mail a perfect professional package. If you are mailing to 200 printers to sell a $5 million press, you should strongly consider putting a professional package in the mail. What is a single positive response worth to you? $5 million? Get help.

If you leave out a word, or have a spelling error or a typo in your mailpiece, you don't want the recipient to think "Gee, I wonder if they have all the gears in the correct places in the press." How comfortable would you feel if you received a brochure from General Motors that had several spelling mistakes? You'd be wondering how many mistakes they build into their cars, and if your car really would slow down when you stepped on the brake pedal.

If you make a mistake, the only time you can't go back and make a change is after it's printed. So don't worry about last-minute changes; you have all the time before it goes to press to correct it and get it perfect. Have several people proof all your work. First have them read through it for content and flow, clarity of ideas, and to see if they understand the offer and the response you're looking for. Is your product attractive to them? Would they buy it? Did they read the mailpiece willingly? All of it? Was it persuasive, even coercive? Then have them proofread it word for word, carefully, for spelling errors and typos. If you're really paranoid about typos, have someone read it backwards. Personally, I've found nothing I do helps - they still get out. Oh well...

Envelope

Envelopes exhibit the full spectrum, from plain vanilla white with no return address to completely crammed with so much stuff you wonder if the writer was paid by the word. Everyone has their own opinion on what works best. The most common element printed on the envelope is teaser copy: a few words to arouse the interest of the reader to entice him to open the package. When should you use teaser copy to make the recipient open your mailing? When should you leave it plain so they won't know who it's from and will have to open it to find out? It depends.

If you are mailing your pieces first class with a live stamp and a handwritten address, people will open the envelope. So you can just leave it unadorned. Almost the same thing applies to an envelope with a label on it; the key is the stamp. First class mail gets more attention and is opened more frequently. This is especially true if your name and address appear to be typed in the return address block, and the letter looks like it is from you personally.

There are about a dozen options for the bulk mail indicia to make it look like a first class letter. There's even a bulk mail postage stamp that must be applied like a first class stamp (at an additional expense to the mailer) just to make the package look like a piece of first class mail. First class carries clout, and your envelope has an excellent chance of being opened without any copy written on it. For just 42 cents.

As your mailings become more commercial, and look more like mass mailings (bulk rate indicia, Cheshire address label), you'll need to coerce people to open them. Design the components attractively, then entice people to open the envelope with a few words that will be of interest to just about everyone. Just a line or two of teaser copy or a simple graphic will suffice. If not, don't mess it up by trying to be cute.

The same rules you used in writing your ad headline apply here. The teaser copy on the envelope becomes the ad for your mailing package. It's like the headline of your ad, or the opening paragraph of your direct mail letter, but more important. Use only one or two short lines to attract interest. You can use your biggest benefit or most incredible offer—if it's really incredible. Intriguing questions can also work well to get the reader to open the package.

This is your one chance to get your package opened; you have five seconds. This copy had better be good.

Put a lot of time and effort into the few words of teaser copy on your envelope. It's worth it. Like designing an ad and its headline, if you put 25 hours into the inside of your package, spend three or four on just those two lines on the envelope—they're that important. Here's the Jeff Dobkin trick for creating a great teaser: write 100 good lines, then go back and select the best one. They should make the recipient stop cold in whatever he's doing and make him want to open the envelope—no, insist on opening the package. Create a package that demands to be opened. If your teaser copy doesn't stop people in their tracks, don't use it.

Like the headline of an ad, the copy on an envelope has to be great, sensational, and terrific—all wrapped into just a few words. Solicit friends and neighbors to write user benefit lines for you. Remember, these need wide appeal; they must be customer-benefit-oriented (biggest-benefit theory would apply here), and enticing, or teasing enough to make sure every reader is curious enough to open the envelope to look for the answer. They also must remain as general as possible to attract and intrigue the widest range of people. This is your one chance to get your package opened; you have five seconds. This copy had better be good.

General teaser copy for the outside of the envelope may read:

- Free Offer Inside!
- See What's New—Details Inside...
- New Pricing Information—Please Open Immediately!
- New Product Information!
- Free Gift Offer... Please open!
- First Time Offered Anywhere!
- Gift Certificate Enclosed! (My very favorite line!)
- Time-Dated Offer... Please Open Immediately!
- New 1/2 Price Offer Inside!

Keep outside copy short, simple, and non-specific—remember, the objective is to entice as many readers as possible to open the envelope—nothing more. You're not selling anything here. Above all, you should strive for the few words that will make <u>everyone</u> who reads it open the envelope. Make sure you follow this copy line to its logical conclusion almost immediately in the letter inside, preferably in the first or second paragraph.

The Danielle Adams Publishing Company
Box 100, Merion Station PA 19066

This is the gravest danger and the worst that can happen in direct mail...

There is a grave danger in using the wrong lines on the envelope. If your choice of envelope teaser copy doesn't sustain the avid interest of the entire audience you are mailing to, you'll lose people before they even open the package. If you miss your mark here, no one will see that great offer or excellent product you show inside. So it's crucial to make sure your teaser copy is very general to your target audience, and makes your package irresistible to everyone.

The biggest drawback of envelope copy is the chance that it will make your product, package, offer, or benefit sound unattractive, or worse, of no interest to the reader. As a result of a bad choice of opening lines or poor teaser copy, or the wrong benefit shown on the outside, you risk the early death of your entire mailpiece. You run the risk of having your whole piece tossed out without the recipient ever getting inside. This is the gravest danger, the worst thing that can happen in direct mail: the entire package you sent gets trashed before it gets opened. So be careful.

Choose not only your envelope wording wisely, but also the benefits you offer in it, and the reasons to open the package. Think about the vast majority of your recipients—will it be an absolute necessity for them to look inside once they read the few words you have printed on the envelope face? Will it have meaning to them? Will it make them open it? Is there something you can say that will absolutely make that one extra person in 100 open it? Use that. If you had 100 pieces of mail on your desk each morning, what would make you open this particular piece?

If at all in doubt about using some particular copy on your envelope, absolutely do not use it. Follow the outline of writing headline copy in the "Ads" chapter. The wrong choice in envelope copy can be the worst mistake you make in writing your entire direct mail package. If the envelope makes your mailing package appear to be uninteresting, it will go right into the trash, unopened. This signifies the early death of your mailpiece, and a complete eradication of your hope of any response. The envelope is where you can make the worst mistake in your entire mailing.

Surprisingly effective for a standard #10 envelope mailing: Have your own name and your company address printed in the upper left-hand corner of the envelope. Instead of having it in some fancy typeface, have it typeset in typewriter-style type to look like the return address was typed on the envelope. This will make it look like a personal letter. To further this image, apply a first class stamp. Nice. If possible, have the recipient's name and address imaged directly onto the envelope (without using a mailing label). This will really look like a personal letter, and will make everyone who gets it open it. If that is not possible, use a mailing label—this package will still get 98 percent of the recipients to open it.

Better paper stock, colored envelopes, and two-color printing are all good at boosting response a fraction of a percentage point or two, if you can afford them. But a simple black and white envelope with your name and address typed in the corner can be just as effective as anything else if it looks personal and is sent first class. On a budget, black and white work just fine.

You can say almost anything as long as it is truthful, within the boundaries of legality and good taste, and will make the recipient open the package.

Lately I've seen lots of window envelopes in my mail with something that looks like a check with my name on it showing through the window. That usually gets the envelope opened, but the down side is when I find out it's not really a check....

It's tough to use clever or humorous lines in advertising copy because if they don't come out great, they can make you sound too clumsy, too cute, or just plain stupid. I don't really use much humor in most of my mailings. Just as in a business ad, you can be more flexible on your envelope if you are mailing to a list of businesses. Humor, or at least clever sayings, can entice the reader to open the mailpiece. In a business setting, where corporate America is bombarded with hundreds of thousands of advertising messages annually, you can say almost anything as long as it is truthful, is within the boundaries of legality and good taste, and will make the recipient open the package. So the definitive line on teaser copy: Yes and No. Yes, if you can make it great, No if there is any doubt. The real question is, can you make it work for you?

The Offer

The offer is what your customer gets for his hard-earned buck. It should not only be great, it should sound great. Making people put money in an envelope and wave to it as they mail it off to you in response to a piece of paper you've sent them is hard work. It's probably the hardest work a piece of paper can do. You've got to make your offer sound awfully attractive. You've got to wrap it in urgency, drench it in desire, make it seem truly valuable, and include as many customer benefits as possible, as well as a price or payment plan that appears realistic and affordable. People should think that if it goes by them this one time, they'll be sorry for the rest of their lives. Does your mailpiece do that? Let's take a look at ways to enhance "Buy this product for $12.95; send today."

Limited-Time Offer

Offer EXPIRES. On top of everything else, in consumer offers there should be <u>a reason to order now</u>. Otherwise your order could find itself way in the back of the person's mind with all the other products the customer meant to order but didn't.

You should stress immediacy to overcome the law of buyer inertia: A body at rest tends to remain at rest and not order. Give customers a reason to order RIGHT NOW. A hurry-up incentive is an effective addition to any consumer offer. Time limited offers may include:

- A sale tied to a holiday
- A discount price good only until a certain date
- Free shipping until a certain time
- Free gift if order is placed now
- Monthly special—prices apply only this month
- Dated gift certificates
- Discount coupons, date sensitive
- Product only available for a short time period
- Sale with an end date
- Product available in limited quantities

No matter what the offer, the use of a hurry-up incentive is always recommended. If your prospective customer puts your piece down, your chance for a sale may have just passed by. "Order now" is a direct mail rule, and you must press hard to make your customer pick up a pencil and send in the postage-paid card right this instant, while it's still handy, while he or she is still thinking about it. Stress urgency in sending today. Using an urgent lift note to make your customers order is also strongly recommended. Think of it this way—when they put down your mailpiece, they may put it down in the trash. If you include a lift note, it is a good place to have a dash of urgency in your tone and a hurry-up prompt for your order.

Retail stores always have such limited time offers running. You see them frequently, but you don't think twice about them. They're called "SALES!"

There's always a sale going on at any department store in the world, at any time. Sales are rotated throughout the year. They all end, but new ones spring up to take their place almost immediately. Consider this: the pre-Thanksgiving Day sale, followed by the Thanksgiving Day sale, then by the fabulous after-Thanksgiving Day weekend sale. This is followed directly by the big semiannual sale, then the pre-Christmas sale, the Christmas sale (followed by one day of regular prices), then sure, the big, big after-Christmas sale. All limited-time offers end, so buy now—this philosophy works in direct marketing, too.

The Danielle Adams Publishing Company
Box 100, Merion Station PA 19066

My firm was once hired to do the advertising for a furniture retailer. The retailer had sale prices on his furniture all year long, every single day. He normally had each piece marked with a sale tag saying "20% Off." Then twice a year, during the big furniture sale months of February and August, prices were reduced by 30 percent. When customers came in, they saw the merchandise was on sale and were encouraged to buy right then and there, while the sale was going on—before it ended. It worked. The sales were always over at some point, but new sales always came in to take their place. For this retailer, it was usually the same day.

Price

Because you can test every element in a direct mail package, one of the variables tested most often is price. Surprisingly, the lowest price is not always what works best. And the general rule for offers to consumers is to RAISE the price if the offer is not working, and test the higher price. Of course, another part of the test is to lower the price.

This book is too general to tell you what price to market your products or services for. But I can say comfortably that whatever it is, test it—it can make a tremendous difference. Some markets are price sensitive, and a low price increases orders. This is especially true of brand-name products— if you are a heavy discounter, marketing nationally recognized products at a low discount price may increase your sales tremendously. Keep in mind that you need to make sure that as your volume increases, your overall profit also increases. You don't just want to move more goods, you want to make more money, and buy that new sports car you've been thinking about.

Assuming you know the best price for selling your product through the mail is the most common error in mailings.

As true as this, however, so is the other side: some markets demand a premium price or customers won't order. When you are appealing to owners of large boats, price may bring an image of quality, and product ownership one of prestige. Also, the perception that a cheap product may be constructed more poorly than a more expensive one can be detrimental to quality goods that are made and marketed inexpensively. Too bad, because while this may be true many times, it is not true all the time. And the opposite—an expensive product is manufactured to higher standards than a cheap one—is certainly not always true.

Assuming you know the best price for selling your product through the mail is the most common error in mailings. You may have seen your product leap off the consumer shelf at $19.95. And seen catalogs reorder with their retail price set at a $29.95 list. But if you don't test the price in your direct mail packages, you're making a terrible mistake. A terrible, costly mistake.

The price of your product is determined not only by your product, but also by your mailing, the date, the copy, the graphics, your reader's perception of the product's value, the construction of your offer, your free gift, and any of a multitude of things you've never thought of—including the wealth of your audience and their willingness to send money through the mail. It can be as variable as what day of the week they get your mailing piece, or the weather, and can depend on the individual need of each prospect, and your product's perceived value in relation to satisfying this need. And that's just one paragraph's worth of factors. When you get right down to it, there are pages and pages of other facts to consider when pricing your product.

While you may think you know the best price, you will never know or be sure until you test this variable. By testing, you will not only find at what price your product will sell the most, but at what price you make the maximum profit—which may be different. You may be able to increase your profit by a factor of 10 or more just by adding a zero, then running a few tests. So test!

For example, look at the direct marketing ads for window treatments in the back of *House Beautiful*: they are all from heavy discounters. If you offered products at a list price there, you'd get about a dozen responses— and they'd be from your competitors and your own family members. Is your market price-sensitive? If you sell at a discount, will the increase in sales volume make up for the additional profit you would make if you sold at list price? Only you know your market, and only testing will tell you conclusively what price to set. I'm not saying you shouldn't start out with your gut feeling—thousands of products are priced that way. But only testing will give you definitive answers.

On the other side, let's take another example—*Architectural Digest*. Products to the upscale audience here sell best if they're pricey. The reason: When you price a product cheaply, it has a lower perceived value than a higher priced product, and a prospective purchaser may not feel it has any worth. In through-the-mail offers the customer can't see, touch, or feel the merchandise. Buyers may have resistance to a product they perceive as cheap. So raising a price has a chance to drive in more orders from some selected markets, and earn you additional profits. Another example is the seminar market. Sometimes lower prices just drive customers and attendees away. Always test markets and mailings to see if they respond well to more expensive offers.

Don't fool yourself into thinking the price you feel is the best really *is* the best. Let the marketplace set the price.

Finally, there will be a limit—because on the other end, you can price a product too high and have price resistance. So pricing should always be tested—the lowest price doesn't always draw the best response. One simple way to test a certain price is to select a specific state or region, offer your product at a higher cost there, and see if it sells better. Or use selected zip codes to vary and track pricing. Different markets may get different prices.

Larger magazines often offer split-run testing. They print two editions of the same magazine, and you can run your ad with one price in the A version and a different price in the B version and measure the response to each.

Don't fool yourself into thinking the price you feel is the best really is the best. <u>Let the marketplace set the price.</u> The difference in price can make a tremendous difference in your sales volume and your profit. How would you like to offer a product at $39.95, a price that seemed fair to you at the time, and receive 300 sales per 10,000 pieces mailed (gross income $11,985, with a 3 percent response rate), then find out in a later test that at $49.95 you received 520 orders from 10,000 pieces mailed (gross income $25,974, with a 5.2 percent response rate)? It can happen. So let the market set the price. Test.

Complement the Offer

The offer for your product should be complemented as strongly as possible by as many great customer satisfaction benefits as you can offer:

- Guarantees of complete satisfaction.
- Product guarantee.
- Guarantee of safe arrival.
- Promise of fast shipping.
- Delayed billing, or payment plan.
- Easy toll-free ordering.
- Free customer support package included in price.
- Toll-free customer assistance lines.
- Your own personal guarantee.
- Free shipping for orders over a specified amount.
- Free gift with order.

If you can make sending money any easier, now is the time. "Send no money, we'll bill you later in three easy installments of just $29.95 each," sounds much easier than, "Include $89.85 in the envelope and mail today." Some attractive-sounding consumer pricing and payment options you may want to consider are:

- Pay in [three easy] installments.
- Charge your order.
- Send no money—we'll bill you.
- Delayed billing until the first of the year.

~ Probability Chart of Results of Test Mailings ~

If the size of the test mailing is	And the return on the test mailing is	Then 95 times out of 100, the return on the identical mailing to the whole list will be between			If the size of the test mailing is	And the return on the test mailing is	Then 95 times out of 100, the return on the identical mailing to the whole list will be between		
100	1%	0%	&	2.99%	250	1%	0%	&	2.26%
100	2%	0	&	4.80%	250	2%	.23%	&	3.77%
100	3%	0	&	6.41%	250	3%	.84%	&	5.16%
100	4%	.08%	&	7.92%	250	4%	1.52%	&	6.48%
100	5%	.64%	&	9.36%	250	5%	2.24%	&	7.76%
100	10%	4.00%	&	16.00%	250	10%	6.20%	&	13.80%
100	20%	12.00%	&	28.00%	250	20%	14.94%	&	25.00%
500	1%	.11%	&	1.89%	1,000	1%	.37%	&	1.63%
500	2%	.75%	&	3.25%	1,000	2%	1.12%	&	2.88%
500	3%	1.48%	&	4.52%	1,000	3%	1.92%	&	4.08%
500	4%	2.25%	&	5.75%	1,000	4%	2.76%	&	5.24%
500	5%	3.05%	&	6.95%	1,000	5%	3.62%	&	6.38%
500	10%	7.32%	&	12.68%	1,000	10%	8.10%	&	11.90%
500	20%	16.42%	&	23.58%	1,000	20%	17.48%	&	22.52%
2,000	1%	.55%	&	1.45%	5,000	1%	.72%	&	1.28%
2,000	2%	1.37%	&	2.63%	5,000	2%	1.60%	&	2.40%
2,000	3%	2.24%	&	3.76%	5,000	3%	2.52%	&	3.48%
2,000	4%	3.12%	&	4.88%	5,000	4%	3.45%	&	4.55%
2,000	5%	4.03%	&	5.97%	5,000	5%	4.38%	&	5.62%
2,000	10%	8.66%	&	11.34%	5,000	10%	9.15%	&	10.85%
2,000	20%	18.21%	&	21.70%	5,000	20%	18.87%	&	21.13%
10,000	1%	.80%	&	1.20%	100,000	1%	.94%	&	1.06%
10,000	2%	1.72%	&	2.28%	100,000	2%	1.91%	&	2.09%
10,000	3%	2.66%	&	3.34%	100,000	3%	2.89%	&	3.11%
10,000	4%	3.61%	&	4.39%	100,000	4%	3.88%	&	4.12%
10,000	5%	4.56%	&	5.44%	100,000	5%	4.86%	&	5.14%
10,000	10%	9.40%	&	10.60%	100,000	10%	9.81%	&	10.19%
10,000	20%	19.20%	&	20.80%	100,000	20%	19.75%	&	20.25%

~ COSTS TO GET IN THE MAIL ~

Creating the Mailing Package   SUBTOTAL   TOTAL

1. Creative Package
  Letter...$ _____
    Writing   First Draft, Second Draft....($____)
           Edit, Final, Proofing............($____)
    Type   Specs, Typography..............($____)
    Design   Roughs, Final.....................($____)
    Artwork/Logo
  Brochure & Order Form...............................$ _____
    Writing   First Draft, Second Draft......($____)
    Edit   Final Edit, Proofing..............($____)
    Type   Specs, Typography................($____)
    Design   Roughs, Final, Mechanical..............($____)
    Artwork Logo, Illustration, Photography........($____)
 TOTAL COST OF CREATIVE (Letter & Brochure)..........................$
2. Printing (Quantity_____)
    Letter...............................($____)
    Brochure................................($____)
    Order Form............................($____)
    Business Reply Envelope....($____)
    Outer Envelope.....................($____)
 TOTAL COST OF PRINTING ....$
3. LETTERSHOP ....$
4. MAILING LISTS ....$
5. POSTAGE ....$
6. Total Costs of Preparation and Mailing
 (Mailing Package: Creative + Printing + Lettershop + Mailing List + Postal Costs).$
7. COST PER THOUSAND PIECES MAILED...$
8. SELLING PRICE OF YOUR PRODUCT OR SERVICE...................................$

~ COSTS TO FULFILL AN ORDER ~

9. Fulfillment Costs
    Product ....($____)
    Free Gift ....($____)
    Order Processing ....($____)
    Postal Reply Fees.................($____)
    Shipping..............................($____)
    Other (800#, Credit Card Cost, Etc.)..($____)
10. TOTAL FULFILLMENT COSTS.......................................$
11. Returned Merchandise, Cost per Order...............................$
12. Cost per Bad Debts, Bad Checks, Credit Card..................$
13. Overhead Costs per Order..$

~ BREAK EVEN ANALYSIS ~

14. TOTAL EXPENSES (Fulfillment + Returns + Bad Debt + Overhead)....................$

15. Profit per Order (Selling Price – Total Expenses)......................................$

16. Break Even: ___ Orders (# of orders needed per 1,000 pieces mailed to break even.
Cost per Thousand divided by Profit per Order.)

*This chart is reprinted with permission from the Hugo Dunhill Mailing List Company.
They publish some excellent mailing and marketing guides and reference materials, and are a quality list house.
They can be reached at 800-223-6454. Copyright 1988 Hugo Dunhill and Bruce Thaler

1. CREATING THE MAILING PACKAGE - If you hire an outside agency to write, design or prepare your package for printing, write in their estimate. If your staff creates the mailing package, enter the cost of their time. If you do this at night on your own, the cost is your own time; enter zero. Remember - these are one-time costs - you won't have to pay them again if you mail this same package again later.

2. PRINTING - Enter the estimate of each component of your mailing package from a printer. Shop around and get several price quotes - printing is an area where, if you shop around, you can save time and money.

3. LETTERSHOP - Call lettershops and get prices for affixing mailing labels and postage to the envelope, then stuffing the mailing pieces into them, sealing, sorting for third class bulk, and mailing. You can do all this yourself the first time to test if your mailing will work, while costing you as little money as possible.

4. MAILING LISTS - The mailing list house will provide a number of recommended lists. In our example assume the list will cost $50 per thousand and we are going to mail 5,000. 5 x $50 = Mailing list costs will be $250.

5. POSTAGE - Multiply the number of pieces you are mailing by the amount of postage each package requires. Add any postal fees for permits you may need - these are usually annual fees.

6. TOTAL COSTS OF MAILING

7. COST PER THOUSAND PIECES MAILED - This figure computes the total cost of your initial mailing into a usable figure of "per thousand." Increasing the number of pieces mailed will lower your cost per thousand. The creative for the mailing package, and the postal permits, will not be figured into later mailings, so costs for further mailings will go down. With this cost you can figure out how many pieces you need to sell to break even, and what your profit will be when you mail again.

8. SELLING PRICE OF YOUR PRODUCT OR SERVICE - This is the retail price of your product or service.

9. FULFILLMENT COSTS - Enter here what you pay for one product. Don't forget to include everything: manufacturing, labor, parts, material used, printing of the instructions and shipping label, the shipping carton + shipping. If you offer a free gift as an incentive to purchase your products, include its cost. Order Processing includes invoicing and getting the merchandise out to customers. Postal Reply Fees include costs for receiving your business reply mail envelope, if used. Shipping is the cost of shipping both product and free gift to customers. Other Costs: Figure in which miscellaneous costs you must add. For example, an 800 number usually costs about $2 per order, credit card processing usually 4% of the order amount.

10. TOTAL FULFILLMENT COSTS

11. RETURNED MERCHANDISE, COST PER ORDER - Add your cost to handle one return (this cost should be the same as your order processing cost: in our example it's $5), plus the cost to refurbish the return (for example, we'll estimate it costs $4 for repackaging, etc.). Multiply the total of both these costs ($9) by the percentage of orders that will be returned. For this example, we'll estimate the return rate at 5%. So $9 x 5% = $0.45. This result is your cost for returned merchandise.

12. BAD DEBT, BAD CHECKS - Multiply your bad debt rate (we'll estimate 5%) by your selling price $250. The result is your cost for bad debts: $250 x 5% = $12.50

13. OVERHEAD COSTS - This figure includes rent, office supplies, utilities, equipment, collection costs, your own time and your staff's time. Overhead costs usually vary between 5% and 10% of the selling price, but if you are working out of your home office, this may be considerably less. Multiply an appropriate percentage (we'll estimate 5%) by your selling price, $250. The result is your overhead cost: $250 x 5% = $12.50.

~ Projecting Total Probable Returns ~

Week	Average of Total Orders Received	Percentage Range of Orders Received	Median Percentage of Orders Received	Mode of Orders Received
1	3.9%	0.3- 24.7%	17.7%	1.3%
2	27.0	6.5- 77.3	39.5	31.4
3	54.6	13.6- 96.4	66.2	75.0
4	67.2	18.9- 100.0	74.9	68.9
5	77.8	36.5- 100.0	82.5	81.4
6	82.8	46.9- 100.0	87.8	100.0
7	85.8	58.1- 100.0	89.2	100.0
8	92.6	74.3- 100.0	92.2	100.0
9	95.3	87.5- 100.0	93.8	100.0
10	96.2	88.0- 100.0	96.8	100.0
12	99.4	92.0- 100.0	99.7	100.0
17	100.0	100.0- 100.0	100.0	100.0

Definitions: Time intervals are weeks from the day the first order was received.
Percentage range of orders received indicates limit of tolerance one way or the other.
Median column is a standard measurement indicating that 50% of all responses will be greater and 50% lesser.
Mode is the percentage figure of the total orders occurring most frequently.

Source: Direct Mail Marketing Association

Of all the pricing options, my favorite is to reduce the price a small amount and sell two. If it's attractive and practical, offer your product with a quantity discount. The ease of selling twice as much product may be as simple as a line of type saying "Two for" and the amount.

Some products are traditionally marketed in quantity. Tires and shock absorbers are usually buy three, get one free. Books by mail are sold with big discounts for multiple purchases. One of the most effective offers is "Buy one, get one free." Some other ways to express similar offers are:

- Get two for the price of one.
- Buy one, get the second one for half price [25% off].
- Buy one, get the second for a penny (made popular by record clubs and book clubs).

The way you express your pricing can also make a big difference. For example, "Four books for 99 cents" makes them sound like they're cheap books, but "Buy one book at the special member's price of 99 cents and get three more books FREE," sounds very attractive. Think about your pricing options—and make them sound good. At $4.95, most purchasers will still think of your price as $4.00 when it is really so much closer to $5.00.

Plus Shipping and Handling, Of Course

Shipping and handling charges are now used (and accepted by mail order buyers) as a way of increasing revenues without making the advertised price appear higher. "Only $19.95 (plus $4.50 shipping)" looks a lot better than "Buy our product at $24.45." Don't go overboard, but you can add a reasonable amount for shipping to increase your revenue. Compare the shipping and handling prices of the many TV offers you see. You can tell the ones that are trying to gouge you: they are the firms that bury the shipping and handling fee of $6.95 in small type at the very end of the copy—for a product that weighs under a pound.

Some firms, especially catalog firms, increase the shipping charges in proportion to the size of the order. I don't like this arrangement. It penalizes people for ordering more. Does the catalog house really want people to be penalized for increasing the amount they spend with that firm? A larger order amount means more profit; they should be willing and able to absorb more of the shipping and handling charges.

I recommend a small initial S&H amount to cover your costs, which will vary according to your product weight and average sale. Between $2.95 and $4.95 sounds politically correct for a product that weighs less than a pound. If it's heavier, or your product costs over $50, consumers are more likely not to resist a $5 or $6 shipping charge.

Why take chances? You'll get very little price resistance or resentment at $2.95 for shipping and handling. If you charge $4.95 and make an extra $2, is that worth the risk of losing extra orders? Only testing will tell, so use these prices as a guideline for initial offerings. If sales go well at the $2.95 shipping cost level, raise your shipping price to $3.95 or $4.95 and test whether sales drop off to any degree. If you get to keep the extra profit with no sales dropoff, so much the better. The next logical test would be to raise the prices for the items you are offering. I'd raise the item price first; some people won't order if the shipping charges are too high. If the item is big, heavy, or bulky, a larger shipping price can be justified.

If you are marketing many products, like a whole catalog or an entire product line, I recommend that you ship all orders over a fixed amount for free. Write in big letters: "All orders over $40 are shipped free!" This encourages customers to increase the size of their order to reach that amount. If you are a heavy discounter, however, this policy won't work, as you may need the shipping charges to keep your low profit steady.

When pricing a product, I always—in addition to the regular price—give a "twofer" price. Someone always orders two. This larger order has double the value to you. Your marketing dollar is already invested in the first order, so the only marketing cost to you for the second order is the line of type you give it in the price section. In addition, the second order increases the size of your average order. As an added bonus to you, it usually ships in the same package. Getting a double order is important to your profitability; think of it as additional free money at little or no marketing expense.

To further increase response and increase the cash amount of each sale, consider offering other extras with the sale of two. Maybe ship the second item free. Maybe offer it beautifully wrapped when sent as a gift to a friend. Or throw in free shipping for both when two are ordered. Make the increase in the order attractive enough for people to order two. It'll be a good value for your customers, too, because they get both items at less cost for each.

Make It Easy to Respond

The easier it is to respond, the more response you'll get. At the end of your creative session, ask yourself, What else can I do to make it easier to get a person to send money or place an order? Can I offer a toll-free order number? Should I take credit cards? Is there an envelope I can provide? Is the order form easy to fill out? Make it easy to respond, and your sales will improve.

These thoughts turn into sales:

- Send in the postage-paid reply envelope with an order.
- Pick up the phone and place an order.
- Call right now. We're ready to take your order or answer your questions.
- To place an order anytime—24 hours a day—call toll free... operators are standing by right now.
- Fast shipping, plus order now and get a full three-year guarantee.
- Fast Federal Express delivery means you can have this slicer in your hands tomorrow morning, and start using it right away.
- You'll be receiving your product by Friday—in time to use it for a weekend of sun. So send today, or better yet, call TOLL FREE right now...

Don't forget to write in terms of user benefits. I don't have to list all the very commercial lines from the successful catalogs, just get the catalogs and see for yourself.

Of course, if you are just starting out, or testing the waters for a new product, you may not have all the advantages of toll-free order lines, charge cards, or one-day shipping. But in more limited mailings, you still can provide a post card or envelope for a response, or offer payment options like "No money up front—we'll bill you" (if you know your audience), a low down payment, or easy-to-pay monthly installments.

Everyone has a swipe file. Everyone.

Your mailbox is a constant source of new ideas. Select and use the best ideas for increasing response. Don't lift full pages of catalogs or copy. But don't feel guilty about abstracting small parts or good ideas from other mailers' packages. In the beginning of direct mail there was only one order form; every order form you see today is a variation of it. Everyone has a swipe file. Everyone. And everyone looks at other packages to see what looks like it's working. If it looks like a winning idea, it'll show up everywhere. Like the lift note. Or the Johnson box. Extract isolated ideas from here and there and put them to use in your own piece. Don't consider it stealing, consider it flattering the originator.

An order form, a reply card, and, if people are to include money, an order envelope will increase your response. If at all possible, these important elements should be included in your mailings. If you can have a reply envelope postage paid, so much the better. If not, the envelope in consumer mailings (where a response includes an order or money) is a good idea, and absolutely will increase response. That's why you see reply envelopes so often in mail responsive packages. If the option of sending money is offered, an order envelope is more than a response builder—it's a virtual necessity. Does Publishers Clearing House have one? You bet—in every package. Notice how every big catalog house has an order envelope? The reason is simple: it increases response.

The Danielle Adams Publishing Company
Box 100, Merion Station PA 19066

— Lists —
~ The Most Important Element in Any Mailing ~

Unlike other media, in direct mail the list is not the way to reach your market—the list IS your market.

While the letter is the most important part <u>inside</u> a mailing package, the list of names you mail to is <u>the most important element in the entire mailing</u>. With the wrong list, you get no orders. Nothing. Nada.

Unlike other media, in direct mail the list is not the way to reach your market—the list IS your market. Let me say that again: In direct marketing, <u>the list is your market</u>. By mailing to the wrong list, you reach people outside your market—people who have no interest in, or no use for, what you sell. Snowshoes to Texans. Steel wrenches to candy shops. Valve tags to dress retailers. Car floor mats to motorcycle shops.

No other medium targets your market as precisely as direct mail does, with so little wasted expense. While an ad in *Car and Driver* may give you a good base for owners of high performance cars, a direct mail list of owners of 2001 Corvettes may just be your cup of tea if you are marketing a new spoiler for that model.

It is only through the precision of direct mail that you can send material to your exact market without waste—if you dig deep enough and find the right list. In direct mail, the correct list is the most important element for instrumenting the success of your mailing. This is the beauty of direct mail— and why, dollar for dollar, it can be the lowest-cost advertising

medium: with the correct list there is absolutely no wasted advertising expense. Spend extra time finding the best list to reach your market. Mail to the best list you can find.

List Criteria

Once a person makes a purchase, signs up for your offer, takes your course, or inquires about your service, you have captured his name, and he becomes your own customer. His name and address become part of your database. After a while, you will have your own list of people you can mail to, called your "house list." It is compiled by your firm in-house.

Your house list is, by far, the best list you have for your new mailings or new offers. Composed of your own inquirers, customers, and accounts, this list is the people and businesses who know you and trust you. They have purchased from you, received your literature, and know you are a real business. If your shipping is fast, and your products are of good quality, they are usually happy to hear of new or repeat offers. This is the beginning of relationship marketing. Hang onto these names, and you will find that the lifetime value of a customer far exceeds the expensive acquisition cost.

You can now also rent your house list of purchasers' names to other mailers to create additional revenues for yourself. Renting a mailing list four or five times a year, or more, is not uncommon. A quality list can be rented out well over a dozen times a year.

Your mailing list should be at least 5,000 names strong to be handled by a list broker and rented to merchants in the markets you serve. Other mailers and businesses may also be interested in your list because of its unique characteristics. When renting your list, depending on its uniqueness, it's possible to charge $65 to $150 per 1,000 names. Bear in mind, the broker's commission is always paid by the list owner.

Most lists go through a two-tier distribution network: 20 percent of the rental fee goes to the list handling broker and 10 percent goes to the purchasing broker of the client. So if you sell your list for $100/M ($100 per 1,000) names, you will net 70 percent of the revenue or $70/M names ($70 per 1,000). If you're buying a list, a broker's services won't cost you anything.

The Danielle Adams Publishing Company
Box 100, Merion Station PA 19066

List sales are big business. But unless you compile your customer lists yourself, before you start selling your names you'll probably be buying lists of names from other companies for your own mailings. This is where you do your hardest work and your deepest digging.

Of all the elements in a direct mail campaign, the most important is the list.

Your selection of the best list for your mailing is far more important than your offer, the creative (art and copy), or your price. If any of these last three are not quite right, you can still achieve some sales. But if you try to sell your product to the wrong list of names you won't get any sales, regardless of anything else. In direct mail, the list is the market. The best copy and graphics in the world won't sell Chevy mufflers to Buick owners, dog collars to cat owners, lawn mowers to apartment dwellers, lace curtains to catfish farmers, or bottle caps to a bowling alley.

The examples I have outlined above are extreme; you won't always be subjected to such extreme ends of the scale. If you're selling an airplane pilot's bag, it's more likely you'll see lists of airplane owners, compiled from plane owner registrations; pilots who own parking spaces at airfields, compiled from airport owners' billing statements; people who have made purchases from aviation catalogs; pilots, compiled from flying license registrations; and people who have subscriptions to aircraft magazines. If you dig deep, you'll also come up with aircraft charter and leasing services, aircraft dealers, aircraft parts and auxiliary equipment dealers, aircraft schools, aircraft service organizations, airline ticket agencies, air transport services, and airline companies—to name just a few places to start your marketing.

If you recall from the beginning of the book, part of the definition of a market is that it can be defined and can be segregated from the general population. The purpose of the list in direct mail is just this: to maximize the number of hot prospects and narrow the number of cold ones. So in your quest for the perfect mailing list, first define the exact group of people you want to reach. Distill larger groups into smaller groups, and gradually tighten your parameters. This narrowing of your mailing list will ensure a better return per number of pieces mailed.

Are your prospects location-specific? Do you need a list in a certain geographical area, such as cold climates, to market ski equipment or heavy gloves? Is your market nationwide? Do all your prospects live in New Jersey? Are you looking for Miami residents only? Or people in your own neighborhood?

Does your target audience have a particular occupation, such as doctor, lawyer, plumber, or accountant? Do you want to target homeowners or apartment dwellers? Are you only after people of a certain age—like teens or retired folks? Do you want to mail only to people within a certain income bracket? Or only to people who own certain types of cars or boats?

In business, are you looking for plant managers? Or presidents of manufacturing firms with a certain number of employees or a certain annual sales volume? Do the people you want to reach have a certain job title? Are you searching for manufacturing firms or service companies? Are you looking for firms in specific industries?

What exact characteristics does your target audience have? The closer you can come to the precise definition of your market, the closer you can specify your list parameters. The more precisely you specify your list, the greater the percentage of orders (and your results and sales) from the number of pieces you send out.

The Danielle Adams Publishing Company
Box 100, Merion Station PA 19066

The most likely person to purchase something through the mail is a mail order buyer who has purchased an item through the mail recently.

If you are selling a retail product through the mail, one of the most common lists to purchase is the names of people who have purchased similar products through the mail. Is the list you are buying of people who have purchased a similar product, from a similar offer? If, for example, you're selling a new bag or widget directly to pilots, people who have purchased from a mail order catalog of aviation equipment would probably be the best list to buy and mail to.

The rule in direct mail for an offer to consumers is to buy your list with consideration to Recency, Frequency, and Monetary. The most likely person to purchase something through the mail is a mail order buyer who has purchased an item through the mail <u>recently</u>. The next most likely candidate for a purchase is a person who buys through the mail regularly (<u>frequency</u>). Third in importance is the <u>amount</u> they spend; the larger the figure, the better. Recency, Frequency, Monetary—RFM. A direct mail rule. Remember For Money, RFM.

When buying a list, you'll probably be dealing with a list broker—so make him earn his commission (which comes off the list owner's side of the sale; the broker's commission is <u>never added onto the cost</u> of the list). Make him poke around and inquire from all his resources exactly what is best for you.

Make sure you buy the absolute best list the broker can find. This will increase your orders/M; for every 1,000 mailers you send, you will have a greater percentage of people respond.

To find the perfect list or segment of a list for your product, make inquiries and do your list research and homework. If you are looking at mail order buyers, when was their most recent purchase? Is there a list of "hotline buyers"? These are people who have made purchases within the past month, two months, six months; these people are apt to make another purchase right away. Hotline buyers lists are usually available from list brokers and mail houses at an upcharge, and can be worth the extra money. Ask how often these people buy.

How recent are the names? Ask what the "average purchase," or what these people usually spend, is. Or is the list just of inquirers—not NEARLY as good as actual purchasers? A list of inquirers only is much less responsive, and these names accordingly sell for less. For your mailing of commercial products, stick to the best mail-responsive names you can get: buyers only.

Is the average unit of sale similar to your offer's? Can you select male or female buyers? Is there a multiple buyers list? (This is one of my favorite requests. There are people who have made multiple purchases and may be considered very mail responsive to product offers.) Is the list you are considering rented repeatedly? And after a few initial rentals (called tests) of parts of the list, do most firms who have run these tests rent the rest of the list, or at least more of the names for a level two test (called continuation)? This will give you an idea of how many mailers this list is working for.

How many mailers roll out to this list (rent all the names)? When was the list cleaned of undeliverables? What is the guarantee of the list owner as to percentage of deliverables? These are just a few of the questions; a good list broker will have tons more. Find a broker who will tirelessly ask them before purchasing a list for you. But be aware that brokers work for the sellers—that's who signs their checks. Get specs from several of the list companies, pick the best of the best, and mail to those lists. Even if the better lists cost more (within reason), they are usually worth it.

Spend some time getting the best list you possibly can. Dig deep for all the information you can get about the list you are considering. I realize list research is not like including a glitzy new brochure in your mailing that everyone will "ooh" and "ah" at. But research here won't be wasted time; it will show up on your bottom line: response. Your response percentage of orders per pieces mailed will go up. Revenues will increase. You will make more money.

Just like when you are selling your list, you may purchase rental names from $65 per 1,000 to about $150/M depending on the recency of the customers' purchases, amounts they have spent, any unusual specifics of the names, and if a phone number is included. I never, ever sell phone numbers with the names of any of my customers, and I recommend you don't. I don't like getting soliciting phone calls at home and I don't think my customers do, either. Average lists range from $65 to $85 per 1,000 names. List brokers are found in the direct mail trade magazines (some have full-page ads) and in local phone books.

When ordering a residential list, if there is no name on the label I always have the computer house add a line above the address that reads "To Our Friends at" or "To Our Neighbors at...."

Since the broker's commission is paid by the list owner out of the purchase price, you shouldn't be paying additional money for a broker's services even when they work extra hard for you. A good broker will be knowledgeable about which lists should work for your offer, they'll know which list worked for similar offers. Be careful, and make your broker do his homework and get the very best list for you to test.

The Danielle Adams Publishing Company
Box 100, Merion Station PA 19066

~ Direct Mail ~

Even though it's in their best interest to sell you the best list for your offer (because if it works, you'll be back for more names), some brokers don't always dig deeply enough in researching the market for the very best names for you to mail, especially for a small list order of test names. Other brokers may have favorite clients they give all the business to. Be careful.

If you are mailing to a neighborhood, residential lists are usually much cheaper to purchase, as low as $20/M. These may or may not contain a name, they may just have an address. When ordering a residential list, if there is no name on the label I always have the computer house add a line above the address that reads "To Our Friends at" or "To Our Neighbors at...." This always makes the piece friendlier, and the feeling is not that of a mass mailing.

When you order residential lists, they are selected by zip code. Be prepared to have all the zips you want at hand when you specify the order. You can specify selected zips or a range. As an example, all zips in Pennsylvania are between 15999 and 19699. To mail to all of Pennsylvania, you'd give that range. To mail to the entire Philadelphia area, you'd mail to all zip codes with the 191 and 190 prefixes. If you give brokers zips, they will give you a count of how many names are in those areas.

Computer output from a list house to a mailing house is usually nine-track tape, but almost all lists are available on Cheshire labels (not gummed) at no additional charge, or pre-gummed mailing labels for about $7.50/M more, in any order you specify (usually zip code sequence for bulk mailings).

When you mail bulk rate, you must order your list in zip sequence. A minimum of 250 pieces is required for bulk mail rates, and the mail must be sorted, rubber-banded and bagged by the first three digits of the zip. The first three digits direct the mail to the Sectional Center Facilities (SCF) of the post office for further distribution. It isn't tough to do this, but additional post office rules apply to bulk rate mail. So before I get too technical, I'll just give a single paragraph about bulk and first class mail.

If you are mailing through a mailhouse, they'll sort the bulk mail drop for you; just order the list names in zip sequence. It'll take from one to three weeks for most of the bulk mail to arrive. If a piece gets mislaid at the post office, it's my belief it'll be trashed. Most people, including most postal workers, feel bulk mail has little value. About 15 percent of it will never arrive. First class is much faster, one to four days, and a single piece will be delivered if it's out of sync. No presort is necessary, and your list may be in any zip order, but bundled zip codes will ensure faster delivery.

List Specifications

Lists originate in several ways. "Compilers" get phone books and other name resources from everywhere you can possibly imagine and compile the lists themselves. As an example, you can buy a list of all TV repair shops in the U.S. that has been compiled from phone books across the country; you can also buy a list of any of the other phone book headings. Or compilers get registrations (such as those of car or airplane owners) or extractions of other data (as you can imagine, the government is a big source for this), then merge this data into list form. These lists become outdated quickly if not maintained, and you can have lots of returns because this information gets old as businesses and people move. Many list vendors offer a refund of your postage if you send them the mailing pieces that come back to you. But that's not much help when you are staring at a carton of wrecked returns that have gone through the rough handling of the postal service.

Some list owners have their list regularly "cleaned," meaning the bad names and addresses are removed from the list. This can be done in several ways. The two most common methods are deleting the names that are on mailing pieces that come back from a mailing, and passing the list through the post office's National Change of Address (NCOA) file. Bad names are referred to as "Nixies," and clean lists have more value than lists that are not purged of undeliverable addresses. No one likes to get returns from a mailing, and it's especially upsetting if they were planning on using the list again.

Industry and trade associations usually have much tighter control of their lists. The roster of member, persons and businesses that belong to the organization or fraternal group, are generally kept reasonably current. Local organizations, such as the Chamber of Commerce, have local businesses on file, and industry groups such as the American Medical Association or the National Association of Hot Dog Vendors maintain fairly up-to-date lists of current members. Some associations are more diligent than others at upkeep.

Magazines usually have up-to-the-minute subscriber lists and are one of the better sources of lists. Because they mail regularly, when they get an undeliverable magazine back in the mail it's expensive for them, and they delete a bad address or name quickly.

When you rent a list, it is generally rented for one-time use. Unless you contract for multiple uses (and pay more for this privilege), you get only one shot to mail to these names—make it a good one. To prevent additional uses of a one-time rental, list owners and managers seed the list with names of friends and family members and insert special spellings and codes to make sure their list isn't used again without authorization. It's difficult to prosecute offenders in states other than where your office is, but I don't recommend using a list more times than you have paid for. It's stealing.

To prevent this from happening to the lists my firm sells, I wrote a tough contract so people wouldn't reuse our list without authorization. The agreement states that if the firm renting our list uses it again without authorization, they "agree to pay all court costs and attorneys' fees" if we sue them and they lose in court. List renters sign it before we send them the list.

When you rent out your own list of names, if you don't have this phrase in your list rental contract, you can still collect the additional rental fees you're entitled to. But even if you win a court case from someone using your list twice, you're still without compensation for the aggravation and the costs of your attorneys. If you have this clause in your contract and you win, at least you get your court costs back, and the other party has to pay your attorney for the privilege of being sued by him. If you can collect. Ugh.

This clause also gives you additional leverage: If you tell someone that when they lose the court case for abuse of your list they will be paying your attorney as well as their own, they're more likely to admit to the additional usage without a court battle and 'fess up to the additional usage charges. Or at least to think again about using your list twice if they read your contract. By the way, did I mention I typeset this contract so no one would read it, and no one does? I have included a copy at the end of this chapter for your use.

The Danielle Adams Publishing Company
Box 100, Merion Station PA 19066

While you may not have heard much about the business of selling lists, if you want to see how big this industry is, just visit the library and get a copy of the SRDS directory of mailing lists. Or get a copy of *Direct Marketing* magazine, *DM News, Catalog Age,* or *Target Marketing,* and call the list suppliers in these magazines. Some list brokers have full-page ads, and ad space in these business journals can be quite expensive. You can also find local firms that sell lists by looking in the phone book.

Most of the bigger list houses will send you a free catalog of the types and specifics of the lists that are available from them. You'll be amazed to discover you can buy a list of:

- Doctors by specialty, income, and/or state
- Businesses by SIC
- Businesses by number of employees
- Businesses by income
- Attorneys by type of practice
- People who own boats, aircraft, or both
- Firms by product
- Personnel by title
- Businesses by zip code
- Businesses by type or industry
- Magazine subscribers by interest or group
- Credit card holders by balance and type of card
- Computer owners by age or type of equipment
- Single parents by income
- Golf enthusiasts
- Association members
- Seminar attendees
- Pet owners by breed of pet
- Trade show attendees
- Hunters by type of license
- Mail order buyers by
    date of purchase
    type of merchandise
    frequency of purchases
    dollar amount of order
    purchases from multiple catalogs

...and all combinations of the above. For example: attorneys in corporate law who have boats; or heads of households by income, state, zip, and magazine interests (called *psychographics*). You can get almost any selection of businesses, or people sharing common traits or interests, that you can name. Bear in mind each qualification (called select) you specify narrows your marketing universe and increases the computer search costs. If you want golf enthusiasts who are members of the USGA, own a German Shepherd and have purchased a bow through the mail within the past 30 days to shoot deer, you are going to pay a lot to a list house for those names. But you can get them.

You are only as good as your last mailing. Your last mailing is only as good as your list.

If you'd like to be more instrumental in the selection of your list, go to the library and get your hands on the *Direct Marketing List Source*™ from SRDS. There are 50,000 lists indexed in this reference manual. It's a monthly publication, compiled by the same people who compiled the SRDS for periodicals. It is the bible of the mailing lists industry, and after a few hours with this publication in your hands, you'll be well acquainted with the list industry. If you are going to rent a mailing list, or sell your own mailing list, this will be time well spent.

SIC

Another common way to specify a business or industrial list is by SIC code. This stands for "Standard Industrial Classification." The SIC system was created by the Bureau of the Census of the Department of Commerce as a system to identify the function of every business, institution, and professional service. The system categorizes business activities by more than 3,000 separate four-digit numerical codes.

The Danielle Adams Publishing Company
Box 100, Merion Station PA 19066

The SIC system uses two digits to define 10 major industry groups:

01 thru 09 Agriculture, Forestry & Fisheries
10 thru 14 Mining
15 thru 17 Contract Construction
20 thru 39 Manufacturing
40 thru 49 Transportation, Communication & Utilities
50 thru 51 Wholesaling
52 thru 59 Retailing
60 thru 67 Finance, Insurance & Real Estate
70 thru 79 Services, Business & Professional
80 thru 97 Services, Professional & Government

SEASONAL VARIATIONS IN DIRECT MAIL

Which month is the best for mailing? Since direct mail can be tested so precisely, several book and magazine publishers mailed the same package month after month to determine which month drew the most response. With 100% as their average response, their results:

Month	Response
January	125%
February	108
March	97
April	90
May	89
June	87
July	100
August	108
September	104
October	97
November	103
December	102

Many smaller direct mailers may find it more profitable to mail outside the peak response times of January and August; their mail has less chance of getting lost in the clutter of the big direct response agencies' packages. These figures represent specific offers; your results may be very different from those of these magazine publishing industry giants.

Source: Direct Mail Marketing Association

There are also third and fourth digits to further divide the major groups into more specific categories. For example, SIC classifications 60-67 cover Finance, Insurance & Real Estate. Within that group SIC 63 is specifically for insurance carriers. Breakdowns within class 63 that define a market more narrowly are SIC 6311, life insurance carriers; SIC 6321, accident and health insurance; SIC 6324, hospital and medical service plans—and so on. Some industries have been so developed, a fifth digit—a letter—has been added to define them even more specifically.

You can specify an industrial mailing list by its SIC code. If you were marketing to motion picture theaters, you'd find classification 7800 for the motion picture industry, and SIC 7833 for drive-in motion picture theaters. If you wanted to target it further, you could address your mailing piece to the owner, the projectionist, or the food concession stand manager.

Any way you can define your market, you can probably buy the list exactly for the segment you wish to market to. In direct mail, the list IS your market. Good lists cost more money. Dig deep and buy the best. You are only as good as your last mailing. Your last mailing is only as good as your list.

Testing

Every element in direct mail can be tested to see if it increases or decreases the response.

Direct mail is a unique medium because you can test it ad infinitum. If you have enough money and time, every element in direct mail can be tested to see if it increases or decreases the response. That's the beauty of direct mail. And that's exactly what the big mailers do—they test every single

The Danielle Adams Publishing Company
Box 100, Merion Station PA 19066

element in their mailing packages. They learn what works best, and you can, too. Just watch your mailbox. Successful packages show up again and again. While everything you see in your mailbox is not a winner (some are test packages), if you see the same or a similar mailing piece show up a few times, you can bet it's making money for the mailer.

For instance, when big magazine promoters mail several million subscription solicitation direct mail packages, they always have several tests going along with the mailings of their control package. Fifty thousand pieces may have a letter with no date, 50,000 may have a salutation of "Dear Reader," while another 50,000 may start with "Dear Magazine Enthusiast" or "Dear Winner." Others have no letter, some have no brochure. Each of these variables is tested against a "control" package: the direct mail package that has been working best for the company. If one of the new test packages beats the control by pulling a greater response, it becomes the new control package against which all other packages are tested.

Mailing a huge number of pieces gives you a rather quick readout of what works best. For example, the mailers you sent with no date may have drawn .05 percent less than the mailers with a date, and the package with no brochure drew 8 percent less than the package with a brochure, but when you received a full 17 percent less response when a letter wasn't included, it wouldn't take you long—or too many additional mailings—to include a direct mail letter in every single mailing you send. When running your own test, keep results measurable and accurate: test only one variable at a time.

It's easy to see what's working in the direct mail industry. Look closely at your mail. You can see the winners every day. With results being measured so carefully over the years, the large direct mail houses don't make the big mistakes anymore such as leaving out an element as important or effective as a letter with their 1 million-package rollouts. (A direct mail package "rolls out" when it tests successfully in small quantities, then is mailed to everyone or every business on the entire list that was successfully mailed to initially.)

Some Packages Fail

Not everything is a winner. In fact, lots of packages fail. All this testing doesn't mean the large companies don't make mistakes or have losers in both advertising packages and products. New products may not be attractive at a price that is profitable to the manufacturer and desirable to the consumer. New mailers may have no control packages, or any idea of what will work, or what the best benefits are to mention, or what will turn the customer on. While you always have to test, test, and re-test to find the maximum draw for your mailing, everybody's gotta start somewhere, and not everything pays for itself. Some packages just plain lose money.

If you're looking for ideas, borrow only from the best. If you are trying your hand at direct mail for the first time, don't get too far away from the mainstream. Later, when you are wildly successful, you can try to break new ground. Day Timers, Publishers Clearing House, L.L. Bean, Sharper Image, Eddie Bauer, and Land's End—these companies know what they're doing, and you'd do well to emulate them. While some of their packages don't work, those packages are certainly in the minority. When they don't work, chances are it's because of product or price resistance, not copy or format mistakes.

Following this advice, you'll never lose big money in a mailing.

A failure in direct mail means that a mailing piece didn't cover its cost or is not profitable enough to mail again. It is the nature of the direct mail business to be able to recover from failed mailings, although to smaller firms the loss may be more dramatic. To cut your losses, do smaller test mailings. This is the beauty of direct mail. If the giants can fail, if the best talent at writing sensational copy, with great art direction and super-duper four-color brochures can fail—you can too. So make sure your first mailings follow the format and procedures in this book for the greatest chances of success. As you grow and create more and more mailing packages, you'll find yourself creating your own style from these basics.

The Danielle Adams Publishing Company
Box 100, Merion Station PA 19066

Mail only test quantities until you know if a mailing package and list can sustain a larger mailing. Following this advice, you'll never lose big money in a mailing. When you test, you are only at risk for the amount of money in the current test. If a list tests poorly, you'll only have mailed a few pieces. Always remember you can limit the amount of loss you may incur by testing the waters with limited numbers in your early mailings.

More packages fail to a lesser degree by drawing only marginal response. To the small mailer, some packages fail because "although it was profitable, it was more trouble than I thought it would be, and I'm not going to do it again." You should be able to recover from the "too much work" syndrome if a mailing is profitable but the profits are small. What did you learn from the mailing? Can you fine-tune your next mailing to draw more? Can you mail more to make more money?

A friend of mine invested $1,000 in a small mailing that returned $1.40 for each $1.00 he invested, so his gross was $1,400. Sending customers the parts they ordered cost $100, so his net profit was $300. He got tired of handling it himself and gave up because he only made $300. When I asked if he would consider an investor so we could invest $100,000 and make $30,000 in profit with each mailing, he changed his mind and went into the direct marketing business. You should see his figures now. He makes a lot of money. A lot of money.

Let the marketplace set the price.

You can make money too—just start out like my friend did, and just like lots of people start in direct mail: mailings right off your kitchen table. When you get a successful mailing package, stay with it, and reinvest your profits for growth—to mail more and more. Direct mail is the only industry you can start on your kitchen table with almost no money; create a winning mailing package and a fortune all with a few strokes of your pen. It's not a get- rich-quick scheme. It's the way any prudent business grows: logically and from the profits of early successes.

The Danielle Adams Publishing Company
Box 100, Merion Station PA 19066

More on Testing

All the variables should be tested continually in direct mail, but a few are key to getting response. One is the price: Let the marketplace set the price. As much experience as you may have in your area of expertise, as best as I can figure out there is not one way to accurately predict the best price of a product when entering a new market. Not one.

Sure, everyone has feelings about what price is best, and what will work. But the only way to know for sure is to test. If you don't test, your sales may be off by as much as not 50 percent, not 100 percent, but you may make a 500 percent error. Or more. There are formulas and formulas about pricing your products. They are all different, and they come up with different answers—which should give you an idea about their accuracy. The only way to be sure is to let the marketplace decide at what price it will purchase the most product, or show you the most profit you will make with a product. So if you want to be in the direct mail business, you'd better get used to the concept of testing.

The opening acts of your direct mail piece are other important elements to test. These include the teaser copy on the envelope, the message before the salutation in your letter, and the first paragraph of the letter. The weight of any of these elements in the success of your direct marketing efforts can be as much as 85 percent. If you create a poor headline in an ad, your ad can sink like a stone. Poor teaser copy on your envelope, and your mail never gets opened. Change your teaser copy from bad to good, and your response can increase 10 or 20 times. Ten or 20 times!

In direct selling ads, headlines are the single most important element. They deserve to be tested in a campaign of any sustained length. The headline is the ad to the ad. It should be so powerful your reader will want to—have to—know more. It must force him to read the rest of the copy. Without this immediate bond, the body copy and great offer are never even seen.   Same with the opening of your direct mail piece—without an electrifying start, nothing happens. Jump-start each piece. Test these variables one at a time, and continuously lean toward the winners that generate the most response.

How Simple It Is to Start in This Business!

The difference between direct mail and a traditional business is, in direct mail you can start the whole business on the basis of mailing a few hundred letters—right from your home. When you start a traditional business, you need an office or a storefront. You need money for advertising, rents, phones, hired hands. You need checking accounts, and a cash flow to keep it all alive from day one.

In direct mail, you can start right out of your home, from your kitchen table. If the product and mailing package work, start mailing more of the same package to the same list. Keep growing based on the success of your initial mailing. It's totally predictable.

Even if you mail just 100 pieces, if you are mailing to part of a select list, your next mailing of the same package to a different part of the same list should be just as successful. If you are on a shoestring budget, first mail 200 pieces. If the results are successful, mail 400. If that's successful, mail 1,000. Then 2,000. Then 5,000. Easy. When you start out with small numbers, you'll never lose a lot of money. Just keep testing till you find a winner!

This is the beauty of direct mail. It's really this simple. Just keep growing from your successes. If the first package fails, change the copy. Raise the price. Lower the price. Insert a lift note. Make the offer more enticing. Try a two-step sales approach. Write new teaser copy for the envelope. Make the package work harder. Try a new list. All are low- or no-cost changes that can make your mailings successful and profitable. Always remember, you can limit the amount of your loss by testing the waters and mailing in limited numbers in the early stages of your mailings.

Results

To measure the results you get from each mailing, tracking where each response came from is one of the most important aspects of direct mail. Each direct mail package must be keyed or coded so you can tell which test package, price, or list the order came from. You may recognize this tracking procedure when you place an order from a catalog house and the telephone sales representative asks for your "control number," your "personal code number," the "customer number," or the "key code" on the mailing label. This tracking number is the reference for any combination of list, package, or pricing variables to determine which is working best. But usually it's the list that concerns catalog mailers.

If your small mailing doesn't allow for a mailing label key-code imprint, the code can be as simple as directing the customer to write to a special department (Dept. M, Department 529H, etc.). If you include a reply envelope, use a different color envelope or order form for each market segment you mail to. For example, if you mail 5,000 pieces, 2,500 at one price, and 2,500 at another price, you can have different colored order forms or envelopes in each package. If the person calls to place an order, ask him what color his order form is; tell him it's so you can have the same form in front of you and they can just start reading from the top down. This will secretly tell you the price. My firm did this for years. When we changed the price of our product but had millions of old order forms on the street (with prices we still honored), we always asked the color of the customer's order form and never had any trouble with this procedure.

As you send out more direct mail packages, count, compile, and compare the response from each package and list to every other test package. Also compare with your control package and house list of your own customers or your own hand-picked prospects. Keep a chart of the draw of each package so you can tally the results. I know you think you'll remember, but I guarantee that in six months, you won't. Write it down, and keep track.

A question I'm often asked is what percentage of response is good. The truth is simple: If you are selling a $5 million printing press, and you mail out 25,000 mailing pieces and get 10 responses, one from a printer who later buys a press, it was a successful mailing. But if you're selling magazine subscriptions at $19.95 a pop, you'd better sell a slew of them to be profitable. Direct mail can work on very small percentages, and success can be as simple and as fast as guessing the correct offer and profit margin in your very first mailing.

For a consumer mailing, you should consider mailing a few thousand pieces to figure out with dependable results the return you'll receive from a roll-out. Offers to the general public should be profitable at very low percentage points. A 2 percent or 3 percent draw means that for each

The Danielle Adams Publishing Company
Box 100, Merion Station PA 19066

1,000 pieces mailed, you'll get back 20 to 30 orders. So if your mailpiece costs 50 cents, or $500 per thousand, to mail, and you get 30 orders at $19.95 each ($598.50), you'd need a product that costs less than $3.33 (30 x $3.33 = $100) to fulfill the orders, with no returns, to break even. But if you're selling a $300-a-year newsletter, any subscriptions over the first two make you profitable. That's a .02 percent response rate to break even.

You can send quite a bit of mail from the comfort of your own home to test the markets.

When a consumer orders a product from you, include a flyer for an additional offer with the customer's order when you ship it. Be sure to include an order form and envelope; it'll be worth the additional cost. Customers who are pleased with your product or service are most likely to purchase from you again almost immediately. They are the very best prospects to buy additional products from a brochure, if you enclose one.

Getting Help with Production

Your initial market testing may be done right from your home. Thousands of direct mail industry people have started this way, right in their own living room, dining room, or kitchen. You can send quite a bit of mail from the comfort of your own home to test the markets and the response. And with the overhead of just your own heat, light, and labor, it's cheap. Why spend money until you see orders and revenues come in on a regular basis?

When you start sending mailings of more than 3,000 pieces at a time, I recommend you think seriously about getting help with the physical production. It's easy to lick one envelope and stamp, and maybe even 100. But when you multiply that by 3,000, the chore becomes much greater. Your tongue will get cut within the first 1,000 pieces, and your saliva will dry up at about 2,500.

September, 2008

«Salutation» «FName» «LName»
«Title»
«Catalog»
«Street»
«CityStZip»

Dear «Salutation» «LName»:

If words like "Increased Market Share" and "Brand Loyalty," "Customer Service" and "Additional Profit" sound good to you, please take a moment to read this letter.

If not, just feel free to skip it.

But please use the FREE ORDER FORM enclosed for your own <u>free sample</u> of our product. And perhaps we may be of service to you in the future.

Our firm is a manufacturer of _____ products.

Our tradition is fast, friendly service: All orders are shipped within three days of receipt. Everyone likes a well-made product. Each item is made to the highest industry standards, and beyond. If this extra care is what you are looking for in a manufacturer and vendor, please call.

If our products are offered in your catalog, your customers will always be pleased with their purchase; we guarantee it. When buying our products, your customers will (insert benefits here).

What makes us so special?

Our <u>Guarantee</u>: We guarantee the complete satisfaction of every customer. You receive no returns - because if any customer is not happy, we instruct the customer to send the product back here for any reason. You keep their payment.

Our <u>Free Replacement</u> policy: If an item we sell ever wears out, if returned to us we will replace it, free.

continued...

The Danielle Adams Publishing Company
Box 100, Merion Station PA 19066

Free Gift: All our merchandise is delivered with a free gift, to thank customers for their purchase.

Product Literature: A complete set of literature is delivered with each item, showing assembly if required, detailed instructions for use, and full warranty information. You don't have to instruct customer.

800 TOLL-FREE Customer Assistance: So you don't have to deal with any questions or problems - at any time.

High Quality: Because some things you just have to see for yourself to believe, please use the handy card provided to get a free sample for yourself.

Dedicated to Excellence: In customer service. Every order and every customer is important to us every day.

Offering our merchandise is an opportunity for you to provide your customers with exceptionally high-quality products. There are no service or repair headaches, ever.

Fast shipping means you need purchase only a small amount of inventory. On drop ship items there's no inventory expense at all. Your firm always profits with our fair margin pricing.

Thanks for your consideration to offer our products. Please call me toll free: 800-876-5432, or send the enclosed card for your own free sample. See for yourself what a pleasure it is to do business with us. Thank you.

Kindest regards,

Jeffrey Dobkin
President

P.S. Call me personally TOLL FREE 800-876-5432 at any time. We are holding your FREE SAMPLE for you, and will ship promptly on request to your home or office.

For help, first enlist members of your family; they won't leave you when they find out how much work it is, and at the end of the mailing they'll still be your family. Next, get friends to help you, although you will periodically lose them if you have big enough mailings. I figure with a 3,000-piece mailing, you can lose about six, maybe eight, good friends by asking them to help. Finally, if you have over 5,000 pieces, give the mailing assembly to a mailhouse, or actually hire people to get the mailing out. It's a lot of work.

Once you get the copy and art composed, and the letter-style ad and collateral material printed, you should get everything for a larger, more complex mailing assembled and sent from a mailing house. One of the prime reasons for this: When it becomes so much personal work, you stop doing it. Although mailings of a few thousand pieces don't sound like an unmanageable amount, when you assemble them on your dining room table, it can be surprisingly time-consuming and even overwhelming.

Everything that goes through the mail first goes through a printer.

Once you see how much physical work it is to mail 5,000 pieces, you won't be tempted to send another mailing. But if you hire it all out, as you would for a mailing of 10,000, 25,000, or a couple of million, you'll have a better comprehension of direct mail. You'll view it not as "Oh, it is too much work trying to lick 5,000 envelopes," but will see it as "so much money spent for services, and you need so much of a return to break even." As in any other medium, when you have promotional material created in any large volume, you're going to need help sending it.

Printing

Everything that goes through the mail first goes through a printer. Printers can be your best friends or your worst enemies. But either way, you've got to live with them if you are to be a successful direct mail merchant.

The printing business is unusual because you can get one price from one printer, then go about two blocks down the road and get a price that is one-third less for the exact same job. There are four reasons for this:

> • First, every printer has different printing equipment. One key in getting the best price for printing is having a printer whose press is the most efficient for that particular job. No printer has all the different presses—so no printer can always give you the best price.
> • The second reason is some printers do better work— quality checks and slower running speeds take more time.
> • Third, some offer faster delivery service—you may pay a premium for a quick turn-around.
> • Fourth reason: Some printers work on a higher mark-up.

Short runs of 1,000 to 5,000 pieces in one or two colors are cheaper when run on a small press. This is because of the shorter and easier "make-ready," a term used to describe all the steps necessary to get the press up and actually printing your piece. Longer runs and multiple color work are cheaper on a larger press, where the make-ready is longer and more expensive, but the actual press running time is shorter. The press may print two or more colors in a single pass of the paper through the press, and/or may have much higher printing speeds, measured in impressions per hour (or IPH).

For example, if you have a printing job of 100,000 letters, and the local printer quotes it on a slow printing press that prints 5,000 sheets per hour, that's 20 hours of press time (plus one hour of make-ready). You know that's got to be expensive. But if you give it to a printer and he runs it two at a time (called two-up) on a larger press that runs at 20,000 IPH, that's 2 1/2 hours of press time (and two hours of make-ready). You can see there will be a difference in price.

Be careful in the printing industry. Especially with low quotes: some printers charge a low initial bid, but if you make any alterations after you are locked into their workflow, you can get stuck with some very expensive additional charges. If you complain that an extra charge is unfair, some printers may refuse to release your artwork until you pay in full (which is

The Danielle Adams Publishing Company
Box 100, Merion Station PA 19066

illegal). Some printers use low-cost paper that has been subjected to high humidity and has a curl to it. The range of what you may get as a final printed piece is wide. The worst part is, the money you pay may not have any correlation to the type of job you receive. Be careful. Going to a new printer is like taking your car to a new mechanic, or taking your TV to a repair shop—you never quite know what you're going to get until it's too late.

For first-time print buyers, I'll cover some basic highlights that will give you just enough information to be dangerous. Only a few paragraphs. If you purchase printing already, you can skip this part.

Since printing is price sensitive, get several quotes—as many as four or five. Printers will have different paper in stock, so when one printer shows you a certain paper, write down the name and ask for a similar grade of paper at other shops so the bids will be comparable. Buying paper "on the floor" (on hand) is cheaper; every printer likes to use up his on-the-floor stock.

Paper comes in different grades. The best are premium grades, or sheets whose whites are measured in brightness; the ratings measure from 85 to 94 (94 being the brightest, measured against Titanium white). Number 1 standard grade sheets have a brightness of 85.0 to 87.0; number 2 grade, 83.0 to 84.9, number 3 sheets, 79.0 to 82.9; number 4, 73.0 to 78.9; and number 5, a brightness of 72.9 and below (newsprint). There are coated sheets, calendered sheets, coated two sides, and 25 or so other variations. When you get a printing quote, get the name of the paper or a paper swatch from one printer, and another printer should be able to come pretty close to a match in terms of price, texture, brightness, opacity, color, hue, and weight, not to mention the other characteristics that make each type of paper so unique.

If you go to an instant printer, ask the printer if they use paper, plastic, or metal printing plates for short runs; metal plates are recommended for crisper printing (only really cheap printers use paper or plastic plates). On longer runs, no one should use anything but metal plates. Ask about the lead or delivery time to see what kind of service you're going to get. When dealing with any printer, always demand your artwork be returned with the finished job. Negatives are usually retained by the printer unless you negotiate with him up front to give them to you when he is through with your job. Some will, as the negatives are of no use to the printer unless he runs the job again. Other printers won't give them up. Curious.

Some printers offer the additional services of artwork and typesetting, but I would purchase these from an ad agency or design shop. The artwork and typesetting should be entirely independent of the printing, so feel free to get them elsewhere. Art is highly personalized, and you may not find a quality artist associated with the printer of your choice. The printer you select may be excellent, but he may have a mediocre artist on staff with little or no direct mail experience. For a printer, having an artist on staff may just be an accommodation to him for his own layouts. A design shop or ad agency usually depends on unique designs and good creative to stay in business—so your chances of getting a better layout will be greater.

I've known great artists who work for printers, and horrible artists as well, so look carefully at their samples if the printer will be doing the layouts, mechanicals, or typesetting for your material. If the samples are great, and you award this aspect of the job to the printer, make sure the same person whose samples you saw will be working on your project. Say no if the art isn't great (say you are going to take the art to an agency), but if you feel comfortable with the printer and his quote for printing, order the printing. If the printer does the artwork, the layouts should be yours—you paid for them. Settle this in advance to avoid a sticky situation later.

Once you find a printer you can work with, one who gives maybe not the lowest, but consistently low to moderate, quotes and delivers a crisp printing job on time all the time, stay with that shop. As one of the key elements in the production of direct mail, a good printer is a necessity. Shop around to find one who does printing reasonably well, has a few different-sized presses in his shop, offers consistent, moderate pricing, and is always honest and up front. This relationship will serve you well.

Conclusion

In direct mail, you achieve success before your product is ever seen. Your sales depend on your mailing package, not your product.

Well, now you have the basics. All that reading about the letter, the package, the envelope copy, and the list—this is where it pays off. If you've got the product, now is the time to try your hand at direct mail. You have a terrific foundation for producing benefit-oriented copy, envelope teaser copy that compels the reader to open it, and an award-winning package that sells the response. You just need to plug it all into a quality list that will pull a tremendous response.

Notice I haven't said much about the product? I know, I know, your product is terrific. In direct mail, you achieve success before your product is ever seen. Your sales depend on your mailing package, not on your product. People don't see your product until they've already ordered, so the product isn't as important to the sale as you may think. The type of product is, but the product itself is not what has sold your customers. Your direct mail package is what sold your customer. Hopefully you will sell a product of good value. And guarantee every product you sell.

The hardest part is now upon you: starting. Now is the time—while it's all fresh in your mind. Just take a pencil and start anywhere. Or sit down at typewriter or computer and crank out a rough draft—that's always the hardest thing. The sooner you start writing, the sooner you'll be able to get your package in the mail.

The Danielle Adams Publishing Company
Box 100, Merion Station PA 19066

You don't have to wait until you have the ultimate perfectly crafted package ready to go; don't let this stop you or bog you down. Everyone starts out with a first package, maybe a bit unrefined as you look back on it when you mail your 50-millionth mailer. But the challenge is to give it your best effort. Show it to a lot of people before sending it, finalize a package everyone likes, and mail it. Get a short list of just a few hundred and mail your best offer. Or go for it and buy a list of a few thousand, and mail to the first 1,000 on it. Get some mail pieces to the post office and feel the excitement of getting a response: receiving money and orders. It's thrilling. It's still thrilling for me.

The only way to get orders to come in is to send some mail out. If I can do it, you can do it. If you need some help, just keep this book handy, and use it as a reference tool. If you really get stuck, give my office a call. Heck, I usually wind up answering the phone myself anyhow. Good luck. Always feel free to drop me a note and let me know how it's going. Twenty-five years in the business, and I still look forward to getting mail every morning.

Personalized Direct Mail Campaigns

Another direct mail strategy is the personalized letter. This campaign is the most effective you can be for 42 cents per prospect. Its low cost makes it the most effective advertising you can buy, bar none. The campaign applies to targeted mailings of just a few hundred pieces, although as you grow or invest more money, this figure can be multiplied by thousands. As your firm grows, the techniques you use in these personalized campaigns can work in larger and larger mailings for you. The campaign is referenced here with small numbers because that's the way to start out on a limited budget. If it works, no reason it can't be expanded 10, 20, 100 times.

Keep in mind that the fewer pieces you mail, the more targeted the group you are mailing to, the more personal the letter can be. The rules I've outlined in this chapter hold true for personalized letters: letters with the name and address of the recipient on them. Personalized letters needn't be quite as commercial looking or sounding as the mass-mailed letters in larger direct mail campaigns. Since these letters fit a tighter group, you can direct them to the precise needs of your reader.

Personalizing your mailing with the name and address of the recipient on each letter is the best and the ultimate use of direct mail. The fully personalized letter takes a slightly different style and approach than others do. This letter really is one to one: you can make it look like the real letter that it is. With a personalized letter, no one has to know that anyone else received the same letter.

A campaign is not a single mailing of anything. Why do you think they call it a campaign?

People read commercially printed direct mail letters (Dear Reader) as letters, but they also recognize somewhere in the deep, dark recesses of their minds that these letters are printed. With a personalized letter this restriction does not apply, as the letter is specifically addressed to only one reader: the person holding it. If done correctly, the beauty of the personalized letter is that the reader feels he or she is the only person receiving this personal piece of correspondence.

When you send a general solicitation mailing to consumers, a single mailing must stand on its own to produce a profitable response immediately. When making targeted personalized mailings to individuals, or to buyers in big companies to distribute or purchase your products in quantity, a direct mail campaign is not only a single letter and a brochure. With the potential for larger sales, you should plan on mailing a campaign of several pieces to secure an order of a larger size. A campaign is not a single mailing of anything. Why do you think they call it a campaign? A campaign is more than one letter, and in fact, more than just one piece of correspondence.

Just as it may take five or ten sales calls to make a big sale in person in most industries, it may take five or ten letters to make a big sale through the mail. So don't be discouraged if your first mailing does not generate many responses. Sure, it's possible to make a big hit the first time out, but I wouldn't bet the ranch on that possibility. If you're trying to market on that premise, it's going to be a long, dry, hot summer.

This is the only medium where you can start to market a product with a few hundred dollars.

The advantage of direct mail is, if you are trying to market a product on a very low budget, you actually can start on your home typewriter on the kitchen table. This is the only medium where you can start to market a product with a few hundred dollars, and get very effective results if the letters are well produced and carefully directed. The reason? The precise aim you can take with your money; no wasted advertising expense. Personalized direct mail campaigns are aimed at catalog houses, product distributors, mass merchants, chain stores, large retailers, and businesses that have the need, and the purchasing power, to buy your product in quantity. Some larger businesses and catalog houses purchase goods in trainloads.

Finding Prospects for Volume Purchases

Personalized letters are for people who can make volume purchases. Or for when a sale involves a substantial amount of money. Taking precise aim with your personalized letters requires more than a good guess. You have to make sure you are writing to the correct person: the one who has the power to make the decision to purchase, and the authority to sign the check.

Probably the best resources for names of the bigger industry players who purchase products in volume or large-check items are the industry trade journals, the annual directories, and the industry resource guides put out by almost every trade magazine publisher. These reference magazines contain the names of the major distributors and the larger

manufacturers in the industry, who will probably be your biggest purchasers for volume sales. Magazines are usually my first choice for where to find names and addresses because they keep industry information current.

Whether searching a specific industry or a geographic region, there are trade journals that will give you current names for your direct mail marketing campaign.

Using the trade journals, finding buyers from larger companies or purchasing agents of distributors is easy. Get the industry magazines, as explained in the "Marketing Through Magazines" chapter. Keep your eyes open for articles about firms that you think might purchase your products. When someone is listed in the article as a president, VP, buyer, or purchasing agent (PA) for a company you think might need your product, give them a call. If the phone number is not listed, call the magazine (the magazine's phone number is always given in the masthead in the first few pages). Since they did the research, they'll have the phone number on hand. Ask for the editorial department at the magazine, mention you read their article (and it was very interesting and well done; thanks so much for the great article), and ask if they would happen to have the phone number of the company mentioned. In all the times I've done this, I've never heard them say, "No, we don't have that."

When you get the phone number, give the company a call. Ask the operator if the name you saw in the article is responsible for purchasing your type of product or service. If yes, there's your answer. If no, get the correct name. If you want, ask to be connected to him; when he or his assistant comes on the line, ask if he is the person to whom you should submit your product for consideration. It's that easy. If you like, you can say that you'll be sending a letter to him, and ask if you should submit a sample, if your product lends itself to sampling.

In addition to feature articles, most trade magazines usually have personnel news, and this can be an excellent source for figuring out who's who in the different corporations.

Finally, most magazines have a directory or annual reference issue. The names of the higher company personnel can be found in this issue. The reference issues usually name the top personnel in each firm, along with their corporate address and telephone number.

Following the trade journals' example of bringing you current names in the industry you serve are the associations. Almost every industry has one or several, and their rosters are usually good, up-to-the-minute compilations of industry personnel. Sometimes you have to do a little fast talking over several phone calls to get a list from an association, but the list can be a perfect market match, filled with nothing but heavy hitters in your industry.

Another option for finding qualified people for larger product sales is to use the SIC code, which has more value than merely specifying a list to a list broker. It can play an important part in a more personal direct mail campaign.

Here's an example of how to use the SIC code. Suppose you are creating a campaign to sell paper to commercial printers. You go to the reference section of the library and find the *Directory of Leading Private Companies*, then check the alphabetical listing of the SIC classifications shown in the book under "P" for printers. It's somewhere after pickles and relishes, poultry production, and popcorn farms, but before psychiatric hospitals.

You learn that the major SIC code for printers is 27, and you find that in the numerical SIC listings. SIC 27, Printers and Publishers. You skim the breakdown of the printing category until you reach SIC 2752, Commercial Printing.

In the next section, the SIC Index, you look up classification 2752 and find a list of large commercial printers. Using this list, you can find more detailed company data in the front section of the book—which lists company headquarters, annual sales volumes, number of employees, and names of all their top personnel, including the buyers.

Once you get the names of the top employees, my advice is to call and verify that you have the correct person, so you don't waste your time sending a great campaign to someone who has left the firm. Once you call and verify that the person is there, and has the capacity to specify and buy your product, then put them on your personalized letter list. In our example, if the organization is really large, you'd probably need to find the paper buyer; you won't be contacting the president. Call and ask who is responsible for specifying and purchasing; get the buyer's name and the correct spelling, then write to the buyer. In smaller firms, the president is a good bet.

This process of using the SIC code is so simple, you can go to the library, find this book, and within a few minutes find the list of large potential accounts. Then it's just a matter of copying their names from the listing, and you can run the entire campaign from your home. So bring a few quarters for the photocopy machine. You can complete all this market research in a single evening's work at the library.

The Catalog Campaign

One of the best uses of direct mail is to get your product in catalogs. It's easy, using the multiple exposure marketing technique with the personalized letter campaign. It's described fully in the final chapter, "The Ultimate Campaign." The campaign starts here, with the research to find the correct person to mail your solicitation to.

A few of the larger catalog houses mail upward of 50 million catalogs a year. Imagine if your product were included in one of them.

If you think your product is strong enough to survive a solo mailing, call a catalog house that sells to your product's market niche, and ask if you can buy its mailing list of customers. Most catalog firms will sell their list to you (often through their list broker). Usually, the only requirement is to send them a sample mailing piece of what you will be sending their customers so they can make sure you're reputable. But it will be expensive to purchase their list and mail to everyone with your own direct mail package. So I recommend another tack for entering the catalog market: selling through the catalogs themselves.

The Danielle Adams Publishing Company
Box 100, Merion Station PA 19066

There are more than 10,000 firms that publish catalogs. Some of them have millions of customers. A few of the larger catalog houses mail upward of 50 million catalogs a year. Imagine if your product were included in one of them.

Catalog merchants buy hundreds of thousands of items. Some catalogs are in specialized fields and offer unique goods not found elsewhere. If you have a specialty item associated with their specific marketplace, these catalogs are most likely to be interested in carrying your product. Most catalog merchants continuously look for new and exciting products. What good would a catalog be without new products to keep it lively? It would grow stagnant.

Some catalog merchants stick to the mainstream, offering a retail product mix that is just like your local department store's. Their particular audience may be people in Alaska, Montana, or the remote areas of Texas where there are no department stores. Their catalog success is further fueled by people who don't get out much, and by people who enjoy shopping from home. Other catalogs specialize in products that are unique to their specific niche. With over 10,000 catalogs published each year, I won't go into what the specialties are, but you can be assured there is a catalog that will be able to fit your product into their mix, no matter what it is. Check later in this chapter for the excellent directories that list all the catalogs.

Once your product is in a catalog and selling well, it may stay there forever, producing income for you every month for the rest of your life.

If you have an item that is marketable, chances are good there are some catalog houses that will offer it. The large catalog houses are always adding new items to their magazines. New products are the lifeblood of some catalogs, and the merchants constantly search the marketplace for new goods or a better design of a product already on the market. What would catalogs like The Sharper Image's or Brookstone's be without a constant supply of new products?

Catalogs are an excellent means of distribution with very low up-front costs or marketing expense. The catalog market is very lucrative if you have the right product and approach the correct catalogs. Once your product is in a catalog and selling well, it may stay there forever, producing income for you every month for the rest of your life.

Ship a quality product on time, and sit back and get checks in the mail every month from each catalog your product is in. This is not only possible, many people earn their living by doing this. Other than your initial contact and your on-time delivery of a quality product, no further work is necessary. Your whole business can be run from your kitchen table. One morning a week.

To get into a catalog, you can take out an ad to attract catalog merchants in one of the several magazines that serve the catalog community, such as *Catalog Age, Direct,* and *Catalog Success.* But they're expensive.

A better idea is to get the names and addresses of the catalogs that serve the people in your market, and write to the buyers of each firm. This is one of the greatest uses of a targeted, personalized direct mail marketing campaign. Sending buyers a personal (or personalized) letter, that may be exactly the same to each person, is a terrific short direct mail campaign composed of 100 or so letters you can send from your home or office.

Overview

As with any direct mail campaign, first define your markets. If the markets you've selected are served by numerous catalog companies, find all the catalogs you possibly can that serve those markets. Are they the correct vehicles for your product? Does your product fit in well with their product mix?

The Danielle Adams Publishing Company
Box 100, Merion Station PA 19066

For the larger catalog houses, I'd call the catalog merchants and ask how to submit your product to them. The usual response: You'll be given the name of a buyer and instructed to send literature or a product sample to their attention. A sample and a persuasive letter may result in immediate inclusion in the very next catalog. This would be at almost no cost to you, and if they accept you'd have instant sales and product distribution. Find all the merchants in the catalog directories.

There is no charge for having your products listed in most catalogs. The catalog house buys at a wholesale cost and sells at retail prices, just like most other retail merchants. Usually catalogers want to mark up a product three times, so be prepared to see the product you sell to them for $10 be listed for $30 in their catalog. Although some catalog houses will work on less profit, for the best chance to be included in their book, try to give them this margin. Some catalogs charge for advertising space. When you run into this, I'd look elsewhere.

If a three-times markup is not acceptable to you or presents your product at too high a price to sell well, most catalog houses will still work with you. If they believe in your product, most catalogs will work on a more traditional margin of two times their cost (100 percent markup). The more attractive your pricing, the more likely they will be to offer your item. But if they think it's a great product, they may accept a lower margin. Remember, they earn this markup by being both distributor and retailer. Some catalogs buy in huge volume, so be prepared to supply large-quantity orders—or at least know how you will be able to manufacture or purchase and ship a good quantity of merchandise quickly, if they ask.

Several reference directories list the majority of the catalogs published, and they can be purchased, or found in the reference section of larger libraries. Most contain a breakdown of catalogs by product line. Since some of these books are very expensive, the library may be a less costly way to research your market and come up with catalogs that may be interested in carrying your product. If you find you're looking for catalogs all the time, their purchas price may be justified Depending on the depth of the market penetration you want, you may wish to use them all. An hour or two at the library photocopy machine may pay off in a deeper catalog market penetration. As a marketer myself, when I market a product, I dig for all the names I can get and as you would suspect, I spend a lot of time submerged in directories like these.

Besides using directories, another way to receive samples of catalogs to evaluate for your product placement is to buy a few consumer magazines that cater to the specific industry segment you serve and send for all the catalogs listed in them. You can probably get a few dozen catalog names and addresses from a product-intensive magazine such as *Modern Aircraft* or *Woodworker's Journal*. If you were looking for woodworking catalogs, for instance, a bookstore with a large magazine section would have a selection of woodworking magazines. Buy them all ($25 dedicated to market research), and call all the catalog houses shown in them—you'll receive about 20 to 25 woodworker's catalogs from one evening's work. For industrial markets, use the trade magazine directories and get the trade woodworking publications.

If you want to be placed on a mailing list, order a small item from each catalog, and you'll get on some of the mailing lists for that industry and start to receive more catalogs. (It's common practice for catalogs to sell or exchange their list of names of customers with similar catalog houses.) This last step will take more time, but it can yield the names and product mix of some of the smaller, more esoteric catalogs in that industry.

The Specifics of the Catalog Campaign

When you receive each catalog in the mail, call the catalog house and ask for the name of the person who purchases or reviews new products. Be sure to ask the correct spelling of the name; nothing destroys the beauty of a direct mail piece more quickly than a misspelled name. And get the spelling of the buyer's name from the operator, to prevent the awkwardness of having to ask for it when you are speaking to the buyer personally. If the buyer is available to talk, transfer to them and ask them the procedure to submit a product. Then send a letter and any literature you may have (or just the letter by itself) about your product. If you called on an 800 number, get the business phone number too; when you call back on a sales call, use the regular number. While buyers in some large firms may not know or care what line a call comes in on, nothing makes me more angry than when someone calls me at my expense to make a sales call.

It's amazing how long your post card will hang around on someone's desk— even if it isn't sent back to you—while they try to figure out what to do with a live stamp on a post card addressed to your firm.

If a sample of your product is inexpensive, send it; if not, let the buyer know samples are available on request, and enclose a postage-paid card they can use to get one. If you don't have a business reply mail permit, include a post card with a live stamp on it. It's amazing how long your post card will hang around on someone's desk—even if it isn't sent back to you—while they try to figure out what to do with a live stamp on a post card addressed to your firm. There's just something forbidding about throwing out a live stamp.

It's OK to write this post card by hand in these highly personalized, limited mailings. Anything you can do that's legal and in good taste to make it easier for a buyer to respond or inquire is permissible. While a handwritten post card probably says your firm is not as big as General Motors, people will recognize and appreciate your effort and won't hold it against you. If it is easier for them to respond—like if you write their name on the back of the card for them—it will increase the apparent value of your service, and your response.

Very large catalog firms will need to know if you can supply them with your product in large quantities. Before you jump for joy when you receive an inquiry, think: Can you really fulfill an order for 4,000 pieces right away when they make a big catalog drop? How about 10,000? If they don't think you can, they won't use you as a vendor. So when marketing to the larger catalog houses, all your communications should make you look like a major player. You've got to convince them you can deliver all the goods they need in a timely fashion.

To find out if there is even minor interest in a product, I usually put a line on business reply post cards sent to catalog companies with a check box that says "___Yes! Keep me on your mailing list!" It's a noncommittal way for even casually interested parties to express their interest.

Before any catalog house runs your product in their book, they're going to want to see a sample to (1) make sure you really have a product; (2) make sure you can deliver as promised; (3) see if it's of good quality; and (4) see if you are responsive to their needs. If you get a request for a sample, break out the champagne: it's the first step in the process, and you are strongly being considered for a catalog.

Personalized letters are ideal for marketing to catalog houses, distributors, and other major buyers. A phone call to the merchant and the offer of a sample is the fastest way to get your product in a catalog; you can get an early readout of results in just a few weeks. But if you don't want to make soliciting telephone sales calls to these places, you can use the direct mail techniques described in this chapter, then continue your campaign as detailed in the last chapter of this book.

Meanwhile in a world of shrinking catalog resources, here's refreshing news about some of the best catalog directories available. We use these in our offices for our own clients. They're well marked up. Come visit - see for yourself.

The Oxbridge Communications National Directory of Catalogs

One of the best, in-depth resources for finding catalogs is *The National Directory of Catalogs* from Oxbridge Communications. Well over 1,000 pages, crammed from head to toe with marketing data about catalogs. This is the dog-eared source book we use around here for in-depth product marketing to the catalog industry.

The four-page Table of Contents shows over 200 catalog categories listed alphabetically by product line, along with the number of catalogs in each category. So at a glance, you can readily look under the heading "Food" and find over 400 food catalogs to place that new line of salad dressings you've been thinking about making. Or immediately find over 60 pet catalogs you'd like to contact to get your new pet brush sold through.

The table of contents, as well as all the other indexes, points you toward the main 800-page Data-Reference Section of the directory—dedicated to each catalog's essentials: name, address, phone numbers, fax, key personnel. Also included is data such as number of catalogs mailed, frequency, retail cost for catalog, whether it's a business or consumer publication, printing info, publication size, list management company, list data (hotline counts, number of 12-month buyers), and sales volume. A detailed description of its product line as furnished by the catalog company, also appears here.

Next is the Company and Title Index. If you know the company name, look it up here, find the page number referenced for the catalog in the main section, and on that page—and surrounding pages—you'll find all the other catalogs with similar product lines. And you thought marketing was hard, when it's really this easy. This section is followed by the Title & Company Index: if you know the name of the catalog, look here to find the page it's shown on in the main section of the directory as outlined above.

The Oxbridge Communications National Directory of Catalogs also has a Geographic Index of catalog publishers by state. If you were thinking of pitching your product in person to some local catalog merchants, this is the place to turn to. The index by state runs slightly under 100 pages. This directory is now available online along with the rest of Oxbridge Communications Directories for a cost starting at $50 a month. Please see the reference section for details of this excellent value.

The Directory of Mail Order Catalogs

Grey House Publishing steps up to the plate with two incredible directories: *The Directory of Mail Order Catalogs* and *The Directory of Business to Business Catalogs*. Updated for 2007, this edition of *The Directory of Mail Order Catalogs* is larger than life and bigger and better than ever. It's 1,500+ pages, 8 1/2" x 11", over 13,000 entries of nothing but catalogs, all arranged, abstracted, dissected, taken apart, and put back together again with one objective: to make your catalog research easier than ever.

Sections include a <u>Table of Contents</u> containing 44 major classifications (e.g.: boating), broken down into their subdivisions (accessories, boat kits, boats, equipment and supplies, radio and navigation equipment). Finding information in this catalog directory is a breeze.

Having trouble finding your markets? Try the <u>Product Index</u>, where catalogs are listed under their product lines. For example: the "Children's" listing contains catalogs such as Talbot's Kids, Land's End Children's Clothing, Wooden Soldier, and so forth; plus the page number of where the full write-up of each catalog can be found in the main data-reference section of the book. All indexes point you to this main section.

Still looking for a particular catalog? Find it fast in the <u>Catalog and Company Name section</u>, indexed alphabetically by... catalog and company name. So while the product section shows the Bass Pro catalog under "Fishing," this section shows it under "B."

Of particular interest to the new breed of I-merchants, computer wizards, and Internet geeks is the <u>Online Directory</u>. Indexed by product classification, each catalog is shown with its Web site address, so an immediate look-up is at hand to find competing products or evaluate the product mix. Such rapid access to this broad range of information—merchandise, distribution, and pricing data—is one of the highlights of the usefulness of the Internet.

The bulk of *The Directory of Mail Order Catalogs* is the <u>Main Data-Reference Section</u>, where you can find all the information about each catalog, such as its name, address, phone/fax numbers, website, president's name and top staff, credit cards they accept, cost, circulation, mailing list, sales data, number of employees and printing information. Also includes

The Danielle Adams Publishing Company
Box 100, Merion Station PA 19066

Target the Catalog Industry!

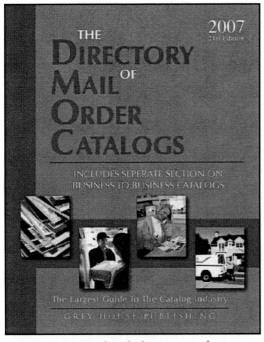

Published since 1981, the **Directory of Mail Order Catalogs** is the premier source of information on the mail order catalog industry. It is the source that business professionals and librarians have come to rely on for the thousands of catalog companies in the US.

New for 2007, *The Directory of Mail Order Catalogs* has been combined with its companion volume, *The Directory of Business to Business Catalogs*, to offer all 13,000 catalog companies in one easy-to-use volume.

➢ Section I: Consumer Catalogs, covers over 9,000 consumer catalog companies in 44 different product chapters from Animals to Toys & Games.

➢ Section II: Business to Business Catalogs, details 5,000 business catalogs, everything from computers to laboratory supplies, building construction and much more.

Listings contain detailed contact information including mailing address, phone & fax numbers, web sites, e-mail addresses and key contacts along with important business details such as product descriptions, employee size, years in business, sales volume, catalog size, number of catalogs mailed and more.

Three indexes are included for easy access to information: Catalog & Company Name Index, Geographic Index and Product Index.

The Directory of Mail Order Catalogs, now with its expanded business to business catalogs, is the largest and most comprehensive resource covering this billion-dollar industry. It is the standard in its field. This important resource is a useful tool for entrepreneurs searching for catalogs to pick up their product, vendors looking to expand their customer base in the catalog industry, market researchers, small businesses investigating new supply vendors, along with the library patron who is exploring the available catalogs in their areas of interest.

This is a godsend for those looking for information." –Reference Book Review
"The organization, scope and continuous updating and revision of this work ensures its place as a standard reference." –ARBA

Pub. Date: December 2006 13,000 listings; 1,300 pages Softcover ISBN 1-59237-156-6, $350

Grey House **P**ublishing

Grey House Publishing
PO Box 860 ◆ 185 Millerton Road Millerton, NY 12546
(800) 562-2139 ◆ (518) 789-8700 ◆ FAX (518) 789-0556
www.greyhouse.com ◆ e-mail: books@greyhouse.com

how long the company has been in business, and an editorial description of the catalog's contents.

The sister publication, *The Directory of Business to Business Catalogs*, is 8 1/2" x 11", with over 6,000 entries. Like *The Directory of Mail Order Catalogs*, this book also has an <u>Online Directory</u> and a <u>Catalog and Company Name Index</u>. In addition, *The Directory of Business to Business Catalogs* has a <u>Geographic Index</u> where catalogs are shown by state.

The Power of Direct Marketing

─────────────────────────────

Direct mail is the lowest-cost way to enter a market without a big commitment of funds.

─────────────────────────────

As you have probably surmised, this book isn't just about direct mail; rather, it's a general overview designed to get you started in high-yield direct marketing of a product or service. Its orientation is toward direct mail and direct marketing because it's a very effective way to test a market to determine whether there is interest in your products without a big capital investment. Direct mail is the lowest-cost way to enter a market without a big commitment of funds. Direct selling is also the fastest way to enter a new market when you have no established distribution channels in place.

If you can write a good letter, and perhaps follow it up with a few more direct mail pieces or even a phone call, you can feel out the marketplace without even having a sample of the product ready. You can do this on a budget of less than a couple of thousand dollars. Keep in mind that, more than in any other means of selling including the door-to-door vacuum cleaner selling of days of old, you'll get a lot of "No thank you's," "Be-backs" ("I'll 'be-back' in touch with you"), and coldhearted buyers who won't give you the courtesy of a return phone call.

The Danielle Adams Publishing Company
Box 100, Merion Station PA 19066

Any salesperson will tell you that you get paid for hearing "no," and this is even truer in direct marketing. But 95 "No's" and 5 "Yes's" out of 100 sounds great to me! Fortunately, direct mail is a game of numbers. The way to make those numbers pay off is to test as many markets as you can until you find the profitable ones. The way to keep costs down is to take careful aim. A few 42-cent stamps can go a long way in discovering sales opportunities.

If you're like me and aren't the kind of person who can take a lot of "No thanks!" whether by phone or in person, this book and these campaigns are perfectly designed for you. Just keep mailing, and if you take careful aim, you have a chance of success. Once you get some response, adjust your aim toward the responsive markets.

All direct mailers know they will receive a majority of "No thank you's." That's OK, it's part of the game. Lots of people don't want or need your products and services. There are plenty of people who want and need your products that you can sell to, and this book is devoted to defining them as our target markets, finding them, and making our offer to them, so we can devote our attention to those who are most likely to purchase our products and goods.

Draft your best letters and drop them in the nearest mailbox: In direct mail, success may be just 42 cents away.

Mailings are the cheapest way to market to a specific audience. Multiple mailings are the basis of a campaign. A campaign, by definition, is not a solo mailing. A campaign is a sustained effort over time. The basis for the campaigns in this book is multiple exposure marketing— specifically, using a series of letters. Letters are the most effective of all direct mail formats. So crank up your favorite pen. Draft your best letters - in direct mail, success may just be just 42 cents away.

There are many books about direct mail, and the direct marketing industry is served by several excellent trade journals. If you find your interest piqued by this chapter, or by the thought that you can send a letter to almost anyone in the United States and have that person read it and respond, get the direct marketing industry magazines. In a very short time, you'll have a deeper knowledge and understanding of what makes the industry tick and where the opportunities lie. You'll also have a fresh idea of what's working in direct mail, and a constant source for new ideas. Did I mention most of the trade journals are free.

After reading just a few of the magazines, you'll get an idea of the depth and span of the markets served by the tremendous direct mail industry. You'll learn about the specific types of offers made by the various companies, such as the "negative option" from the book and record clubs (you must write "no" to their offer to not receive their next selection) or the "front-end loader," which offers six records for one cent up front; you purchase twelve more later.

In the direct mail trade journals, you'll see which catalogs are working and the analysis of what makes them work. You'll learn why their formats are successful. You'll read the industry dirt on who's mailing what, and who is getting sued. If you feel this industry or the direct marketing media calling you, call the trade journals and get subscriptions. The education to follow will be worth it. If you have any further questions, write to my office.

One of the most valuable aspects of direct marketing is that you should be able to figure out the original source of 99 percent of your orders or inquiries, and you can market harder to those successful markets. You can increase the volume of the winning packages that work well and are profitable for you. You can continually enhance your marketing budget by increasing only your most effective advertising dollars.

Yea, it's crucial to measure and track your response carefully. Keep a written log of responses: which market, which package it came from, which envelope and copy, and how many responses you received from how many pieces mailed. The date when you mailed and the date when each response came in can be important for later analysis. The price at which you sold your goods, the special offers, and especially which lists the orders came from are all elements to track. Track them so you can repeat your successes and cut out unprofitable mailings.

The Danielle Adams Publishing Company
Box 100, Merion Station PA 19066

Keep tabs on the profit or loss from each mailing, as well as the general results. Write it all down—I know you think you'll remember what came from where, but I guarantee that if you don't write down everything as it happens, it will all blend together when you add the element of time. If everything is written down, in six months you'll still be clear as to the results of each effort.

Finally, create each direct mail package as if it's your last—as if the success or failure of your entire company depends on it. This is especially true of the first package you mail, but it still applies to every mailing you do. Write each mailing package as though your business depends on it. Be as convincing as you can, and make it as easy as possible to respond. Make every effort to draw the maximum response the first time out—so you can taste the success. There's no magic in marketing—or in direct mail. Just thousands of hours of hard work, followed by instant success.

Conclusion

If you need help, this is where to go. Direct marketing agencies, freelance marketing agents, and direct mail copywriters are my first choices when I need to have an expert direct mail package professionally prepared. If you are making any major investment in your mailing package, there is no substitute for having a seasoned professional compose a direct mail letter that will go to 1000's of people, or a hard-hitting direct marketing ad that makes the phone ring off the hook. Some are expensive and excellent; some are expensive and lousy. You never know what kind of creative you are going to get until you see their samples. Look over plenty of samples and select your creative team with great care.

Since direct mail lives or dies by the written word, check each candidate's writing for effectiveness, and how it conforms to the rules stated in this book. Better writers are worth their weight in additional response, and I recommend you hire the best you can find if you outsource your writing. You can check to see if it's cheaper to write the copy yourself and submit it to an outside firm for a tune-up; this may be much less expensive than having an agency start from scratch. Who knows, your stuff might just need a few light pen strokes. In any event, make sure you present the writer with a list of features and benefits, as outlined earlier in this chapter. Doing so will help a copywriter considerably. And remember, your direct mail package is only expensive if it doesn't work. If it works, the orders offset the up-front costs.

Call around and get samples from copywriters and agencies alike. Photocopies of direct mail letters and ads they have penned are inexpensive and easy to send to you. While a writer may not have a sample letter or brochure directed to your specific market, any good copywriter or agency will have a number of random samples on hand. The samples should explicitly show you the quality of the talent you are buying. When you find someone whose work you like, make sure that if you hire that agency, you will get the same writer or team to create your piece. When you receive the samples, ask what the costs were to the client for each piece.

A copywriter is only expensive if his copy doesn't work.

For larger runs of promotional direct mail letters, you need a specialist who can follow the direct marketing principles that have been tried and tested. You would be better off sticking with a professional direct mail copywriter. While some professionals are quite costly, many are worth their weight in additional orders and generating additional income—and profit—for you. Some are worth many, many times their weight in orders. Remember, like your mailing package, a copywriter is only expensive if his copy doesn't work.

In larger cities there is usually a direct mail association. In Philadelphia it's called the PDMA—Philadelphia Direct Marketing Association. It's kind of a loose-knit group which has monthly dinners, and organizes a local trade show once a year. The association also publishes a monthly newsletter. Associations like this will have the names of direct mail specialists, such as copywriters, lettershops, printers, or artists who are involved with direct mail and the organization.

You are always welcome to call me, too. While I ain't cheap, I have seen my work make money for clients by increasing their orders, revenues, and response. My firm offers marketing, copywriting, and design and consulting services. I am always pleased to send samples of my work upon request. Thanks.

~ **Marketing Through Magazines** ~

Examine the markets, the magazines that serve them, the tools to determine the scope and depth of each market, and how to reach them. You will find out how to select markets from these reference directories, analyze the different market segments, and undress the magazines that serve each particular industry. Here you'll also learn how to figure out which magazines to send press releases to for a publicity campaign.

The conclusion of a successful PR campaign is placing ads. You'll learn which magazines offer the best chance of success if you place an ad, how to negotiate for a good ad placement price, and how to get the best ad position. Get free samples of all the magazines to analyze, and get ready to place ads in your final magazine selections.

I hope you've enjoyed the extensive chapter on direct marketing and direct mail, and found the many tips and techniques I've tried to cram in there useful and helpful in your marketing. If you get a chance, call or drop a note to let me know if this has been really helpful.

BOOKS
THEY'RE EVERYTHING
YOU'VE EVER IMAGINED...
AND MORE!

DANIELLE ADAMS
PUBLISHING COMPANY

~ **Introduction** ~

Since the world, or at least the United States, is too big to cover by foot, and there are certainly too many people to call on the phone to personally introduce to your product, man has created magazines. Almost every niche of every market has its own special periodicals. Most industries have several; and larger, richer markets have so many it's tough (translate that into "expensive" or "impossible") to figure out which magazines will work for selling your product, and which ones won't.

This chapter will show you how to make your magazine advertising and publicity campaign as effective as possible at the least cost. This means you'll generate the most inquiries and the most sales (and make the most money in return) for each invested dollar in your budget. You do have a budget, don't you? A written budget? If not, don't worry. If you're a small firm, or marketing from your home, you don't need one until you get larger. Isn't it a refreshing surprise to hear that?

There are so many ways to figure out a budget, all of them can't be correct because each of them leads to a different answer. Or none of them is correct, for the same reason. Take your pick of the all or none theory. But remember, as long as there is so much confusion on the matter, anything you choose is right if it works for you. Don't get bogged down in the tall grass grappling with how to figure out a budget. The basic plan in this book can be enacted with so little money, a budget is irrelevant. When you have established a good stream of income, you can worry about how to slice it up in a budget. For now, no budget is fine. And don't worry about that slight shaking of the ground you just felt, it's just all my old marketing professors turning over in their graves.

If you're a large firm and have no budget, you probably do need to go back and address the issue properly: make one up, like everyone else does. It can be in the rough, or off the cuff, but you should have a general idea of what you'd like to spend, more defined than "as little as possible."

I've heard every rationale for the amount of advertising and PR money a firm is going to spend. Two percent, 8.5 percent, one-tenth of the net, 15 percent of the gross. In small firms—I don't care what anyone says—there is no one formula that defines a way to select a reasonable advertising budget for every company. Young firms usually spend more to get the word out. Certain industries require you to spend more. And in some smaller market niches, you can spend less.

A small company's budget figures don't play by large-company rules. With $100 million in sales, a 2.5% ad budget ($2.5 million) will get you a good presence in a lot of markets. With $100,000 in sales, 2.5% ($2,500) won't get you very far. With $50,000 in sales, 2.5% ($1,250) for ads won't get you very much to look at. It will, however, get you a great creative PR and letter campaign, as outlined in this book.

Ads are the logical conclusion to a successful PR campaign.

I once was called for a consultation by a rug cleaning firm. Incredibly, the owner spent one-third of his gross income on advertising, mostly on half-page ads in the yellow pages. I cut his yellow page ad budget by two-thirds by deleting his half-page ad, and expanding his listing ad specifically in his township (everyone likes to shop in their own back yard, and most people give preference to local service companies). Then we sent letters to all his old customers, plus generated some free write-ups in the newspapers by donating free service to area children's hospitals. Business went up, his ad budget went down, and he had a great formula for staying busy that worked year after year at a low advertising cost.

Ads are the logical conclusion to a successful PR campaign. Ad budgets pay for the composition and placement of the ad, which is the last avenue of attack. Magazines give you wide exposure but little depth. Reader service card lead sheets dominates the type of response you get in most trade magazines. Lots of these leads are worthless, but a few good ones can sneak through. If you've ever had sheets and sheets of mailing labels and wondered what to do you're not alone here: dealing with them efficiently is difficult for everyone.

This chapter is mainly about marketing a product nationally. It supplies a means of examining and evaluating each different market (where the product may be needed) for potential, and selecting the segments of each market where people are most likely to buy your goods. You'll find and choose different magazines that target specific groups you are interested in reaching within each market, and evaluate the different publications that serve those groups. The chapter is designed to show you how to find, select, and analyze the individual magazines that serve your markets. You'll send press releases to the broad field of periodicals that match your audience profile. If you are successful with your PR, you can use the specific instructions I've included on how to place an ad at the best rate, and how to get the best position.

Marketing

The definition of "marketing" runs only five words, if you count the "a": "Selling to a defined audience."

Just what the heck is marketing, anyhow? People talk about marketing niches, target marketing, selecting markets, primary markets and secondary markets, this market and that market. What the heck is all this about?

It's simple. A market is a definable portion of people in the population who are most likely to buy your goods. The definition has a key word: "definable." You must be able to identify your customers and set them aside from everyone else. The definition of "marketing" runs only five words, if you count the "a": "Selling to a defined audience." When you offer your product to anyone, that's sales. When you select your audience, thereby narrowing the field to include the most likely prospects needing your goods or services, that's marketing. Let's look at these terms more closely.

The Danielle Adams Publishing Company
Box 100, Merion Station PA 19066

While all your prospects may not be easy to locate, they all have a common denominator: the desire or the need for your product. You can separate your market from the general population by a specific set of criteria that you set up.

Let's take an example. You're a manufacturer of firearms, and your market is hunters. But that is just one part or segment of your entire market, or "marketing universe." Hunters can be further broken down into several smaller market segments, or market niches, based on their quarry: large game hunters, small game hunters, and bird hunters. Each is a unique segment of the hunting population that would buy a specific type of firearm from you. So now we can see that the single firearms market we started out with can be broken down into several smaller market segments or niches that are all different.

Sometimes a market subset for a product is so large, it's also a whole industry in itself. The law enforcement industry is an example of another market for your guns and rifles. Police officers and security organizations constitute an entirely separate market from hunters.

Security guards are only one segment of the security industry. Smaller niches in the security industry include people in bad neighborhoods who use guns for personal protection; private detectives; SWAT teams using long rifles; and the FBI and the military, which use automatic weapons.

The federal government would be a market in itself. And all the different markets within the government organizations: FBI; Secret Service; Alcohol, Tobacco and Firearms; and so forth. Foreign governments and foreign markets, too.

Target shooters are still another entirely separate market for your guns. Target shooters also can be broken into several smaller market fragments: skeet and trap shooters, and marksmen who target shoot at a range. People who shoot pistols and rifles are another subset of that market.

In addition, in each gun market to which you already sell, collectors are still another segment of the overall marketing universe of purchasers of firearms. And survivalists. And—well, you get the idea.

You can see there are a lot of market niches in what at first appeared to be a simple example of a market, the firearms industry. In all these instances, "market" is a noun meaning a defined audience of people who are likely to purchase your product.

The word "marketing" can also be used as a verb, meaning "selling to a defined audience." But marketing is also the umbrella for all aspects of sales. It encompasses the entire spectrum of selling, and incorporates all the different sides of business: planning, pricing, targeting audiences, merchandising, retailing, packaging, wholesaling, direct selling, and so forth. Marketing is one of three major functions of all business; the other two are finance and operations.

This is starting to sound like a textbook. I don't want to get too technical—you're probably just interested in selling products, and I never did have the patience for schoolbook learning. So we'll get right back to what we need for selling a product in a moment. After a brief overview of the chain of traditional distribution, we'll go back to really useful information on direct marketing.

Distributors and Wholesalers

For firearms manufacturers, for years the traditional way of selling guns has been through a two-step, or two-tier, distribution system: you sell to wholesalers, who, in turn, sell to retailers. Those are the two tiers. The retailers, in turn, sell to the end consumer. Very traditional. Let's take a closer (but brief) look at this.

You market your firearms to wholesalers, who act as your distributors and sell to dealers such as range owners, sport shops, and firearms retailers. They all stock your guns and rifles. Wholesalers buy in large volume, and when a dealer orders a pistol, they ship it right out of their own stock.

Every step in the distribution process costs you part of the retail price. Wholesalers usually make about a 33 percent mark-up. If you sold a gun to a distributor for $100, he would sell it to a retailer for $133. Wholesalers have to buy in big quantity to get this price. Some of the larger wholesalers have sales personnel on the street, and the biggest wholesalers or distributors may sell to 1,000 dealers.

To sign on a big distributor, your initial sale can be very large. They can move a lot of merchandise if their sales force gets behind your product. You may only need half a dozen or so large wholesalers to have your product distributed across the entire country.

Or you can market to retailers directly. It's more expensive to advertise to each dealer, because there is a multitude of magazines serving each specialized fragment of the gun industry at the retailer sales level. You probably won't have sales people calling on each retail account like the bigger distributors do, which is also a disadvantage. But you keep the 33 percent commission the wholesalers get, to support these additional marketing costs.

You can hire an independent representative to be your in-person sales force to the retailers. Independent reps generally get between 8 percent and 15 percent (sometimes more, sometimes less), depending on your sales volume, the industry you serve, and your negotiations with them. Manufacturer's reps are common in almost every industry, and very prevalent in some. They take your product around and show it in person to wholesalers or retailers (or both) and try to secure sales for you.

In my experience as a small marketing agency, I've never had much luck with a rep firm. So if you think that's the way to go, be careful. Most rep firms I've dealt with have had big product lines they push, and as far as I could tell, our product never made it out of the trunk of their car. Although some firms are good and can deliver, I've had some mighty big promises broken by rep firms. You should be aware, if you are a small manufacturer marketing a single product, your representation to the marketplace may not get a fair shake through a rep firm. But in fairness, some rep firms can generate large sales to both big distributors and chain stores on which they call regularly. Just be careful and choose wisely. And keep a close eye on them and their expenses.

Retailers can make anywhere from 35 percent to 100 percent mark-up, depending on the industry and the individual dealer's policy. If a retail store bought your gun from a distributor (or you) for $133, they would sell it anywhere from about $180 to $266. With all these steps in the distribution field, you can see why a product costing $10 to manufacture usually costs the consumer $30 to $40. After looking at these figures, you may also feel that direct marketing is a more profitable way to sell your product.

Some industries are a little different. In the jewelry industry, mark-ups can run as high as 300%.

If you sold your guns directly to consumers, you could sell them for whatever you wanted: $133, $180, or $266. You would just have to be aware that if you sold a gun for $133 to end users, you would never be able to sell through wholesalers and retailers. If they saw your retail price was $133, they'd want their price discounted from that figure. So retailers would want to pay about $66, and wholesalers about $50, to make their mark-ups. Some wholesalers and retailers wouldn't want to handle your line because since you sell direct, they'd feel they are missing purchases from consumers who bought directly from you.

Some industries are a little different. In the jewelry industry, mark-ups can run as high as 300 percent. A list price showing three times the jeweler's cost is called "triple keystone" ("keystone" meaning the retailer's cost). So it would be common for a jeweler to buy a ring for $100, post the list price as $300, and sell it at a discount of 20 percent off list, for $240. In the jewelry industry, discounts and sales are a very common way to market. During a really steep sale, like an annual clearance, the price may drop to half off the list, or $150. The retailer still makes a 50 percent mark-up even at this sale price. But let's go back to the firearms industry.

If you sold to retailers directly (not through wholesalers), you'd need to give additional consideration when selling to small mom-and-pop-type store retailers: whether each dealer has a good credit record, and if you are going to get paid on time for goods they purchase. Dealer credit is a factor in any industry, as is the shipping and handling of hundreds of small orders, and the seasonality of your merchandise. The paperwork can be incredible.

The Danielle Adams Publishing Company
Box 100, Merion Station PA 19066

As a firearms manufacturer, you can also market through mass merchants like Sears or WalMart. Since they buy goods in large quantity, they get the low prices the distributors get. Because they have their own retail stores right in their supply chain, they can sell your firearms at a pretty low price and still make a profit. They are both retailer and wholesaler. As you can imagine, the buyers for these stores are approached by everyone. But that's OK; by the end of the book you will see that the techniques we use in our campaigns are especially effective in selling goods to these large merchants.

Here's an interesting aside: During the growing years of mass merchants and heavy discounters in the '50s and '60s, small retail firearms dealers could actually buy a firearm from a mass merchant who was a discounter, right off the shelf, for less than they were paying for it from their wholesale distributor. Since the mass merchants were buying in such quantity, they got the very best quantity pricing. They could then sell products at these low costs and still make a profit. This shook up the firearms industry quite a bit and forced numerous small gun shops to close. Many other industries were affected also.

The smaller shops survived by forming industry buying groups: large numbers of firearm dealers banded together specifically to purchase goods in the same huge quantities as the mass merchants, so they could get the best pricing. Industry associations sprang up everywhere. The same revolution occurred in a multitude of other industries. To counter the big discount stores, many dealers started positioning themselves as servicing dealers, a function the mass merchants couldn't meet. Smaller stores also purchased specialty items that people couldn't get at a mass merchant, so price comparisons couldn't be made, and customers could purchase unique products. These practices continue today.

The problem still exists for small mom-and-pop retail stores in many industries all around the country. Heavy discounters such as WalMart, BJ's, PACE, and Sam's Club come into small towns and take over all the business with their incredibly low prices.

Catalog merchants also fall somewhere between the categories of wholesale and retail merchants. Some are heavy discounters. Still others sell at full retail. Some have incredibly huge distribution, and others are small operations mailing from their home and still making good profits. We will address these mail merchants over the course of the rest of the book, with several ideas on how to market to them, and suggestions for campaigns specifically for catalog merchants.

These are just some of the pieces of the marketing puzzle. Marketing actually encompasses all the different aspects of selling your products: finding the right audience, positioning your product and your firm (are you the cheapest, the brand leader, do you provide the fastest service), pricing your products correctly, distribution methods, merchandising, packaging, advertising, press and press relations, and, ultimately, follow-through with customer service, and the next level, repeat sales.

Considering all these separate elements, with unique market segments and different ways to sell to each, which piece of the puzzle of the firearms purchasers universe do you go after first? Which is the most profitable? To which can you sell the most easily? Each segment has to be addressed in a different way and with a slightly different approach, product, and presentation. You wouldn't try to sell hunting rifles to the police market. Or shotguns to the target shooters. Or handguns to bird hunters. The firearms industry is fragmented into many different market segments. Each unique segment of gun users must be defined, and in this case it's defined by the use of the product.

If it all sounds too complex, don't worry. All the pieces will unfold in an easy-to-understand and easy-to-use plan of action by the end of the book. Although all markets are different, they are somehow all the same. And the marketing methods that work for one segment work for all the rest, too.

Marketing Through Magazines

In this chapter we'll look at marketing through magazines. We'll explore trade journals, which are used to sell products directly to businesses in almost every industry. We'll also use magazines to get dealers and distributors to purchase consumer products for resale, and consumer magazines as vehicles to get retail customers directly.

In the rest of the book we discuss direct marketing techniques for PR, ads, and direct mail. You can apply the direct marketing techniques to both consumer and business-to-business campaigns. While direct marketing in its purest form usually implies selling to, and getting orders directly from, end users, I won't hold to that tight limitation here. For our purposes, your customers can be consumers, retailers, or wholesalers.

The term "direct marketing" describes a campaign that will move your product off your shelf and onto someone else's shelf when you have no physical presence in their office and no sales personnel to call on them. I'm not too concerned about whose shelf it is—whether it's a retail or wholesale shelf. In this roundabout way, I address sales to consumers, wholesalers, and retailers, directly and through catalog merchants. To me, direct marketing means selling without having a live sales agent show up at the buyer's door. That's the only restriction.

You steer the entire direct marketing campaign from your driver's seat, whether it's in your home, office, car, or wherever else you happen to be. You can mail 10 letters in this campaign, or 1,000, or 50,000. Send one press release or a hundred. Take out one ad or a complete campaign. You won't need anyone else to help you until you get busy...busy making money and seeing profits.

In direct marketing, you'll sell your product in a direct mail package, or right from a page in a magazine. Most likely, it will be in a two-step sales campaign: you'll place an ad or have a press release printed, generating free publicity (as outlined in the "Free Press" chapter), and you'll send literature to inquirers who respond. From this literature, people will purchase your product. If you don't have any literature now, don't worry, you will! You'll learn how to create a data sheet or spec sheet by the end of the book. Finally, you'll make up a strong sales letter and mail it with your literature to a list of potential customers.

While the profits can be great when selling direct, the downside is your advertising costs can be incredibly high, because each specific market has its own magazines. You can't take out an ad in a magazine and tell your potential customer to go into a neighborhood store in his area and see the product, touch it, feel it, and buy it. No one gets the recommendation of the dealer to buy your product. And selling off a page in a magazine is a tough way to move many types of products.

This book addresses a multifaceted campaign to wholesalers, retailers, and end users. In a publicity campaign to the trade, we'll pick up dealers and distributors as well as direct sales. We'll also devise a direct mail campaign specifically aimed at catalog merchants, wholesalers, and your largest prospects. If your product is consumer oriented, we'll go after direct sales with an additional publicity campaign directed through consumer magazines.

One way to reach a particular market on a national level is to find the magazines that serve the precise market segments you have selected and submit a press release or take out an ad. This is the heart of a national marketing campaign. This chapter will show you exactly how to find the correct magazines, so you can send them a press release. If the results are good, you can take out an ad. That would be the next logical step in a successful product launch.

Let's go back to the firearms industry. You're a firearms manufacturer. To reach hunters, you'd advertise in a consumer hunting magazine like *Field and Stream*. You may also consider *Hounds and Hunting, North American Hunter, Pennsylvania Sportsman, Deer and Deer Hunting, Louisiana Game and Fish*, or *Outdoor News*, to name a few more. Feeling rich? There are 107 magazines that are directed toward hunters and outdoor enthusiasts at the consumer level.

To reach police officers who purchase their own unique types of weapons, you'd take out an ad in or send a press release to *Law Enforcement Product News*. You may also consider *Law and Order, Drug Enforcement Report, Crime Control Digest, Police and Security News, Police Times, State Police Officers Journal*, and so forth. There are 18 trade publications that serve the police market.

For security personnel, there are *Security Journal, Security Dealer, Security Sales*, and *Security Magazine*, just to mention a few.

For the handgun enthusiast, magazines include: *Guns and Ammo, Hand Gunning, Guns Magazine, Shooting Times, Precision Shooting, Gun Week*, and, well, there are a bunch of them.

To market a product to any of these groups, you don't have to be clever. You just need to know which reference books to use, and how to use them.

The Danielle Adams Publishing Company
Box 100, Merion Station PA 19066

In a single evening at the library, you can find all the markets and the media that serve them, and outline the basics of an entire marketing plan.

_____

But the one day marketing plan and execution...well, it's very fast. And because of its speed, very good.

_____

As you read this book you'll find a section where you can create and execute an entire publicity campaign in just one day. Incredible, but true. The depth of knowledge you'll acquire of the markets you are entering is in your favor. Your publicity coverage, as printed in your choice of magazines, will be much greater. And your depth of understanding of the marketing process will have much more time to evolve as you learn from your early mistakes.

Warning: But the one day marketing plan and execution...well, it's very fast. And because of its speed, very good. It definitely can get the job done. If you're in a hurry, like most people today, you can profit from my 25 years of experience. Find the one-day campaign discussed later in this chapter. It's presented as an option.

A word of caution: I don't recommend it, it's cheating. It's like jaywalking. It can get you to the other side of the street in a hurry, but you risk getting hit by a truck on the way. You may not have time to see your mistakes since it all happens so fast. Like the truck coming at you at 80 mph when you're in the middle of the street, you may not have time to react correctly to all your options. Still, it's always nice to have a few different routes you can take. You decide.

First, Target Your Market

In magazines, as in direct mail, even the best ads or the most-likely-to-succeed campaigns won't generate a significant response from the wrong audience. A successful campaign is one that pays for itself and leaves money left over for growth and profit. Money for growth will be used for entry into other markets, for a deeper penetration of your current market, or to test new magazines. It's also useful to cover your mistakes—which if you didn't make this time, you will make next time.

A very successful campaign is one that pays you a handsome six-figure salary on top of all the above. But forget that for now, unless you're unusually good, lucky, or both. Let's just concentrate on finding the people who are your best prospects. We'll initiate a winning campaign in a later chapter.

This chapter assumes you know at least a few of the primary people who will need, or at least purchase, your product at the beginning. Later in the chapter, we'll go over the magazine selection process in detail.

The first step is to define your markets. Who are the groups of people most likely to purchase your products? Do you know everyone who may need or want your product? To make sure you are clear on this, take a sheet of paper and write down every group of people that can use your product. List everyone, no matter how silly or remote they are. This is tonight's assignment.

When you have filled up a blank sheet of paper, go back and rank your entries in descending order of their need. Rewrite the list with the people most likely to buy your goods on the top, then those less and less likely to purchase your goods further down on the page. Always remember, you are encouraged to continuously discover needs and desires of people and open up new markets. Explore other markets and segments by phone and with press releases that may later prove to be profitable. When starting, go with the easiest and most profitable market most likely to ensure your success.

Some products have customers so difficult to locate, you need pinpoint accuracy to find and address them. Even though the initial research to find them may be tedious, it may be highly profitable to sell to this audience because you can target them without wasted advertising expense. These are the unique market niches you hear so much about.

The Danielle Adams Publishing Company
Box 100, Merion Station PA 19066

Other products, like telephones, have unlimited marketing prospects because everyone needs them. I believe these are the toughest products to sell because of the great marketing expense associated with reaching everyone to introduce them to your new product. And ooh, the competition.

Marketing Through Press Releases

Now that you have an understanding of press releases—what they are, how to write one, and how they work—let's assess the selection of industries, and which publications in those industries to send a press release to. If you have the money for an ad campaign, we'll specifically discuss how to analyze the magazines and how to choose the right ones for placing an ad.

A press release is the lowest-cost and easiest way to get free publicity and generate interest and sales for your product.

Press releases are unique. Unlike ads, which can cost quite a bit to place in magazines (and therefore must be aimed with the precision of a marksman), when you send press releases you send them *en masse* to just about any industry or market where you think you may experience decent sales. It's the shotgun approach.

A press release is the lowest-cost and easiest way to get free publicity and generate interest and sales for your product. The only costs are the photo, the envelope, the paper your release is printed on, and postage. You can generate tons of inquiries from a single press release sent to a list of magazines that serve your markets.

Just remember, you have to respond to all those inquiries in a prompt fashion with additional marketing material. If the respondents are not really part of your market, you'll generate only requests for literature and no sales. This can get pretty expensive. So here is just a simple word of warning: Don't go crazy—stay within your own well-defined marketing areas with your press release campaign. It can be profitable to explore secondary and tertiary markets using this low-cost approach, but don't go completely into left field just to see your name in print.

Also keep in mind that when you generate inquiries and leads through magazines (especially through reader response cards), they will not all be potential buyers. Some will just want to see what you send, others will be literature collectors, and all your competitors will probably respond. If you throw a loose qualification net, most respondents can be defined as the "Just Curious."

Trade Publications

Trade magazines are probably the greatest resource for information in any industry.

Trade magazines are the meat and potatoes of marketing any new product nationally. They are the inside-the-industry view of the industry. There are usually several trade publications serving every industry. Trade journals contain industry news, industry standards, industry statistics, work procedures, personnel and company gossip, suppliers' ads, buyer's guides, industry technical information, and a resource guide. Each magazine usually publishes an annual directory.

Trade magazines are probably the greatest source of information in any industry. If you need in-depth information about any industry subject, the trade journals or the industry association can usually supply you with good answers and/or good directions to find it. Besides the annual directory issue most journals put out, the editorial coverage has probably answered most of your questions at one point or another.

In business-to-business marketing, trade magazines show both new products and industry standards that keep that particular industry's machines running smoothly. They are the industry's source of information about unique products and services sold to a specialized industry's needs. Unless you read *Modern Bottling*, it's difficult to find a manufacturer of a machine that does nothing but capping and corking.

Trade publications are responsible for introducing products to the marketplace by way of distributors or wholesalers, jobbers, and retailers. If you can sell a product to any one segment of this distribution chain, consider yourself initially successful. If you can sell to a few of these distribution channels, you are successful. Keep in mind you'll eventually need pricing for each of these levels if your products are to reach the retailers' shelves. If you can supply wholesale levels in the distribution chain for an industry, you will have a strong base for all sales.

As you might suspect, consumer publications supply the general population with knowledge about products. Although there are many similarities between trade and consumer publications, trade magazines are much easier to negotiate with for ad rates and to get press releases printed in, simply because they do not have the gigantic numbers of readers that the consumer publications do. The consumer magazines need more before they will print your press release.

When marketing consumer products through traditional channels of distribution, the last step is to advertise in a consumer publication. Consumer publications seek to persuade the end user to buy the product from the retailer's shelf or catalog. In direct marketing, consumer magazines are brought into the picture much earlier. While some products may skirt both direct and traditional ways of marketing, it may be better to start out in these established channels. Then you can decide if you wish to make an unusual market entry from another direction. Well, we've had our potatoes, now let's have some meat. Here's how you do the marketing.

~ Research Tools ~

The SRDS Business Publication Advertising Source™

When marketing through magazines, you can find publication tools in most libraries that break down the various trade and consumer publications according to the different markets they serve. Each has its own peculiarities, strengths and weaknesses, level of depth, and ease of use.

One if the most common reference tools for magazines and marketing found in most libraries is called the *SRDS Business Publication Advertising Source*™. This big book, which contains well over 1,000 pages, lists the name and address of almost every current business periodical printed, along with the publisher, published ad rates, and circulation data. Neat.

The *Business Publication Advertising Source*™ from SRDS (formerly Standard Rate and Data Service) is published quartly, although for us regular folk, a copy in the library that is up to a year and a half or two years old is still pretty current. A two-year-old copy won't list the newest publications, but it'll have plenty of industry standard magazines that are tried and true from which to select your marketing and PR lists.

_____

The publication is about the size of the Manhattan phone book, so you won't run out of reading material before the library closes.

_____

Unless you're in a volatile industry like computers or desktop publishing, where new products are invented daily and major magazines are coming out weekly, the older copy of the *SRDS Business Publication Advertising Source*™ found at your local library is a pretty good bet for beginning your research into finding industries, markets, and additional sales opportunities for your products and services.

The publication is about the size of the Manhattan phone book, so you won't run out of reading material before the library closes. If you like to stay up all night, you can buy a subscription for a year for $821 and online access is $390 per quarter. Whew. If you own a woodburning stove, the subscription is a better value because you can heat your house with the old books.

The SRDS book weighs about six pounds. Once you get used to it, it's a fairly straight forward and easy-to-use reference tool, although there are certainly more user-friendly directories. The depth of information you can find in this book is excellent.

Three Sections of the SRDS Directory
Overview

There are three sections in the SRDS directory. The first is the <u>Alphabetical Index</u> of magazines by title, which is approximately 10 pages long. If you know the name of the magazine you are looking for, you can find it here in just a few seconds, along with the market class of similar magazines.

Example:	**Class**	**Magazine**
	47	Fire Engineering Directory
	47	Firehouse
	47	Fire Protection Contractor
	47	Firefighter's News
	47	Fireman's Journal, The
	H3	First Databank Blue Book
	19A	First Tuesday
	46	First Wall Streeter
	50	Fish Trader
	48	Fisheries Product News
	48	Fishermen's News, The
	48	Fishing News International
	137	Fishing Tackle Retailer
	137	Fishing Tackle Trade News
	48A	Fitness Management

Next, the <u>Marketing Classification Section</u> shows magazines grouped by industry. The industries are shown alphabetically. This section also runs approximately 10 pages. This section is where you do your market research, finding the industries you will be marketing your product to and the magazines that serve them.

Example: Class 47, Fire Protection
    Magazines   Audited
                         Fire Chief
                         Fire Engineering
                         Firehouse
                         Firefighter's News
                         NFPA Journal
                    Non-Audited
                         American Fire Journal
                         California Fire Service, The
                         Fire Engineering Directory
                         Fire Protection Contractor
                                etc.
               Class 48, Fishing, Commercial
                    Audited
                         Alaska Fisherman Journal
                         Aquaculture Magazine
                         National Fisherman
                         Pacific Fishing
                    Non-Audited
                         Commercial Fisheries News
                         Fisheries Product News
                                etc.

Market classifications are alphabetical. Following "fishing" would be Class 48A-Fitness Professional, Class 48B-Floor Covering, Class 49-Florists & Floriculture, Class 50-Food Processing and Distribution, and so on.

Finally, the main section of the book, the <u>Business Publication Listings</u>, is where each magazine is broken down into components such as ad costs and circulation data so you can study and compare one magazine to another. The Business Publication Listing section runs well over 1,000 pages. This is where you do an analysis of the magazines you are thinking about using to market your product. Here, the classes are listed by number. If you were interested in marketing a product to the fishing industry, in the alphabetical index of the Marketing Classification Section you'd look up "Fishing" and find it is class 48. In the Business Publication Listing section you'd look up class 48, and you'd see the details of all the magazines in the fishing industry.

From "Advertising" to "Woodworking," and everything in between, there are about 155 different industries or markets that are segmented, listed, classified, cross-referenced, and shown in the SRDS directory. In addition, there is an entire separate section just of health care magazines. The health care market is so huge and so rich it demands its own section.

Alphabetical Index

The book starts with a bright yellow index, which references all the publications alphabetically by title and shows in which class they appear in the Business Publication Listings.

So in this yellow index, *Journal of Photography* would be listed under "J" for "Journal." Before the magazine title, you'll find the Business Publication Listing class reference number. For photography, it's class 113. This is where you can find *Journal of Photography* in the Business Publication Listings section, along with *all* the other trade journals published specifically for photographers and retail camera stores. If you were marketing a camera lens, your initial marketing research would be mostly done now as far as finding the major publications in the photo industry. If you were marketing a new camera bag, you'd continue looking for other markets that may have an interest in your bag, such as the luggage industry or bicycle industry.

The alphabetical listing is especially handy if you know the title of the magazine, because you can find it quickly in the yellow index. If you need to find all similar publications serving that particular industry in the Business Publication Listings, the class they are all located in is shown with the title. This is a reference section that simply makes it easy and fast to find magazines, and to quickly find their class in the Business Publication Listing section so you can analyze them.

Marketing Classification Section

The next section in the *SRDS Business Publication Advertising Source*™ is where you do your marketing research. Here, magazines are grouped by industry, and the industries themselves are shown in alphabetical sequence. So in this section, all the publications that are specific to the banking industry are listed under "B," under the heading "Banking." *Journal of Banking,* instead of being listed under "J" for "Journal" as in the yellow index, is grouped with all the other magazines serving the banking industry, like *Modern Banking, Banking Today, American Banker,* and so forth. In this section you'll do all your market investigation. Here you'll find the various industries and markets, and decide which ones you'll serve and approach with your product or service. Again, this is a reference section that simply makes it easy and fast to find markets or industries, and to find their class in the Business Publication Listings section so you can analyze them.

Simple and easy so far. But your market search just started; it gets more difficult from here. If you were going to sell a product to the banking industry, there are over 50 magazines that go to bankers each month. Ugh.

Auditing the Circulation

The audit bureaus, like radar detectors, just keep honest people honest.

As you look over the magazine classification section, you'll find that magazines listed under each industry classification are divided into "Audited" and "Non-audited" categories. To prove to advertisers that the publishers mail as many copies of their publications as they say they do, independent auditing firms are hired by the publishers to verify that all the copies are sent, and that the recipients have the qualifications that the publisher states. For example, audit bureaus verify that *Modern Printer* is actually sent to printers, in the same counts the publishers tell their advertisers. The audit bureaus, like radar detectors, just keep honest people honest.

Suppose you own a firm like General Motors, and you wish to reach the service station market with your new brand of aftermarket headlights. There is a market universe of about 125,000 stations. Some publications say they mail to all 125,000 service stations, but how do you know? Since a count is out of the question, you would look to their audit bureau to verify how many subscription copies they mail each month, and that the subscriptions indeed go to service stations. With unaudited publications, you just have to rely on their word. And with some, you can. The trouble is figuring out which those are.

SRDS Business Publication Listings

This is the main section of the book. The preceding sections make up the first fifty pages in the SRDS directory. The remaining one thousand, four hundred and some-odd pages are filled with the details of the magazines, grouped in their respective industry classifications. As in the Marketing Classification section, each magazine is shown in its numerical marketing class with all the other publications for that particular industry. For example, all banking journals are shown under class 10, "Banking." Here, each magazine is shown with a detailed breakdown of its composition, ad costs, publication data, addresses, main editors, publishers, phone numbers, and circulation figures.

In the Business Publication Listings section, each magazine is divided into 18 components to help you analyze it. Here you can compare a magazine to every other magazine to see if one particular periodical is more anatomically correct for your product. Once you get familiar with this section, you can tell quite a bit about a magazine in a very short period of time.

Thrown in with this breakdown is an assortment of ads the magazine publishers purchase from SRDS (now you know why it's published—for the ad revenues) with reasons, data, charts, and graphs that show why their magazine is a leader in its field, and why the intelligent person with marketing and advertising money to spend should spend all of it with their publication.

Individual Magazine Listings in the
Business Publication Listings Section

Each magazine listing begins with the magazine title. The magazine names in large print are spots paid for by the magazine publishers. Like in the phone book, listings are free, but anything else costs the magazine publisher plenty.

The editorial profile is probably the most important paragraph in the whole listing.

Following the magazine title is the name, address, and phone number of the publisher. Then, just a few lines down, is the magazine's editorial profile statement. In a single paragraph, this statement highlights the purpose and feel of the magazine, its editorial direction, the market it attempts to address, and the magazine's features.

The editorial profile is probably the single most important paragraph in the whole listing. Written by the publishers themselves, it gives you the editorial orientation and audience profile of the magazine. From this single paragraph, you can get clues about whether the product you are marketing will reach your target audience through a particular magazine. If you read it carefully, it will also tell you if the publication accepts press releases.

A student of mine once designed his firm's ad campaign. The company manufactured architectural plaster: sculpted ceilings, light fixtures, and beautiful, ornate doorway arches. They sold to architects and builders, and the marketer recommended they place an ad in *Architectural Digest*. It seemed pretty natural—it's a beautiful consumer coffee-table publication that showcases this kind of work. The result of their ad campaign that cost thousands of dollars was...no sales. The reason: *Architectural Digest* is written for little old ladies who like to look at pictures of beautiful houses.

It even says so in their editorial profile, if the firm had only looked. They needed to address architects and building contractors.

It's not too late for you. When researching your markets, look closely at the publisher's editorial profile. See if the magazine clearly targets the audience you are trying to reach: distributors and retailers who will stock your products to sell, or consumers who need, and will buy, your product or service.

Most important for our initial campaign is to see if the publication accepts press releases. If it does, it is usually noted in this paragraph when the publisher states that there is a column called "What's New," "New Products," "New Equipment," "Product Reviews," and so forth. "Newsmakers" usually denotes the publication's acceptance of releases about people: new positions, personnel advances, etc. (it can be a good source for names of new people to market to—see the last chapter, "The $500 Campaign," for a sales campaign to these prospects). If you look for these key phrases, you can easily see which magazines accept releases on products, people, news, events, etc.

This editorial profile paragraph is a good place to start your magazine review. In the industry classes you are marketing to, place a large red check mark next to all the magazine editorial profiles that show they accept releases. We'll come back to this in a moment.

Directly following the editorial profile is the breakdown of each magazine into 18 categories (numbered for ease of use) showing the editors, ad rates, production specifics, and circulation details. Once you get familiar with these sections, you can skim through them to get to the three or four sections that really matter for marketing.

This is the beginning of your search in earnest for qualified magazines to send releases to. At the conclusion of your PR campaign, if it is success-ful, or if you have the money, these are the magazines in which you will place ads. The first challenge you face is to decide which markets, which segments of those markets, and further, exactly which specific magazines in those segments you should send releases to or invest your ad dollar in. In the marketing classification section, you found all the markets. Now you are selecting specific magazines within these markets that you'd like to be represented in.

Carefully look over the magazines that are sent to the markets you have selected. You're now going to make up a "press release list" of all the magazines in which you'd like to see a release printed about your product.

Information in the magazine industry, like products in the fish industry, has a way of becoming old very quickly.

Obviously, some markets and some magazines will be better suited to your product. Some will be perfect, and you'll want to make sure your release gets printed in them. Those magazines deserve a phone call before sending a release. We'll call this our "A" or "Must Get In" publication list. Put a red star with the check mark next to their listing. Our "B" list will receive press releases without the added value of a phone call, unless you have the time or enjoy making calls.

If you're strongly considering sending a press release to a magazine, after reading the editorial profile to see if they'll accept it, skip down to the first heading in publication listings: Personnel. Direct your release to the editor by name. If this particular publication is very important, before sending the release I'd at least invest the quarter and call the magazine to make sure the editor is still the one listed. Information in the magazine industry, like products in the fish industry, has a way of becoming old very quickly. Like everyone else in the world, the editors like to receive mail specifically addressed to them by name. It also gives your correspondence a higher perceived value.

Color ad rates are shown in section 6 of each listing, and a special mail order rate, if available, is found in section 11. Skip down to the last heading in each listing, heading #18, which is Circulation. There are two noteworthy figures in circulation: non-paid subscriptions, and paid subscriptions.

Unlike consumer publications, over 95 percent of subscriptions to trade journals are free to subscribers, if you qualify. The publication specifies the qualifications of the readers, and it's usually reported in the audit. An example of a qualification for a printing magazine may be, "To receive our magazine, the printer must have at least one 11" by 17" press, and have printing sales over $50,000."

Some magazines send free subscriptions to anyone even remotely related to an industry. Ads in their books are worth less to you because the market they serve (very broad-based) may not be your exact choice of tightly qualified industry personnel. Their subscription figures drive their ad space rates higher, and in these cases, if you placed an ad in their book, a lot of your marketing dollar would be wasted. In fairness, I must say some free publications have very, very tight controls over their subscription list, but they are very few in number. I can count on one hand all the extremely tightly controlled publications I have seen in the past 20 years.

When subscriptions are paid for by the subscriber, they are of slightly more value than non-paid subscriptions. When a subscription is paid for, you know it has value to the recipient and he or she probably takes a closer look at it; you should, too.

The exception to this is when the subscription is included with, or is an addendum to, membership in an organization. This is an important point to remember; when the space salesperson for the magazine calls you to sell you ad space and constantly reminds you the magazine has a paid subscription base, you have to keep in mind it's only paid because it's part of the association dues.

But always remember: The media responds kindly to a well-thought-out and properly executed publicity campaign.

Remember, each market has a "universe"—the total number of customers, shops, or businesses who may need your product. To get an idea of the size of the universe of the market you are researching, check the magazine circulation figures (section 18) of several of the industry magazines. The larger publications should all have about the same figures. This is approximately the size of the population you are marketing to at this level of distribution. So if you are selling a new type of dog collar to pet shops, if you sold to 15,000 shops, you'd know that almost every shop in the country would be carrying your collar. If one publication states its circulation is much higher than the rest of the field, question its authenticity and check its requirements for receiving free copies in the audit bureau circulation statements you'll receive with their media package.

It only makes sense that the larger-circulation magazines are the hardest to get press releases printed in. They're sought out by almost everyone, including the industry's major suppliers, for free press. But always remember: The media responds kindly to a well-thought-out and properly executed publicity campaign.

As a final step in evaluating magazines for either press release or ad potential, go back to heading #5: Black and White Ad Rates. Check out a few ad rates. Wow. Pretty expensive, huh? These costs are for one issue, one time. This is the most you will pay for an ad in this publication; it's their published rate. Like when you buy a car, you negotiate off these rates. Generally speaking, if you submit a press release and it's printed in

---

the magazine, the value of having your product release printed is about the same as taking a one-sixth- to a one-third-page ad in that publication. This gives you some sense of the value of a press release that is printed in various publications.

The *SRDS Business Publication Advertising Source*™ is a good book for information about placing ads and planning an advertising campaign because it gives you ad rates for most of the magazines. It's an excellent resource for analyzing which industries you will be marketing to, as the SRDS for industrial magazines lists no consumer publications. It's certainly a valuable resource.

Its strong points are excellent depth of information, and good accuracy. The SRDS directory itself also has good penetration in the library market, and you can usually find it, even in smaller libraries, although the copy may be fairly old. The breakdown of markets is easy to use, but it supplies no cross-referencing if you are looking for secondary markets. Business publication listings are long, and if the publisher doesn't spring for the bolder, larger, or logo heading, the magazine's name can be hard to find. Important parts of the listings include the editorial profile, ad rates (#5), and circulation figures (#18). It's not the easiest resource to use, but it can be pretty fast once you get used to it. Although it probably has the best selection for analyzing advertising rates, it may not be the perfect choice for a press release campaign.

Sections new to the SRDS directory are the Geographic Index, which shows a breakdown of each magazine published in a particular state, and the Keyword Subject Classification listings, just a couple of pages showing where classes of magazines can be found by keywords or buzzwords. This new section is growing, and will make your marketing easier.

SRDS also publishes several other directories, such as the *Consumer Magazine Advertising Source*™ and a directory of newspapers, both of which are fairly strong suits for them. But since I've included an analysis of the newspaper directory that one of their competitors publishes, I'll just mention this in passing. The *SRDS Newspaper Advertising Source*™ is a very comprehensive resource tool.

Finally, SRDS publishes the *Direct Marketing List Source*™, one of the most comprehensive and valuable resources for finding mailing lists in the direct mail industry. Although difficult to find in small libraries, it's a very thorough book that every list house, as well as most major libraries, will have. When you start marketing through the mail, spending a few evenings with this book will be well worth your time. It's the industry standard.

The SRDS folks are most famous for their directories of periodicals and mailing lists. The manuals are good resources, and I recommend their use in any marketing campaign. I grew up with these reference tools, and I am very comfortable using them. If I had to pick just one publication vendor to work from, SRDS would be a strong contender, but not actually my top choice.

Bacon's Directories

Before I start sounding like an ad for SRDS, I'd like to give you a few more options on selecting print media directories. One of the best is *Bacon's Newspaper/Magazine Directory*.

This reference set is dedicated to being easy to learn and use from the get-go.

If SRDS's book is the bible of the magazine industry, Bacon's is the New Testament. SRDS books are oriented toward placing ads in magazines, but Bacon's is the ultimate service provider for press release campaigns. Bacon's directories provide several reference manuals for publicity, and offer an unbelievable array of reasonably priced services, besides just the listing of markets and magazines.

The two-volume set of their media directories contains one book for newspaper listings, and one for magazine listings. Each book contains over 750 pages of reference material. This reference set is dedicated to being easy to learn and use from the get-go. Their stated missiom is to have you be able to find your markets easily, and place your product and news releases (or ads) in the markets you select. Unlike with SRDS, both consumer and trade publications—and newsletters—are mushed together in one magazine directory. I originally voted this a minus, but after working with this format, I've concluded that it has its benefits. It is especially nice that both trade and consumer publications are featured in one book, at one price. Unlike with SRDS, you don't have the additional expense of separate reference manuals for trade and consumer magazines. A big plus, since the books cost several hundred dollars each. While the magazines are blended together on the pages, consumer and trade publications are marked with a "C" or a "T" to designate their status.

Bacon's directories are well designed for press release campaigns. The books don't give the ad costs broken down into partial pages, as the SRDS does; each magazine's ad rate is shown for a full-page black-and-white ad. This will give you a general idea of the cost of advertising in the periodical.

Bacon's books give circulation figures and publication frequencies for over 9,200 publications. They show the publishers, magazine addresses, phone and fax numbers, editors, reporters, and writers. If the publication is large enough, Bacon's gives you the name of the specific editor to send each release to, such as the news editor, health editor, travel editor, or new product editor.

Bacon's directories also give you an editorial profile for the larger magazines, including the mission statement describing editorial interest, and a description of the magazine's audience. This is very similar to the SRDS directory. Bacon's also contains a Publicity Use Profile, which indicates exactly which types of publicity releases are accepted at the magazine: new products, personnel announcements, letters to the editor, industry news, coming events, etc., and also if the publication accepts photos with releases. Very handy. Very, very handy.

Bacon's Format

In the front of Bacon's magazine directory are approximately 228 market classifications in 90 categories, condensed into two pages called the "Numerical Index of Market Classifications." Here, magazines are broken down into 90 specific major categories and subdivided into 228 minor classifications, from advertising to woodworking, according to the markets they serve.

For example, in Bacon's, all computer magazines are listed in the alphabetically organized main section under classification 18, "Computers." At a glance, you would see there are 620 trade and consumer computer magazines in classification 18-Computers. There is a further breakdown of this classification into subgroups: 18A-Computer Technology/Data Management (95 publications in this subgroup), 18B-General Interest (113 publications), 18C-Software/Operating Systems (142 publications), 18D-Internet (63), 18E-Industry Applications (109), and 18F-Related Interest (48), 18G-Computer/Video Games (23), and 18H-Marketing/Retailing/Reselling (27). Obviously, the computer market is a huge, huge market. It's probably second only to health care.

Another example: women's magazines (all 218 or so of them) are listed under classification 89, "Women's." Directly following the major heading of "Women's," magazines are further broken into subgroups: 89A is women's general interest magazines (115 of them), 89B-Brides (59 publications in this subgroup), 89C-Beauty and Fashion (36), 89D-Romance. Your selection of markets can be pretty quick and easy if there is a narrowly defined market segment you are targeting. It's especially helpful that Bacon's shows you up front how many magazines serve each market (and each subcategory of that market). In just a few seconds, you can get an idea of the number of releases and photos you'll need to send in your campaigns.

Numerical Index of Market Classifications / Bacon's

These two pages give you an incredible amount of market information in a short format. This index is found in another part of the book you are reading, and a full market selection guide is on pages is in here too. Starting with "1" and in alphabetical order, you'll find the group number the magazines are in, the magazine count in each group, the market classification, and the page number where the magazines are found. Each main classification heading is in bold, and after it is the breakdown for that classification. For example:

Group	Count	Market Classification	Page
1	**(108)**	**Advertising/Marketing/PR**	**9**
1A	(49)	Advertising	9
1B	(19)	Public Relations	12
1C	(40)	Marketing	13
2	**(95)**	**Amusements and Motion Pictures**	**17**
2A	(51)	Amusements & Motion Picture Trade	17
2B	(12)	Movie and TV Fan	20
2C	(23)	Performing Arts	21
2D	(9)	Casinos and Gaming	22
3	**(43)**	**Architecture**	**24**
3A	(26)	Architecture	24
3B	(17)	Interior Design	26
4	**(358)**	**Automotive**	**28**
4A	(57)	Automotive Trade and Service Stations Etc.	28

As you can see, it's pretty easy and fast to do your marketing research here. If you were marketing a product to the architecture trade, you'd find all 43 magazines that go to that field, starting on page 24 of Bacon's Magazine Directory. You can discover all your primary, secondary, and tertiary markets in just a few hours of easy work. Select primary markets first, then choose secondary markets on the edge of your universe, where people may still show an interest in your product.

If you want to send press releases for a carpentry product, you'd find that releases may be sent to secondary markets in classifications 3 (Architecture, 3B-Interior Design), 11 (Building), 37 (Hardware), and 61

(Paint, Decorating), and to tertiary market classification 67A (Heating and Plumbing). Just in case you are still having trouble figuring out additional markets, Bacon's shows related industries at the beginning of each classification in the main section of the book. A very handy feature for finding secondary and tertiary markets.

Alphabetical Cross-Reference

Immediately following these two pages of dense, compact marketing information is an easy-to-use "Alphabetical Cross Index of Market Classifications." While the name sounds fairly imposing, this section is there to further assist and simplify your marketing efforts by linking 600 specific products and reader-interest subjects with their related markets. For instance, the heading "Baby Care Products" is shown with the market section 89B, which is "Parenting." For example:

AAA Motor Club Magazines	86B
Abrasives	41A
Accessory Merchandising	32A
Accident Prevention	41D
Accounting	12D
Actuators	41A
Adhesives	41A
Administrative Management	12C, 58A
Adventure Magazines	49C
Advertising	1A
Aerobics	29A

Etc.

Another example: If you were marketing a new building tool to the carpentry trade, you'd look up "Carpentry" in this Cross Index of Market Classifications and find the market classifications of 11A (Building), 49B (Do It Yourself), and 90A (Woodworking). You'd then look up each magazine in the main section, "Magazine Listings by Classification," and read their editorial profiles to see if these are the people you want to reach. Then you would either call each publisher whose magazine you suspect you'd be interested in, or send a form letter requesting a media kit to each of the publications to get a sample copy. When you received the sample copy, you would see if it fits your market profile. Of course, you could also simply mail releases to all the magazines in the market classifications you found in the Cross Index of Market Classifications (11A, 49B, and 90A).

Main Section: Magazine Listings by Classification

It's possible to figure out a broad-based press campaign using just the front of the directory. But for those of us on a budget, the specifics of each magazine, as found in the main section, will help you pick and choose individual magazines for free editorial coverage with more precision and accuracy.

_____

Each magazine is given an inch or two of write-up, and you can scan and summarize the information and assess the magazine in just a few seconds.

_____

Before you waste your money sending releases to publications that don't specifically address the niche you wish to market to, turn to the main section of the directory, "Magazine Listings by Classification." This composes the bulk of the book, almost 700 pages. Using Bacon's directory as a reference manual is not unlike flipping through an L.L. Bean or Eddie Bauer catalog: in the front you find the page number that shirts or sweaters are on, then you look up that page to see all the different kinds of sweaters to decide what you like, and what you think would fit. The main section of the book is where you do your shopping and selection.

If you want a quick overview of the magazines to send releases to, you'll be in heaven. Each magazine is given an inch or two of write-up (three inches if it's a really big publication), and you can scan and summarize the information and assess the magazine in just a few seconds. It's

everything you, as a free publicity seeker, could want in an encapsulated form. The book serves the reader well. That's exactly what it's supposed to do: make your life as a public relations director and marketing whiz easier. And it does.

As in other magazine directories, each magazine has an editorial profile. In Bacon's, this is the paragraph from which you can glean your press release list. It gives this whole section, and these reference manuals, true worth and value. If you send a lot of releases, send releases on a regular basis, or are a marketing, PR, or advertising professional, buy the book. After immersing yourself in it for just a few days, you'll find the cost is justified. If it's too expensive to purchase, annoy your local librarian till he or she gets one in stock for you. It may be an old copy, but that's OK.

Bacon's magazine directory also features a list of multiple magazine publishers in alphabetical sequence with each of the magazines they publish and their related markets (this runs about 20 pages).

The grand finale in this publication reference tool, and taking up the remainder of the book, is an "Alphabetical Index of Publications." Each and every magazine is listed alphabetically by its title. Very handy. Referencing a publication class is fast and easy if you know the title of one of the magazines that serve that particular market.

Bacon's magazine directory doesn't have the ad rate depth of the *SRDS Business Publication Advertising Source*™, but for a press release campaign, you may not need to wade through the half-page magazine listings of the SRDS directory in a laborious market search. So while knowing what a quarter-page ad costs in each magazine (as found in the SRDS directory) is nice, prices will be for reference and comparison only. The layout in Bacon's is fast and easy to use right from the start.

Between both reference manuals, you have the best of two worlds: The SRDS directory offers in-depth market research, with comprehensive ad costs, while Bacon's offers a broad overview and a quick way to summarize market facts, which you can use to analyze your markets and print media. Using either, you can create a precisely aimed press release campaign that will give you all the free publicity you can use, and probably all the sales leads you can handle, at a minimum cost.

The Danielle Adams Publishing Company
Box 100, Merion Station PA 19066

After only a few hours with either of these media tools, you'll obtain a good depth of understanding about marketing, and of the size and scope of the markets you are seeking to serve. Once you get copies of the magazines themselves, you'll see the number and strength of competitors in the trade press. You'll also be able to make an educated guess about which industries, and specifically which magazines in those industries, offer a good potential for sales. And you'll discover where you may wish to place an ad when your PR campaign is successful.

Geographical Marketing Through Newspapers

For the most part, trade magazines address a national marketplace within a single industry, trade, or profession.

While magazines separate the markets of potential targets or prospects into vertical segments by industry (e.g., all paint shops, or all car washes), they are almost always national in scope. A few magazines are regional, and a few others have demographic editions. For the most part, trade magazines address a national marketplace within a single industry, trade, or profession. Consumer magazines address a broader—but still audience-specific—market.

Newspapers, on the other hand, break out markets by geographic regions. With regional marketing, you get more of an "across the board" or horizontal type of market: you trade reaching a specific industry for reaching all people in a geographic location.

While newspapers can be used for national campaigns, I have written more extensively about magazines as the medium for most product marketing. Trade magazines show a product to a industry. Since most products are industry-oriented, or specific to a certain field or target audience, the most direct route to exposure of your product to the industry you serve would be through magazines. Consumer magazines also introduce a product to a select and defined end-user market. Unless your product is exceptionally broad-based, time-dated, particularly newsworthy, of tremendous human interest, or specific to a geographic area, magazines are my first choice of media vehicles.

Regional marketing is excellent for local services. Even large firms use regional marketing to test new products. If it's successful, they'll roll out and introduce the product on a national scale. For instance, Procter & Gamble may introduce a new type of breakfast cereal to the Philadelphia area with local TV ads, direct mail product sampling, and coupons in the local newspapers. If it sells well, they'll take it national.

Among Bacon's Information Services publications is a newspaper directory for both broad-based national and local geographic campaigns. It's a book that is similar to the magazine directory (it comes with the magazine directory as part of the set) and, in a logical sequence, gives a breakdown of newspapers, just about any way you can slice them up.

If you were a printer trying to market a book called *How to Sell Printing* to other printing firms, the trade printing magazines would be a good bet. It wouldn't matter where your customers were; the only qualification would be that they were printers. If you wished to test market your book locally to see if it would sell, a newspaper campaign would be a tremendous waste of expense: only a small percentage of newspaper readers would be printers, and you would be paying to reach people outside your target market, most of whom have no interest in your product. You'd be better off starting a local direct mail campaign, targeting printers in your area, from phone book listings of printers.

But if you were selling your own general printing services to businesses, your only criterion would be that your customer base of people who buy printing be close to your shop. The common denominator of businesses you would advertise to would be the close proximity of their office to your firm. Since you could sell your printing services to a full range of businesses, a newspaper campaign would be a fair choice. An ad or press release in a local newspaper would reach many types of businesses, all in your community. Since most firms need to buy printing, local newspapers would be a good place to take out ads or send press releases.

The Danielle Adams Publishing Company
Box 100, Merion Station PA 19066

Without the specific department, or the name of an editor, the release has less value and can float around the newspaper office for quite a while, landing on different desks where it will be of little use, until it eventually gets thrown out.

It is possible to get free press coverage from newspapers on a national basis. There are sections on business, travel, finance, op-ed, health, food, and so forth that are commonly found in most large papers. You can submit a press release to the specific department heads of these sections at as many papers as you wish. You can also submit the release to some of the syndicated writers for United Press International (UPI) or the Associated Press (AP), which run a number of specialized columns in a multitude of papers on a daily basis. If one of these columnists picks up your story and runs it, it will appear nationally in all the papers the syndicate serves.

When you submit news stories or press releases to newspapers, it's even more necessary than it is with magazines to direct them to a specific department. For the best chance of having your release published, try to send it directly to the editor of the department where it will appear. Without the specific department, or the name of an editor, the release has less value and can float around the newspaper office for quite a while, landing on different desks where it will be of little use, until it eventually gets thrown out. If you direct it to a person or a specific department, it will take a shorter, more direct route to the correct person, and is more likely to be printed. Newspapers deal with a great volume of information, and you have to be specific in the direction you send your press releases to get timely action and the favorable review you are seeking.

Almost 10,000 daily and weekly newspapers in the Bacon's directory are listed with editorial address, phone and fax numbers, circulation, ad rate (for one column inch), and the names of editors and staff writers for the different departments. Since newspapers print such a huge volume of information on a frequent basis, larger papers usually have a writer or editor at the helm of each individual department. For larger newspapers, the names of sports writers, business and financial writers, entertainment editors, travel editors, and so on are also listed. In addition, Bacon's lists daily and weekly papers, news services and syndicates, syndicated columnists, and Sunday supplements, and top geographic newspaper markets are broken down into an easy-to-use format.

If you are interested in marketing through news releases directed to newspapers, your stories should have more of a human interest slant. Press releases about products, which you send to trade publications, won't run well in newspapers. But newspapers are an excellent way to market, if the approach you take can make your product or persona "newsworthy" and interesting. The advantage of newspapers is the speed of dissemination of information into the hands of the public. Because of the enormous amount of material they publish every single day, day in and day out, including Sundays, newspapers are always looking for good stories to print.

Other Media Publications from Bacon's Mentioned In Passing

Another directory published by Bacon's is their *Radio/TV/Cable Directory*, a publication of listings (as you would suspect) of all radio and TV stations, including names, addresses, target audiences of different shows, syndicators, program content and profiles, and people to contact to appear on the show. It's printed in the same style as the newspaper and magazine directories. The *Radio/TV/Cable Directory* needs little explanation of how it is used, and you won't get that here. The directory's clean and simple layout makes it apparent.

If you would like to be on a talk show to hawk your product, this is one of the books that shows you whom to contact, and where. The same rules apply to press releases sent to talk shows as to newspapers and magazines, although you should definitely orient your release more toward the human interest side of your product.

Bacon's also publishes several other directories shown in the reference section in the back of this book. They also—as most directory publishers— now offer their data on the Internet. I like the printed versions as I can flip through the pages and scan pages very quickly. But the Internet offers the ability to form mailing lists withough rekeying the data, you just download what you need. And the databases are always up to date. My personal feeling is that as the directory publishers find the books and paper more costly and time consuming to print, they'll all move to online publishing only and we'll all have to accept that as the way the information is available.

But beyond the Internet, Bacon's offers some additional services that can make your life easier.

Additional Help from Bacon's

Bacon's now shows contact pitching profiles on most of the editors mentioned in their directories. The newest directories show you how, when, and what to pitch to specific editors—their likes and dislikes, the best times to call, and when not to call. If you've ever spoken to a grumpy editor because you've called too early in the morning, you know the value of this information.

Bacon's publishes two of the most in-depth, comprehensive media books ever, and now markets them as *The New York Publicity Outlets* Directory and *The California Media Directory*. These are an insider's media tools, the ones the professionals use when they need depth of coverage.

The NY media book shows almost 3,000 media listings, all in New York City and the metro New York City area. The depth of the media coverage is unbelievable. This reference resource even has direct-dial phone numbers for almost every media contact person. There's a breakdown of media by type: broadcast and cable TV networks and local stations; newspapers, daily and weekly; consumer magazines; radio networks and local stations;

radio network syndicated and local programs; news services; special interest and Sunday supplements; and ethnic and foreign publications. A two- or three-line listing indicates each magazine's area of interest, or what a show centers around, and their range of audience interest.

To give you an idea of the depth of information this book contains, it has over 300 listings of editors and their assignments for *The New York Times* alone, and over 160 names of editors and personnel for *The Wall Street Journal*. Their listing for *Good Housekeeping* magazine shows over 25 editors and departments.

Like its East Coast counterpart, the California book gives a wealth and depth of information on newspapers, both daily and weekly, and consumer magazines published in California. I don't know of any reference guides that are more in-depth for their specific markets than these books.

Bacon's Press Release Service

An additional beauty of Bacon's is that they will actually send out your press releases for you for a pretty reasonable charge. A nice feature if you are short on staff, and not a bad idea if you just need some extra help in getting your press releases to the correct people in a timely fashion.

You send Bacon's a one-page release, and they reprint it on white paper and send it to the list you specify from their database of magazines, newspapers, or electronic media personnel. They'll address it with a person's name or a title and mail it for you.

If you send them a release and 5" x 7" photo, they will reprint the release, make duplicate prints of the photo, and enclose both in an envelope and mail it. (They will also fax your release to the list you select.)

Both are pretty straightforward services. If you send them your release and they mail it for you, you have the advantage of their most up-to-the-minute editorial changes, as the mailing list comes right off their database that day. If there are any recent changes in media personnel, you get the benefit of the new, updated entry. Their service is very prompt, and they place your release in the mail within about a day of when they receive it. If you're an entrepreneur or a small business, you get all of this done for you without the headache of hiring someone or "Now I've gotta do this myself."

The Danielle Adams Publishing Company
Box 100, Merion Station PA 19066

Since all their information is in a database, Bacon's can split up any markets you select, any way you like. For instance, you can mail to the major magazine classification "Automotive" (with over 350 entries), or restrict the mailing to any of the individual segments of this market: Automotive Trade and Service Stations (62 entries); Buses, Taxi Cabs and Public Transportation (11 publications); Motor Trucks (65 entries); Trailers, Mobile Homes, and Recreational Vehicles (15); Auto Sports and Racing (62 magazines); General Interest Auto: Consumer (11 publications); Special Interest Auto: Consumer (35 magazines); Aftermarket Parts and Repair (51); or Tire and Rubber magazines (5 entries). Whew.

If you elect to run a newspaper campaign, you can select a particular state you would like to mail to, or specify mailings to names of editors, to personnel titles, titles of newspaper or magazine columns, or to any selected departments. You can slice up the media just about any way you want.

Bacon's will also sell you a list of any of the editors or media personnel found in their directory books on computer disk or on mailing labels. When you buy the names on disk, you purchase the rights to make multiple mailings to these people for one year. Labels, on the other hand, are for a single mailing and one-time use.

You can specify options for contact personnel on the daily newspaper lists. If, for instance, you want to mail releases to newspaper financial editors, book review editors, outdoor editors, or food editors, you can mail to just those personnel at the publications you select. You can also buy Bacon's list of food editors or medical editors for all papers or magazines, as well as the list of the newspaper publishers themselves.

You can select newspapers, radio stations, or TV stations by the criteria of circulation or audience, or select geographic markets by city or state. You can select only news services and syndicates, or syndicated columnists. Specialized media outlets are also offered, such as freelance food writers or college newspapers. Any way you slice it, you can probably purchase it. It's a pretty extensive and thorough service.

The One-Evening Marketing Plan

And the execution of it the following day.

For those who are in a hurry, and most of us usually are, here is the shortest course in marketing I have ever taught. You won't get this in any college or graduate class. It's something you only get from someone who has been in marketing for twenty-some years. It's instant marketing.

But before I divulge this little trick, I want you to know this isn't the way you're supposed to learn marketing. You see, a great depth of market knowledge comes from reading the trade journals associated with each industry. Trade journals are the greatest source of industry information. The only way to get a deep understanding of every market is to read about and study each one.

If you intend to figure out what drives a market, reading the trade journals is a necessary evil. This is where you acquire inside information and learn who's who in each marketplace. The lessons of who the major players are, and where the industry is, and is going, come dearly: by required reading. Your best sales prospects and the deep market penetration you'd like are also found in the trade magazines. So be warned, by using this shortcut technique, you don't learn much about the industry to which you are marketing. Of course, on the good side, if you make a lot of money, it may not matter to you.

The bottom line for this program is: If you don't want to spend the time, and you have the money, you can do most of your marketing in one evening, and execute the entire plan the next day. Here's precisely how.

Call Bacon's Directories, and get the current Bacon's Mailing Services and Media List order form (free). This single form is exactly the same as their market classifications, found on page 348 - so feel free to just use that! It's compact, yet incredibly rich with marketing information - these are the exact markets. Just by studying the few pages of this form, you can learn about marketing what would take you about half a year in any school (a full year if it's a state school, and double that if you're a senior) to learn. It will give you a broad base of marketing knowledge: what markets there are, their relative sizes, and how to reach each of them.

The Danielle Adams Publishing Company
Box 100, Merion Station PA 19066

It's Not Only Possible, It's Practical and Easy

To select your markets, spend a couple of hours with Bacon's market classification listings (page 348). This is where you do your marketing. Select all the market classifications you feel will align with your hit list of who will need, want, or buy your product or service. The classifications you select will contain the magazines that serve your markets.

Call Bacon's and order the labels for all the magazines in your selected markets by checking off all the classes you are marketing to. Then simply copy the pages and send to Bacon's, saying you'd like to order labels for all the magazines in these broad market classes, and include payment. You'll send press releases to them all when the labels arrive several days later. Your marketing is done. Now's a good time for a beer. I'll have one too.

_____

You know, for a press release campaign, it's damn near perfect.

_____

This method doesn't target your markets with the precision you would get by reading all the editorial profile statements in the main classification listings, but it's fast. And since you're buying all the publications in the markets you select, the campaign is probably much broader-based than you actually need. If you took the time to analyze the magazines in more depth, you wouldn't be adding many, you'd only be deleting the ones that don't look like a good marketing fit or are too far out on the edge. For your initial campaign, I recommend you go with the most likely, most potentially profitable, best mix of markets, with the best fit with your product.

You know, for a press release campaign, it's damn near perfect. Unlike placing an ad, when you need the precision of an expert marksman, press release campaigns are meant to be conducted using the shotgun approach: Send what you can, wherever you feel it may be appropriate, and whatever gets in is a major plus. This is the nature of a free press campaign.

If you want to be more selective but still send releases as soon as possible, you should still use this campaign and order the labels. Since you'll have a few days before they arrive, you can use that time do the "zero-in targeting" research: reading the publication listings to see exactly which magazines are best to send releases to. While you'll find you have ordered some extra labels, the cost of these will be minimal. Send only to the magazines you select after doing the additional research.

As with anything that happens too fast, there are a few drawbacks to the instant marketing approach. If there are specific magazines or newspapers you "should" or "must" get into, they may not stand out from the rest when you are just looking at the overall marketing picture on the order form. Also, you don't know which magazines to call to alert the editor that the release is coming. Since releases are sent in one day, there's no time for personalization, and this could be reflected in a reduced number of magazines and newspapers that publish your release. By not calling the editor, you miss showing the extra amount of personal, sincere desire to have your release printed in that particular magazine, and the chances of its being published decrease tenfold.

Since this is a non-personalized campaign, you don't address the editor by name or mention the name of their column, so your chances of actually having a release published falls back to the 5 percent range for unknown companies and first releases, and to about 20 percent for industry-familiar releases.

Because you'll be buying additional names and magazines that aren't precisely in your target market, you will have some wasted expense. But there's some justification for this added expense in the speed and ease of the campaign. As a bonus for cheating like this, you may wind up being able to order your release lists without having to purchase any directory books (some of which cost $500 each) or spending several nights in the library. If you feel really good about this, send me the $500.

The order form provides a fast and handy way to perform the overall marketing research and the marketing function, all in one fell swoop. You can read and study this list, and have your entire marketing campaign laid out in an evening. At no cost. Of course, I said you could be through with your marketing in an evening, and I just told you that you had to wait for the labels. For readers who would call me on this, here's the rest of the plan.

~ **The One-Day Execution** ~
of Your Campaign

The execution of your press release campaign can be accomplished in its entirety the next day. With the completed order form from Bacon's directory in hand, write your release and your cover letter. It's a good idea to have a photo for all releases, so if you elect a photo release campaign, this should be arranged beforehand. Send your photo, release, and cover letter to Bacon's with the specified lists checked off, along with the money to cover the costs. Bacon's Information Services will duplicate your photo, reprint your letter and release, and send them to all the magazines you have checked on your form. Now you really are finished with your marketing and press release campaign, and you should definitely open that bottle of champagne you've been saving for a special occasion.

In about three months you should start receiving inquiries from the releases that made it into print. If your release is well written, the photo clear and sharp, and the cover letter convincing, magazines will publish it. The number of magazines will vary with the industry, submission time, appropriateness of the release, and so forth, as discussed in the "Free Press" chapter.

If you choose to run a newspaper campaign, you can expect to see results in one to two weeks. Newspapers are very prompt in running releases. Press releases to newspapers should be sent only about two to three weeks at the very most before you want them published (sooner if it's time-dated material). Since newspapers work on supplying immediate news, they always leave room for late-breaking stories. News, press releases, and feature stories that can be run at any time are held back if the papers get a hot news story. When things quiet down, they run the releases that firms and PR agencies send. In fact, newspapers rely quite heavily on outside sources for this manufactured, semi-newslike material.

The part of the campaign you miss here is the depth of knowledge of the industry needed to sustain your product marketing. The deeper magazine analysis, the calls to the editors of your "A" or "Must get in!" press list, and the personalized letters that go with the release ensure a higher ratio of releases printed in the magazines you really targeted. But for a night's work, this campaign isn't bad. Not bad at all.

Addendum. If you run a newspaper publicity campaign and want to see what is printed in the papers about your company or product, or even about your competitors, Bacon's offers a clipping service. They scan thousands of newspapers and magazines daily and clip articles, ads, or press release blurbs (what your write-up is called in newspaper language) about your product or firm. If you want to compute the value of the publicity you have received in your campaign, you can count the number of lines of your write-up, then multiply that by what the cost of each line would be if you placed an ad in that particular paper. There are 14 agate lines to an inch in most newspapers. Or, if it's a long article, track by column inches, another standard way to purchase newspaper space.

Before I start sounding like an ad for Bacon's, there are a few more excellent reference manuals absolutely also worth mentioning.

The National Directory of Magazines

Published by Oxbridge Communications, this large, 1,600-and-then-some-page book is on a level with the SRDS and Bacon's directories and then some. The layout is a little different, but it's easy to use and supplies a wealth of information, some of which is not found elsewhere. It's very comprehensive, and shows data broken out in slightly different fashion.

The *Oxbridge Communications National Directory of Magazines* starts out with an alphabetical table of contents of markets such as Advertising, Baby, Dairy, and so forth. Following the market name, the number of periodicals sent to that classification is shown. You gain an immediate idea of the size of each market by seeing the number of its magazines.

The next few pages contain a cross index to subjects. It covers a lot of ground and is very easy to use. The cross index is where you look up a market, such as "Coins," and are referred to sections on Coin Operated Machines, Food, Laundry, Dry Cleaning Equipment, Cleaning and Dyeing, Music and Music Trades, Vending Machines, and Numismatics.

The directory has and unusually good depth of coverage in the multitude of magazines it lists. The next section, and the bulk of the book, shows magazines arranged by markets. There are well over 1,000 pages in this section alone, with about 12 to 15 magazines presented per page. Wow. That's a lot of magazines.

This one figure makes it terrifically easy to compare the costs of advertising in one particular magazine with those of all the other magazines in its field.

The publication list is presented differently than in the other resources, perhaps because of its magnitude of scale. The Oxbridge reference manual shows all industrial and consumer publications in each heading, so there are a lot of magazines. On the top line of each listing, the magazine is shown as a Business, Association, or Consumer publication to help you scan the publications quickly and pick out which part of the market is served by the magazine. If your product is designed for industrial use, only the business trade magazines would be of interest to you.

On the right edge of the top line of each listing in the *Oxbridge Communications National Directory of Magazines* the CPM is shown. This stands for "Cost per Thousand." Cost per thousand is an incredibly handy figure when you are analyzing magazines you're considering for an ad schedule. The figure shows at a glance the cost to reach 1,000 readers with a full-page black-and-white ad in that magazine. This one figure makes it terrifically easy to compare the costs of advertising in one particular magazine with those of all the other magazines in its field.

Suppose you found two magazines in an industry that looked like good vehicles in which to place ads. One publication has a circulation of 19,000 readers, and would cost you $745 to take out a full-page black-and-white ad. The other magazine you are considering has 23,478 subscribers, and the cost of a full-page ad is $1,995. Which is the better deal? In the first publication, your cost to reach 1,000 people with a full-page ad is $39 per 1,000. You reach 1,000 people with a full-page ad in the second magazine at a cost of $84 per thousand readers. The CPM figure makes it easy and fast to instantly compare ad rates and readership of different magazines, which have different circulation figures and different ad costs.

As you would suspect, each magazine listing contains the names of the publisher and other selected staff personnel. In addition, there is a one- or two-line editorial profile, slightly shorter than those found in other directories: sufficient to let you know if the magazine fits your markets, but not quite enough to tell you if they take press releases.

Circulation figures are given, as are costs of a full-page ad, in both black and white and color. Other miscellaneous data are given, such as subscription costs; percentage of paid subscribers vs. controlled (free) circulation; printing specs, such as paper, size, and binding; and whether the magazine's subscribers are available on a mailing list to direct marketers, the cost, and through which list company you can purchase the records. Some of the listings, but not all, also tell who prints the magazine.

What makes this directory stand out is the incredible depth of different magazines shown. Magazines not found in directories elsewhere can be found here. For example, Oxbridge has a section of club publications, showing magazines published by groups like the Sons of Italy. They also have a listing of college alumni publications, broken down by state. I've never seen anything like that in any other directory. Incredible depth.

In a section near the back of the book, the *National Directory of Magazines* lists publishers by state. This is handy if you are looking for local or selected state-oriented publications like those of the New York Department of Schools or the Pennsylvania Game Commission. It's also handy in finding publishers who may be close to you, so you can call them and perhaps visit them for better press coverage. A live and in-person visit will almost ensure a favorable write-up if you present your material well.

Also included is a title ISSN (which stands for International Standard Serial Number) index, which is used by libraries to find a periodical by title, and a multiple publisher index for publishing houses that offer more than one magazine.

What sets Oxbridge's *National Directory of Magazines* apart is the awesome number of magazines it shows: over 20,000 titles. Since this information is warehoused in a database (like Bacon's), information in this directory is available sliced up as you like it. For example, you can order "editors of automotive magazines" by name or by title; selected state publications with circulations over 30,000; publishers or editors of magazines under 10,000 circulation, and so on. Everything in the directory is available on labels or disk for your media publicity campaign. And now, on line. Nice. Simple. Easy. And you thought marketing was hard.

The Oxbridge Communications Directory of Newsletters

Newsletters are probably one of the most overlooked marketing publications to send releases to.

Another valuable resource published by Oxbridge Communications is their *Directory of Newsletters*. More and more newsletters accept advertising, today, and most will publish a release if it's of interest to their readers. Some newsletter editors rely heavily on press releases for timely information they can publish first, before the real media gets hold of it and it becomes common knowledge.

Newsletters are probably among the most overlooked marketing publications to send releases to through traditional marketing methods. Newsletters are deep in the heart of niche marketing. Some newsletters have a circulation of only a few hundred people, but if they are your selected target market, you can experience good fortune by sending a press release to the editors or publishers. Great fortune.

Most newsletters are small affairs. For many, the editor and publisher are the same person—who also writes the newsletter, designs it, has it printed, and is the same person who licks the stamps every month to put it in the mail. Since it's such a personalized vehicle, if you call the editors, chances are pretty good you will be able to get your release printed if they feel it is newsworthy and of interest to their readers.

Every once in a while you'll find huge circulation figures next to a newsletter listing. Some fill a market niche and have tremendous market penetration. If you can get in these bigger newsletters, you can generate substantial sales. The good newsletters are read word for word, and the editors' recommendations usually carry tremendous weight in their industry. The newsletter format raises newsletters' believability over that of magazines, and better newsletters carry substantial credibility.

The layout of the *Directory of Newsletters* is similar to that of the *National Directory of Magazines*, so I won't go into unnecessary detail explaining it all over again. I'll just give you this short version: There's a table of contents showing the newsletters in an alphabetical index, followed by the actual listings—over 1,000 pages of short descriptions of each newsletter.

Listings contain the editor, publisher, editorial description, circulation figures, frequency of publishing, printing specs, and also show if advertising is accepted. The next few sections follow the pattern of Oxbridge's other book: multi-publisher index, publishers by state, telephone contacts by name, and title ISSN index. I recommend giving serious consideration to supplementing your magazine publicity campaign through the use of newsletters. Don't overlook this unusual, but highly effective, resource for additional market coverage and deeper market penetration.

Between their directories of Magazines, newsletters and catalogs, the online database of Oxbridge Communications (called the Mediafinder®) make the data of over 77,000 publications available to you. See the reference section for details and prices.

The National PR Pitch Book

While the directories you were reading about are comprehensive, an interesting ripple has been happening in the time-space continuum of PR: Enter the *PR Pitch Book*.

The Danielle Adams Publishing Company
Box 100, Merion Station PA 19066

Just because some media directories don't have the distribution the larger magazine directories have - like being in every library, it doesn't mean they aren't as good—or better. Take the *National PR Pitch Book* series, for example. Published by the Infocom Group in California, the *Business & Consumer Edition* has the weight (over 4 lbs.) and feel (over 700 pages) of any of the other major directories. But there's a big difference, and a new angle. A new pitching angle, to be exact.

The editors of this series of PR pitch books have interviewed the nation's top editors, writers, publishers, producers, syndicated columnists, reporters, and journalists on what stories they are looking for, and how they like to be pitched. The responses they received—in many cases the direct quotes from the journalists themselves—are reprinted in each book.

Imagine knowing the inside track on how, when, and what to pitch; editorial hot buttons, quirks and peeves, deadlines, and best times to call. Imagine having the insight to correctly pitch your story or product for the best possible chance of media placement. If you'd like to use the press in your favor consistently, this is valuable information. What a great tool to let you know exactly what to send, what not to send, how and when to follow up, and the editorial mission of each journalist.

The *Business & Consumer Edition* contains over 170 newspapers with circulation of over 100,000, over 460 top business and consumer magazines, over 350 talk radio stations in the largest radio markets, over 100 nationally syndicated radio shows, almost two dozen wire services, over 200 of the top nationally syndicated TV news and consumer shows, and over 450 syndicated newspaper columnists. Granted, the *National PR Pitch Book* doesn't have the breadth of 10,000 business magazines or the tremendous depth of some of the other media directories, but it does have all of the top publications, shows, and news bureaus—plus in-depth contact listings that include personal phone lines, fax numbers, and e-mail addresses.

In frank and brutal reality, the *National PR Pitch Book* simply contains *contact dossiers* on the nation's top editors, producers, bookers, and journalists. It's inside information and advice that can get your PR consistently placed in the top markets.

The *National PR Pitch Book* contains *contact dossiers* on the nation's top editors...

This PR reference tool makes an excellent supplement to your PR library. While other media directories are now capitalizing on the great idea of pitching profiles, these folks have it down to a science.

Talk Show Circuit

The directories from SRDS, Bacon's, and Oxbridge Communications all give you tremendous details of media contacts. In addition to print media, they all have a television edition showing stations, shows, programers, booking agents - everything you need to contact a station or show.

Appearing on talk shows is a nontraditional way to market, since only a few people (compared with the enormous number of write-ups people and products receive in magazines and newspapers) actually get on a show. The number of talk shows aired pales in comparison to the number of magazines published. But...

If your product has a strong human interest element, or aligns closely with the audience profile of a particular show, don't discount your chances. Like the print media, TV and radio shows constantly look for fresh new ideas, new products, and new people who may be of interest to their audience. If you think this is for you, the campaign is similar to what we have already discussed. The key to getting on a talk show, similar to submitting an article to a newspaper, is to show a human interest side of your story.

A press campaign directed to talk shows is drafted like any press campaign to the print media, but with more personalization. Since the value of being on a show is so great, your best chance to make a great first impression is to compose a personal letter to the booking agent for the show, and precede it with a phone call, just like your "A" press list for magazines. The letter you send with your release should be benefit-oriented and detailed to show why you or your product would be of **significant interest** to their viewers and listeners.

Never, ever be boring to the high-tech television market.

The directories from SRDS, Bacon's, and Oxbridge Communications, as well as *New York Publicity Outlets* and *metro CALIFORNIA media*, all give you tremendous details of media contacts. But you may not need such great depth of media knowledge if you are aiming your publicity to a few select TV shows.

If you are offering a product that you think will make an interesting news item, or you think you would make an interesting guest on a news, talk, or magazine-type show, an easy-to-read directory comes from Bradley Communications (800/989-1400). It's called **Harrison's Guide to the Top National TV Talk Shows** and contains detailed profiles and contact info for the nation's top 235 national news and talk broadcast programs. For each show, up to twelve individual contacts are listed along with phone numbers and the topic(s) they cover. You get a printed directory plus a database file to create mailing lists. Cost is $347/single-copy with no updates, $697 for a one-year subscription with monthly updates. Info at www.AppearOnTopTVShows.com.

Bradley also offers a **National Publicity Summit**—a twice-yearly conference limited to 100 attendees who get to personally meet 70-80 journalists from top media outlets like ABC's The View, Today Show, Good Morning America, Time, Newsweek and other publications and radio/TV shows. Info at www.NationalPublicitySummit.com

Gebbie Press All-in-One Directory

While not providing as much depth in information about the media as some of the other books, this reference guide is a bargain at $165. It starts out with 69 publication classification groups unpretentiously arranged alphabetically, from "Advertising" to "Woodworking." Directly following the market classifications, individual publications are shown in an alphabetical listing with reference to the classification sections they are in.

Magazines and journals are shown in the main publication listing section, about 25 to a page. Information includes the publication name, publisher, address, phone and fax numbers, the main editor, circulation, and a short description of whom the magazine is sent to. This is bare-bones information, but enough to enable you to send a press release campaign directed to the main editor, or to call the editor to inquire about market fit or about publishing your release. That's the first third of this small-format, 6" x 9" spiral-bound book; it includes business papers, trade press, farm publications, and general consumer magazines.

The middle section of the book is exclusively newspapers. It includes news syndicates, magazines distributed with newspapers, daily and weekly newspapers, and the black and Hispanic press. Newspapers are arranged by state, and listings show newspaper name, address, city, and phone and fax numbers, along with circulation figures. Papers are separated into daily papers and those with weekly distribution.

The final third of the *All-in-One Directory* is all electronic media, and includes listings of TV network headquarters, news services, and television stations. The bulk of this section contains radio station information. As you would suspect, all the necessary data is shown to allow you to find a station, then send them a press release.

Gebbie Press puts out this reference tool for people who need basic information across different media platforms in a hurry. You can get lost in some of the other larger reference books; I find this easy-to-use, easy-to-carry, smaller reference book very handy. It's meat and potatoes stuff with a no-nonsense approach to the media. A pro version is also available. Contact Gebbie Press at Gebbie Press Inc. http://www.gebbieinc.com. PO Box 1000. New Paltz, NY 12561, 845/255-7560 Phn; 845/256-1239 Fax.

Conclusion

I don't know of any marketer who doesn't use one, or several, of these directories in his marketing process. There are other marketing reference publications, but these are the best. Through the largest of the media directories—from SRDS, Bacon's, Oxbridge Communications, or all three—you can figure out an entire print marketing campaign, compile a comprehensive list of media names for publicity or news releases, target specific market segments, and mail releases to them to get free publicity written about your product. The other specialty directories offer you a choice of great depth of coverage, multiple sourcing of different media, or exceptional low cost with terrific ease of use.

If you follow the format and recommendations outlined in this book, your publicity campaign will be successful. The exact same campaign has worked precisely as outlined for hundreds of thousands of firms and public relations agencies. They've done nothing exceptional to get this free publicity, certainly nothing you can't do simply by following the candid advice I have given you in this book, just as I have given to clients and friends.

These manuals and directories are at the heart of any campaign, and worth every minute you spend on them. Bacon's services that mail your releases for you are a wonderful treat. They can free you and your time for more creative matters, and take some of the chore out of this end of marketing a product. They offer fast turnaround and reasonably priced service.

In marketing, no one can tell you the depth or breadth of the markets you wish to span with your products without this research. These reference books make it easy to find your primary prospects, as well as secondary and tertiary markets, and narrow down, if not pinpoint, your target audience.

But only you can arrange the people to whom you wish to market in your own descending order of value. First, start with the people who really need your product. Only then should you explore other markets to see which ones work best. Track all your responses, and constantly lean toward where the money is coming in from. These reference tools are as valuable to a marketer as a hammer is to a carpenter. Take a little time to learn how to use them, and they will serve you well for a lifetime.

~ Marketing Through Magazines ~ with Paid Advertising

Paid ads are the next logical step in marketing if your press releases generate interest and revenue. They are the conclusion of a successful PR campaign. If your press release is published in a magazine, and successfully brings in enough orders or inquiries to make you feel an ad would pay for itself, you can go on to the next level. You have just passed GO, and have collected the $200. An ad is justified and successful when it generates more than its placement cost and the cost of fulfilling the orders (product plus shipping).

Outside of offering free publicity, some magazines work very hard to generate sales for your products when you purchase advertising space. Like a surgeon, you should carefully carve out from the slew of publications you are considering a select few in which you will actually place an ad. Only a few magazines will work for you profitably, with your product and your method of selling. Of these, only one or two will be the best: bringing in the most responses and the highest sales for the money spent. You'll want to be in these FIRST. When you are making enough money to test the less profitable media, you can place ads in the others.

Some magazines, even though they may be the best in their field— delivering the most readers at the lowest cost per thousand for an ad— may not be effective for direct response advertising. Others will be poor at lead generation. Some will give you a multitude of leads and inquiries, but the quality of respondents will be so poor, you'll have little back-end conversion of leads into sales. Selecting whom to send press releases to is easy compared to selecting where to place an ad. Whether it works or not, you pay for each ad placement. If you miss your mark here, it gets very expensive, very fast.

That notwithstanding, there will probably come a time in your marketing program when you will wish to place an ad, and you should know how to buy magazine advertising space.

In the beginning of each campaign there comes the educated guess as to where to place your ad. This is where your study and analysis of the magazines leads you to, hopefully, a correct decision. The educated guess can narrow the field down quite a bit. After that, the press release, when published in a magazine, will give you a good indication of market fit and whether an ad will be profitable. The final way to find which magazines are the best for generating income and leads is to systematically test them. If you are in a market long enough, eventually you will wind up testing all the magazines that serve that market.

Never take out an ad without reading several copies of the magazine to ensure an exact fit. Or a precise fit. Or at least a close fit. You should have done most of this for your press release campaign. It is even more critical in an ad campaign.

Negotiating Ad Rates

When you are serious about placing an ad, make sure you get the lowest cost for any ad you place, and the best position for your ad in the publication. Like car salesmen, many, many publishers will discount their ad placement price. This is especially true if they think you'll be a long-term advertiser.

Perhaps a better analogy for buying ad space is buying a stereo system: rates in the magazine industry can be negotiated.

It's standard industry practice for magazine publishers to offer a one-time rate (for an ad that will appear once) and a lower three-time rate, six-time rate, or twelve-time rate (when you contract with them to take out an ad in every issue of their monthly magazine for the year). These rates can be found in the ad rate sheet in the magazine's media kit. This is the magazine's standard list price (like the list price on a car).

These published prices are the "list" or full rate prices, similar to the list price on a chair or piece of clothing in a department store. Perhaps a better analogy for buying ad space is buying a stereo system: rates in the magazine industry can be negotiated. In addition, they go on sale (like furniture) if the magazine has unsold space left right before an issue closes. It can be a very steep sale.

Standard Industry Practice: Take 17.65% Off the Top

It's also standard industry practice for most magazine publishers (98 percent) to give you the advertising agency discount: 15% (or 17.65%, which takes the discount off the net) if you submit camera-ready art. Even the publishers who won't discount their published ad rates will usually give you this discount without any fight, if you ask. You can pretty much expect this discount, but only if you ask. It usually applies to everything except the classified section, and is subtracted from your negotiated rate.

Many more publications will give you the agency discount if you squabble with them enough, even if you don't submit camera-ready art. While no one likes a moaner, it can be effective. This discount is still not the negotiated rate, but it's traditional industry practice...and the asker's price.

Still a good many more magazine publishers will readily negotiate off their published ad space rates. Some will not, but you can always try. For selected smaller publishers, it's not an uncommon policy to charge what the market or individual advertiser will bear. Buying ad space in magazines is not like buying a ream of paper or a dining room table that has fixed material, manufacturing, and other hard costs. Once publishers cover their costs for writing, composition, printing, and postage, all additional ad revenues are "gravy." Once their quota is met, your additional ad dollars can look plenty attractive. So I always (politely) try to negotiate prices.

With smaller publications you can usually bargain hard and receive a discount on the ad. With some, a very steep discount is available to those with good negotiating skills. Larger publications are somewhat more inflexible; they can afford to be.

The Danielle Adams Publishing Company
Box 100, Merion Station PA 19066

I recommend you DO NOT place two or more ads in your first insertion order without seeing the results from your first ad.

Ad space salesmen are usually allowed to deal and offer discounts, but, like car salesmen, some have to go back to their managers when the dealing gets tough, and they may need approval for the final figures. That's usually a clue you are approaching the limit. If a salesperson asks the manager if they can give you that steep a discount, it's usually a good sign.

Magazine personnel are always more willing to try to deal if you commit to a longer-term contract rather than just a single test ad. But yes, single ads are still discounted, so don't get hog-tied into running a big schedule in an unknown magazine to get a lower price. I DO NOT recommend a long insertion schedule be placed before the magazine is tested heavily up front. I recommend you DO NOT place two or more ads in your first insertion order without seeing the results from your first ad. Unless you know the ad will work and (at least) cover its cost, go for only one ad insertion up front. Or you could be losing twice the money over several ads, instead of just once in a single issue. More on this in a minute.

All magazine publishers hope for long-running advertisers. They know if your ad in their publication is profitable, you'll be back with another insertion. But they can't afford to give space away, and they can't run every test ad for free.

In addition, their regular advertisers who pay list price would get mighty angry if they found out they've been paying full price while others regularly receive large discounts. So it's a fine line for publishers to maximize their revenues, satiate larger clients, sell out all the space in each issue, make a profit, and still have flexibility in their rates for new marketers to test new products. Be kind to them. But hey, you can be frugal: it's your money.

The Specifics of Rate Negotiation

The first discount I ask for almost without blinking an eye is the 12-time rate, even when I know I'm placing just one ad. Lots of smaller magazines will extend this rate to you if you simply ask. You already know this rate is profitable for the magazine because they offer it to longer-term advertisers. And the fact that they have various rates on their rate sheets tells you they'll deal.

They're not going to tell you, "Yes, we made up the ad rates by charging what we think our advertisers will bear." But I've never seen any scientific way to come up with a rate schedule...

If nothing's doing there, I always ask directly for the six-time rate, thus setting up a good fallback position of the three-time rate. Again, this is even if I am just placing an ad one time. Depending on how well the publication space sold for that particular month, or how hungry the publisher is, this may work, and is definitely worth asking for every time you place an ad. Space salesmen hate me. Keep in mind these are all early negotiations, and are preparing your salesperson for what lies ahead: good placement.

Rates in magazine publishing aren't set in stone. And while most magazines publish a rate chart, plenty of magazines will work with you. The ad rates at most magazine houses are simply made up by the publishers. They're not going to tell you, "Yes, we made up the ad rates by charging what we think our advertisers will bear." But I've never seen any scientific way of coming up with a rate schedule, other than a bunch of people sitting around in the back room discussing their best guesses as to what the magazine delivers in terms of performance, audience, readership from that audience, numbers of copies sent, percentage of current ads to editorial, what the traffic will bear, and how deep the pockets are of the clients in their advertising base. Cram all that stuff into a spreadsheet, mush it around a little, then add the five P's—paper, production, printing, postage, and profit—and you've got the sixth P: your ad price. It's not rocket science. And it's not set in stone.

If the publisher or space salesperson you're working with won't deal by giving you a discount, you might also try requesting the next larger size ad at the smaller ad price. Obviously, you won't be bumped up to a half page from a quarter page, but from a sixth-page ad to a quarter-page ad may be possible. It's pretty inexpensive for a magazine to do this once they have made their margin and covered their costs for publishing an issue.

If you've been negotiating hard for a discount with the magazine and find you're not getting anywhere, don't give up—just change your tack. Negotiate a discount off the published rate by asking for the "mail order rate." Surprisingly enough, lots of magazines have this rate, and for some it's even listed in the SRDS directory. If they don't have a mail order rate, there's a chance they'll make one up and give it to you. That's right, I said they'll make one up. It gives them an excuse to discount their ad rate and still make a profit. This way they won't look bad to their national accounts, and they'll still be able to close the sale to you.

_____

If your ad pays off, it is a win-win situation. You could possibly become a long-term advertiser in the magazine, and your ad may run for years.

_____

Tell them you are a mail order merchant, and simply state that you sell a lot of merchandise through the mail (if you do) and you'd like to know the mail order rate for display advertising magazine space. Publishers know that if their magazine brings in more than an advertiser's cost in direct sales, the advertiser would be foolish to not run again and again until the ad stops producing, and some ads never stop producing. True to your word, your ad for this magazine, if you get in under this guideline, should be direct selling–oriented, or a strong hard-hitting direct response–type ad for customers to request your catalog, brochure, or sales package.

Test Rate

If you're really not selling at all through mail order, ask for the "test rate." Lots of magazine publishers will extend a lower rate as a courtesy to allow new advertisers to test their publication to see the draw. Remember, both you and the magazine are looking for profit over the long term. If your ad pays off, it is a win-win situation. You could possibly become a long-term advertiser in the magazine, and your ad may run for years.

To get this rate, simply say you are thinking about running an ad, and ask if they can give you a test rate to test the magazine to your market. Surprisingly, lots of magazines will do this and it's definitely worth a try. Once you establish they are willing to negotiate price, you have set the stage for further advertising discount negotiating.

_____

The Danielle Adams Publishing Company
Box 100, Merion Station PA 19066

Subtly remind the publisher that if your ad works you'll be running more ads—but remember, they hear this all the time, so don't emphasize it because it's probably pretty annoying to them.   Everyone calling for a discount says this. I always hated it when a client of mine said, "Do this one cheaply and next time...."

When placing a half-page or larger ad, I usually ask for an additional color at no charge on top of any discount. It's a good opening bid, and maybe a long shot with some publications, but worth a try if you can casually slip the question into a conversation to feel out whether or not the magazine is going to negotiate.

_____

Before committing to a long run, you absolutely must see the results from your first insertion.

_____

I might phrase this second color free request like this: "I'm thinking about a third of a page ad, but if you think it's possible to get a second color thrown in, a half-page ad would be better for our product recognition."

Through all this bargaining and negotiating, the sales reps will inevitably offer an additional discount (steeper than on their rate sheet) if you commit to a longer schedule, placing your ad in more issues. Be aware this will come up fairly soon after you mention the word "discount" to them. But before committing to a long run, you absolutely must see the results from your first insertion.

While it does take a few ads and some regularity to be noticed and have your space advertising run at maximum effectiveness, if your first ad doesn't draw anywhere near the break-even point, more ads of the same kind aren't going to help. Absolutely do not schedule more than one ad up front. Wait till you see the results of your first ad before placing more advertising. I know in many instances this takes up to three months, but would you rather pay for one ad that didn't work or three months' worth of ads that didn't work? Don't do it. Better to be a couple of months late with your next ad placement.

I know, I know, the special "Show" issue is coming up and it's closing fast. Or the gala "Christmas Preview" issue. Or the super special issue of...well, you get the idea—these special issues always come up. In fact, special issues come up every single month, and always will. If a magazine is going to work well for you, it'll work well just about every issue, although summer months are usually weaker.

If the space salesman absolutely won't let you discount the price without committing to additional ads, and you feel it's a wise investment to commit to these ads, book the additional ad space SIX MONTHS in the future. If it's December, book the next ad to appear in June. That way, before the second ad appears, you'll know exactly what the first ad did. And if the first ad didn't draw, you still have time to cancel the next insertion. You may have to pay the full rate for your single ad instead of the three-time or six-time rate you negotiated (they will "short rate" you for running short of your insertion schedule). But it'll be better than paying for three nonworking ads.

If you schedule three months of ads all in a row, you'll be stuck. By the time the first ad appears and you figure out that it's not working, the rest of the ads will already be in production and in print...and it will be too late to cancel. Feel free to remind your sales personnel (if they get pushy about your taking a three-ad schedule) that if your ads don't work, you still have to pay for them. If they tell you that you don't have to pay for the ads until they appear in print, remind them that that time always comes around, and their telling you that is not much help. It's not their money. The full amount always comes around, due and payable.

Remnant Space - Every Publisher's Nightmare

Remnant magazine space is leftover space in the magazine that becomes available at the last moment. Remnant space is always sold in the last few closing days of the publication as the publisher finds out there is a white hole: a page or other space with nothing in it. In addition to the discount you can get when placing a regular ad, remnant space is always discounted fairly steeply. Sometimes very steeply.

The Danielle Adams Publishing Company
Box 100, Merion Station PA 19066

Most publications, despite pushy salespeople, a great reputation, and reasonable or unreasonable ad space costs, still wind up with unsold ad space right before the issue closes, and will deal. The deals and discounts can be substantial - 50%, 60% even 70% off the published rates!

At the end of each month, if a space in the magazine isn't sold or an advertiser backs out at the last moment, the publisher usually places a house ad or service ad in the "remnant" opening. These can be nonpaying house ads for the magazine, which usually say how great the magazine is, or have an obscure fact about the magazine or the industry. They can also be nonpaying ads for any of hundreds of great causes like the American Heart Association, the American Diabetes Association, and so forth. The magazines always have ad slicks (pre-composed ads) for these groups (usually made up by the Ad Council) ready to drop in at the last moment so there won't be a blank spot in the magazine when it's printed, which would look pretty unprofessional.

The deals and discounts can be substantial - 50%, 60% even 70% off the published rates!

To buy remnant space, do your homework beforehand to make sure the magazine and ad size will work for you. Then ask your salesperson to contact you if any remnant space comes up in the near future. This can be the cheapest space if you bargain hard, and are prepared to move fast and take an ad out at the very last second. You'll probably need camera-ready art on hand so the publication can just drop it in the open position. If you don't have camera-ready art, the magazine will probably compose an ad for you, but deadlines are already tight and they may fax you an ad they had to make up at the last moment—which you may not think is so great.

I never give blanket permission for an ad to be published without my seeing it. Ever. And I recommend you do the same. If the ad the magazine makes up is unsightly or appears it will be ineffective, you may have to make a decision between a poorly produced ad the magazine conjured up at the last moment, and giving up the space. If you give up the space because the ad is unsatisfactory, you won't be able to buy remnant space in that publication again. I guarantee it. You'll also make a few people on the magazine staff fairly angry, but hey, it's YOUR MONEY.

Here's my recommendation: Don't run a poor ad. If the ad is not satisfactory, it's their fault. Don't give away your money to keep someone from getting angry. I wouldn't. Deadline or not, there is no reason to present a poor ad to a client—and I don't care how tight the deadline is. If there wasn't time to make up a good ad, they shouldn't have sold you the space or made you the offer. Fast work doesn't necessarily mean poor or sloppy work. If the ad is poorly composed, you won't get your cost back from its placement. So don't do it. Even if it's cheap to run, this only means you will lose less money. But you will still lose money. There's not much worse in advertising than an ad that loses money. Whatever the price of an ineffective ad, the cost was too much.

If you really feel bad, offer to reimburse the publisher for the composition of the ad at their actual cost. Actual cost shouldn't be much, since they didn't have time to use any costly special effects or fancy screens. The costs should only reflect the small type charges they actually spent money on, which are cheap. Remember, it's THEIR actual cost you are reimbursing them for, without any profit or mark-up. I can't advise you what to do here because it depends on how the ad looks, and how much it costs to place.

Again, if you have any bad feelings at all or don't think the ad will draw, forget it. It'll be cheaper in the long run to not run it, and not cost you anything, than to lose money on a bad ad. While your costs for a remnant space ad may be discounted up to 50 percent or more, even this cheap price won't justify a poor draw; and if the ad doesn't pay for itself, it's not worth anything to you as a loss.

Ad Position

Like when you buy a car, once you agree to the amount and say you'll take it, the game is over. You don't get another thing. Not one.

Position is less of an issue with remnant space. The space you buy as a remnant will fill a void in the front of the magazine only if the magazine is already laid out and on the very edge of being shipped to the printer. This would be the luck of the draw, but don't count on it. More likely, your remnant space ad will appear in the back of the magazine. The magazine will run full-paying advertisers in the better position of farther forward. I wouldn't count on good position for remnant space purchases, ever.

When you buy space for your traditional ad, after all the rate negotiating, haggling, and jousting is done, and <u>just before</u> you are ready to say "Yes!" to the insertion, you are ready to talk to your salesperson about where the ad will be positioned in the magazine.

Just <u>before</u> actually placing the ad I always—yes, always—bargain hard for good position of the ad: in the front of the book. Once you commit to placing the ad, you lose all your bargaining power. Like when you buy a car, once you agree to the amount and say you'll take it, the game is over. You don't get another thing. Not one.

Customers, prospects, and competitors can see my ad <u>in the front of the magazine</u>, as readership always falls off toward the back...

Space salespeople will tell you everyone reads the book (magazine) cover to cover. If you listen long enough, they'll tell you everyone reads the book back to front, too. If you stick around, after that they'll probably tell you their readers read it with their checkbook in their hand looking for your ad. I don't know this for sure—I never stayed around long enough for the encore.

For my money, and my client's money, potential customers, prospects, and competitors can see my ad <u>in the front of the magazine</u>, as readership always falls off toward the back of the magazine. How many times have you picked up a magazine, read a few pages, and even with good intentions of finishing that great article on how to double your money in under five seconds, never picked it up again? I am usually fairly insistent on this point, and am prepared to walk away from a magazine that won't favor me with good position. But again, larger publications are less flexible and must appease their long-running national accounts first. Still in all, no one likes to see a customer walk.

Most magazines offer a "premium" position and have a special rate for it on their rate card. This can be called a "guaranteed position rate," or "premium position rate." Unless you are on the outside or inside cover, or the first one or two pages, don't pay a premium for position. It, too, is negotiated. In fact, even these best spots can be negotiated at times.

For example, if the magazine finds the inside cover has not sold at its premium rate, they may use the ad space for one of their full-page regular advertisers, saying they're giving him a perk or bonus position for being so consistent. Or it may go to a first-time advertiser whom they may want to impress. Or the space salesperson (knowing the inside front is open) may tell an advertiser that if they move up to a full-color full page, they can get the inside cover. The negotiations work two ways.

By the time you're ready to take out full-page ads in *House Beautiful* or *Playboy* for well over $50,000 an issue, you'll have had a chance to rethink this philosophy and form your own opinion. If a magazine gets sticky about good position, just say no to placing your ad, and that you aren't willing to chance a bad placement in the rear of the magazine. Tell them they can call you back; if they change their minds, you are willing to talk. I've never known a small publication not to call back over a position requirement. If it's important to you, call them back a few days later and tell them you are still willing to place your ad if they promise good position.

Far forward is always best, and to me, left or right facing page doesn't matter. In reality, the right-hand page is usually a stronger position for better readership. If I have an illustration in the ad that requires a left- or right-hand page, I definitely ask for that. Most illustrations have a direction, and the direction should always face into the center, or gutter, of the magazine. If there's someone's face in the ad, the face should look inward toward the center; a person walking should walk toward the center. Finally, the top of the page is a much better position than the bottom.

If you're placing smaller ads, they're usually pushed more toward the rear of the magazine by the publication's layout artists, but with a one-third-page ad or better, you should be able to get close to the front. Each magazine is different, so before you negotiate, get a copy and check to see if they run small ads up front. This is valuable information for you when speaking with the person who sells ad space for the magazine.

The designation for Far Forward Right Hand page is "FFRH." If you're placing a full-page ad, you should be able to get in the first 10 pages or so. Here you are dealing with a strong hand of a good size ad and can demand more. While the first 10 pages may be all full-page ads and the table of contents and such, it loosens up shortly after that for smaller ads.

If you're placing an ad that is smaller than a full page, start by asking for your ad to appear in the very front of the book, and if the magazine rep agrees, ask for the specifics of exactly where. They may not be able to give you an exact page number, but they should be able to give you a fairly tight range. Otherwise your idea of the front (first 20 pages) and their idea of the front (first half of the book) may be different, although both will be correct. If this happens, by the time you see your ad in print it will be too late for you to clarify your definition of far forward, complain effectively, or get the better position you wanted, as the magazine has already been printed. What they'll offer you at this time will be for you to place another ad that they'll run in the front. Humph, old magazine trick. They're certainly not going to give you a full or even partial refund, because your ad did run.

With a third-of-a-page ad, start by asking for the first 15 pages and tell them it's a must. When they complain and moan, you can back off to the first 25. No luck there? Drive hard for the first 50 pages. The first quarter of the book would be a final fallback position. I wouldn't go further back than that; your response will fall off dramatically.

If they give you a tough time about this, and tell you no third-of-a-page ad is that far forward, tell them OK, as long as you are the first one-third-page ad (or the first black-and-white ad) in the publication, you'll be satisfied. You can also be armed with the exact count of how many pages in you saw the first one-third-page ad in their last issue, and ask for that page or better. Space salesmen really hate me.

Don't let the space salesperson tell you he or she has no control over where the magazine places your ad. If they tell you this, immediately ask for a different salesperson. I always like someone who is straight with me. I can be tough, but I'm always honest, and I expect the same.

Keep in mind that although these strategies work with lots of publications, some of the big consumer magazines and even some of the bigger trade publications won't deal. They are already very prosperous and don't have to make deals. No one likes to turn down additional business, but ad revenues in a publication like *PC Magazine*, one of the most popular computer magazines, are well in excess of $10 million an issue. If you demand too much, they can make themselves mighty hard to reach on the phone, especially if they think you are a one-shot advertiser. Some

The Danielle Adams Publishing Company
Box 100, Merion Station PA 19066

magazines are very profitable for the publisher, and the spoils are they don't have to do anything they don't want to do. Hrumph. Must be nice not to need business.

Good Advertising Months, Bad Advertising Months

There are a few bad months for both consumer and trade magazines: June, July, and August. These are the months when the magazines are sent, not necessarily the cover dates, which may differ by up to three months. On a nice summer day in early July, would you rather be at the pool or beach with a cold drink, or reading a trade magazine with a pen in your hand to get information? I like marketing and magazines, but they don't compare with a cold drink at the beach. Same goes for consumer publications. There are a few seasonal exceptions, but readership and response, for these months, goes down. Way down.

_____

Like streetcars, if you miss one issue, lo and behold, another comes along next month.

_____

Just as you would suspect, the converse is true. The cold months of January, February, and March enjoy the best magazine readership. On a cold winter day people stay inside reading magazines, pen in hand to get information or place orders. This is true for both consumer and trade publications.

When space salesmen speak with you they all pretty much tell you, "You should be in the very next issue," and "It closes within a day." Or next week. Or on Tuesday. I dislike this rush-rush attitude of how and when to spend my money, and recommend you don't place an ad under their insistence of "This is the issue you should be in," or "This is the big show issue," and "It's closing fast." Like streetcars, if you miss one issue, lo and behold, another comes along next month. Every month. There are always more magazines. As long as there are new months coming up on the horizon, there are new issues coming out.

If a magazine is going to work well for you it should work well for most issues, the summer issues being the weakest. Space salesmen who have client longevity on their minds know this and won't rush a prospect. But if you get a salesman who is trying to make a quota or fill up a particular issue, well, a little word of warning: Never rush into spending your money. Don't worry, you'll spend it soon enough without rushing.

Unless you can afford an expensive ad campaign that may not promptly pay back the ad dollars you spend, your advertising campaign should comprise taking out ads that will be your very best bet to give you an immediate good return. For smaller businesses (sales up to $50 million) there is no such thing as institutional advertising. Institutional ads say, "We are." "We are here." "We exist." Or "We are an institution." If you want to take out an ad like this, without asking your readers to call you, you're reading the right book. There are three words you should listen to very closely—you're only going to see them once: Get over it. Unless you have all the money and business you need, don't even consider an institutional ad. Every ad you write needs to work as hard as it can to bring in response: calls, mail, leads, inquiries, orders, and money. If you are not advertising for additional business, why are you advertising?

Use the press release as your weapon of choice for testing all the other magazines to see if they and their market segments will work for you also. From the results of your press releases (if printed) you will be able to determine how effective an ad would be in that vehicle.

It's possible to run an entire campaign on just press releases. But it's a hard campaign to manage because there are no guarantees of maintaining consistent lineage in each journal, or having an ad appear consistently so you are able to judge response accurately. But if you can live with this, and execute a clever campaign to get your press releases published regularly, a campaign can be run without bearing the exact placement structure of ads and their cost.

Ads can be powerful because you can design them any way you want to elicit the exact response you are seeking. Press releases are effective because they give the credibility of being written and presented as editorial.

The Danielle Adams Publishing Company
Box 100, Merion Station PA 19066

The right campaign would be a good mix of ads and press releases. The ads maintain consistency in your placement, and also encourage the editors to pick up your releases. The releases offer your products through the magazine, balancing the editorial coverage your product receives with ad space. This gives you added industry credibility, and supplements your ad campaign when ads aren't running.

The most important part of any ad is the response, and the most important part of any campaign is to track the response.

I'd place about 30 percent ads and try to have run about 70 percent releases for an inexpensive campaign. This ratio is ideal, if you can attain it. The less money you have, and the fewer ads you can take out, the more releases you should send. If you have the money, be consistent in your advertising. If your ads are working well, work up to running every issue in every magazine that pays off covering the cost of the ads.

Response

Sometimes it's tough to figure out what's working and what's not. The most important part of any ad is the response, and the most important part of any campaign is to track the response. Otherwise you keep spending money on advertising that doesn't work.

Suppose you run two ads, each costing $300. One works and draws 30 responses and two sales, and one doesn't and draws four responses and no sales. Unless you track your advertising, you will be running those two ads all the time, getting 34 responses for $600, and two sales. Your cost per inquiry (CPI) is $17.64 each, and your cost per sale is $300. If you tracked your response you'd soon place one ad with a CPI of $10, and a cost per sale of $150. Then you'd have the other $300 a month for several nice dinners. If you had 30 ads like this running, the results would be multiplied by 10, and at the end of the year you could buy a new car.

The best way to track ad response is to ask everyone who calls you for information, "How did you hear of our company?" Write the answer either in a log book or on a piece of paper that you put in a selected file. Also include the date and the name of the firm, along with the source. Every month, count the slips in the file. If you fulfill literature requests with a computer, have the computer keep track. You can tell which savvy firms do this because when you call them to inquire they ask you at the beginning of the conversation how you heard of them. You can identify the firms that don't need to save on their advertising expense, or find out the efficiency of their marketing or advertising, because they don't ask.

Coding Ads and Releases - This is Important!

When responses come in by mail from magazine ads or press releases, they should all be coded so you can tell which magazine they came from. The code is put in by the magazine when your release is published and is in the form of "Department___" followed by the magazine initials. So "Department PIB" in the incentive industry means your release was published in *Premium Incentive Business* magazine.

The way you should track magazine response from your ads is by assigning a "mail to" or "Department" code in the form of a department number or letter for each release or ad. So your address in an ad may say "ABC company, Box 10, Dept. PIB, Merion Station, PA 19066." If you run lots of ads in *PIB*, you might show PIB7 for your ad that appeared in the seventh month, July, and PIB8 for the eighth month, August.

At the very least, code everything with a letter or suite number after the address. P.O. Box 100 becomes P.O. Box 100-A, or Box 100-G. Boxes can also have a MailStop code, as large companies do, such as P.O. Box 100, MS-222, or a room number: P.O. Box 100, Room 304. The street address of your home on Baker Street becomes 23 Baker Street, Suite 212. Code everything. Track everything. Keep a chart, and make it a habit. It's the only way to tell what's working and what isn't.

~ Finding and Analyzing the Magazines ~

Read the marketing section of the media directories. They are only a few pages long and contain all the market classifications. Write down any classification that seems like it will be read by candidates likely to purchase your products. Let's assume for your new campaign you feel there are two primary industries you want to reach, and six secondary markets that may give you some sales. It is not uncommon to have multiple target markets. If you feel your product has only one market, go back and look again. Dig deeper. Who else uses your product? I'm not specifying a product here because this formula works for any product and almost any industry.

You've done your homework and read all of the publisher's editorial profile statements and marked them with a red pen if they are in your targeted markets and they accept press releases. In all, let's say there are three markets, and about 60 trade journals where you feel you would either like to place an ad or send a release. Sixty to 80 releases would be a good size for a campaign for a product spanning two or three smaller markets. Most campaigns for products in a single industrial market will be smaller, say about 20 releases. With smaller markets and fewer releases, the campaign can be more personalized. What's next?

_____

Never, ever place an ad without seeing a copy of the magazine.

_____

All in all, you've really got to see a publication to know its true worth. Is it a glossy, four-color coffee table magazine? Are there lots of four-color ads, making your black-and-white ad look lost or reflect poorly on you and your firm? Is the editorial crisp and tuned in? Does it have a cohesive, intelligent layout? Is the magazine thick or thin?

Before you seriously consider placing an ad, you need to get a few sample copies of the publication. It's easy and it's free. Just call the publishing house and say you're thinking about buying ad space in the magazine, and you'd like a media kit and a couple of recent sample copies sent to you. Never, ever place an ad without seeing a copy of the magazine.

The media kit contains all the hype about why this magazine is so terrific, and why you should spend your entire ad budget in this publication. Publishers know that when a media kit goes out, money comes in, so they send them right out. While you're on the phone, also ask for a copy of any circulation bureau audit reports to which they subscribe. This will give you a confirming, detailed breakdown of their circulation. Some media kits will be sent overnight.

I also always ask at this time if the magazine has a directory issue or special annual issue, and request that they kindly enclose it and any special advertising rates for that issue, too. I may not advertise in it, but it usually gets me a valuable resource to the industry for free. If you called and asked to get this through normal channels you might have to purchase it, and some are quite expensive. The directory issue also shows you the publication's strength, and their depth of knowledge of the industry they serve.

When speaking to the people at the publishing offices of the magazines you feel will definitely be of help to you in your marketing, or ones that you want to examine closely over time for advertising potential, ask the sales rep to start you on a complimentary subscription. It is standard industry practice to give advertisers and potential advertisers a complimentary subscription even if the magazine is generally a "paid for" subscription in the industry. There are only two or three publications I have seen in the past 20-some years that don't give complimentary subscriptions to potential advertisers. You can also fill out the reader service card bound in the magazine itself and check the box for starting a new subscription.

So what's next? Before placing any ad, call or write to all the publications. It's more homework. There's no magic in marketing, it's just hours of hard work followed by a long term of success. Would you rather place your hard-earned money for an ad in a publication you've never seen? Or would you rather place an ad in a mediocre magazine when there is a better one easily available...if you had only taken a moment to find out?

The Danielle Adams Publishing Company
Box 100, Merion Station PA 19066

Gentlemen:
   We are interested in a possible ad insertion schedule
in your publication.
   Please send your media kit for _____ magazine.
   Kindly enclose two <u>recent</u> copies of the magazine, along
with any reference issue, directory issue, or annual summary
issue you may publish. Please include display and
classified advertising rates.
   In your correspondence, please advise us of your
editorial calendar, along with the closing dates of each
issue.
   Please also let us know if you publish a card pack,
newsletter, or similar style publication to this industry,
and if advertising space is available in it. Kindly include
a recent issue, also.
   Thank you for your prompt response.

I have a standard letter that can be used as is and sent to each publication being considered for an ad or a press release. IT IS OK TO SEND A FORM LETTER OR A COPY REQUESTING MEDIA KITS, AND I RECOMMEND IT. It can even be faxed. Big ad agencies do it all the time for every market their clients enter. Your request doesn't even have to look good. You only have to be believable, and convince people that you can pay the bill if you take out an ad. If they smell an ad placement, which is revenue to them, they'll send a media kit right out. So sound convincing.

Analyzing and Evaluating the Magazines

In about two weeks you're going to have about 60 media kits and 150 magazines on your desk, or worse, on your kitchen table. What a mess. Rich or poor, I don't know anyone in marketing who hasn't had this selection of magazines on his kitchen table at one time or another.

To keep all the magazines from becoming overpowering when they arrive, separate them into primary, secondary, and tertiary markets. Hey, that's just a lot of fancy jargon for saying stack them in three piles or put them in three boxes. Then sift through the litter later and evaluate them all at once, when they have all arrived.

Look through the amazing amount of paper you received. Ugh. If you don't have a wood burning stove, now's the time to consider getting one. You'll find, along with the tremendous amount of fossil fuel every media kit contains, a circulation statement and a rate schedule. Glance through all the rest of the stuff, then throw most of it out, saving any extremely important parts, but relieving yourself of the numerous folders the prolific magazine writers have included in their packages to seduce you into buying advertising space in their magazine. Keep the rate card, at least two copies of each magazine, and the annual or directory issues for references.

Circulation figures represent the number of magazines sent out; the number of people actually reading each issue is smaller.

By the way, many of the magazines will show two circulation figures in their literature. One is their actual circulation, as found on their audit statements. The other is usually expressed as "readership" or "pass-along" circulation. I suppose this was dreamed up by a clever ad man who saw a way to triple the circulation figures in one afternoon. Take this number with a grain of salt. It's what some magazine sales personnel calculate their circulation to be if every issue is given to two or three more people. Every magazine has a pass-along copy audience, but there is no way to judge what this is, let alone measure it accurately. Be careful this "readership" figure is not given to you on the phone by an overzealous sales person and quated as a real figure.

Also remember that the circulation figures represent the number of magazines sent out; the number of people actually reading each issue is smaller. With the poorer quality magazines, it's much smaller. And in the hot days of summer when everyone is at the beach, the readership figure is much, much smaller. The magazine publishers never tell you this.

Thoroughly read or look through the magazines in your primary markets not only to evaluate them, but also to find similar products and your competitors' ads. If you find one, turn up the page by folding it vertically in half at a slight angle. Notice that a small part of the page sticks out of the top for easy reference. Next time you speak with a space salesperson for that publication, ask how long and how often that ad has been running. Or check older copies to see if the ad is included. If it's been in there a while it probably means it's working, and this magazine should start to look more attractive to you for your ad.

When examining the magazines, see if the other ads and the editorial align with profiles of your own customers or your product audience. Whom is the magazine written for or directed toward? What audience is being addressed? If you have any doubts, call the editorial department and ask who reads the publication, then see if you think this is your market. Also, ask if they think the magazine is directed toward your market. You can simply call up the publication and ask for "Editorial" or "Editorial Department." I have always found the editors to be frank and helpful, and they are usually a pretty straight and honest lot.

If the market isn't a good one for your products, you have a better chance of finding this out from editors than from a space salesperson. No offense meant (I've already offended space salespeople quite enough, thank you). A space salesperson is trained to focus on sales, and on showing prospective advertisers the magazine's fit to almost any product—even if the fit is only partial. It's like asking a surgeon who is trained to cut, who spends eight hours a day with a knife in his hand, for a solution to a medical problem. Naturally, he thinks in terms of cutting, slicing and dicing.

In fairness, some space salespeople are truly friendly and very honest, and can be a tremendous asset in your corner. These people can be accurate when discussing industry matters since they spend eight, ten, or twelve hours a day immersed in it. If they aren't overzealous with sales, some will supply you with a good depth of quality industry knowledge at no charge. While most will not recommend competitors, the honest ad reps are worth their weight in gold and will at least steer you away from their industry if they think your market lies somewhere else. I'm very friendly with a few, and I don't believe they would ever make a bad recommendation. Sadly, they are the exception, but I have to let you know there are some great folks in this position out there.

Final Selection

Lots of magazines will fit in with your product marketing to some extent. Your mission, should you decide to accept it, is to determine the best magazine, with the best fit, and the best possibility of the most qualified responses and the most sales. Would you rather place an ad in a magazine that gives you 100 inquiries and six sales, or 40 inquiries and one sale? This is the difference between an accurate and a partial market fit. Or worse, a non-fitting market: 100 inquiries and no sales. Ugh.

Still have those magazines on your kitchen table? Good. On the face of each magazine write in a very bold marker the cost of a full-page black-and-white ad, the cost of a one-third-page or one-fourth-page ad (whatever you think you may buy), the circulation, whether they accept press releases, and the name of the column in which press releases are printed. Turn up that page in the magazine. If you see a competitor's ad or release, turn up that page, too.

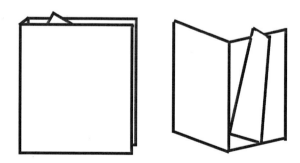

Turn page up, like this.

Place a preliminary letter grade (A through F) for ad potential on the cover. Then you can throw pretty much everything else out. At a glance, you can see the magazine, go or no-go on releases with the name of the column and editorial style, and your competition. If a magazine isn't right for an ad or press release, keep just the cover. In six months when you're wondering if you've reviewed that publication or not, you'll have a record of it. A thin record. Now read and analyze the magazines from other markets in the same fashion.

Now that the magazines are fairly separated from the paperwork that came with them, you can make an intelligent comparative decision as to which magazines address your markets, appear to be a good value, and will result in sales of your product to that market. Further separate them into magazines for advertising consideration, and magazines for press releases only. Next, pick out the top 10 and divide them into your "A" press list and your "B" press list. Assemble your press kits, and mail.

Just think, after all the hard work you have just done, no one has noticed. No one has thanked you. And you have nothing to show for it but a bunch of magazines littering your kitchen, with some scribbling on the covers. I know the feeling well.

But now you are coming into an exciting time—sending releases, and if they are successful, placing ads. It's always exciting to see your name in print. Seeing an ad or release for your product actually printed in a magazine is still exciting even for me, and I've been doing this for... umm.... ahh... umm.... years! Jeez, am I that old already?

It's now time for the visible part of all your hard work. Send your releases, see the response, and get the results of all your efforts. Placing ads and doing your best to see that your releases are printed is the next-to-last part of your magazine campaign. The results will tell you how well you did your homework and research. The final part will be evaluating the response, sending letters, literature, and perhaps samples to qualified prospects, and placing inquirers in some kind of marketing campaign. If you're successful, the conclusion of your campaign will be counting the money. Congratulations—you've just learned the art and science of marketing. The markets are out there, and they are ready when you are.

Notes...

The Danielle Adams Publishing Company
Box 100, Merion Station PA 19066

~ Ads ~

An ad is the logical conclusion to a successful PR campaign. This chapter shows you how to write your own ad, design it, then lay it out graphically in rough form. From there you can take it to an ad agency, printer, or typesetter and have it typeset professionally. Or you can try this yourself on your computer. The closer you get to the final concept, copy, and layout—the less expensive it will be for you, and the more likely you will get exactly what you want. The focus is on direct selling ads. Most of the chapter discusses the copy, which is what sells the product. Then the graphic design is addressed, which in direct selling ads serves to attract the reader and support the copy.

~ Ads ~

All my ads say the same thing: call, write, or come in.

If a customer hasn't done any of these, we didn't get his business. At some point the advertisement has to stimulate this response, or the ad fails.

The process of writing every ad starts exactly the same way. Just as in a direct mail letter, write your objectives in the upper right-hand corner of a blank sheet of paper. It should say one or more of the above: call, write, come in. This is a reminder that the response you are seeking is the reason for your ad. If you don't ask for a response, what is the purpose of the ad? I always ask my clients, "If an ad doesn't pay for itself, why are we doing it?" This brings the issue into focus.

Triple Your Phone Calls in a Week?

The importance of writing the objective of the ad can be demonstrated best by example. I was once called in for a consultation by a large real estate company whose sales were slipping. After an hour's discussion with the owner, who had over 50 years of experience in selling real estate, I outlined the consulting agreement: We'd meet for 10 hours or so and I'd outline a plan to increase his sales. Disbelieving, he flatly stated: "I have over 50 years of experience selling real estate—do you mean to tell me in 10 hours of meetings you're going to show me how to sell more houses?"

"Yes," I replied.

"Sir," he said, in continued disbelief, "I have forgotten more about selling houses than you will ever learn in your life." He was right; it was true.

Too bad the reply, "Sir, I have forgotten more about advertising than you have learned in 50 years selling houses," didn't come to me till months later. Isn't hindsight wonderful? It always lets you know you could have said something more clever, now that it's too late. Since he wasn't sure he'd get practical, usable information, I proposed a unique way to bill. "I won't charge you for any idea you don't use," I said. This always appeals to clients because they know they'll get usable ideas. It's one of my favorite ways to bill.

The Danielle Adams Publishing Company
Box 100, Merion Station PA 19066

I've had other clients take me up on this option. It's an expensive way for them to do business. For one, it always leaves an open budget. The client is free to pick and choose the best of the best, and it's always their option not to use anything I write. But each idea has a price tag on it. Ideas are more costly priced this way than as part of a package such as a working action plan (also known as a marketing action plan).

The objective of each listing was to generate a phone call. The objective of the entire ad was to generate phone calls. I've never known anyone to see a listing for a house in a newspaper and send a down payment.

The client enthusiastically agreed. I enthusiastically agreed. Upon acceptance of the plan, we spent a good deal of time reviewing the listings for houses in the real estate sections of the local newspapers. Like it or not, this is where the action is in the local housing market. When I asked him the objective of the very expensive one-third-page ads he ran day after day, month after month, he told me quite sincerely: "To sell houses." When I asked him the purpose of the individual listings within these ads, again he replied: "To sell a house."

He was partly right: he had forgotten even more about selling houses than he thought. The objective of the ad was not to sell a house. No one sees a four-line listing and buys a house. The objective of each listing was to generate a phone call. The objective of the entire ad was to generate phone calls. I've never known anyone to see a listing for a house in a newspaper and send a down payment. They see the ad and—if it works—they pick up the phone.

The objective of an ad is generally not to sell the product. The objective is to generate phone calls.

So I proposed a format change in each listing. *Call now*, the new ads said. *Call for an immediate appointment to see this new listing. Call for our free brochure! For information, call!* And we gave the phone number in a multitude of places, along with the house descriptions and stronger call-generating copy. After customers read our ads, with all the boxes and listings saying "Call now!" and the phone number showing repeatedly, they called. My client's phone calls tripled the very first week. That's the value of first writing the objective of the ad, then writing the ad to fulfill the objective. This lesson was much more expensive for him than for you. You've learned it for the price of this book.

The next step in writing an ad is to take a sheet of paper and draw a line down the middle. Write your product's features on one side, and the purchaser's benefits on the other. If you are not sure how to do this, you can find detailed instructions in the "Direct Mail" chapter. Unless it's in a very technical journal, your ad will offer benefits, and sell the phone call or the write-in response. The objective of an ad is generally not to sell the product. The objective of the ad is to generate phone calls. Now you are ready to write the ad.

Direct Selling Ads

Direct selling ads are necessary when you don't have your product in stores where potential buyers can see it, touch it, feel it, and purchase it. Many firms market their products solely in this way. Direct selling means you'll be taking out an ad in a publication, or you'll be sending a few sheets of paper to your customers and asking for an order. The paper can be in the form of a mailing package, a magazine ad, an article or write-up, or simply a letter.

If you have little or no distribution for your product, you have little or no choice but to make your ads direct selling ads. Before you can run an ad that says, "Buy this product at your local supermarket or hardware store," your products need to be on those retailers' shelves.

Direct selling in this context also means you have no sales force to knock on a customer's door. You also have no strong manufacturer's rep force to service your customers.

In this chapter we'll focus more closely on ads. While an ad is the last choice for where to spend money in a low-budget marketing plan, it is the logical conclusion to a successful PR campaign. And sometimes it is the only efficient way to reach a large portion of a specific market in a timely manner.

In addition, circulation figures don't tell you who read that particular issue of the magazine, they just show how many magazines were mailed out.

Magazines give good reach. This means they have the potential to be seen by a lot of people. Measured in CPM, or cost per thousand readers, some consumer magazines have circulation figures of over 10 million. While the circulation numbers for trade journals are smaller, their audience is more targeted. Trade magazines may have fewer readers, but more readers may be focused within your specific target market. So their CPM may be higher, but your overall marketing costs will be lower.

The downfall of magazine advertising: most offer very little depth when you buy an ad. You only get a fraction of a second to alert people to your product. In a single glance, you have to grab their attention, impress them with your product, show its outstanding qualities and benefits, convince them to purchase or inquire, and finally leave a brand impression of your company name on them. All this is very hard to do in a third- or quarter-page ad, run in one issue, one time. In addition, circulation figures don't tell you who read that particular issue of the magazine, they just show how many magazines were mailed out.

So the frequency with which your ad appears in a magazine is also important. To reach the entire magazine subscriber base and have them actually read your ad, you've got to appear regularly. Depending on the quality of your ad, the quality of all the ads, and how well the editorial is

---

The Danielle Adams Publishing Company
Box 100, Merion Station PA 19066

written—which will dictate how well the magazine is received—I'd guess this figure ranges from two to six times over the course of a year for a monthly publication. Whatever it is, it's part of a multiple exposure marketing campaign that says you need more than one exposure to make your marketing work.

As mentioned in the "Marketing Through Magazines" chapter, ad salesmen will tell you that you need three exposures for maximum results from your ad. That may be true for maximum results, but I'll guarantee you one thing: If one ad fails miserably, the next insertion of that ad in the same publication isn't going to do much better. **Hence, Jeff Dobkin's One Issue One Time rule: When running an advertising test, place only one ad, and wait for the results to come in before scheduling further ads.** I don't care what the ad salesman says. If he's so sure the second and third ads will do better, let him pay for them.

If the first ad isn't close to breaking even, the second and third ads in this series will continue to be an incredible waste of your money. While one exposure in one magazine is not a campaign, if your response isn't even close to breaking even, don't run the same ad again in that publication. Your results will be similar. If you are determined to continue advertising even after you see the poor results, be prepared to regroup. Start thinking about a radical change in your ad, your headline, the magazine, the offer, or the price. Consider additional space ads only if you are close to breaking even in your initial insertion. Multiple exposure marketing works, but only if it is done correctly. A poor ad shown repeatedly will still produce poor results.

If successful, some ads run for years. Ten years, 20 years are not unheard-of figures. To create a winner, the expense of the ad plus the cost of fulfilling the orders needs to be less than the money the ad brings in. It's a fairly simple equation. For example, if your ad cost $5000, fulfilling the orders it generated cost $3000, and the ad brought in revenues of $9000, you made $1000. If you own a large firm, add a zero to these figures.

There are several successful formulas for creating great, hard-hitting ads, so let's jump right in. A similar axiom in writing direct mail copy also holds true for advertisements—even more so: AIDA. <u>A</u>ttract attention, generate <u>I</u>nterest, stimulate the <u>D</u>esire, and <u>A</u>sk for a response.

A magazine ad is a tougher selling proposition than a direct mail solicitation. With a direct mail package you have several seconds of your prospect's undivided attention to simply get them to open the package—a relatively easy task, since they are holding it in their hands. With a magazine ad your time is shorter, and the response you are seeking (pick up a pen, find an envelope, go to the phone, or send in an order right then and there) is much harder to initiate. This is because of (1) more limited selling space, and (2) reader inertia (a body at rest tends to stay at rest). In addition, your competition is fierce for both time and eyeflow. Your ad is surrounded by distractions from your prime objective.

If your ad is not the most attention-attracting ad on the page, it's only slightly noticed or just glanced at in passing. It is the harder-hitting ads that command the reader's attention and focus. If none of the ads on the page is exciting, the page is turned. If either of these scenarios happens, your investment promptly goes down the drain. Your fantastic offer gets as much attention as last week's *TV Guide*. So your ad must not only attract attention, it has to actually command attention, and command the most attention of any ad on the page. You have about two or three seconds to entice the reader to stop, look at your ad, and read your headline. Which brings us to the first rule of making an effective ad: Create an effective headline.

Types of Headlines

Use a headline that will stop the reader dead on the page, capture his attention, and force him to read the rest of the ad.

The headline is
the ad for your ad.

The headline is, by far, the most important line in the ad. The headline is the ad for your ad. If it isn't catchy, if it doesn't capture readers and compel them to read the rest of the copy, don't use it. If you work on writing your ad for 25 hours, make sure to spend 10 of them on the headline. Ten hours on one line? You bet! It can be worth it. It is the single most important line in your ad.

The Danielle Adams Publishing Company
Box 100, Merion Station PA 19066

The difference between response to an ad with a poor headline and one with a great headline can be 10 times, 20 times, even 30 times! In certain instances, 100 times! Imagine that you take out an ad and get 100 responses. Then, keeping all the other elements of the ad the same, you change the headline, and now you get 1,000 responses. That's the difference between a so-so headline and a great headline.

Don't write just one or two headlines and pick one. Don't write a dozen. Write 80 or 100. Yes, that's what I do. That's why my ads are expensive— they take a lot of time to compose - and you don't see all the stuff I toss out. Write even more if none looks good. Write from different directions and perspectives. Take the page of benefits you wrote and study them. Write several headlines based on each benefit.

Ask friends to write snappy headlines. Better yet, tell them they'll have the pleasure of seeing their words in print in a magazine if you select their headline to use. If that doesn't work, offer to pay them if their headline is used.

The headline is the ad for the ad, and it accounts for about 80 percent to 90 percent of the effectiveness of the ad. Of all the elements to change in a failing ad (assuming you're in the correct market), consider a new headline first. If your headline is really off base, by correcting it (to make it a great headline) it's possible to draw 10 to 20 times the orders. Your ad that marginally drew 100 orders now draws 1,000 orders. So let's spend a moment discussing headlines. There's a way to play it safe.

Benefit-Oriented Headlines

The most powerful headline you can write contains your biggest reader benefit. One of the best ways to write a benefit-oriented headline for your direct marketing ad is to ask, "What is the biggest benefit of using this product?" In the answer lies the headline of your ad, or the envelope teaser copy and first sentence of your letter in a direct mail campaign.

The best headlines inform the reader of their biggest and best benefit. It's a good thing you have that page of benefits your product offers already written down from the "Direct Mail" chapter.

What is the one outstanding benefit you'd like everyone to know? Why is your product better than any other similar product in the field? What is the benefit that goes along with this difference? For example, if you are selling lawnmowers and yours is the fastest or has the most horsepower (these are features) you might write in the headline: Mow your lawn in half the time! What is it that makes your product unique and different? This is called your Unique Selling Proposition or USP, and it is an effective way to merchandise your product or service in an ad.

What specifically separates you from the pack? Is your product longer-lasting? Lower-priced? Can you use that difference in terms of user benefits in the headline to make people stop shopping and buy your product? Does your product have a sensational, outstanding benefit that can be crafted into a "catch everyone" headline? To be safe, stick with the basic approach of offering the best benefit. It's one of the safest, most effective ways to attract your prospect.

Examples of headlines that promise a benefit:

> End rust forever!
> Drive like a professional race car driver.
> Remove even the toughest stains instantly!
> Double your money overnight.
> Wax your car in half the time.
> Meet more women than you ever thought possible.
> Stay at any hotel for half price.

Headlines should be self-explanatory. Readers should know from just a glance what's in store for them. Keep it simple and drive home a singular strong point: the biggest benefit that happens when your product is used. It's an effective way to write headlines. A headline that shows the biggest benefit is one of my first choices, and the safest.

Benefit-Happened Headline

Rather than showing what the benefits are, you may use the benefit-happened style of headline. This variation of the biggest-benefit headline shows that the benefit has actually happened—as a direct result of the product's being used.

The Danielle Adams Publishing Company
Box 100, Merion Station PA 19066

To write this, imagine the best thing that can happen when a person uses your product. What is the best result they can possibly achieve? If your product works like a charm, what happens? For example, if your product is a piano teaching method, your ad could say, *Everyone at the party stood up and applauded when I played my first song on the piano!* Picture the biggest benefit—the greatest, very best result that can possibly happen—and write it in the headline. If you were speaking to a friend to relay the story of what happened, this would be your first sentence.

Several examples are:

Suddenly I was playing golf like a pro!
I started playing tournament tennis almost overnight.
I never ran out of hot water again.
Plants just seem to grow like wildflowers.
He mastered his computer in just a single weekend.

Notice something about all the examples? They all show action. A driving force. Something is made to happen. Action words increase readership and response. Action words create excitement. Never write a passive headline.

"How To"

Another safe yet effective headline style is the "How to" format. *How to prepare over 80 meals in under 20 minutes! How to buy any airline ticket at a 50% discount. How to make dinner using only one pot.* If your product lends itself to the how-to-do-it market, even people with mild curiosity will read the ad if it shouts "How to!" For example:

How to learn to play the guitar in just one week!
How to change the oil in your car without getting dirty.
How to look years younger in just a few minutes.

The "How to" format is usually the beginning of a harder-selling ad, and is a safe recommendation when you're sure your audience will be interested in your topic. It's also an exceptional way to define your target audience. For example, an ad that gives away a free booklet and has the headline *How to select shock absorbers for your car* would appeal to people thinking about purchasing shocks. *How to install a new roof* would appeal to people who need a new roof. And *How to keep your tellers happy* would appeal to bank managers.

Attention Arrester

An attention-arresting headline makes an incredible statement. (It is called "teaser copy" when it's placed on the outside of an envelope.) Use copy that stirs the reader's interest to such a degree, it forces—or "teases"—him to read the rest of the ad. Make your headline so irresistible that people just have to read the body copy to see how you support it.

A perfect example is our lawnmower ad. *This lawnmower is so easy to use, I bought it for my wife!* The copy that follows says that she's a professional landscaper - but too late, the reader is already hooked. Since it's unusual for a man to buy a lawnmower for his wife, the headline will attract attention and "dare" people to read the rest of the ad. The ad doesn't disappoint: it resolves why the lawnmower was purchased.

Following a successful direct mail campaign, I created an ad for a financial investment firm with the headline *A safe and easy way to instantly double your money.* The copy that followed talked about the firm, what they did, their services, and so forth. The way clients could double their money appeared later in the copy, after we made them read the selling pitch. The technique had been invented by the founder of the business, the father of the current owner: "Fold it in half and put it in your pocket." But if that wasn't enough for them in today's market, readers could call. The same line was used in our direct mail campaign as a teaser line on the envelope. As far as we could tell, everyone opened it. Everyone. While it didn't translate to the ad with all the impact it had to make you open the envelope, we did get an excellent draw from the hard-selling ad.

The Danielle Adams Publishing Company
Box 100, Merion Station PA 19066

New

Some words work like magic in a headline to attract readers and increase readership. Everyone likes something that is NEW, and NEW is always an attention-getter. Just check the product shelves at the supermarket.

If your product isn't new, is there a new benefit you can show for it? Or a new feature? Or a new offer you can make? *Now* is almost as effective. If you can't use *New*, using *Now* or *Now Get* can increase readership and response, as *now* is closely associated with *new*.

Price

A price in a headline can also be an effective attention-grabber that forces price shoppers to read the copy that follows. If you are in a price-sensitive market and you are the low-priced competitor, a price in the headline will attract buyers. Even in non-price-sensitive markets, all product-oriented people look at price. After seeing a price, customers will read the copy to see what they get.

Violator

New Low Price! combines headline elements for additional effectiveness. Can you reduce your price just a little so you can justify *New Low Price!* in your ad? But a new low price isn't enough of a benefit to sustain a headline by itself—it's too general. The best place in an ad for *New Low Price!* is in a graphic element called a violator. Made famous in the retail packaging industry, a violator goes against the rest of the graphics in the ad and offers an additional spot for unconnected copy. A violator could be a starburst, circle, strip, or oval set off to the side. This is where you place additional copy such as *New Low Price!* or *Call Now!* A guarantee also works well in a violator to increase response. Or, if you are in the nacho business, *Now Made with Real Cheese!* works well. For examples of package violators, please see the potato chip section of your supermarket—it's loaded with them.

The Danielle Adams Publishing Company
Box 100, Merion Station PA 19066

FREE!

A free offer increases response. Although overplayed and overused, *free* remains one of the most effective words you can use in a headline.

Some words really are magic in advertising. Use of the word *free* in the headline, or in the subhead, beats anything else for attracting attention and keeping people interested. Also include it in the first line, and again in the close. And reinforce it in the violator. It's the single most powerful word in advertising. So your offer for *Five books for just $,* becomes *You get three books for just $5—order now and get two more books absolutely free!* If you're digging around for something to offer for free in your ad, your old literature has just become much more valuable as a free informational booklet. I like to set FREE in all caps for added visibility. See for yourself. Examples:

> FREE brochure shows you how to repair your oven.
> Free tax analysis and planning guide. Sent FREE to
>   homeowners (yes, I know I used the word *free* twice).
> FREE gift just for calling and listening to our tape!
> Free Coke with any full dinner purchase!
> Free pinstriping with any paint work.

A free offer increases response. Although overplayed and overused, *free* remains one of the most effective words you can use in a headline. A free offer will attract readers who are only mildly interested in your product and produce a better response of additional leads, more inquiries, and more sales. This fulfills the ad objective: more people respond.

Additionally, when customers call to get something for free, they are usually very, very friendly at this time—because they are getting something free. It's a good time to extract the marketing information that you need from them. Once they are on the phone, you can see for yourself if they are actually in need of your product or service, just thinking about it, or just fishing. Prepare for this by writing down several questions to ask every caller who claims your free offer.

Not nearly as strong, but still worth mentioning, are other effective words like *Introducing* and *Improved*. Everyone likes a just-introduced new model, or a newly improved old model. Look through the detergent section of the supermarket. How many boxes, bags, or bottles have these words on them? After 40 years on the shelf, Tide still says *New and Improved*. Why?

Secret Formula Revealed

A great formula for success in an ad headline is "New Feature makes Benefit, Benefit, Benefit." It's probably the greatest formula ever for a headline. For people who didn't read the "Free Press" chapter, this formula makes a great press release headline, too.

Show your final headline choices to all your friends and ask which ones they like best. Show everyone. If you have a lot of money, you can afford to test dozens of headlines in actual ad placement. But on a tighter budget, you've got to hit it on the head the first time out or the ad won't pay off, and that will be that. You'll come away knowing only that your product didn't sell. But you won't be any wiser. You won't know if it was the headline that didn't work, if the market wasn't correct for that product, if the price was wrong, if the body copy didn't sell the phone call—or any of the multitude of reasons ads and products fail.

Here's another example to show you the value of a headline. Same real estate client as in the beginning of the chapter. With the downturn of the real estate market, he was having trouble getting good sales personnel. In our newspaper I spotted an ad that began *FSBO* (pronounced "fizzbo"), and inquired what it meant. He told me it meant, "For Sale by Owner." Out of curiosity, I asked if any of the owners ever sold their own houses. My client said it is difficult to sell a house by yourself, and very few people do. He also said that almost every salesperson in the industry who sees that

"This Lawnmower Makes Cutting the Grass So Fast and Easy, I Bought It for My Wife!"

Cut your lawn in half the time with the new Wide-Path Excel Lawnmower.

Now on sale at our lowest price of the year!

Imagine having a beautiful lawn year after year, but spending only half the time mowing it... and doing only half the work you do now. No matter how large or small your lawn, spend less time mowing it, and more time enjoying it. Guaranteed!

Just ask my wife!

Earlier this year I bought my wife the new Excel Lawnmower. As a professional gardener she needed a powerful way to cut lawns fast. Now she comes home for dinner earlier. She has more time to spend with me and the kids. And more energy at night.

Cut your grass in half the time!

The new Excel Lawnmower has almost double the horsepower of ordinary lawnmowers. So it's faster, and easier to use even in deep grass and up steep hills. And it cuts a 34% wider path because the blades are longer - so you can cut more area in a single sweep. Makes cutting faster than ever before.

Get a month of FREE lawn care!

We're so sure you'll cut your lawn faster, we'll make this guarantee. Buy the new Excel Lawnmower at our lowest price of the year (this week only, during our spring sale). If you don't cut your grass faster and with less effort than ever, I'll send my wife over to give you a month of free lawn care service. Of course, you'll have to cook dinner for her, and take care of the kids.

The new Wide-Path Excel Lawnmower - on sale now and in stock for immediate delivery - just call and we'll bring one right over! Or come into our showroom this week for our biggest sale ever - and get the lowest price of the year. Call 876-5432 for more information.

Call now for our FREE booklet, "25 Tips for Nicer Lawns!" Sent FREE on request. Call 876-5432 today for your free copy!

Old McDonald's Lawnmowers
Sales • Parts • Service
5432 Empire Street • Philadelphia, PA 19004
Call 215/876-5432
Call for fast FREE delivery!

Benefit-oriented, attention-arresting headline.

Benefit subhead.

Hurry-up incentive.

Benefits and guarantee.

Added benefits.

More benefits and guarantee.

Free offer of incentive aimed at precise market.

Strong call to action. Says "Call" 4 times and "Free" 4 times.

headline calls the owner to see if they will list the house with their agency. Listing brokers get half the commission when a house is sold; the other half goes to the selling agency. Converting a FSBO into a listing with your agency can mean fast and easy money.

Now that I had a headline every salesperson in the industry would read, it didn't take me long to create our own version of the FSBO ad: "FSBO—For Salespeople Beyond Ordinary. We have immediate openings in our growing agency…" We found that all the sales positions in his organization could be filled within a week. He never, ever had to run short of sales people again.

There are many types of ad headlines: funny, clever, cute, sincere; they are all over the map as far as being creative. Forget them. Forget being the copywriter for the old Volkswagen bug. Forget writing headlines for Budweiser or *Sports Illustrated.* It's too risky. You are interested only in fulfilling an objective: getting your prospects to call, write, or come in. You are interested only in making sales.

You aren't in a contest to see who can be the most unusual, or win an award for being the most different. You just want to make money, and have a good, solid ad, built on a traditional format, that has proven time and time again it will pay for itself. Ads that draw the greatest number of qualified responses have the best chance of success. This is your objective, and the basis for a short ad campaign on a limited budget. If you have a long-running campaign, you can be more flexible in your style and content. If you have an unlimited budget, let's talk.

This isn't saying you don't want to create an attractive, clever, and intelligent ad in an atmosphere that encourages a direct response. In this game of numbers, every single response shows up on your bottom line. You are trying to convert the maximum number of people to purchasers. They all have a common denominator: they all must read your ad. So in your headline, promise a benefit, offer something free, show something is new, give a price, or make an incredible statement with teaser copy—and hook the reader to read the rest of the ad. Get that one extra reader in 100 who was going to whiz right by your ad to stop and read your headline, read the ad, pick up a pencil or the phone, or, as that great American institution Bob Barker says, "Come on down!" The headline is the most important line in your ad. Don't be satisfied with a good one. Make sure it's a smashing great one.

The Danielle Adams Publishing Company
Box 100, Merion Station PA 19066

The Second Most Important Line in Your Ad

The second most important line in your ad is... the second line in your ad: the subheadline. This is a transitional line before the body copy, usually in slightly smaller type than the headline, but larger than the body copy.

In some ads this transitional line is the first line of the body copy. It depends on the space you have in your ad, and the amount of copy that needs to fit. This subhead clinches the reader's interest, then—much like the quick yank on your 15-pound test line when you feel a bluefish nibble on your hook—it leads the reader, without pausing, directly into the body copy.

The role of the subhead is to keep the reader enticed. Like the headline, its purpose is to drive people to read the rest of the copy. This line usually expands on the main benefit of the headline, or is itself heavy with additional user benefits.

For example, the headline of our lawnmower ad might read *Cut your lawn in half the time!* The photo would be of a large lawn with a house waaaay in the background. If you used that headline, now would be a good time to use an interest-arousing subhead: *This lawnmowing system makes cutting the grass so easy, I bought it for my wife....* Since it's unusual for a wife to mow the lawn, this line stops people and forces them to read the rest of the ad even when it is used as a subhead. They will continue to read the supportive copy that follows. The role of the subhead is to keep the reader reading. If it fails, the ad fails.

The third most important line in your ad (no, we aren't going to do this with every line in your ad) is the first line of the body copy. It serves to get people to jump into reading the rest of the ad. So it, too, needs to be catchy and make the reader continue. The body copy for our lawnmower ad may begin *The clippings were mulched and spread without my wife even breaking a sweat!* Support for the headline, subhead, and first line of the body copy might explain that your wife is a professional gardener and that she now endorses the lawnmower. We wouldn't want our ad to get us in trouble with the largest segment of the population, would we? But we do want everyone to continue reading.

As readers are drawn into the copy and continue to read, it is less important to coerce them to read further. By the middle of the main copy block, they have invested the time to get that far and are fairly committed to reading the rest of the ad. So you can gradually shift to important things, like getting an order if you have a direct selling ad, or generating a phone call if it is a two-step selling process. Once they are hooked, people interested in buying your product will continue to read your ad, even through the boring stuff like product specs and testimonials.

People who are about to make a purchase want as much information as they can get for two reasons. First, they want to confirm how great your product is so they can justify its purchase to themselves. Second, once they have made the decision to make the purchase, they look for support and reassurance that they have made the right choice. The copy now confirms and supports that their decision to purchase is the correct one. Go ahead, pat them on the back.

Design Ads for Three Levels of Readership

Level I. The first level of readership is for the people flipping through the pages of the magazine. To attract their attention, create a big, catchy headline so they will stop flipping the pages and look at your ad a little longer. To attract the most attention, the headline area generally should occupy one-fifth to one-third of the ad; it can be smaller for a direct selling ad where longer selling copy is more necessary (and requires more space). The headline area includes the type and the white space around the type. You have about two seconds, if that, to capture the attention of a skimming reader. This is where a photo or illustration comes in: to keep your ad space visually exciting and graphically interesting—enough to make the reader pause and look. The purpose of the graphic is to stop the reader from turning the page by creating interest, then direct the prospect to the headline.

Unlike traditional ads, direct selling ads usually don't have a large illustration. It wastes too much space that is better used for selling copy. Sometimes they have no graphic at all. A small graphic is recommended, to give the reader a visual reference. Direct selling ads need to have an exceptionally stimulating and enticing headline, good typographic design to pull the reader into the ad, and exciting copy. In direct selling ads, the copy is what drives your orders. Strong copy sells.

The Danielle Adams Publishing Company
Box 100, Merion Station PA 19066

Level II. The second level of ad readership is when readers start to casually browse around your ad after they have stopped to read the headline. To encourage Level II readership, I try to design the eyeflow of the ad to direct readers to the subhead immediately after they finish reading the headline. If they are at all interested in the headline, they will continue reading the subhead if it is properly placed and inviting. The subhead is placed directly above the body copy of the ad, so the reader's eye continues reading the body copy in a comfortable and natural movement. Direct the eyeflow for this immediate transition.

Following the body of the ad, give less visual emphasis to the name and address of the company at the bottom of the ad. The reader's eyes will dance around to these elements for just a fraction of a moment after reading the headline, and will find the name of your firm, no matter how small it is. Your logo (if you have one) doesn't need to be big, either—it's not a benefit to the reader. Your logo is important only to you, not to your customer. In a direct selling ad you can use this space more efficiently for selling. Give a larger phone number to make it easy to respond by phone, fulfilling the objective of the ad: generating phone calls. Always give preference to the elements that fulfill the ad's objectives.

If you are running a series of ads, your logo should be large enough for people flipping through the pages to see it easily and recognize it in just a glance. This is not so much for the people reading your ad, but for instant brand recognition by the people leafing through. Additional exposure of your logo through repeated ads give you additional credibility. It's one of the bases of multiple exposure marketing, the founding principle of this book.

Write the body copy in terms of action benefits from the reader's point of view. Readers see things in terms of what they will get.

Level III. Potential customers who are reading the body of the ad are at the third and final level of readership. These people are interested in the product, the benefits, or what you have to say. Hopefully, by the end of the ad they will make a decision to purchase your product, call for more information, ask for your free brochure, or come in to your store and look you or your product over more carefully. If they are really interested, they'll get the free brochure and read every word; people intending to buy are hungry for information. Draft your brochure for them—they'll be reading it.

The body copy style is the same for your ad as for your direct marketing package: write the body copy in terms of action benefits from the reader's point of view. Readers see things in terms of what they will get. So *We're going to send you* is not of great value, nor is it a benefit to the reader—it's what "we" are going to do. *You will receive* is of value to the reader—it puts the reader first. Take your writing out of the first person ("I" or "we") and involve the reader ("you"). Use direct action words. Thus, *We'll send you 5 tickets for only $5* becomes *You get all five tickets for just $5.* Or *Buy just 3 tickets by April 3, and you'll get 3 more FREE!* Keep up the high interest level of your copy, especially at the beginning, so you don't lose readers.

Two-Step Selling

Probably the best way to market from an ad is to offer a free booklet or brochure. This gives your customers an easy, non-threatening, and no-obligation reason to call. Offering a free brochure changes the nature of a

---

The Danielle Adams Publishing Company
Box 100, Merion Station PA 19066

direct selling ad from a one-step selling vehicle (people see the ad and call to order the product) to a two-step selling vehicle (people see the ad and call for the brochure; then, after they receive the brochure, they purchase the product). Everyone has their own opinion about which is better, and what works best and where. Regarding the one-step and the two-step selling process, I have two opinions myself. Both are effective at different times.

If a direct selling proposition can't be made fully in an ad—for example, if you are selling a pricey service, or a complex item that needs more selling copy than space will allow—a two-step selling process is a logical choice. If you are selling from a small ad, like one-sixth of a page, or a classified ad, you have narrowed the choice for yourself: a two-step selling approach is a necessity.

In selected media, you can sometimes sell a product effectively with a one-step approach. It happens in catalogs all the time. And lots of business-to-business ads are direct selling. Direct selling long-copy ads have run for years in some magazines, attesting to the success of this method. But magazine space is expensive, and testing can still break the bank if you're not well financed or your ads are not written well. For more expensive items, more complex products, or items that are more technical in nature, a smaller ad followed by a bigger direct mail package is more likely to convert prospects into customers than using only a small direct selling ad.

In a two-step selling process, your ad concentrates on just one goal: getting the inquiry. Your follow-up direct mail literature gives you more time to introduce more benefits and a more powerful selling proposition to your customer. When prospects receive your mailing package, you are not competing for their attention like you are when they are leafing through a magazine with other distracting ads and stories on each page. When you send them a piece of mail, you have their undivided attention, even if it's for just a short time.

The formula is simple: Free booklet offers benefit, benefit, benefit.

If you opt for a two-step selling ad, offer a free booklet. In the ad, sell the value of the booklet, and stress how easy it is to get it for free. The booklet may be your own, from a manufacturer you deal with or from an industry trade association, or an industry publication. You can even offer a single typed page (called a data sheet or specification sheet) about your product, service, or industry and still have dramatic success in fulfilling the objective of your ad: making the reader pick up the phone and call.

Think of the brilliance of this: A moving company writes a headline that says *Free booklet shows you how to pack your house and valuables for moving.* The offer is a free booklet that directly benefits the company's ideal audience: people who are ready to move. I'm sure it produces a ton of the highest-quality, most well-qualified leads.

Change our earlier formula, *New feature offers benefit, benefit, benefit,* by bringing the magic word *FREE* into the picture for added response. The formula is simple: *Free booklet offers benefit, benefit, benefit.* Or *Free booklet explains how to get benefit, benefit, benefit.* Or *Free booklet shows you benefit, benefit, benefit.* This formula is the secret to creating a successful ad. Any ad. If you want to be safe and effective, this works. If you are having trouble writing effective headlines, this one formula is worth the price of this book.

Increase your response rate by offering free literature that is informative, contains "how-to" information, or explains something useful about your industry, product, or service. Can you find some "how-to" or useful information related to your service or product that potential customers will want?

For example, if you sell radios, you may wish to offer a local program guide to your city's radio stations: their call letters, frequency, phone numbers, addresses, type of music they play, special programs, and... well, you get the idea. With your typewriter, you can create a single page of paper that becomes a valuable resource and free gift. Of course, it has your name and phone number on it.

If you can include this handy reference chart on an adhesive label that readers can stick on their radio, so much the better. Make it as useful as you can, so your gift has a high perceived value. In your ad, make your free literature or information sound so great customers will feel they are missing something if they don't call right away to get it. Use *FREE* liberally throughout your ad. If you create a gift of lasting value, in eight months or a year, when your customer needs a new radio, they'll still have your literature handy—and will call you, this time to use your services. As a lead generation device, an informational brochure is an excellent marketing tool. Probably the best.

There are two focus points of any ad. One is to get a response. The other is the quality of the response.

When marketing a local product or service, a more active free offer involving the use of your time can be very effective. This might be a free analysis, estimate, or inspection of your customer's present equipment, stereo system, car exhaust system, building, roof, or whatever your specialty or service is. Free estimates, appraisals, assessments, and evaluations are very effective in service offerings. Once you are at the customer's house giving the estimate, the selling becomes very different from selling from a page. It's much more personal, one-to-one, with feedback and direction on how to approach the sale if you listen closely. The technique of a free gift or free appraisal can get you an appointment. After that, you're on your own.

Qualifying the Response

Teaching or instructional aids are one of the best giveaways because they are low in cost, high in perceived value, and can qualify a prospect and boost your draw to give you an excellent response, all at the same time. Free booklets like *How to lay a floor* or *How to set up your computer printer* are tremendous aids to getting highly qualified leads.

There are two focus points of any ad. One is to get a response. The other is the quality of the response: making sure the response is from a bona fide prospect. In qualifying the response, finding someone who is actively looking for your product is certainly a great start. This is why the Yellow Pages are effective.

Offering a teaching aid revolves around both focus points. The free offer generates a response, and at the same time qualifies the lead as someone who has a specific interest in your product or service. With the higher quality of the respondents, you'll be sending literature only to interested parties, and following up with less wasted time and expense.

While a free offer may seem like you are giving too much away, especially if it's instructional in nature, I have never found this to be a deterrent to getting further sales. If anything, instructional material makes you look better. If you are a roofer, a booklet called *How to install a roof*, written by roofing material manufacturers, isn't going to cost you any business if you give it away to potential customers.

It's unlikely that people are going to read the book and put on their own roof. They will just see how difficult it is, and you'll get the work. If you ran an ad, or had a press release published that featured the free booklet *How to install a new roof*, you can imagine who'd call: people who are thinking about replacing their roof. Since you gave them a booklet written by an expert, most people will assume you are an expert also. They assume you'd install roofing as specified in the booklet if they hired you.

This applies to almost any industry. Bearing manufacturers can offer a booklet called *How to test bearings* or *How to tell if your bearings are wearing*. Suit manufacturers can offer *What to look for in a top-quality suit*. Two questions: (1) What free product information could you offer in an ad or press release that will make people call? (2) What's the holdup? Why aren't you working on this right now?

Marketing with Free Gifts

Marketing with a free gift, or premium, is certainly not new. In fact, every year there are two giant trade shows—one in New York in May, and one in Chicago in October—that feature premiums: free gifts and incentives used by almost every industry to inspire sales. Exhibitors at these shows are familiar names such as Sony, Chrysler, Nikon, Sears, Best, Canon, Panasonic, Columbia House Records and Books, and Black and Decker, to name a few. All these manufacturers exhibit their wares with great fanfare, showing how to encourage sales using their products as sales incentives, premiums, and gifts.

Here's an example of marketing with a premium. For years, banks gave away toasters, clock radios, and other such gifts when you opened an account—until the Feds came down on them with so many rules and regulations that it wasn't worth it to them. Bank marketing with gifts was pretty hot for a while, but now you mostly just get free checks when you open an account. It's still a premium, but how boring.

An example of a free gift with purchase in a consumer offer is the way *Sports Illustrated* markets their magazine. You get a free gift with a subscription. The particular gift rotates during the year. Their TV ads offer their magazine for about 15 seconds, then tout the gift for the rest of the ad. In the spring it's the swimsuit issue, free with your regular subscription. Eighty percent of the ad shows pictures of the swimsuit issue, touting how it's free with your regular subscription, how great it is, and oh, those almost-nekked-ladies photos.

At other times of the year *Sports Illustrated* gives away videotapes of football or basketball highlights using a similar format: 15 seconds of their TV ad is about their magazine, and the rest of the ad shows the best parts of the videotape—which you get free with your subscription. At other times they offer a phone shaped like a football, free with each subscription. (A phone shaped like a football? Get a life.) Well, it increases sales.

Many successful firms offer free gifts when customers place orders over a certain amount, or a free bonus when certain merchandise is selected and purchased. On the smaller side of premiums, McDonald's®, Burger King®, and Wendy's® all offer kids' toys based on current movie themes.

Insurance companies offer vacation getaways to their agents for increasing sales or meeting quotas. And small gifts with a company name imprinted on them abound, such as mugs, pens, and key chains. Who hasn't gotten a key chain from a car rental agency or dealership?

I recommend that you offer a free premium along with your customer's purchase, no matter what you are selling. Yes, when they buy anything. The gift doesn't have to be fancy or expensive, but it should have a high perceived value. When my firm started marketing pet ID tags, we offered the gift of a free "Fireman Save My Pet!" sign with each ID tag customers purchased. We generated some nice numbers with our pet ID tags, and some of our customers ordered ID tags from us just to get the fireman alert sign. Our fireman alert signs cost me under a dime each. (Of course, we buy them 50,000 at a time.) A premium doesn't have to be expensive to work well.

Direct Selling Ads

In a traditional ad, the use of a large illustration or photo captures eyeflow and thereby increases readership. Just check any magazine to confirm this. A good photo or illustration is the fastest way to capture the attention of the fast-paced page-turning reader. In a direct selling ad, a small photo of a person or product will also work as a graphic enhancement. But, even though a picture is worth a thousand words, make sure to leave plenty of room for copy. You don't have to have any graphic element (photo or illustration) at all in a direct selling ad IF you lay out the type so it's extra attractive. But my recommendation is, even a small photo, graphic, or illustration is a good idea—it gives the reader a visual reference in your ad.

If you use a photo, be sure to include a caption—it will have the highest readership of your entire ad, outside of your headline.

No time for a photo shoot? No budget for an illustration? For an ad with no graphic, you just need a large and exciting headline to attract the reader. Support this with well-designed and captivating copy, and your ad can still work. Entice your readers to keep reading. **Never forget: In direct selling ads, the copy is what makes people respond. The copy creates the response. The graphics serve only to attract the reader, and support the copy.** You can use an exciting headline to accomplish the same goal.

If you use a photo, be sure to include a caption. After your headline, the caption will have the highest readership of your entire ad. Everybody reads the caption of a photo. You need only pick up a newspaper to find this out. Flip through a couple of pages, and you'll notice you are reading each photo's caption.

Since the caption is widely read, make sure it's a most powerful selling line. You don't necessarily need to describe the photo—it's probably apparent what it is. If it's a picture of Bob and Mom in the sun, what a waste of this high readership area to say *Here's Bob and Mom in the sun.* It's much more effective to say *Enjoy being outdoors on your own private golf course.* Reader benefits are the key to effectiveness, and this is a great place to sneak one in. <u>Above all, the copy in any direct selling print medium should be a set of customer benefits pointing readers to the action you want them to take</u>: Ask for the response.

Incentives for Immediate Action

If at all practical, a "hurry up" incentive to prompt the reply should be part of the offer, to overcome the law of "reader inertia": a body at rest tends to remain at rest... and not order anything. Instill a sense of urgency for the response. If you don't wish to put a specific expiration date on the offer, you may consider:

> Hurry, sale price ends...!
> Hurry, supplies are limited!
> For a limited time only, get this free gift
>   with each order!
> Sorry, no rainchecks.
> First come, first served!
> Special One-Time Offer!
> You MUST order now to get this...

Prompt a quick response by saying *Send this ad today with your order and get...* People will hold onto the ad until they send it, hopefully sooner than later. To ensure immediate action, stress a limited-time offer:

> Free gift to the first 100 people!
> Mention this ad for a free gift!
> Free gift—just bring this ad.
> Coupon for $20.00 off, expires...
> Now on Sale!
> Gift Certificates Valid Thru...

Soft sell of the product, heavy on the benefits, hard sell of the call. It's another great formula for success.

The Danielle Adams Publishing Company
Box 100, Merion Station PA 19066

Most ads are directed at making the reader pick up the phone. It's the path of least resistance, and usually the easiest, most immediate action the reader can take at any given moment. To place an order by mail, the respondent has to find a scissors, paper, pen, an envelope, and a stamp, write down the information... how much easier it is to just pick up the phone! Credit cards are easily located in a person's wallet.

Getting readers to call is the usual objective of most ads I write. Following suit, I sell the call in a fairly hard-hitting fashion in most of the ads I create. Soft sell of the product, heavy on the benefits, hard sell of the call. It's another great formula for success. "Call now"—whether it's for free information, immediate assistance, a price quote, or information fast—focus on selling the call. And have a big phone number. Convey an image that your entire organization is eager to help, and is sitting by the phone. It's been an effective technique for lots of clients.

Coupons

If your direct selling ad is big enough (half-page or larger), consider using a coupon. A coupon serves two purposes. First, it immediately alerts casual readers that they can—and are encouraged to—send for something directly from the ad. When they see the coupon, they immediately know there is an offer, a product, and a price somewhere in the ad. Anyone even remotely interested will look through the ad for the price. Most folks will read the coupon to see what the offer is.

Secondly, the coupon gives the reader of the ad a structured vehicle for purchasing the product or requesting information. Even a small coupon increases direct response. People who otherwise exhibit good sense will use even a very small coupon. I am always amazed they do this instead of taking a sheet of plain paper to write down the necessary ordering information. But they do. Make it look like a coupon by using a heavy dashed border. This will encourage and increase direct response orders.

All these little things increase the response by a percent or two. By the time you've made all these enhancements to copy and graphics, you have the difference between a successful ad and one that won't break even. Don't try to make your coupon look like a beautiful full-color dessert, make it look like a coupon. The goal is to draw the maximum response possible from whatever size ad you have. Use every square inch effectively.

In direct selling, each ad is tested to see its exact dollar draw. Certain results have become consistent and predictable over time. A coupon on the bottom right always draws better than a coupon on the upper left. Time after time. So after a while, you realize the formula for the maximum draw in a direct selling ad is common to all direct selling ads. Don't try to break new ground by putting the coupon in the upper left. Follow the traditional formula for successful direct selling ads, and position your coupon on the lower right.

The form and style of your ad is always your choice. But styles are also dictated by:

1. The product you offer
2. The industry you serve
3. The ad size
4. Your budget
5. Your type of company
6. Duration of the ad campaign
7. The competition
8. The medium
9. The particular advertising vehicle
10. And, of course, the audience you are writing to—which gets prime consideration.

Common sense prevails. If you have a serious product, don't get funny. If your product permits, be clever. If not, just sound intelligent, show your biggest benefits, and don't forget to ask for the response. Cute or witty ads are rarely effective for direct response sales, where a reader is asked to send money. Placing money in an envelope and sending it away is serious business. Your customers don't want to take a chance when they do this, so don't you take a chance that your humor may be taken the wrong way. Check out our Internet site, that can be funny. Send me $25, that's serious.

The Danielle Adams Publishing Company
Box 100, Merion Station PA 19066

Business to Business
Inquiry-Generating Ads

The response is the most valuable part of your ad. This part of the chapter discusses how to determine the value of the different types of response. It also discusses how to sell your car.

Believe it or not, business ads can be a little less formal. In business-to-business ads, the advertiser is generally only looking for an inquiry. Even if seeking a direct sale, the business ad—because of the competitive environment of a business journal—can be a little less formal. Lighten up, dude.

I've written about the importance of the headline, illustration, placement, product, and free offer. But the most important part of your ad is the response you receive. In a direct selling ad, it's the envelope with the money, or the call with the charge card. In retail, it's the people who come in. In a business-to-business ad, it's the inquiry. Without a response, your ad failed. Generating a response is the ad's only reason for being. And in business, it usually comes to you in the form of a mailing label.

Business Ads

Most of this book is about direct marketing, which incorporates direct selling advertising. The reason the subject is important? If your product is not on store shelves the moment the ad breaks, the press release gets printed, or the direct mail package lands in the hands of potential customers, no one can buy it unless they contact you directly. That's why all the ads and mailing pieces discussed here aim toward selling direct.

Without any sales personnel on the road, and no established channels of distribution, you have no choice but to sell direct. But what a nice option direct marketing is—you can market a product without any chain of distributors and retailers. If you don't have to set up a chain of distribution, you can bring a product to a national marketplace almost instantly. You can establish yourself almost overnight. And you don't have two pay cuts out of each sale for a distributor and a retailer.

With the invention of the magazine reader service card, the primary function of business ads is became generating leads and inquiries. When you are placing an ad to generate an inquiry, since you are not asking your audience for a death-defying feat of trust (placing money in an envelope and sending it to you), you can be a little less formal.

In business to business marketing, the ad gives you the opportunity to present inquirers with a more comprehensive, harder-hitting package.

This is called a two-step selling process. The ad brings an inquiry. That's the first step and primary function of the ad. The direct selling package you send to inquirers (step two) is longer and harder-selling. It brings in the order.

In business-to-business marketing, the ad gives you the opportunity to present more qualified prospects with a more comprehensive, harder-hitting package. Unlike with a magazine, all the pages in the brochure you send are about your products. You can make a hard offer that requires money at the time of placing the order, or a soft offer with billing terms—such as send no money, we'll bill you, or pay nothing for 30 days.

I know it sounds odd, but business-to-business ads can be a little looser, and a little more fun. They don't have to be as structured, when the objective is to produce only inquiries for a two-step selling process.

The most common response to a business two-step ad is for the reader to request information. Although the different types of responses you'll get will vary depending on your offer, I'll take a shot with some percentages. A rough guess would be, reader service cards will constitute about 93 percent of your total responses; customers calling, 5 percent; and customers writing in, 2 percent. A nice free offer can change these percentages quite a bit. There is necessarily more paperwork in almost any business-to-business sale, and more back-and-forth correspondence created by inquiry generating ads.

Usually business products are somewhat complex in nature, and demand a deeper explanation than can be crammed into a small ad space. This need for additional information creates an opportunity for you to send a better- qualified prospect benefit-oriented marketing material such as letters, brochures, and specification sheets. The same rules for writing direct mail copy apply to business-to-business brochures, regardless of industry, products, or offer. The message is always the same: *You're going to get these benefits. Buy our product... It's easy to order. Just pick up the phone and call now.*

If your product doesn't lend itself to an immediate sale—if it's very expensive, complex, or there's just too much left out of an ad to secure sales directly from the ad placement—structure your ad solely to generate an inquiry. Inquiries are opportunities: narrow your prospect base, and direct your expensive marketing material only to people who have shown specific interest.

When the recipient doesn't purchase the product immediately, their name is filed—to be contacted again somewhere between later and never—and the lead is eventually lost, forgotten about, or thrown out.

The value of receiving an inquiry is that you may now send a more powerful advertising package to a more qualified recipient. Afterward, you or a salesperson can follow up with additional mailings or phone calls. See if the interest is genuine, if the inquirer is considering purchasing your product, or if a particular feature, benefit, or specification is needed.

This is the most common type of business advertising, called "lead-generation" advertising. Unfortunately, this is also where the worst mistake in marketing is made. The most common type of follow-through to an inquiry is to send a letter and a brochure. Then, when the recipient doesn't purchase the product immediately, their name is filed somewhere—to be contacted again sometime between later and never—and the lead is eventually lost, forgotten about, or thrown out. Some people call this marketing. I call it a waste of money.

Direct selling ads are rigidly formulated and structured, and they have measurable results. While there are less restrictions on business ads, some basic rules apply. Some things never change: the directions for the layout, a photo or illustration to attract attention, a large headline that demands reading, benefit-oriented copy, a large phone number, and (unless you are Mercedes-Benz) a small company logo, name, and address on the bottom.

Showing the benefits is not mandatory if you can create a stronger way of generating high readership and serious inquiries. But showing the benefits is still the safest, most sure-fire way to receive the maximum number of qualified responses to an ad. This approach is the safest way to write ad headlines and copy. Even in business ads, I strongly recommend benefit-oriented headlines.

Because of the limited space, the hardest selling of any kind is directly off the page in a magazine. It's impossible to say everything you want in the magazine space you buy, if for no other reason than much of the space has to be dedicated to the design demands of getting readers to stop and read the ad. All that wonderful space you could have crammed with user benefits must instead have something that attracts attention and stops readers from turning the page, with a headline appealing enough to motivate them enough to read the rest of the ad.

While I don't usually recommend humor or trying to be funny, you can be clever, intelligent, direct—or anything in between that compels readers to look at the ad, read the copy, and inquire about your product. Simply getting an inquiry is pretty easy compared to actually selling a product off the page.

Magazine space is expensive. What you are paying for an ad is probably tremendous. A small, five-inch square of one side of a sheet of paper can cost thousands of dollars. It's not possible to list all the benefits of any product that costs more than $50 in this small space.

The magazine's format also makes it difficult to sell a product directly. Your ad is sandwiched between all the other ads that are crying for attention, just like yours. This format does little to encourage people to sit down and read every one. Magazines promote "skimming and scanning" for information.

The Danielle Adams Publishing Company
Box 100, Merion Station PA 19066

Your ad is nothing like the direct mail package you can send to inquirers. You can address your reader personally in a letter. Just the two of you, taking a moment to examine your goods and how they can be of benefit to him. You can address your prospects by name, show them all the ways your product will help them, let them see the biggest benefits (while you emphasize and explain every benefit in your own detail). Your prospects can read this material at their leisure, uninterrupted by other advertising and editorial clutter.

When inquirers receive your direct mail package, you can direct them toward your strongest features in your data sheet or brochure. And you can do so without competing for their eyeflow like you did in the magazine, which was strewn with other ads and deterrents to reading your ad. For however long they stay in your mailing package, you have your prospects' undivided attention. Unlike with a magazine, if they turn the page in your direct mail piece, it's just to see your product from another point of view, or to see more benefits, or better yet, to find your order form.

So now we're back to where we started: sending a potential customer a piece of mail, with something in it that looks like a letter, asking for the order. Déjà vu. We just took a different route, that's all. You now have someone who is interested in your product, as expressed by their inquiry to your ad.

Qualifications of the Respondents

It's up to you to decide how you want to qualify the people who respond. In your ad, you can throw a loose or a tight qualification net. A loose net attracts everyone. Even those remotely interested in your product are invited to respond. A tight net is when you limit your response intentionally to people who meet your more stringent qualification requirements.

With very few exceptions, I recommend a loose net. Once you have established that you are marketing to the correct audience, let your ad attract everyone's attention and bring every response it can. Let them all call—you can sort them out later. Ultimately this will be a source of more sales, and better feedback. If you think this is too much work, you are either too rich or have enough business. If you're too busy to respond to the results of your advertising, maybe you should take a closer look at why you are advertising.

The Danielle Adams Publishing Company
Box 100, Merion Station PA 19066

Let's take an example of qualifying your respondents. You are selling franchises. Your franchisee needs $40,000 cash on hand to start up. In your ad you rave about the great value of a franchise, how easy it is to own, how lucrative it is, and you end by saying *Call us toll free.* This is a loose net. The callers will be all over the place with their interest, let alone their financing. Some will have it, and some won't even know what you mean when you say "financing."

For better-qualified respondents, you might insert a tag line in your ad saying *Financial Investment Required.* This will scare off some of the people, and help cut down on the calls from people with no money. You may also lose some of your real prospects—you never know.

If you wanted a tighter qualification, you might include in your ad *Investment required: $40,000,* which will cut out almost everyone except very serious inquirers with that much to spend. This is a very tight net. You may not get any calls at all with this limiting factor printed in your ad. But if you do, every respondent will have money.

Face it, the easiest kind of selling is face-to-face. In this situation you can ask probing questions, and get visual and verbal feedback through interaction and body language. The next easiest selling situation is on the phone. Third, in ease of getting an order, is with a piece of direct mail. Fourth—and this is a long way from the first three—is an ad in a magazine. The toughest type of selling is off a page in a magazine. All reach, no depth: you can have lots of people see your ad, but you can't give them a good understanding of you, your company, or your product. Magazine communication is like watching TV with a remote in your hand—if your ad isn't sensational right from the start, it only lasts a few seconds in the viewer's eyes.

When you limit your ad and throw a tight qualification net, you lose the ability to feel out the customers who never called. You don't get to see why they didn't respond, let alone purchase. You can't see their objections, or whether there's a way to circumvent them. For example, if you say *$40,000 cash needed* and a person doesn't have it handy, they may pass right by your ad. But with a loose net, if they call, maybe you'll find they've been working at a stable job for 20 years, own their own home, and are an excellent prospect for a bank loan. You'll never know. With a tight net you don't get the opportunity to find out, because these people never call.

It's similar to placing an ad for a car in a newspaper. Do you put the price in and limit your calls? Or leave it out so that anyone who is at all interested will call for the price? My recommendation is, give no price in an ad, unless your price is a fabulous selling feature because it's exceptionally low. I say let everyone call. Sure, it's a little more work. But you're not selling your car in the paper because it's less work; you're selling it there to get the best price, and to sell it as fast as you can.

This goes back to the basics. What is the objective of the ad? It's not to sell the car. No one sees your ad and buys your car. The objective is to generate phone calls. I've never seen a used car sold where the customer didn't call first. If they don't call, they are not going to buy your car.

Once you have your prospect on the phone, you can tell them how great the car is: its low mileage, the perfect paint, and how your grandmother only drove it on Sundays. Sure, you'll get some people who are only looking for a low price. Those phone calls will be fast. But you'll have generated calls. This is the first step in the sale.

By the way, when people call, there is only one objective to the phone call...

Now let's follow that objective a little further. What can you say in the ad instead of the price to generate phone calls? *Will accept best offer. Low price. Make reasonable offer. Priced for immediate sale. Will negotiate fair price. Call 876-5432.* This is in addition to the rest of the sales copy: *One owner. All service records provided. Call owner 876-5432 anytime. Ready to sell. Priced fairly. Drive this car home tonight. Dealer-serviced. Excellent shape, ready to drive home. Garage-kept. Showroom condition. Low mileage. Reason for selling: purchasing new car. Need to sell, please call now 876-5432.* Kind of makes you want to pick up the phone, doesn't it? Sell the call.

When you sell the call, if your ad works well you get lots of response. You can then tailor your telephone selling technique to the callers, and make adjustments along the way. If everyone who calls says your price is too high and hangs up, consider lowering your price. But if people hang up when you tell them your car is lime green, you'll know not to mention the color. When they ask the color, just say it's environmentally friendly.

By the way, when people call, there is only one objective to the phone call: getting the person to come out to see the car. Just as no one buys your car from seeing your ad, no one sends you a check from just your phone conversation. They've got to come out and see the car before they can purchase it. So your whole sales pitch should be designed to have the caller come out to see the car. Phrases like *We can talk more serious pricing when you get here,* and *You really have to see this car to appreciate how well my wife kept it,* come into play.

In business, when you limit the inquirers to your ad, you also miss the opportunity to present a more powerful sales vehicle. In our franchise example, when someone calls, you have an opportunity to describe all the benefits of owning a franchise that you didn't have space for in your small magazine ad. Benefits like being your own boss, being a respected community leader with your own business, securing lucrative government contracts, or dating your secretary. You never know what the hot buttons are that will turn a prospect into a customer. You have a much better chance of a sale when you can tell potential customers all the benefits on the telephone, or better yet, in person. If someone wants your $40,000 franchise enough, they'll find the financing.

You'll also get more feedback when you use a loose qualification net. If your franchise ad included *Minimum $40,000 Investment,* and no one responds, you'd never know if it was placed in the wrong magazine or section of the paper, if it was unattractive or poorly designed, or if the $40,000 figure scared people off. Let's say you leave that line out. When you speak with people on the phone and you mention it costs $40,000 to start up and they all pass out (or hang up), you'll know it's because of your price. If there are still no callers at this point, then it's your offer, placement, design, headline, selling proposition, or ad copy.

If you are selling kitchens, you wouldn't put *Minimum Job, $20,000* in your ad, would you? When you receive a call, you can ask what they have in mind, and then decide if the job would bring in sufficient revenue and you want to pursue the lead.

Sure, you'll get more worthless inquiries with a loose qualification net. But offsetting this, you'll receive more feedback, and more sales, too. Isn't that what you want—the most sales from each advertising dollar?

The Response

The value of each response to your ad is the opportunity to further pursue an interested potential customer, without the constraints, limitations, expense, and distractions of the small ad space in a magazine. You can entice potential customers to look over your data sheet, read your letter, and see all the benefits. You can overcome their objections and help them feel great about you, your firm, and your product. Did I mention you can motivate them to place an order?

If you are a direct marketer, response also comes in the form of envelopes with money in them. This is the very best response you can have from any ad. Customers simply send you their money. You receive an envelope with a check. No headaches, no hassles, no salesperson is necessary, and processing is fast.

Track each response from its source (which ad and where it was placed) to see what's working. Then place more ads in that medium or industry. A simple formula for successful advertising—and it only happens when you track your advertising.

If you're a retailer, an ad is successful when it brings people in. So the next-best response to an ad is when people come into your store. This result is of great value because (1) it's easier to sell something face to face; and (2) the serious shoppers usually bring money. They are pre-sold, and they've come to make a purchase. In addition, they can see, touch, and feel your merchandise. How easy to make a decision to purchase something in person, compared to looking at a photo of it in a magazine. And oh, how convincing you can be in person.

The Danielle Adams Publishing Company
Box 100, Merion Station PA 19066

To measure the effectiveness of a retail ad (which is harder to track than a direct marketing ad), place a small line on the bottom that reads *Bring this ad and get a free gift with any purchase* or *Mention this ad and get a 3% discount*. A dollar-off coupon also works with low-ticket items. This will give you an idea if your ad is working, and to what extent.

You should also ask customers who come into your store if they saw your ad, and where. Write each response on a slip of paper and place it in a box or drawer; count them later. No matter how much you think you'll remember, if you don't write them down you'll forget. I guarantee it. And in six months you won't have a clue as to which media drew what responses. Close tracking is a necessary part of any cohesive advertising and marketing campaign.

This list does not just contain your market, this list IS your market.

As a retailer, be sure to have a "Sign up for our mailing list" box next to your cash register. Encourage people to fill out the mailing list form by telling them they'll get something wonderful in the mail, like advance notice of sales and discounts, and receive special preferred customer status. When they fill out this form, ask them where they heard of your store. This box will produce the highest-quality mailing list.

Your current customers already know where your store is; you don't have to explain to them how to get there. They already like your merchandise. Mailing to them can be very effective. Because it's your house list of your own customers, mailing to them is better than mailing to any list you can buy. This list does not just contain your market, this list IS your market. Of all the people in the world, your most likely prospect is a satisfied customer.

The third-best selling opportunity is when your prospects call you on the phone. This is certainly not as good as having someone come into your shop for a live demonstration, where they can touch or feel your product, and face-to-face selling. But at least the phone gives you a chance to speak with your prospects and find out if they have special needs, how serious they are about buying your product, or how imminent a sale is. You can slant your sales pitch to address their needs. You can overcome their objections. It's the third best kind of response you can have.

The fourth response level, in terms of value, is people who write. You don't get any feedback from these folks, but at least they own a pen and can afford a stamp. They're not my favorite, but the inquiries are worth the paper they are written on, and each and every one deserves a serious and prompt answer. It takes a lot of motivation for someone to write. The write-in lead is a necessary evil. Just remember, the more requests for information you get, the more chances you have to sell your merchandise, and the more sales you'll have. The conversion rate is much lower than for phone or in-person sales; but the good news is, replying to these inquiries is far less time-consuming. One thousand phone inquiries couldn't be handled in a week by a small office, but 1,000 leads can be sent product literature and a letter in a single day.

Reader response card leads. Ugh. These are the worst-quality leads.

As the past owner of a direct mail firm myself, I used get lots of written correspondence with questions and comments, along with orders. My firm got more than 1,000 pieces of mail a week. Ugh. Everyone on the staff wrote a lot of letters responding to these inquiries, and our turnaround time for sending a reply was less than two days. We answered every inquiry. Be timely with your correspondence, and sales will follow. Although the percentage of conversion is much lower than with call-ins (whose needs are urgent and whose orders are more immediate), written inquiries convert to real sales if you pursue them in a timely fashion.

The Danielle Adams Publishing Company
Box 100, Merion Station PA 19066

If I haven't alienated all my friends who publish magazines, I will now do so. Last and least in the pursuit of sales leads, we have magazine reader response card leads. These are the worst-quality leads, but the most prevalent in any industrial or business-to-business magazine marketing campaign.

Reader response cards are included in almost every trade publication. An ad, press release, or write-up appears with a small number at the bottom of it and a statement such as *For more information circle number 147 on the reader response card.* Called reader service cards, RSCs, or "bingo cards" (because they have so many numbers printed on them), they are post cards that are bound into the magazine and contain groups of numbers. Interested readers circle the number on the card that corresponds to the number that appears with your ad or press release.

The magazine publisher gets the cards back in the mail from readers, sends them to a data processing house for data conversion, then sends you the name, company, address, and phone number of everyone who circled your reader response number on the card. Additional information is sometimes included, such as business size, number of employees, title, and sales volume. One of my favorite pieces of information included by a few magazine publishers is how many other inquiries the person made. I wish all magazines did this, but only a handful do.

While some of these leads are of value, the majority are not. Too bad you can't figure out which ones are which, up front. It's easy for someone with a casual interest and a pencil to circle as many numbers as they feel like. Many of these people have no intention of buying your product. Some are just literature seekers. Some like to get mail. Your competitors are in there, too.

Reader service card leads from the magazine are usually supplied on ready-to-mail labels. Phone numbers are included so you can call inquirers if you like. You might try to qualify them in some way. You might send all of them literature, send them partial literature, or just pick out the best of the inquiries and mail to the people who made them.

But beware. I once directed a campaign marketing a product to teachers. We were receiving 600 to 700 names of reader inquirers from every sixth-of-a-page ad we ran in a particular child care magazine. After a few months, when $12,000 in literature that was sent to these inquirers resulted in an unnaturally small handful of sales, I called the magazine and asked them to send me some of the actual reader service cards they were receiving. Of the cards they sent me, fully half had every number circled. Some even had all the numbers on the card circled *en masse* with one big circle. It seemed teachers just liked to get mail. I guess if you're a teacher in rural Nebraska, you look forward to that once-a-day mail delivery. They wanted to see everything, including our costly literature.

I didn't consider these qualified leads, and I told the magazine publisher so. How dare they send us a name of a person as a "qualified lead" interested in our product when all the numbers on the RSC were checked! It cost us a lot of money to learn this lesson; hopefully it will be less expensive for you. All magazines and all industries are not the same. While some RSC leads may convert to profitable sales, you should be aware that the value of these leads and their conversion rate is not nearly as high as from respondents who make the effort to write, call, or come in.

Ad Design and Procurement

How to design your ad, and get it into a clean, tight rough draft, ready to be typeset and printed. The options you have in this procedure, and the design processes, are discussed, as are selecting and working with an ad agency.

Determining the Size of Your Ad

Ad size should not be based solely on how deep your pockets are. Take the duration of your campaign, your commitment to the industry and product, the size of your market, how many ads you want to place, in which publications, their costs, and the length of the run—throw all that into a folder and shake it up, and these factors will determine your ad size.... No, no one does this. The only scientific method is to test, test, and test again. Without this historical research (that most of us won't do), you have to guess. Your guess will be based on some estimate of the above formula. Since every ad placement costs you money, on a limited budget an accurate first guess is crucial.

Most small firms besides yours don't have a set budget in mind when they start marketing a product, either. So you're not alone. For now, let's

The Danielle Adams Publishing Company
Box 100, Merion Station PA 19066

concern ourselves with the ad size and the duration of the run. For starters, you should run your ad only once as a test. There, that was simple. If the first test ad is anywhere close to being successful (meaning that it covered its cost), plan to run three or four more times as a continuing Level II test. If successful, you'll continue to run the ad as long as it produces profitable results. If it isn't close to breaking even, don't run it again. The same ad in the same publication will produce the same results. I don't care if it is the annual big issue coming up.

What about ad size? If you're rich—make that really rich—or if you have a lot of investors, if your product needs to be set off with an image (like a new car), if it's an exotic product, or if you have a sponsor for a co-op ad, OK, take a full page. I generally don't recommend this to anyone else, although there are a few exceptions: (1) you bought the page at a steep discount, (2) you need the ad in the front of the magazine and the publisher only places full-page ads up front, (3) you have deep pockets or are exceptionally well financed, or (4) you are placing a direct selling ad.

With a full-page ad, right off the bat you've got to create a superb, winning ad, and it should be financially successful the first time out. If it isn't, you're going to get kicked in the butt as soon as the bill comes in. So if you are thinking full page... realistically, unless you are financially strong, forget it. Most ads lose money the first time out.

The only time I recommend a full-page ad is when clients can sustain the cost for six to eight months up front, and have that in a written budget. This shows a superior market position, strong cash availability, and a formal written marketing and advertising plan. By the time you are this big, chances are you know what you are doing and what to expect. Which is not to say you are going to get what you expect—even the best ads, writers, products, and offers sometimes fail miserably. And the biggest firms make plenty of mistakes (but they have the money to cover their losses).

If you can't afford this six- to eight-month campaign up front, don't take a full-page ad. Forget taking a full-page ad for one issue, thinking it will pay for itself. Most ads don't. And first ads are even less likely to do so. And unless your name is General Motors, forget a four-color ad. It's too expensive for now. This is a book about low cost techniques. So let's look around...

For those of us not well financed, the biggest ad I recommend is an ad of "dominant page size," slightly bigger than half the page. This size is always offered in newspapers, and in some of the tabloid-size magazines. Traditional magazines usually offer a two-third-page size. With this size you can be certain that no other ad on the page will be larger than yours. So if it's visibility you're looking for, readers will probably see your ad.

When you are marketing a product direct, there are no distributors or retailers to take a hefty cut out of the list price. When selling a product directly from an ad in a magazine, you have only the advertising bill to pay. You keep all the money that is sent in, including what you would have spent on distribution costs if you had sold through traditional marketing channels. So larger, harder-hitting direct selling ads may be necessary. Direct mail ads are necessarily larger to accommodate the longer selling copy. But they can pay off because of the added net revenues you get to keep.

Magazine circulation figures show how many copies are sent out, not how many copies are read, each month.

If your ad is not a direct selling ad, instead of a full-page magazine ad, I'd recommend two half-page ads. Don't let your ego get in the way and buy a full-page ad because the space salesman says your ad would look good as a full page. Actually, my preference is one-third of a page with good positioning, run more frequently for more exposure. If you're running a direct selling ad, you've got to test all these variables. You need to establish your breakeven point and test smaller ads first—it's cheaper. Unless a client is very rich, I usually recommend a smaller ad placed more frequently, and "growing into" a larger one.

Realistically, everything depends on your product, goals, objectives, breakeven point, and budget. If you're well financed, go for the full page; I have nothing against it. It's just that most new product marketers aren't that well backed. Plan on the longer run. A single shot in a magazine (even a full page) doesn't capture the readers who may need your product but didn't have time that month to read or even pick up the issue. Magazine circulation figures show how many copies are sent out, not how many copies are read each month. Remember this, because you'll never hear this from a publisher.

Design

Now that you've written fabulous copy—a great headline that will stop even Billy Joel in his tracks, a subheadline that will retain his attention, and supporting copy that will hold even the most casual reader's interest (and hopefully motivate him to pick up the phone and make an inquiry or order your product), you'll need to get the graphics and layout of the ad close to what you want in the final version.

If you don't have the time, or if there is design money in the budget, then take your ideas, any copy you may have written, and the features and benefits page (along with any initial market research you've done) to an ad agency. If you're going to make your own ad, here's how to do it yourself. You don't need to be an artist.

Make a rough. All ads start with a rough draft, usually just called a "rough." Get some inexpensive paper and make a few thumbnail sketches (small enough for four to six to fit on a page) of what your ad will look like. These sketches will give you a quick idea of all the elements you will be dealing with: the headline, copy, illustration if you have one, logo or company name, and phone number.

These initial thumbnail sketches should be done quickly. Spend 10 or 15 minutes at most on each sketch. They'll be very rough at this point, only showing you what will probably work, and lots of what definitely will not work. Select your best two or three, and quickly sketch them in a slightly larger size on a fresh page. If none looks good, draw some more. Work up several ideas, each from a fresh point of view. Then get away from it—take a short break. When you return, you'll see all your roughs in a fresh, new light. Boy, they look terrible. But that's OK, they're just working sketches. They're roughs.

Make any notes on these working sheets. Copy considerations, notes, thoughts, ideas—anything that will help you get to a polished, finished ad. These are work sheets; don't be afraid to mark them up. They are only as good as the ideas you write or draw on them—they serve no other purpose.

Next, draw a border for the ad in the size you are considering, and sketch all the elements of your best thumbnail sketches in the approximate size they will appear in your final. It doesn't have to look good at this point, either. You just want to see if everything will fit, and where. Pencil everything in: mark where the photo goes; add the coupon, if you have one; make the headline as big as it will appear. Don't forget to put your name and phone number at the bottom. This is the actual rough of your ad.

If it looks unattractive, readers won't struggle to read your ad. They'll simply turn the page.

Take the correctly sized ad and visualize whether everything you have written will fit. You don't have to handwrite every word of the copy; just run parallel lines to show the visual weight of the typeset characters. You want to get a feel for how the copy will appear in that space. Some limitations apply, as you would reasonably expect: a full page of typewritten copy won't look good in a quarter-page ad, no matter what. Typeset copy can be much smaller than typewriter type, because you can adjust the size. But three pages of typewritten copy won't shrink down to a four-square-inch block. Well, it will, but you'll need a large magnifying glass to read it. Remember, if it looks unattractive, readers won't struggle to read it. They'll simply turn the page.

The Danielle Adams Publishing Company
Box 100, Merion Station PA 19066

So... better edit your copy again. I say this from much past experience. The copy for most of my ads still gets edited again after I have ordered the type and find out it doesn't all fit when I lay out the ad. You'd think after 25 years I'd have learned; yeesh, talk about a slow learning curve. I am getting better, though. Now I lay out the ad on the computer, and I know fairly early what will or won't fit. I still edit substantially before I send it out for final typography.

After you have made this rough, do it again. Sorry, everybody does this several times. Refine your artistry in an attempt to get closer to the final ad. Again, start with a border of the correct size, and enter all the elements. This time, be a little more careful in your layout. Does the headline fit? If it runs across two lines, does it break in a good spot? Does the body copy fit? Is there room for your logo, address, and a large phone number at the bottom? If you are using an illustration or photo, mark off where it will go and shade it lightly with the side of a pencil, just enough to get a feel for what the photo will look like in that position. Shading puts something of visual weight in the photo block to help you visualize how a photo will look there.

Does the copy block look better in one or two columns? Is the photo better on the left or the right? Does the headline break in a good spot? Get all the kinks worked out. Do this several more times, until it looks good enough that you can show it to someone without embarrassment. You can trace the first ads you drew—this helps to get the final drafts on paper quickly. For accuracy and speed when drawing the border, it's easier and faster to find the same size ad in a magazine and trace the border. I do this. I'm one of those visual people who needs to see everything. So I usually draw about a dozen roughs to get something close enough to a final that I can show a client. Don't be disappointed if you have to do more. It's all part of the process, and everyone does it.

If you need ideas for your ad, there are plenty of examples in hundreds of thousands of magazines. Get a magazine, flip through it to find an ad style you like, then make your ad similar. Cut out several ads you like and keep them in a reference or "swipe" file. Every artist has a swipe file. Mine is about five hanging folders crammed with reference material and is over six inches thick. I have reference files for good shadowing effects, good folds for brochures, great ads, well-written copy—you name it: if I liked it, I saved it. Pack rat, huh?

While I don't copy directly from the file, I do use it as a reference guide, for inspiration, as an idea starter, and as a resource for well-executed ideas. Don't worry about someone recognizing the ad you emulate. If you are marketing a desk calendar to the office products industry, no one who sees your ad will say, "Say, this looks just like an ad I saw for hammers in *Popular Science*." It ain't going to happen. There are tens of thousands of magazines printed each month. By the time your ad gets into print, it will appear far removed from the original that inspired it. I guarantee it.

After making about a dozen roughs (more if necessary), each one progressively more detailed and closer to the final, you are going to end up with a very tight draft of your ad. Once you have this nearly final version, there are three choices. First, you can send the draft to the magazine to set the type and run it. Most will usually do this at no charge to get the space placement. A few will charge you. Find out up front if there is a production charge. This can usually be negotiated—unless it is presented to you after the fact. Then it can be very hard to shake off.

You'll have more bargaining power when you ask if there's a charge for typesetting and laying out your ad before you commit to advertising space. To get your ad business, the publication will probably be willing to work with you on costs, or set the ad for free. After they have your confirmed space commitment, you lose all your bargaining power. Just like when you buy a car: once you say "Yes, I'll take it!" the game is over and you don't get anything else.

If you send your ad to the magazine for composition, you may not get to see it till it's in print—too late to correct any mistakes. Insist on a preview: this may be a blueline, a brownline, or a print. If the magazine tells you there's no time for a preview, insist they Federal Express it or fax it to you when they are finished typesetting it. Never authorize the publication of an ad without seeing it. Never. I've learned this from experience. You are at the mercy of the layout artist the magazine assigns, and while some are excellent, some are not so good. Do you want to take this chance? If you forgot anything, too late, and too bad. The rule of the magazine is "Follow the copy the client has submitted to the letter," and if there is a mistake, even a glaring mistake, it's the client's.

The Danielle Adams Publishing Company
Box 100, Merion Station PA 19066

Option #2: You can go to a typesetting house and have them set the type, or go to a quick copy shop (like Kinko's) and set it yourself. Most copy shops, and now a multitude of other small print shops across America, have Macintosh computers that you can use right there for your own desktop publishing, all for a low hourly rate. You can type your ad copy in and lay it out yourself on the spot, or bring it in on disk. The shop may have someone on staff to help you.

Option #3: You can take your rough to an ad agency to be composed and typeset (and possibly get some suggestions for improvement). My advice is to go for door number three, an advertising agency.

Agency Selection Criteria

If you have a rough ad, with or without finished copy, or just a page of features and benefits, advertising agencies can be of great help to you. They can lay out your ad from either of these forms, and they should be able to give you a handsome, well-designed ad. If you employ them to do more than just set type, like if you want them to get more involved with the creative or the marketing of your product, they can be of help there, too. They can also be a tremendous hindrance. So be careful.

There are lots of ways to find a good ad agency, and there are lots of good agencies. The selection of an agency can be instrumental to your success—or failure. To err in the selection of an agency is easy, and a poor decision will greatly increase the possibility of (or even ensure) your market failure. You will also incur additional expense in the execution of the agency's poor plan. Whoa, pretty harsh review for bad agencies! But there's a simple reason: It's true. Your ad campaign can fail miserably if it is handled incorrectly by a bad agency. Poor suggestions about media, choice of headline, pitch, offer, or style all lead to expensive mistakes agencies can make with <u>your</u> money.

In addition to the agency selection criteria of "good" and "bad," there are many shades of gray. There are also agencies that are too big or too small for you, and agencies with different strengths and weaknesses. Take additional time to select a PR firm, advertising agency, freelancer, or consultant with great care.

With too big an agency, your small account—as important as it is to you—won't mean much to them. You won't get the best talent or their top staff. And your bills—although expensive to you—won't be enough to warrant outstanding service from them. This doesn't mean you can't get lucky with the choice of a big agency and have your product land on the desk of someone who is exceptionally creative, and practical with their ideas and your money.

I don't recommend a big agency if you're a small account. Top guns at the big agencies will be working on the big accounts. Your chances of receiving great help are a long shot, at best. The creative services you purchase will usually be from the new employee, inexperienced lower-echelon personnel, or, worse yet, people who never got to the top for a good reason.

If (even after all this) your heart is set on a big agency, almost all libraries have a book called the *Advertising Red Book* (published by National Register Publishing, a Reed Reference Publishing Company). It lists almost every agency whose billings are over $25,000 annually. Look up several—preferably in your neighborhood—and interview them.

Freelancers and Consultants

On the other side of the coin, too small an agency—such as a one-man show (consultant or freelancer)—may not have the knowledge or in-depth marketing expertise to correctly handle your account and market your product. Among the freelance advertising agents or advertising and marketing consultants I know, three are excellent, a few are "so-so" in terms of effective campaigns and ideas, and one or two are just nice people. And one or two aren't.

To make matters worse, it's very difficult to tell who's who, and who will perform well for you, based on the initial interview or even the first several meetings. After that, it's basically too late. By that time, you have probably invested several thousand dollars in their campaign. Firing someone is always tough, especially if they are nice.

However, to endure the remainder of an ineffective campaign is much worse. You'll watch as your product fails in the marketplace and your money runs out. You may think your product is a failure, while the real

The Danielle Adams Publishing Company
Box 100, Merion Station PA 19066

reason you're not selling anything is a poor plan, the wrong market approach, a poor ad, an ineffective headline, the wrong magazines or newspapers, or even the wrong section of the newspaper. All your money will have been spent, but it will have been spent in the wrong direction. You'll get no sales, no feedback, and no information about why your product failed. The only person who will make money on your product is the agent.

On the plus side of selecting a freelance agent, if you know how to select quality people to have at your side, a freelancer can be your best choice. If you are fortunate enough to find a great freelancer, all the ideas come right from the top. You get the top talent 100 percent of the time. He or she can make you successful almost regardless of your product, or ensure your further success. For example, it's not unusual for me to come into an existing campaign and double or triple the response. If the campaign is really bad, a 10- or 20-times increase in response can occur. With a top-notch freelance agent you can be almost positive of having a winning campaign. <u>A referral from a business friend may point you toward someone who is tremendously effective, consistently</u>.

You may wind up getting experience— which is what you get when you don't get what you want.

On the down side, if you make a poor selection of a freelance agent, you end up with one person's poor opinion. If that person is off the mark, you can get stuck with some very bad advice that will sink your idea like a stone.

Without knowing the track record for successful campaigns of the freelancer you select, you can get hurt very easily. Some might recommend a pretty brochure because that's what they specialize in, when what you really need is a shrewd marketing campaign for your limited budget. If a bad idea is recommended and you aren't familiar enough with the range of possibilities to know that it won't be your most cost-effective marketing option, you may wind up getting experience—which is what you get when you don't get what you want. And this may be a particularly expensive way to get experience.

The best freelancers or consultants will give you the straightforward and effective advice you need at the very beginning of the campaign. To save money, consider hiring them on a consulting basis. You can then carry out the campaign they recommended by yourself. Some consultants can be pretty darn clever at creating great low-cost campaigns, increasing sales, and saving you money at the same time. The real trouble is figuring out which ones are good, which ones are great, and which ones will just be expensive. If you are good at choosing talent, it would be most worthwhile to investigate this possibility. The talent is out there.

Selecting an Agency

One of the best ways to find creative talent is by referral. A good recommendation from a true friend is always the best. If you know someone who has a small business that markets products, or who has an idea they are bringing to market, ask them if their agency is any good. If you get a "Fair," or a "They're OK, but..." rating, keep looking. The great ones are out there.

In the absence of a terrific referral, a fair way to find an agency is to pick up the local papers or magazines, and decide which ads are the best and the hardest-hitting. Remember, when you see a great ad, it has little to do with the product; credit goes to the agency that created the ad. (You won't know if the product is great until you see it in a store or purchase it through the mail.) Call the business and ask who created the ad. Most people will tell you. Ask if the ad was effective. Then call the agency and ask for samples of its work.

Another option: If you don't know anything about the agencies you are choosing from, go for the ones close to you—especially ones in your neighborhood. Everyone likes customers in their own backyard: you'll get a fairer shake, and at least you won't have to go far to check them out. A local agency is especially nice if it snows; your cold, wet commute will be short.

The Danielle Adams Publishing Company
Box 100, Merion Station PA 19066

Being close has other advantages, too. If you hire a nearby agency to handle your work, each trip there will be just a few minutes' commute. It'll be easy to drop stuff off and pick stuff up. It will be easier to get a quick approval of art or copy, without having to trek across town. And their travel time will be minimized, too—which will translate to lower fees, so you'll get more frequent, less costly meetings for your money.

Some of your local printers are sure to know good agencies—they get to see their artwork all the time. They also know who routinely designs brochures that are impossible to print. Better agencies and freelancers are knowledgeable in the field of advertising art. They give printers ad compositions with clear directions, good layouts that are easy to follow, and work that is realistic to print within budget.

When scouting agencies, check out brochures they've created, as well as ads. Very accomplished designers take into consideration how the art will be printed: what type of press, press size, size of print run, age and speed of presses, paper selection, and capabilities of the printer. A good designer who knows how a printed product will run on-press can be a printer's best friend, ensuring the job will run smoothly. Inexperienced artists can be a printer's (and client's) worst nightmare: designing a piece no one can print at a reasonable cost, or an ad so poorly laid out that no magazine can reproduce it. A good designer should be able to design an ad or brochure within your reasonable budget constraints.

In the old days (way back in 1985), typesetters used traditional methods of keying in copy from your longhand or typewritten original and outputting this onto special resin-coated paper or film. But I don't think there are too many old-world typesetters left anymore. About the only ones I know of are specialty type houses that offer the exotic typefaces you can't get anywhere else. Modern-day typesetters (now called service bureaus) set type from your computer disk. They print out your scanned-in graphics and output the type you've already keyed in on your computer.

The people who run this new breed of typesetting service can probably recommend a local ad agency that is creative and easy to work with: they deal with them all the time. For the most part, even with this recommendation, you'll need to assess the agency yourself. Look closely at its creative work, art, copywriting, ideas, marketing skills, and fees, and evaluate its performance. Ask about the objectives of each piece it has created, and the response each received, so you can evaluate the effectiveness of the agency's overall campaigns.

As you call around to several ad agencies, you'll get a feel for what it would be like to work with them. Getting along well with the agency is half the experience of working with it. Make sure you speak with a marketing or design person. A salesperson may not be the one to ask about marketing ideas or design; they may only be good at sales. You need to find out if the agency is good at marketing, copy, and art, while still being thrifty with your budget.

My Personal Recommendation

A freelance advertising or marketing agent may give you the best campaign, but I recommend going with a small ad agency. It's safer. Because several people will be looking over each campaign, your chances of receiving better talent and a broader range of ideas are greater than if you work with one person. In a small agency, when you have three or four people looking at your campaign, a poor idea has a chance to be rejected by one of the other players. And if there are two or three people generating ideas, you'll get more ideas and a better selection of them. Hopefully, you'll select the best of the best.

If you decide to work with an agency, my recommendation is an agency with just a few employees (three to ten). Your chances of getting the most and the best resources for high-quality suggestions and concepts for your campaign are excellent with a team of this size. Make sure you ask for everyone's input, and get it. In addition to receiving a broader range of better ideas, there is less risk of an off-the-wall concept failure. Let your agency know what risk factor to dial in for your campaign. If you want a traditional, safe campaign, let them know. If you're comfortable with higher risk—and perhaps a chance at bigger money—let them know that, too.

Having your campaign reviewed at the top level of a small ad agency is more likely than in a big agency. You have a better chance of the top team approving a quality campaign, or nixing an ineffective one. Smaller agencies can have quite a lot of talent at all levels, since the owners usually work closely with all the creative staff. In fact, at a small agency, the owners usually read and review your plan, if they don't write it themselves.

Exceptional strategic marketing plans and campaigns are out there. You can get one from an excellent agency at a reasonable price if you shop around.

Selecting an Agency, Part II

Once you figure out you really need some help with creating your ad, marketing, or a letter campaign, call at least six advertising or marketing agencies. Remember, half the agency experience is how you relate to them and how they relate to you. Give them an accurate picture of the help you may need. Tell them exactly where you are, and what you have done so far (ad concept, rough, markets researched, media assessed, press releases written, etc.).

Be specific about your needs on the phone. Ask them if they will look at your completed work, make any suggestions in case it's missing something major, and give you prices for the final typesetting and layout. When it comes to costs, make sure they are specific. Ask their hourly rate, and get an estimate, or at least an educated guess, as to what each phase will cost. Find out if they bill by the hour or on a per diem basis, and get itemized estimates for everything. If they publish a price list for their services, ask for one.

When you show your rough layout and copy to agency personnel, most will know right away if there is a glaring error. They should tell you straight out at this point, when they see it. No agency you plan to deal with should be so stingy with help they won't give you some up-front suggestions when it may be apparent to them your piece needs a change.

When I see an ad, I can spot a big mistake in about 10 seconds, maybe less. It will take me another 10 seconds to advise my client. The same applies if a firm has a big hole in its marketing plan. This 20-second review is always free. Unless you're speaking with a lawyer, a courtesy discussion is always a precursor to a good business relationship. (Lawyers have their own set of tough billing rules... which has led them to be the butt of about 50,000 lawyer jokes).

If you contract with an agency for the final layout and typesetting of your ad, it would be politically incorrect for them not to tell you about any mistakes they see. In fact, if they see an error or problem area and don't mention it, you don't want to continue working with them. All agencies should have your success foremost in their mind. If your ad works, chances are you'll come back.

Make an appointment with at least two of the best agencies you find in your phone interviews. I recommend meeting with more if you can afford the time. It's an important decision. If you have the time, see them all— you won't regret it. Bring your idea or ad, no matter what form it's in, and listen closely to the advice each agency gives you. Have them review your ad. Most small agencies have only a few people working in their shop, so if you've done your pre-screening well, chances are pretty good you'll get someone knowledgeable and creative in your first meeting.

During the meeting, the people at the agency should give you some tips to fine-tune your ad even further. If asked, they should be able to speak briefly and knowledgeably about your marketing program. So with each meeting, you'll get some valuable marketing and advertising advice—or at least you should. Good agencies that have been in the business for years aren't worried about divulging what they've learned over 20 years in a 10-minute conversation. The information just won't fit. They should give you a good sample of what they know and where they would go with your ideas, products, and concepts. Kind of like reading this book. With a background of 25+ years in marketing, I am giving you just the tip of the iceberg of what I have learned.

If the agency doesn't make at least a few specific recommendations or outline some kind of plan, consider this a big minus. While an overall marketing plan can't be established without some hard thinking over a period of several days, the first seeds of creativity should show up immediately. Make sure you speak with the person who will be working on your account and will be responsible for your ad. If that person is going to assist you in marketing, he or she will also be responsible, in part, for your success or failure. Anyone who won't give you the benefit of a few suggestions during your first meeting won't be any better in subsequent meetings—or while working on your campaign. Thank them kindly; then leave.

If an agency is too big, you'll probably be given to a salesperson who will try to close you as an account. Chances are you won't meet the "back room people" who will actually be providing your account with creative service. You weren't going to get the top staff at an agency this size for your account anyhow; the top staffers work on the big accounts.

If they really want to impress you, you'll be given a brief meeting with a bigwig at the firm. Chances are this is the first and last time you'll see him, and the last time he'll see your account. If this happens, be very direct with your questions about who in the firm will contribute to your success. If the top gun just goes over the work of some of his "hired hands," it's not a satisfactory arrangement. He'll just be editing someone else's work. Let him know you want some good, creative input into your campaign from an agency principal, not just their editing (which comes at the end). You also want more of the top banana's involvement in your success or failure— which will happen only if he personally designs the campaign himself.

Your chance of getting high-quality talent at a smaller agency is much greater. Actually, it's pretty good overall.

While at the agency, examine their samples carefully. They should have lots of ads about the size of yours. Ultimately you will be buying their effectiveness, and their style and grace in print.

_____

An ad is expensive only if it doesn't work.

_____

Ask what price the agency charged for each ad. This will give you an idea of what's in store for you, so there will be no surprises at the end. If the person you are speaking with doesn't know or can't get the pricing information, either the agency is too big or you are dealing with the wrong person. Pricing is a very fair question. You wouldn't buy a car or a bottle of perfume without knowing the price, would you? Do you want to be surprised when the agency completes your ad and gives you a bill for double what you thought it was going to be? The best way to avoid such surprises is to ask about similar ads, and insist on learning their costs.

Undoubtedly, you will hear that certain elements in an ad make it more expensive. It's true. Drop shadows on the lettering, two colors, four colors, type inside a photo, retouching, screens and tints, unique borders, long copy, direct selling ads—all take more time, and time is money. Some agencies hire special copywriters for direct selling ads. This can be very expensive (but really worth it). So ask about the cost of the ads that are similar to what you want. Most agencies will have samples of low-budget ads, and can explain costs for ads that take them longer to develop and prepare. Only by seeing each ad, poking around at all the elements of the ad, and asking what they cost, can you get an accurate idea of what you will be spending for a similar ad, brochure, or letter.

An ad is expensive only if it doesn't work. If an agency you select charges a high rate, there may be a reason. They may be consistently excellent at achieving spectacular results. The cost is only high if the ad is not effective. So don't automatically throw out all the high-cost agencies. The additional expense may be well worth the cost in terms of additional orders and larger sales.

Important: By being tough on price, I just want you to make sure you know what the price is going to be up front—and not necessarily go for the lowest bidder. Get a competitive bid. A competitive bid is not always the lowest-cost estimate. A competitive bid is a balance between cost and quality. A successful bid should simply demonstrate good value for the amount paid, while delivering superior results. The results are the bottom line.

Like a boat, some agencies can be a hole in the water into which you endlessly throw money.

The Danielle Adams Publishing Company
Box 100, Merion Station PA 19066

One more note on spending money. Be careful you don't get a low up-front bid with a big back-end bill. This is another reason to insist on seeing final prices of other ads. If your ad was quoted at $800 to $1500 and the final cost of all the other ads they show you are $1750 and up, you can suspect the worst: your ad will wind up being more expensive than the original quote.

A good agency can be instrumental to your success. But like a boat, some agencies can be a hole in the water into which you endlessly throw money. Afterward, you sink faster than the *Titanic*.

The advertising agencies you speak with may all sound good based on the sales pitch you initially get. This is why you should stay away from the agency salesperson. Be careful that the back end isn't disastrous. Shopping for an ad agency is like buying a piece of software for your computer: they all sound good up front, but you don't really know what you've got till you run with it for a while. It can be heaven, it can be hell.

While every agency has success stories I'm sure you'll hear about, they also have campaigns that made money, but only for the agency. These "other" campaigns lost money for their clients. You should hear these war stories too, but you never do. As you review ads and brochures, ask what objectives the agency set for each ad, and how the results were measured. Find out how the agency decided on objectives and benchmark criteria, and how it measured response and sales. These are key elements, and a very important part of every marketing campaign.

Only a few agencies provide clients with suggestions on how to measure results and track leads; the better ones usually build in some type of benchmarking system. Get the specific numbers for the response rates of the different ads, and the conversions to sales the leads generated. Get the number and types of inquiries from each ad. Some companies shield their agency from hard data on figures, so don't be scared off if they don't have all the answers. Poke around anyhow. Find out the results of each ad. This whole area of discussion should be designed to give you a better idea of whether the agency is results-oriented. If they handle your account, they should be concerned about your results, too.

If they show you an ad that failed, ask what they did to convert it to a successful campaign (change offer? different market? new headline?). While poor products may be the reason for the failure of some ads, if there is a preponderance of them, it's more likely the ads or placements were incorrect. You don't want your product to end up in that pile, do you?

For the most part, in a direct marketing campaign you find out that a product has failed only after it has been shipped, received by the customer, and then returned. It's easy for an agency to point to the product and say the product didn't work, but in most cases customers never even see the product until they actually receive it. It's the results of the ad or direct mail piece that show you the strength of the agency's work: the number of orders, the calls generated, and the quality and number of the inquiries and leads. If the work was good, there should have been lots of responses and orders—regardless of the product quality. (Returns of the product indicate the product wasn't good.)

When selecting an agency, be tough up front. Then, once you select an agency, be honest and open. You need a good relationship with the agency staff to get the best creative effort for your campaign. Don't always insist on the lowest cost for everything. Eventually, the best creative effort suffers—whether intentionally or unintentionally—if you do this. Nobody likes a constant fight to be paid enough money.

If you see continuously increasing fees as a consistently recurring pattern after you are involved with an agency, consider moving. Truth is, you may not need a hard-hitting (and higher-priced) agency if you come in with a tight rough of an ad, well-thought-out copy, and extensive research about your markets.

Choosing an agency is not unlike selecting a stockbroker. If you need advice or guidance, or if you're not sure doing it all yourself will really be in your best interest, select a full-service firm. Discuss ideas with them and let them make recommendations. Have them look over your shoulder, and ask them to protect you from mistakes. On the other hand, if you know what you want, and just need a broker to make a purchase for you, a discount house will be cheaper, and this may be all you need.

Buying creative services is not like buying a ream of paper or a pound of potatoes. If you need the agency to create the ad or direct mail campaign (not just set the type and give you a simple copy tune-up), remember it takes work, time, research, creativity, and inspiration to produce great ads and direct mail literature. Give the agency enough background about your product's uses, features, benefits, and markets. Then give them enough direction to let them know what you would like. Finally, give them enough freedom to generate and develop their best ideas for your approval.

BUT—and like my Aunt Mildred's, this is a big "but"—always keep in mind that if an ad fails, it's your money that was spent and lost. So if you don't like the direction the agency is taking, let them know—and the sooner the better. If a campaign fails, no one will come to you and say it was your agency's fault. It's ultimately your responsibility to make whatever you are marketing a success.

The good news: If a campaign is a success, you don't give the agency one red cent more for creating a winning package. Just as they don't take a loss in a product failure, they are not your financial partner in a success. Remember this when you receive their bill, which may come way before you find out if the quality of their work was excellent.

It's in your best interest to develop a good relationship with an agency or marketing firm that understands its sole function is to make you a success. Having an advertising agency that truly wants to contribute to your success and turns in an inspired example of its best work will be more likely if you cultivate a good relationship. Consideration must be shown on both sides in order to develop a package that works toward your common goal: maximizing the response and sales of your campaign.

Conclusion

Ads are the logical conclusion to a successful PR campaign. You now have an outline and action plan of several elements and levels that can be used in an ad concept or direct mail campaign. You should also have an idea of what to expect from, and how to work with, an agency if you decide to use one. If you buy the services of an agency that doesn't know what the heck it's doing, use these methods to either direct its people, guide them, show them the opportunities outlined, or give them the boot. Find another agency at the first signs of failure.

As I mentioned at the beginning of the chapter, all my ads say the same thing: call, write, or come in. If a prospect doesn't call, write, or come in, we didn't get his business. These are the only reasons to advertise: to get business, and to make a profit. No ego trips. Not to see your name in print, or in a particular magazine. No institutional ads to "let people know you're out there." Look over your finished ad—does it make the reader want to call? Does it entice him to come in? Is it so powerful he can't put it down? Does it drive him to pick up a pen and write to you for more information or product literature? Or pick up the phone and place an order? Does it fulfill its mission?

Creative Sessions

No matter what you are writing, there are procedures to help you be more productive and get more from your creative process.

Rule number one: When creating copy, write everything down. Creating headlines? Write them all down—even the silly ones. This will clarify your ideas. A headline that doesn't look good now may look better later. Some ideas look better in print. This is the time to get your creative juices flowing, so write down every single idea you think of, no matter how terrible it initially sounds. Do not obstruct your creative thinking process by stopping the flow of ideas, which is what happens when you edit. Generating ideas while saying, "No, this one is silly," or "No, that one won't work!" will stop the flow.

Let all of your words (and ideas) flow out onto your paper in this part of the creative process. Just keep writing everything down. You should have a couple of pages of headlines, ideas for body copy, transitional phrases, and fragments of sentences and ideas. And you should be in a mild sweat when you are through. Fill up at least one page, maybe two. Then take a break. Eat. Watch a movie. Go for a ride. Then come back to this a little later, after your subconscious has had a chance to think about it. Continue writing from the fresh perspective and directions your break allows you to see. This break may seem trivial, but it is a very necessary part of the process.

The Danielle Adams Publishing Company
Box 100, Merion Station PA 19066

Of course, nothing works with the TV on, even if it's only in the background.

When you get stuck, a creative technique I use is to ask "And what else? And what else?" 10, 20 times or so. Then sit there quietly for another couple of minutes. Write down anything that comes into your head. Then put your pen down and get away for a while. Again, let your subconscious have another whack at it without your conscious help.

Over the next few hours, or few days, bring the subject to the forefront of your mind once or twice an hour. Tape a sign to your TV or your refrigerator. So whenever you walk by, you bring the subject to the front of your mind, and think about it for a moment. This opens the pathway between your conscious and subconscious and allows them to talk.

You'll find ideas pop into your head when you least expect them. This is your subconscious talking to you; write these ideas down no matter where you are. Keep a pen by the bed, and in the car. Finally, transpose all the ideas to the paper you were working on. This technique works, and you will find throughout the day and night you will be having more and more ideas. Of course, nothing works with the TV on, even if it's only in the background.

When writing, just start writing. Even if you can't think of anything good—just start writing anything. Still stuck? Write a letter to your friends. Write down old recipes, list all your clothing, name all your high school friends, anything. Just start writing. It's like ketchup: once you begin, the ideas will start pouring out. So just start anywhere, and after a few minutes, start to direct your writing to be of your product. Write as if you were speaking to a friend and telling them about the benefits about your new product. Make notes of new ideas when they come to mind. Start tuning in, focusing on your product, its features and benefits. In another half an hour or so, you should be writing ideas and copy profusely; your pen may not able to keep up with all the ideas your mind is generating.

Then at your leisure, over the next few days, sift through all these ideas and fragments of sentences to get to your final selections. Start organizing this into copy: the crystal-clear line that shines well above all the rest will become the headline of your ad; the important parts will be the beginning of the letter of your direct mail piece. Then edit and polish. Write and rewrite. It takes time to polish and refine your writing, but in the end it'll be worth it. When people see your ad or letter they won't ask how long it took you to write the letter, they'll just order your product.

Best trick in copywriting I've ever learned:

After you're done, go back and cross out the first line of your first paragraph—that will usually pull you through the wishy-washy part and directly into the heart of what you're saying. If you really had a bad start, go back and cross out the first few lines... or the first paragraph. Nice trick, a?

I wish someone had taught me these ideas a few years ago. Heck, I wish someone had taught me all of this a few years ago. Hey, if you like this book buy it for someone, or tell a friend to get it. It'll make their day, and perhaps help them with their success. Thanks.

Many people have asked me about protection when submitting an idea or product to a firm who may want to license it market it. No piece of paper even comes close to keeping you safe - and I've never seen a sheet of paper stop a crook. We use the document on the following page as it is better than nothing (but not much!). It just keeps people honest! Please feel free to use it, but contact your attorney and ask their opinion first.

The Danielle Adams Publishing Company
Box 100, Merion Station PA 19066

~ **Non-Disclosure Agreement** ~

Whereas Jeffrey Dobkin T/A Jeffrey Dobkin and Associates, and the Danielle Adams Publishing Company (hereinafter called LICENSOR) has in its possession certain proprietary, confidential and valuable business information, opportunities, drawings, designs, inventions, letters, patent information, and/or other information deemed to be trade secrets which is the sole property of the owner for the SPECIFIC product "_____."

Whereas _____(hereinafter called Licensee) hereby agrees that in consideration for access to information submitted to Licensee by Jeffrey Dobkin for the purpose of exploring potential business products and business relations between Jeffrey Dobkin and Licensee, Licensee and its employees and affiliates will:

1. Keep all information relative to concept, prototype, machinery, equipment, models, drawings, discussions and printed materials in confidence.

2. Disclose this information to individuals or companies on a need-to-know basis only, for the sole purpose of receiving manufacturing quotations.

3. Not contract with or make any agreement with anyone outside Licensor regarding the development or marketing of this idea without Licensor's prior written approval.

4. Licensee, it's owners, directors, stockholders, officers, employees and/or agents shall not use either directly or indirectly any such information provided by Mr. Dobkin for this product for the personal benefit of any employee, person, persons, Licensee's firm or any other person or corporation without Licensor's written permission.

5. In the event of a breach of this contract, the injured party reserves the right to collect court costs and attorney's fees if this matter goes to court or arbitration.

6. This Agreement shall be constructed in accordance with the laws of the state of Pennsylvania, and contains the entire understanding of the parties hereto.

Understood and agreed this day of _____

Agreed and Accepted for
Licensee_____(Signature)
Print
Name_____Title_____
Firm_____
Address_____
_____
Telephone_____ Fax _____

~ The Campaign ~

To launch your product, follow this effective marketing campaign in the print media on a national basis. As promised, it will cost be low in cost. But you can add value and enhancements at any time. Use these ideas as a springboard for your own campaign tailored to your company's unique objectives and style.

~ **The Ultimate Campaign** ~

Overview

In the chapter on free press, you read how to prepare a press release and submit it with the greatest chance of having it printed in a magazine. In the "Marketing through Magazines" chapter, you learned how to define your markets, and select the magazines in those markets that most closely coincide with your exact audience. In the "Direct Mail" chapter, you learned the value of letters; not only how to write one, but also how to design one. So you've really seen all the pieces of this campaign. Now we'll put all the parts together and see how effective we can be.

The ultimate use of these components is the ultimate campaign: an action plan composed of press releases and direct mail. With a small amount of capital and some time you can achieve a good number of high quality leads and achieve some decent sales. Start with these effective marketing techniques to find and pinpoint your markets, and send press releases. After testing the media with press releases, place ads in the magazines that worked best.

For those of you in a hurry, this campaign may be supplemented with phone calls. Since I hate making telephone sales calls myself, the actual campaign outlined doesn't use any. Since not everyone has my call reluctance, if you like to make calls do so at any time, although I suggest you wait. Here's the reason why.

The Worst Mistake in Marketing

There's a mighty big mistake made by 95 percent of the firms in America. Almost every firm that calls me for a marketing consultation makes this mistake. You can save yourself my consulting fees by reading this chapter. Don't you make this mistake, too.

How many times have I seen it? An inquiry comes in by mail from a highly qualified prospect. Or a serious inquiry comes in by phone about the firm's product or service. It may even be one of their very best prospects from a mailing they've recently sent. What do they do? They send a letter with a brochure. They call a week later and when the prospect fails to make an immediate purchase, they never contact him again. Some people call that a campaign. Then they wonder why their marketing program failed to generate sales.

A letter and brochure are not a campaign.

It's tragic: 95 percent of the firms marketing products make this mistake, following the same exact procedure. They acquire a quality sales lead through an ad or press release. They send a brochure, and perhaps a cover letter with it. Then they wait a week and call - and work on the front end, for a single phone call. Then nothing.

A letter and brochure are not a campaign. A campaign is not a single attempt of anything. A campaign is a selling effort sustained over time. It has frequency. It has depth. It is a repeated series of friendly contacts. Why do you think it's called a campaign? A campaign has multiple exposures of your name, ad, or offer. Repetition, by definition, is a necessary part of any campaign.

The reason to wait before calling your prospects deeper in the campaign is so you are not put in the boat with the thousands of other firms that make this marketing blunder. The marketing technique used in this book is *multiple exposure marketing*. Through consistent use of direct mail, you avoid the #1 marketing error: a single contact. We use a form of frequency or relational marketing that is "repeated friendly communication."

You've probably heard there are a number of contacts needed to sell a product. Five sales calls. Three ads in a magazine. Prospects must see your name seven times before they will buy. Bull. Everybody can't be right. There is no set number. But I can tell you each additional exposure helps build credibility and increases the chance for a sale exponentially. In the real-world industrial marketplace, the price of a personal sales call is about $225, and it usually takes several to secure any large sale. Why people expect results any sooner, better, or faster from a letter, brochure and a phone call is beyond me. The results from a print campaign won't come any quicker, but positive results will be easier to achieve with consistent written communication laying the groundwork for you.

With this campaign, your sales calls are made for you up front, in the form of a series of letters. You have the opportunity to be different; to prove yourself, your worth, and your diligence before you ever speak to your potential customers. Then, when you do speak to them, they already know you and your firm. They know you have attention to detail and good follow-up. They have seen you will be a reputable and reliable firm with which to do business. And faithful at customer service. All this will be known to your prospects before you make that first phone call. If you wait until you've written a few letters, you will be well received when you call, and you'll get the warm welcome of a friend.

Another reason to wait: If you expand this campaign to 5,000 (or 50,000) prospects, you'll have a hell of a phone bill if you call them all. It'll take months. But with this letter campaign, you can contact them all simultaneously, repeatedly. Call only the people who respond to your direct mail package.

When you start marketing your product, while you may have some immediate sales, there is no campaign that happens instantly. Sure, you can achieve some excellent results right away. But for a deep market penetration, it probably will take a year or more. So if you thought your idea would be on the consumer's shelf by the summer, think next summer.

Getting rich instantly has a nice sound to it, but it takes preparation and solid execution to create a demand for a new product in a competitive marketplace. It takes three months just to get a press release to appear in a magazine. After that, there is time needed for correspondence and negotiations. Wholesalers need time to make up their own flyers or selling sheets to show your product through their own link in the distribution chain.

Catalog houses need time to prepare photo shoots and product copy. On the manufacturing side, you need time to get your product created (tooling, molds, dies, whatever). It takes time to create copy and graphics for ads, letters, and direct mail packages, as well as retail packaging. Add to this, time for the product to be transported to the retailers' shelves. And...well, you get the idea. It just takes time. Everything takes time.

One way to shorten this time is to buy help. You can make things happen much faster with hired help, and with specialty firms to take sections of the workload off your hands. Certainly, lead times are shorter if you already market a product and have the distribution system in place. Or have all the marketing completed with letters and brochures, and names and addresses already on your computer and ready to mail.

I mention all this because you should have a realistic time perspective. I've never gone into the office of a client who has shown me a new product and thought it would take 2 full years to bring it to market. Everyone has always thought it was going to be on the market within a few months, and the money would come rushing in. In a few months you can initiate your main campaign and, if you're lucky, make some nice sales; but to make a serious dent in a big market with good penetration, it takes longer.

The Ultimate Campaign—Part I

OK, let's get busy. Every campaign begins by defining the marketing universe: on a blank sheet of paper list all the people or businesses who may purchase your product or service. Now rank them in descending order. You've got to know who your absolute best potential buyers are before you can figure out how to reach them. Then, it's back to the library.

Once in the library, find a seat next to the most beautiful woman (or man) in the place. No matter how hard you're trying to work, it's always nice to have an attractive distraction nearby: it makes the research more enjoyable and the time go faster. Now get to work: get one of the directories for trade magazines such as Bacon's publicity directories or Oxbridge Communications' *National Directory of Magazines*, or any of the other reference tools described in the marketing chapter.

Perform the necessary research on your markets as outlined in the "Marketing through Magazines" chapter to abstract a press release list.

The Danielle Adams Publishing Company
Box 100, Merion Station PA 19066

Draft your press release in correct form, as described in the "Free Press" chapter. The number of markets you are penetrating, and the size of each of those individual markets, will determine the number of magazines you are going to contact. All this information will determine the number of press releases you are going to send out to receive favorable write-ups.

Make copies of the pages that refer to your targeted industries so you can have them as your own personal reference, and mark them up as needed. Analyze the magazines as outlined in the "Marketing through Magazines" chapter. Devise A and B press lists. For each magazine on the A list, call the editor and notify him you are sending a press release, as detailed in the "Free Press" chapter. Magazines on the B list just get releases, unless you enjoy making calls - then call these editors too.

With a bit of creativity the plan outlined here has an excellent chance of successfully (and profitably) marketing a product. It's been the basis of successful campaigns for myself and many clients over the years.

For success to depend on free media write-ups from press releases your magazine your A list must be very strong. This will ensure you will get published in as many magazines as possible. You should call as many magazines as you can, so your release will get published in as wide a magazine distribution schedule within your markets as possible.

The Press Campaign

To begin a press campaign, section out about 80 magazines from which you'd like to receive free publicity. Let's just say you are going to call 20 magazine editors before sending them releases, and send another 60 in the blind faith they may be published. You should call more editors if you don't mind phone work; I'd recommend calling about 40 for more complete campaign coverage, or as many as you can if you are good on the phone and comfortable with bigger numbers.

Before speaking to the editor, ask the person answering the phone for a media kit along with several sample copies of the magazine, and any annual or directory issue the magazine may publish. Be sure to get the correct spelling of the editor's name now, so you won't have to get it from the editor himself and make that part of the call unnecessarily long and boring to him. (Editors stay pretty busy and will appreciate this.) For any journals that will be important to your long-term marketing, tell the operator to have a salesperson from the magazine call you, then have them transfer you to the editor. Give the editor your two-minute pitch as outlined in the "Free Press" chapter.

The directory will be a free, up-to-date mailing list of the big manufacturers' and distributors' names and addresses.

When the salespeople call you back, tell them you're entering their market, and have them start a free subscription of their magazine to you. Also ask them if they have a directory issue that will list the people or businesses to whom you will be marketing. Mention you are considering taking an ad out in the directory, and ask if they will send an advertiser's checking copy (for free). I've never been turned down with this request. The directory will be a free, more or less up-to-date mailing list of the names and addresses of the big manufacturers and distributors in the industry.

You'll need a photo of your product, so call around to various local photographers. Get a good, crisp 5" x 7" black-and-white product shot.

Have contact prints made. You can get them at a local photo lab, or use the one I use—Quaker Photo in Philadelphia. From your black-and-white print, Quaker will machine-make 100 quantity contact prints for about 70 bucks. You don't have to use these folks, but if you do, call first to make sure these prices are still current. You also can take these prices to your local photo lab and see if they'll match them.

Write a quality press release as outlined in the "Free Press" chapter, and a convincing "Thanks for publishing our press release" letter to go with it. Don't forget, the letters to editors whom you've called should be personalized with the name and address of the editor. Make a brief reference to your call at the beginning of the letter ("Thanks for receiving my call, it was a pleasure speaking with you..."). If you can personalize the other letters with the editors' names, it's worth the effort to do so. Mentioning the name of the column or magazine section in which your release is to appear is also a big plus. Now, armed and dangerous with releases, photos, and letters, lighten your load by putting them all in the mail.

Except for the typing of the individual editors' names and addresses, and printing the letters, that wasn't too bad. If editors consider your press releases newsworthy, you can expect to see the releases published in about three to six months. It's always exciting to see your name in print.

The Campaign—Part II

This is where that lengthy chapter on direct mail comes in, and the especially long-winded part on letters.

During the next three months, while waiting for the press releases to appear, take those directory issues the magazine salespeople sent you and start compiling a house mailing list of your very best prospects—about 100 of them (200 if you are interested in a larger campaign, 5,000 if you own a big company). The best prospects are those who represent large sales figures if you secure a sale from them. Put these people on your mailing list. If you have other people who should be on this list, by all means, include them. If you are marketing to catalog houses who may be interested in carrying your products in their catalogs, include them on this list, also.

Here's the heart of the campaign. This is where that lengthy chapter on direct mail comes in, and the especially long-winded part on letters. The campaign is a series of letters. Over the next six to eight months you will be sending your best prospects about a dozen letters.

The good news of this campaign is that you only have to write 12 great letters. The bad news is that they all have to be printed out 100 times–or however many people you have on your mailing list. But hey, that's not really too bad.

In a more traditional campaign, you'd be writing one letter here, one letter there. Each person you'd speak with would get a letter, and by the time you sent correspondence to all your best prospects you'd not only have sent hundreds of letters, you'd have written hundreds of different letters. In this campaign, your initial 100 prospects all get the same letter series. Writing all the letters up front in a planned program of correspondence initially seems like more work, but ultimately it saves you a lot of time, work, and effort over the course of the campaign.

Letters should be perfectly crafted. To invoke a response from decision-makers at major companies for large sales, you have to do some careful work. Hey, I didn't say the campaign would be easy, I just said it would be cheap. Quit complaining.

But really, to whom would you rather spend time writing? Isn't writing to your *very* best prospects worth your time and effort? (If you answered anything but an unequivocal yes, you'd better realign your thinking.) At the end of the campaign, you should have closed at least a few accounts, probably more, and no cold calls.

I hesitate to tell you what some of the campaigns I've created for clients bring in, because so much depends on the list, the products, and the offer. However, it's possible to bring in a 25 percent response rate, and the campaign can produce a higher hit rate if you follow up with a call after four or five letters.

If you want to follow up your letters with phone calls, you definitely will close more sales. But ugh, I hate making calls, and I deal pretty poorly with rejection. Actually, that's how this campaign started. I wanted an action plan that would work without making cold calls. In this campaign, you simply wait for customers to call. And they will. Just be patient.

At the end of some letter campaigns I have surveyed customers and the universal response to the letters has always been the same: recipients are exceptionally friendly. Even if they don't buy my products, they always remember me and have good things to say. After I wrote one person about four or five letters, he called me—just to tell me that even though he sold his company, he liked my campaign so much he wanted to tell me. He even thanked me for writing to him.

By the way, if you do make follow-up calls and get screened by a secretary who asks what you want to speak with the person about, don't say "our product." Instead say, "It's about the letter I have written him." Your call should go right through. Use this technique any time your call is blocked.

The Structure of the Letters

Since you've already read the lengthy dissertation on how to construct a letter, I won't bore you with that again. But the tone of the letters (which are fully personalized with the recipient's name and address in the salutation) is different from commercial letters of mass mailings that begin "Dear Reader."

In the letters for this campaign, talk directly to the person you are mailing to. They really are personal letters you're sending—one to one. No one knows you're sending them to anyone else (not to mention to a few hundred to a few thousand other people). The tone is politely friendly. The objective is to encourage a response; the first letter just sets up a favorable future contact. Initially you just want to get noticed in a positive way—so your letter is almost too polite, too quiet and understated. A harder sell, with a more focused selling effort, will come later.

Your copy platform for the first letter is friendly as usual, introducing yourself and your product to the reader. Inform him, "We make a quality product, sell it at a fair market price, and provide exceptionally fine service." Mention that your firm is dedicated to excellence in customer satisfaction. State a few of the benefits of owning or using the product or service you are selling.

If your letter runs over one page in length (remember, use a lot of white space in the margins so it looks easy to read), use a second sheet, not the back of the page—this is a personal letter. To save time and effort, the second page doesn't need to have the person's name on the top, it can just simply say, "Page Two." This way, instead of running it through your computer printer, which is probably slow and time-consuming, you can just make one computer printout of page two and copy it on a high-quality photocopier for the other recipients in the campaign.

If you are going to call the reader, say so at the conclusion of the letter so he will know to (1) read the letter again so he can speak intelligently about it when you call, or (2) warn his secretary to fend you off when you call.

Make sure the final photocopied second sheet doesn't look like a photocopy, as this will destroy the whole image of "This is a personal letter from me to you, and you are the only one receiving it." If your copier can't make perfect copies, and I mean perfect copies, take it to a quick copy shop or printer. This is important. If the second page doesn't look like the first page, take the time to print it on your computer to be sure of a perfect match. It must look perfect.

The letter concludes with "Thank you for your time, and please call with any questions. Or use the postpaid reply card for more information." It's a soft sell. Feel out the market and fish for an early response. Make sure the post card also has a space recipients can check if they would like to remain on your mailing list. On the face of the post card, put your name and address and a live first class postage stamp. If recipients do not send in this card, it will lie on their desk for about a week—maybe longer—while they try to figure out what to do with a live stamp on a post card addressed to you.

Always try to include a reply vehicle to make the response easier. Included are several samples; please feel free to use them.

____Yes! I'm Interested!

____Please send a free sample -
          and have your representative contact me.
____Please send additional literature.
____ Current interest ____ Immediate need ____ File only
    ____Please keep me on your mailing list. ____Just Curious.

Name _____

Business _____

Address _____

City, St, Zip_____

Telephone _____

                ____Oh, no. Please remove me from your mailing list.

_____**Yes! Please Call!**

Have your representative contact me ASAP.

_____ Please send literature.

_____ I have an immediate need. _____ File only.

_____ Just curious. _____ Please keep me on your mailing list.

Name _____

Business _____

Address _____

City, St, Zip_____

Telephone _____

_____ Save the postage. Please remove me from your mailing list.

____ **Please keep me on your mailing list!**

__ No thank you. We are not interested in saving money at this time.

_____ Please send additional literature.

_____ Current interest. _____ Just curious.

Name _____

Business _____

Address _____

City, St, Zip _____

Telephone _____

_____ Please remove me from your mailing list.

The Danielle Adams Publishing Company
Box 100, Merion Station PA 19066

Remember, the primary objective of this letter is to generate a call, it is not to sell your product... so do NOT try to sell your product. You are the only one who knows you will be writing these lucky people again at a later time, so the secondary objective of this first letter is a bit unusual—it is to get noticed, and whet their appetite for your product. Of course, it would be great if they expressed an early interest—that's why you send the post card. But don't bet the ranch on early returns. Just make sure recipients know who you are. As you conclude your letter, let them know you look forward to working with them and you hope to hear from them soon. About two weeks later you are going to follow up your letter with another mailing piece. And every two to three weeks after that.

If you are going to call the reader, say so at the conclusion of the letter you send just before you call, so he will know to (1) read the letter again so he can speak intelligently about it when you call, or (2) warn his secretary to fend you off when you call. But I'd save the call until after your recipient gets about five letters. As I've mentioned, most salespeople write a letter, send a brochure, and then call. If they don't get anywhere at that point, they move on to someone else. We aren't going to do that. Give the campaign a better chance to work.

Data Sheet or Brochure

If you are selling a product, it's most advantageous to list the features in a brochure. (The benefits go in the letter, the features in a brochure.) You can create a handsome brochure or simply list your features in a "spec sheet" or "data sheet" and include it with the letter. A data sheet looks just great in black and white.

Use anything you have in your arsenal of printed literature that will make your firm look solid and reputable. But if you don't have anything in the way of current literature to send, that's OK too.

Because of time or money shortages, or in between press runs of brochures, some firms include a press release. I don't recommend this. I've never seen a press release that says exactly what I would want to say to a prospective customer. While your new product introduction may be news, you can show more benefits in a letter, and you can show ALL the features in a brochure or data sheet. Additionally, you can orient your letters and specifications to make the customer call you. A press release is not written to this end.

Creating the Letter Series

Spend several days on the letter writing, design, and layout. Spend more if you need it. Remember the letter is your ad, your product salesman, your brochure, and your chance to acquaint your prospects with your product and your firm, overcome their buying objections, get them excited, and make a sale all wrapped up in one or two pages. It's worth the extra time. Make sure you follow the letter-writing guidelines in the "Direct Mail" chapter. Even if it takes you two or three weeks to write and design the letter to perfection, it will be worth it. Even if it takes a month or more for the first one, no one will know it took so much time; they will just see a perfect letter. Take your time. The subsequent letters will go much faster. Practice makes speed.

After you send your first letter, don't be surprised if no one writes or calls just yet. It's early. The second letter starts out with a reference to the earlier correspondence: "Several weeks ago I wrote to you saying how our product was..." followed by your biggest benefit. Continue with "I'd like to now address an additional benefit I have not mentioned...." Now feel free to describe more benefits.

Make it short and crisp. You've already driven your point home by sending the second letter. They'll remember. If not, they will by the third letter. So soft-sell. Show the benefits; if there is time, restructure the spec sheet so it looks new (if not, just include the same one); and soft-sell the response. If your product lends itself to sampling, continue, "Just send in the postage-paid card and we'll be pleased to send a sample to your home or office free of charge."

Maintain a conversational tone, just like when you speak. To make it easier to respond, include a post card. Say their call is welcome, and give a phone number in the body of the letter. I know, it's already in the letterhead, but this will drive home the objective of *calling you* even further. Most of all, the point of this part of the campaign is to maintain consistent, friendly contact, and build a relationship by way of your letters. This is the basis of truly outstanding direct response marketing.

By the third or fourth letter, you can begin to get more serious about getting a response. As the second letter did, the third letter usually takes people completely by surprise. You've introduced yourself in the first letter.

You've started to show you're serious in the second letter. The third letter confirms it. Refer to the previous two pieces of correspondence early in the letter. Start to paint a picture of your firm as a responsive partner in business, that will be a pleasure to work with. State you are offering a quality product, with strong guarantees, and mention that you hope they can see you are dedicated to excellence in customer service. Orient the benefits toward working with your company, and remember—there are still six or seven letters left, so you can take a slower sales pace.

If you're really in a hurry, send letters every two weeks. If you can afford the luxury of time, wait three weeks to a month before sending the next letter. Ideally, the time between the first and second letters is two weeks, with subsequent letters sent every three weeks. After about the fifth letter, everyone will know who you are. If you'd like to call some of these prospects to test the response of the campaign, this is a good time. You can see why it's important to direct this correspondence to a correctly spelled name of a person who can order or test your products and can make the decision to purchase. In a campaign with this much depth (but little cost), you should be sure you are mailing to the right person.

"We'd like your business. As you can see, we are willing to earn it. Over the past three months I have written you several letters; I hope you have enjoyed receiving them. I also hope you can see we are a firm worth looking at and doing business with." Continue, "We produce a quality product, delivered in a timely fashion, at a fair price. I know in our own business we value our better vendors as much as our customers. I hope we may be privileged to serve you...." Over the next several letters the sell gets slightly harder. The push gets more direct. But still maintain that one-to-one relationship in your letters. By this time you should have one or two favorable responses, but be prepared not to have any. It depends on what you're selling, and on how many typos and spelling errors you have in your letters.

Handling a Mistake in Print

Even if you discover a spelling error in a previous piece of correspondence, it's not something that can't be overcome. With all the writing I do, and even with all the proofreading I ask my associates and friends to do for me, errors still occur and slip out. As in all your writing, just be frank and honest.

Turn your spelling error into a positive about your company and products.

When a typo got out in one campaign of a client of mine, it still turned out OK. I wrote copy for him addressing the error in the next letter: "Just a day or two ago I was reviewing all the correspondence I sent to you over the last few months (all those spelling errors—ugh!) and I wanted to let you know that while it takes an owner like myself to mess things up, our production people do a much better job. We have over a dozen quality checks before our finished product gets through the line. We're not perfect, but we're close."

Turn your spelling error into a positive about your company and products. Go through your quality control procedures in the letter. "Since all our work is predicated on the correct product and prompt shipping, before any order goes out it's checked on paper, and checked again at a final product inspection. This is a luxury my letters don't have. The policy of our firm is to ship perfect quality parts, backed by continuing, complete dedication to excellence in customer service." So the minus became a plus. Sometimes typos just get out; don't let that stop you or discourage you from continuing your campaign.

Don't get discouraged, even if you have no response late in the campaign. By the tenth letter, your prospects know you pretty well. I would think you should have some solid and highly qualified responses from your mailing list. But, it depends on what you're selling. Since these recipients represent your largest customers, I would think a single sale would be great. A 2 percent response would certainly be excellent. The sale of your product will be substantial to these larger prospects, and one sale may pay for the whole campaign, and more.

As you approach the eighth, ninth, or tenth letter, stress a strong call to action. "I have enjoyed writing to you, but all good things must come to an end. Without your encouragement, our campaign to win you over as a customer and friend will end with this letter. I hope through my correspondence you have come to understand the way we run our business...."

Continue later in the letter with a harder sell: "Now I ask you only to send in this card—or call—to keep receiving my correspondence—and staying abreast of what's new at our company. Of course, if you'd like to do business with us I'd be delighted. Our diligence and attention to detail is not just limited to my letters. I'm sure you will be more than pleased with business as conducted by our firm." Continue, "I hope you will allow me the opportunity to continue to correspond, and you will call—or send in the enclosed card. Your personal request is the only way I can continue to devote my attention to those interested in our firm, our products, and what we have to say."

As your last letter approaches and you make a final stand, you can also inform the recipient if you are going to call. In your letter, say it in the very first line—or better yet, make this your whole top paragraph: "It's been a pleasure writing to you. Next week, I'm going to call." You can also use a longer variation of this in a form that would appear in the close of your letter: "Just as all good things must end, this is my last letter to win you over as a customer and a friend. Next week, I'd like to speak with you in person on the phone. I hope you can see I've tried to earn this privilege."

To the prospects who don't purchase, leave the door open for a later sale. Write them every few months to stay in their minds. Even a post card is fine; they'll remember the campaign. Conclude by informing them that the purpose of your letters was to show them how you run your business or company; how diligent you are not only with your product, but with your customer service as well. And how you offer them an opportunity to conduct business with your fine firm on a long-term basis. Use a strong call to action to make them send back the reply card. If you can travel, the last letter in your campaign is the time to set up an appointment for face-to-face selling. If not, a call would be in order. But either way, this campaign will open significant doors.

This campaign is a best bet in turning a prospect into a customer, who will recognize your name, company, and product. It is also an excellent way to set up a personal sales call. Not a bad investment for $5 (what we spent on postage for each prospect). So far, you've gotten the attention of an entire industry with your press releases, and the eyes and ears of the largest potential clients you could find. I don't think you can do any better than that with the tight budget you used - or an open budget.

You can, of course, apply this same campaign to a wider audience, and not change a thing. I'd recommend this. Also, there is a surefire extension of this campaign when you have prospects you know are worth the additional money—the Pen Campaign. You can purchase this in the form of the actual series of letters. Just fill in the prospect's name, purchase the pens, and mail. It's easy, since the letters are already written for you. It's kind of instant marketing, just add your own prospects.

To change the campaign around, it's possible to add a few post cards into the mix of your mailings. Post cards are easy to handle and easier to address and mail than letters. They still keep you in top of mind awareness. While you can't get personal with post cards, they serve a different purpose: they can scream out your best benefits and product features without sounding obnoxious like it would in a personal letter.

Four color post cards are now available reasonably priced from a multitude of vendors who offer them with the fast service of a three or five day turnaround. Shop around, great prices are out there.

Back at the press release campaign, by the time you have finished writing all the letters and have started sending them out, your press release campaign should be kicking in and you should be getting a good mix of responses from the different magazines. Don't forget, a single letter and brochure isn't the solution to closing sales with these folks either. You can adapt this letter campaign to a shortened form, depending on the value of each person's response to the press releases that were published.

A single, overbearingly long letter can be more than enough, but when this same copy is sent in two or three individual letters, it can be a substantial part of an effective campaign.

With the lesser value of prospects who responded to the press releases through reader service cards from magazines (but also depending on how the lead came in, and whom it's from), an abbreviated series of printed, but not personalized, direct mail letters may be used with excellent results. Keep these printed letters interesting, and shorter. Better to be too short than too long. Too short gets read, too long gets trashed.

Always keep in mind one letter and a brochure is not a campaign, and certainly not an effective campaign. A single, overbearingly long letter can be more than enough (and not in a good way), but when this same copy is sent in two or three individual letters, it can capture your customer's interest and be a substantial part of an effective campaign. For the extra 42 cents, or whatever the cost of an additional stamp is these days, it's well worth sending the letter in two parts.

This series of direct mail letters, along with the press release campaign, is the basis for this book and the heart of the marketing program I endorse so strongly. The techniques should produce numerous leads from the magazine write-ups. You can hand-pick the higher quality leads for volume sales, and section out these customers for the more in-depth letter campaign. The program can be adapted to just about any company, any offer, and any industry or market.

Money is not the determining factor in the successful marketing of a product.

This chapter presents a coherent <u>plan of action</u> for showing your company in a unique light. It demonstrates a well-thought-out campaign, and that your firm is reliable, customer oriented and diligent in the detail of follow-through. Everyone likes a firm that is easy to deal with, and provides prompt responses to phone calls, questions, and inquiries. Cost isn't always everything in a product, or even a good basis for purchasing, or for a solid business relationship. Money is not the determining factor in the successful marketing of a product. If price were the sole determinant of the purchasing function in every business, many high-priced products would be off the market, and many large firms out of business.

Keep in mind that the letter campaign can be adapted to new prospects and companies at any time. Once you have written the letters, if you see a new name in the marketplace or in one of the trade journals and it looks like the person will be a good bet as a customer, start sending letters from the beginning of the campaign.

Once you have already written the letters, you can add people at any time to receive the same series. You just have to keep a log of what went to whom and when; so the series will be sent in order, and in a timely fashion.

Also remember, direct mail is a game of numbers. Whether you are sending one letter to 100, 1,000, or 1 million people, most of the people

---

The Danielle Adams Publishing Company
Box 100, Merion Station PA 19066

who get your mailpiece won't respond. Some won't need your product. Some will be sleeping with their current vendor. And some of your mail will consistently be diverted, while still more will be directed to the wrong person. These are facts of life in direct marketing.

The purpose and intent of this book is to create a campaign of sufficient breadth to elicit a positive response, enough to pay for the campaign. After the response is created, your real success begins: taking orders and cashing checks. As in any campaign, you have to balance the value of the responses you get, the conversion of those individual responses to sales, and the amount each sale is worth in terms of profit, cost, and risk, with the amount of work you must do to secure these sales. Fortunately, this campaign involves little work other than the initial writing of the release and the letters, about 15 pages total. There is less of a cash investment than in any other campaign I have ever seen, and therefore a very small amount of cost and risk. Is it a lot of work? Yea, it is. You didn't this would be without work or effort, did you?

Constantly analyze your markets and the people to whom you are writing. Only then can you make an intelligent decision as to whether this campaign, with all its depth, will bring in enough profit to completely cover the cost and effort. Direct marketing, when played correctly, is a game of sending ever-increasing numbers of mailings to larger and larger lists. If successful with your initial campaign, you will constantly mail more and better packages, leaning toward your responsive markets since they are the source of profit. This is direct marketing.

Even after reading this chapter over a dozen times (ugh), I still can't think of anyone I'd rather write a series of business letters to, or wage a precisely targeted direct mail campaign at, than my very best hand-picked list of my largest potential customers. This campaign has been a successful formula for many clients, and I know it will work for you. Positive marketing through multiple exposures. Throw a loose qualification net. Achieve a strong pre-sales condition before you even speak with the customer. By the time you call someone, the prospect has been pre-qualified—pre-sold— and your contact is to confirm the delivery of your service or goods and answer any final questions.

Conclusion

Throughout this book, I have tried to outline a series of marketing guidelines to help you initiate or enhance any sales campaign. The ultimate goal is to assist my fellow entrepreneurs and business owners in their marketing. I hope I have shown you several unique, low-cost ways to find your marketing niche. I also hope I have shown you how easy it is to find both old and new markets, and professionally market any product.

Now, I'd just like to say a few words of a more personal nature. If you purchased this book for the business knowledge it can give you, you don't have to read the remainder of the text. The rest is advice that will probably get me into trouble, and does not contain "how to" business information. Thank you for purchasing this manual on marketing. If you'd like to see more works by me (I've only scratched the surface), please drop me a note— I'd love to respond. There are several audio tapes available, a new book (*Direct Marketing Strategies*), some terrible videos, a few speeches, pre-written letters, and a 10-cassette series on classified ads called *The Intelligent Testing System*. If I get enough encouragement, I'll continue writing.

If you use any of these campaigns and have success, please let me know. I'd be delighted to see what you've done. If you write a letter campaign you have personally drafted, I'd enjoy reading it. All material will certainly be kept confidential unless you specifically state in writing that I can use it in a new book. Just as I have done with the campaigns that were most successful for my clients and myself over the years, I hope we can all share in our colleagues' successes.

If you are thinking about running a small business from your home, my personal recommendation is simple: start. Try your hand at any of these marketing campaigns. Whatever reasons you are thinking up for why they won't work, forget them and just move ahead: start anywhere. Worried about taxes? Don't. When you don't make money, there are no taxes. When you are a single entrepreneur, Uncle Sam is not your partner until you achieve some success and generate some income. When you do make money, you'll have money to pay him. Incorporating? You don't have to—just start out of your home. When you start making money, you can incorporate. Don't let all that bureaucracy crap stop you from starting your own business. Don't worry about the small details. I've seen people come up with so many reasons not to start their own business, they don't.

Even the largest businesses run into the unexpected. If you try to cover everything, you'll never get off the ground.

Sure, there are millions of excuses not to start making money from your own business and newly found marketing resources, but no real reasons. I've heard most of them: you don't have enough capital, there is no time, you're too busy with the kids, tomorrow will be better, the line at the post office is too long, the light in your kitchen is too dim. To me, all of these are about the same as the excuse, "There is something good on TV." They are excuses, not reasons. Where would we be if Henry Ford had said, "I'd better not start that motor car company, I don't know much about payroll taxes." You've got to take the plunge; you'll learn what you need to along the way.

What I have tried to accomplish in this book is to take away the single most often-used reason people don't start a business marketing a product: the cost. With the total cost of under a grand and the price of writing about 15 pages of material, anyone can market a product. If you can write a letter, you can market a product. If you can't write a letter, see the direct mail chapter for directions.

No one can anticipate everything they will run into in their business, and you won't, either. Don't even try to cover all the bases. Just cover as many as you can, be honest in all your dealings, and move forward to the next objective on your list. Constantly move toward your next goal. Even the largest businesses run into the unexpected. If you try to cover everything, you'll never get off the ground.

You're right, some products fail miserably. If you think you will fail, realistically, there always is that possibility. I'm not going to kid you about that. So if this is your line of thinking, don't start. Of course, if you have some great ideas, and a desire to be independent and perhaps wealthy, you are making a bigger mistake by not going for it. When I started my manufacturing business, I was filled with fear. I still have scary days now and then, and am not sure every decision I make is correct. But so what? No one makes all correct decisions. Not the president of the United States. Not the corporate wonders and CEOs of the biggest companies. I don't know of any business person who couldn't name four or five big mistakes he's made, right off the top of his head. Look at New Coke. EuroDisney. Remember the Edsel? How about the Ford Falcon or Chevy Vega?

When I started my firm, I was prepared to fail. I could live with that. I wouldn't be happy, but I could go on. What I was not prepared to do was to wake up one day when I was 50 or 60 and look back and realize I hadn't had the courage to try. I couldn't live with that.

Henry Ford had tons of problems before coming out with the Model T. IBM has launched many products to dismal failure. So have GE and Green Giant. Don't you think Black and Decker ever launched a product that never made it off the shelf? Did that stop them from launching new products? No way. Fear of failing is no reason not to start, not to move forward and not to try. It's like not going to a restaurant because they may not be able to seat you. Or not going into town because you may not find a place to park. In fact, the worst possible reason not to start is because you may not succeed. There are no guarantees in anything in life. The only true failure is not to try.

The key question to ask yourself: "How old will I be in five years if I start marketing this product?" This is regardless of whether you are successful or not. Then ask, "How old will I be in five years if I don't market this product?"

If everyone who wanted to market a product stopped because they said "What if I fail?" we would have no innovation. We'd still be using fireplaces for heat, and candles for light. We'd still be in the dark ages. Very dark ages.

Here's the most valuable part of this book!

This part of the book is my gift to you. The original article was written almost 30 years ago. I continually send this media kit to the press.

"I'd like to give this to my fellow man while there is still time." I remember this headline from an ad in *Popular Science* from my youth. Every month I'd get the magazine and see the picture of a gray-haired man, broad smile on his face, and this caption splashed across the page.

You know, I was a kid, and I never did figure out what he was selling. It was a successful long copy ad that ran for years, so lots of people must have sent the $19.95 or whatever he was charging for whatever he was selling, but I didn't. I was young, and $20 was a lot to me then.

But I do know I have this to give to my fellow man. I have a theory of how to save lives. So here it is. If you ever need this, I hope you've read it, and it works for you. It's only a theory. But after reading it, decide for yourself. Let me know what you think. The first part presented is a condensed version of a press release; the original research paper follows.

A TIME-BUYING PROCEDURE
TO DELAY BRAIN DAMAGE

Theory by Jeff Dobkin ©2007

Imagine this: *You've just come into your child's bedroom to tuck her in for the night. Her lips are blue, her face cool. As you reach over to pick her up, her body is limp in your arms. Your child is not breathing. What do you do?*

Thousands of times each year this terrifying scene is repeated. If you are the parent of a young child, without a doubt this would be the most horrifying experience of your life. If you don't know infant CPR, your only option is to watch your child lie there, not breathing, until help arrives. Even if you know CPR, there may be a simple technique you can do immediately to increase the chance of your child's survival and complete recovery. I would think any possible way to help your child at this time would be welcome.

~ Background ~

It was the winter of 1977. A young boy named Brian Cunningham fell into an icy river and drowned. He was submerged for over half an hour. He had stopped breathing after only two minutes. His heart had stopped. He lay motionless under the water. The boy, by all our definitions, was dead. For well over half an hour this child didn't take one single breath.

Thirty-eight minutes later he was pulled from the river by a fire rescue team. Contrary to conventional thought, he was resuscitated, revived, and returned to live a perfectly normal life. There was no brain damage. How could this happen?

I was brought up in the '60s, and was taught when no oxygen was supplied to the brain for a three- or four-minute period, irreversible brain damage occurs. Those were the '60s. Everyone believed it, even me. It was almost 10 years later that my curiosity finally got the better of me.

Of course, while growing up I was also taught the food groups you needed to eat every day were meat, vegetables and fruits, grains, and dairy. Remember the food pyramid? In the '70s the USDA recommended you eat two to three servings of meat a day. Perhaps you remember just a few years ago, they changed all that. Now there are new food groups. Fats and oils are out. Meat isn't really high on the recommended list. Times change.

Just last week vitamins were good for you. This week they're bad for you. All the changes in medical thinking and medical methods indicate the profession has numerous ideas about almost every condition, and about every issue. They can't all be correct, because they conflict with each other. New rules apply every day; just ask a different doctor.

Now there are new food groups, and new theories about vitamins. But physicians still cling to the belief that there is only CPR for heart attack victims. Yet even now, after all these years, the effectiveness of CPR is still in question.

I was surprised to read that article in *Newsweek* in 1977 about a child falling into icy water. When Brian was pulled out of the water with no brain damage after half an hour of being completely submerged, why this happened became a recurring question that haunted me for almost 10 years.

In 1985 I began my research to investigate how some people (especially children) can apparently drown, and upon their resuscitation—sometimes up to 40 minutes later—experience no brain damage. What is it that delays brain damage during this period?

My research showed that hypothermia, created by the cold water, helps delay brain damage. But that's not the reason these people survive. It is the triggering of a specific reflex that is responsible for saving lives and delaying brain damage. It's called the Mammalian Diving Reflex.

Further investigation showed the specific technique of triggering this reflex can be accomplished by a simple facial immersion in cold water. Only the face

The Danielle Adams Publishing Company
Box 100, Merion Station PA 19066

of the victim needs to be placed in cold water to trigger this reaction. All that is necessary to delay brain damage is to trigger this reflex by applying cold, wet compresses to the victim's face.

Specifically, the facial immersion in cold water is what saves victims in cold-water drownings. From my findings I wrote the enclosed paper. Thousands of lives are needlessly being lost each year, and thousands more people unnecessarily suffer brain damage.

Heart attacks are the fourth largest cause of death in the U.S. Victims of suffocation, electrocution, drug overdose, SIDS—all these people—and infants—could possibly be helped by the early triggering of this natural oxygen-conserving reflex. If just one child (the diving reflex is most pronounced in children) with SIDS can be saved with the technique of triggering the diving reflex by application of cold water to the face, it is well worth all the research I have done.

~ **Personal Note** ~

But before I get too far ahead of myself, I acknowledge this is a tough subject. You don't have to run this story. Maybe you don't need to present a controversial theory like this to your audience. Just stuff this article in a file cabinet, and no hard feelings. I hope no one in your audience will ever need this in an emergency. I hope you won't, either.

But if you're interested in helping to save lives, and if you want to present some good news—maybe you should take another look. If you've ever wondered how people survive cold-water drownings, if you are interested in the chance, just the chance, of saving one infant from SIDS, your consideration to bring this story to your audience is appreciated.

One more note. Quite frankly, I can be sued. I know this. I'm ready to be sued. I've held back this theory since 1986 (when I completed my initial research) for fear of being sued. If someone tries this on a dying person and the person does die, I probably will be sued. You can sue anyone for anything; all you need is a lawyer. And there are plenty of lawyers.

In this lawsuit-happy world, where lawyers run hard-sell ads for suing people on TV, I'm sure I will be sued. But do you know what else? This theory is worth all the money I have.

I am prepared to lose the house I live in, my business, and all my money, for the chance—just the chance—to save one child from sudden infant death syndrome. I now realize, although I am at risk of losing everything I have worked for all my life, if this saves just one child, all the wealth I have will be worth it. How about if it were your child?   Wouldn't you want to know about this technique?

"In a terrifying moment you see her on the bottom of the pool. You immediately pull her out, but she is completely lifeless."

Take an example. Just after you rushed into your house to answer the phone and grab a soda, your child falls into your swimming pool. Within a few seconds she slips under with hardly a ripple, and sinks to the bottom. Within two minutes she lies motionless at the bottom of the pool, not breathing. You go out to check on her—remember, just two minutes have passed—and in a terrifying moment you see her on the bottom of the pool. You immediately pull her out, but she is completely lifeless.

To trigger the diving reflex, the water must be 58 degrees or cooler, so this reflex did not occur. Your daughter now has two more minutes before irreversible brain damage occurs, followed directly by brain death. What would you do? Would you want the option of now triggering a natural oxygen-conserving reflex to possibly delay the onset of brain damage?

This technique may not make me any money; but I believe it will save lives. If it does, I will have rewards beyond my wildest dreams. I am no longer willing to hold this theory back in fear of being sued and losing my material possessions. There is nothing I own that has close to the value of the life of a single child.

~ The Life-Saving Technique ~

Here is a description of the Dobkin Technique for delaying brain damage. It can be done by a child. It can be explained over the phone. It can be self-administered. Initiating the reflex takes well under a minute. It is a natural occurrence: nature's own way of protecting her children.

"This one paragraph may save your life..."

In the event of any oxygen deprivation to the brain—such as heart attack, drowning, suffocation, electrocution, drug overdose, trauma, or SIDS—the first action a person should take is to place ice cold water, cold wet towels, or cold compresses over the eyes and face of the victim. Leave the nose and mouth uncovered for breathing. Keep towels or compresses cold, and leave them on the face. The water must be 58 degrees or cooler, which is the mean temperature of the waters of the world. For extra protection, apply iced compresses to the back of the neck at the base of the head to cool the blood in the brain. This is all that is necessary. It's this simple, it's this fast.

This is the whole technique to trigger the Mammalian Diving Reflex, a natural oxygen-conserving reflex found in all mammals. It is nature's own reaction to delay brain damage and sustain life. Unbelievable? This is the whole technique in one paragraph. One paragraph that may save your life. Or the life of someone you love.

Take another example. You are staying at a friend's house, 20 minutes out in the country. On a warm summer night you are sitting on the porch when your spouse—who has been feeling pale and weak all day—suffers a heart attack. You call for an ambulance, 20 minutes away. You don't know CPR. You now have two choices. You can helplessly watch your spouse, who has just stopped breathing, lie there on the floor. Or you can trigger the reflex. Which would you rather do?

———————————————

Let me be more specific about using Dobkin's Technique. "If something isn't done right now, this person will die." This is when the technique is used.

———————————————

With hundreds of hours of research and investigation of the oxygen-conserving reflex, I am available to you and your audience by phone or in person. But even as just a news brief, I would like you to release this information, to offer a choice to those who may stand helpless as their spouse or child lies dying from drowning, heart attack, electrocution, suffocation, SIDS, drug overdose, or any other trauma where there is danger of oxygen deprivation.

~ Final Note ~

This technique is not approved, and may <u>never</u> be accepted by any governmental body or the medical community.

The only way it has even the remotest possibility of being accepted by any medical group or sanctioned by any governmental body is if I can spend the $20 million or so it typically takes to run the tests up the government flagpole. Then spend the next six to ten years collecting empirical evidence, and filling out stacks and stacks of paperwork from the government for its approval. Then waiting for approval while they do the same tests. And spend the same amount of money. Then, since it's not patentable, and is a natural occurrence without the use of drugs, pills, or injections, no pharmaceutical company in the world will take a penny's worth of interest in it. So this technique will be unauthorized forever.

The medical community won't sanction this technique either. The medical community itself can't even agree if vitamins are good for you. Do you think they will, in unison, agree this natural occurrence can be a real rescue tool? To wait for any approval means thousands of lives that can be saved, will be lost. This technique is too valuable to be put in that political arena and bounced around forever. The decision to initiate this oxygen-conserving reflex is within each individual. It's not going to come from the AMA or the government.

The choice is clear to me: this technique will save lives. It will provide an added margin of safety to victims. It is a time-buying procedure to delay brain damage. This paper isn't about whether this technique works. This reflex has already worked on thousands of cold-water drowning victims. This paper is about the knowledge each individual should have to be able to choose for himself whether he wants to use this technique or not. After that, if your audience believes they would like to wait for the government to give the OK, they can choose not to initiate this reflex in an emergency.   Once they have this knowledge, it is up to the individual to make the choice. This paper is about the choice everyone should have.

####

Quite frankly, my list of people saved needs more names. If I had 1,000 names, more people would listen. If I had 10,000 names, everyone would listen. Including the government and the AMA. If anyone has survived a cold-water drowning, please let me know. I'll compile the data into a presentable and accountable document if you send experiences to my attention. If I can get enough response, I can compile the data as proof of the effectiveness of this reflex, and the technique will become an accepted life-saving procedure. Thank you.

A Technique For Delaying Brain Death In Heart Attack Victims

Theory by Jeffrey Dobkin • Copyright 1986, 2007
Box 100 • Merion Station, PA 19066 • 610-642-1000

WHILE CURRENT MEDICAL METHODS cannot entirely prevent heart attacks, there is an emergency procedure that can save lives. A simple technique can reduce or delay the possibility of brain damage and brain death to a heart attack victim for up to an hour—or more.

If this procedure saves one life, it is fully worth all the time and effort I have spent in research.

The Technique seeks to prevent or delay the irreversible brain damage thought to occur when no oxygen reaches the brain for four minutes.[1] It is used as a time-buying procedure to save the lives of heart attack victims and victims of suffocation, drowning, respiratory failure, and drug overdose. Perhaps it will even help SIDS (crib death) or stroke victims until proper medical equipment and personnel are summoned and arrive.

The Technique can be applied by a child or may be self-administered in almost any home. It takes less than 30 seconds to initiate and the results are as immediate.[2] It works on both conscious and unconscious victims. It can be explained on the phone in under a minute.

Almost everyone has heard of a boy drowning in cold water—then, after half an hour of submersion, being resuscitated with no ill effects and no brain damage. The *Canadian Medical Association Journal* documented such a drowning: After half an hour of complete submersion, a boy was rescued from the icy waters where he fell.[3] He was resuscitated and, with proper medical treatment, had no lasting side effects. There was no cerebral damage, although his brain received no oxygen for over half an hour.

Research has provided additional case study after case study of extended cold water submersion with no brain damage to resuscitated victims. Article after article, story after story, of people deprived of oxygen for up to an hour—with no ill effects or brain damage. What is it that protects the brain from damage in cases of oxygen deprivation over the four-minute limit? And can this be applied as a lifesaving technique to heart attack victims?

In all vertebrates, there is an automatic reflex called the Mammalian Diving Reflex. It occurs naturally as a life-preserving mechanism during cold water submersion. More commonly called the "Diving Reflex," it is a protective oxygen-conserving reflex to keep brain and body alive during submergence and possible drowning in cold water. The body prepares itself to sustain life. It is a totally natural protective mechanism serving Homo sapiens, originating from hundreds of thousands of years of evolvement.

Natural engagement of the diving reflex is what has enabled drowning victims to be revived successfully after cold water submersion for as long as an hour, with few or no ill effects. The Technique seeks to trigger this reflex in a crisis. The Technique may never replace CPR. The purpose of this article is not to compete with CPR, but to help sustain the life of the hundreds of thousands of victims of heart attacks or suffocation, thrust into a life-and-death situation, who may not be near people trained in CPR.

If you are not skilled in CPR, and you live in the country where an ambulance is 20 minutes away, and someone close to you has a heart attack—the options are frightening. Without the initiation of the Technique, a person whose heart stops has only four minutes until irrevers-

The Danielle Adams Publishing Company
Box 100, Merion Station PA 19066

ible brain damage occurs. After you call for help, you can watch. If you think this is a horrifying alternative, I couldn't agree more. Or you can try this Technique.

The Technique may work to save lives in conjunction with CPR. There is also the possibility it may not work at all; this is, after all, a theory. But the fact that it just may work makes it worth closer study. When there is no other immediate remedy, this may be put into practice in an emergency. What would you have your spouse do if you lived in the country and you had a heart attack?

"The Technique for Delaying Brain Damage" is simple and easy to initiate. In natural surroundings, the diving reflex occurs when a mammal falls into water 58 degrees Fahrenheit—the mean temperature of the waters of the world—or colder. But this reflex may also be triggered by only a <u>facial</u> immersion in cold water (58 degrees or colder).

The Technique is to apply cold water, wet towels, or wet ice packs to the victim's face—especially the eyes—to trigger the diving reflex in the event of heart or respiratory failure.

This procedure starts the oxygen-conserving mammalian diving reflex. Here is what happens:

Bradycardia can start in as little as four seconds or can take up to thirty seconds, depending on what part of the breath cycle the person is in when cold water is applied to the face. In man, cold water facial immersion usually induces a 15% to 30% decrease in heart rate from normal resting values. The reflex is strong enough to override other seemingly vital reflexes; i.e., it can completely obliterate the tachycardia that accompanies moderately severe exercise on a bicycle ergometer and can abruptly reduce heart rate from 130–140 beats per minute to 80 or less, despite continuation of the exercise.[4] Bradycardia is initiated by parasympathetic vagal activity.

Skin and muscle blood flow decrease through a powerful constriction of peripheral arteries. Peripheral vaso-constriction brought about by sympathetic activity maintains blood pressure. At the same time, systemic arterial pressure, especially diastolic, is increased. This lower heart rate and redistribution of central blood flow supports more necessary life-preserving organs.

The reflex triggers anaerobic metabolism, shown by a fall in arterial pH. There is an increase in concentrations of lactic and other organic acids, and a rise in blood carbon dioxide and potassium. This indicates that the body's cells are using less oxygen.

In a study by Wolf, Schneider and Groover, arterial oxygen saturation fell very little during immersion when the reflex occured.[5]

Because arterial oxygen saturation falls very little, the term "oxygen conserving" is appropriate for the reflex—an animal is enabled to survive without breathing for a much longer period than its supply of oxygen would warrant under ordinary circumstances.[6]

In Diving Reflex experiments, Charles Richet tied off the tracheae of two groups of ducks, then held one group under cold water. The ducks held under water lived more than three times as long as their partners not immersed in cold water.

In further studies of nerve-cutting experiments, Harold Anderson of Oslo, Norway, documented that the Diving Reflex, as manifested by slowing of the heart, depended on the integrity of the ophthalmic branch of the trigeminal nerve. With the nerve intact, a duck would trigger the diving reflex and survive under water for 20 minutes. When the ophthalmic branch of the trigeminal nerve was severed (bilaterally), immersed ducks failed to slow their heart rates when cold water was applied to their faces and survived only six or seven minutes.[7]

Accentuation of the reflex to the greatest degree occurs when the facial immersion in cold water is accompanied by fear. The more fearful the condition, the stronger the trigger to bring about the reflex and the greater the chance a strong oxygen-conserving reflex will take place.

In patients resuscitated by the team of a special ambulance service run by the Department of Anesthesia at Ulleval Hospital (from an article entitled "Resuscitation of Drowning Victims"), the most successful outcome was observed in those with cardiac arrest following drowning.

In an article in *Newsweek,* drowning specialist Dr. Martin J. Nemiroff (Michigan University Medical Center) suggests that the involuntary diving reflex saves lives of drowning victims by <u>delaying suffocation</u>—by shunting oxygen from extremities and sending it toward the heart, brain, and lungs—<u>and reduces the possibility of brain damage and death.</u>[8] A photo in the *Newsweek* article shows Dr. Nemiroff with Brian Cunningham, who was revived after 38 minutes under water.

Dr. Nemiroff has successfully revived numerous victims of cold water drowning who were submerged for 30 minutes or more and were pronounced dead. He says that what saved the victims was the automatic activation of the Mammalian Diving Reflex and the coldness of the water.[9]

It is my conclusion that if the diving reflex can save the lives of drowning victims by delaying brain damage, then triggering the reflex should also delay brain damage in heart attack victims.

A discussion in a *Scientific American* study of the human body's ability to resist drowning states that the Diving Reflex and cold water reduce the oxygen demand of tissues, extending the period of survival <u>without external oxygen</u> to as long as one hour. Previously, irreversible brain damage was thought to occur after four minutes without oxygen.[10]

The Diving Reflex is currently used by the medical profession in conversion of paroxysmal atrial tachycardia.[11,12,13] The Technique is to immerse the face of a person in a tub or basin of water 50 degrees or cooler. Since the technique produces an almost instant conversion to normal sinus rhythm and is not invasive, the use of the Diving Reflex is recommended by many authors and cited as a safe, effective treatment. In one study, nine out of 10 patients converted in 15–38 seconds, with an average of 23 seconds.[14] Its use is also the treatment of choice for converting a supraventricular tachycardia in children and infants, in whom the Diving Reflex effect is most pronounced.[15]

In a letter to Mr. Dobkin, Dr. Linus Pauling surmises there are two ways in which the damage to the brain might be delayed for some time when the oxygen to the blood is stopped.

"The brain can tolerate a certain amount of decrease in the partial pressure of oxygen supplied by the blood. If the circulation of the blood to the brain and to the tissues continues at its normal rate, the oxygen is used up rather fast, most of it (75%) by tissues other than the brain. Accordingly the induction of bradycardia, delaying the rate at which oxygen is brought to the tissues by the blood, would conserve the supply of oxygen and permit anoxic damage to be delayed by a considerable amount.

"There is a second way of delaying brain damage by anoxia. This way is to cool the brain. The biochemical reactions involved in anoxic damage have a high temperature coefficient, so that cooling the brain by a few degrees can slow down the rate at which anoxic damage occurs to perhaps one-tenth of its rate."[16] This letter suggests that ice or cold water also be applied to the neck, so that the blood is cooled and the brain itself is cooled in the region in which anoxic damage occurs. I concur with Dr. Pauling and recommend that after the face is immersed with ice packs or cold water, cold water be applied to the neck and the base of the hairline at the back of the head.

After countless hours of research, I am convinced that the Technique to delay brain damage will save lives. The technique of applying cold water to the face of conscious or unconscious heart attack or suffocation victims should be a known lifesaving procedure. It may be used in the event of any oxygen deprivation to the brain. Its procedure can be explained over the telephone, self-administered, or applied by a friend or child with no training. And while it will not stop heart attacks from happening, it will buy precious time until proper medical equipment and personnel arrive.

The Technique is quick and easy to apply. It is a time-buying procedure—when time is of the essence. It is nature's own way of protecting us—a non-invasive action that can be initiated immediately by someone with no training. This natural, life-conserving reflex is common enough to be found in all mammals and powerful enough to save someone's life in a traumatic moment.

Further investigation and clinical evaluation may be necessary, but from the empirical evidence I have uncovered, I recommend this reflex be initiated in time of emergent need. I hope this article is a catalyst to spur new research. My reward? I would like my name assigned to the Technique; after all, Heimlich has his maneuver. My goal? I hope at least one life is saved.

###

The Dobkin Technique triggers nature's own protective oxygen-saving mechanism to save lives. It is the same reflex that has saved children and adults from drowning even though they were completely submerged in cold water for up to an hour. Your comments are most welcome. If you know someone who has been revived from a cold water drowning, please write to me. Also, if this technique has been used, please let me know the details. Thank you.

Jeffrey Warren Dobkin • P.O. Box 100 • Merion Station, PA 19066

Abstract References:
CPR, Diving Reflex, Heart Attack, Brain Damage, SIDS, Suffocation, Respiratory Failure.

The Danielle Adams Publishing Company
Box 100, Merion Station PA 19066

~ Abstract ~

Help for heart attack victims—when no one is around who knows CPR, initiate "The Dobkin Technique for Delaying Brain Death": Apply cold water or cold wet towels (58 degrees or colder) to the face and eyes of victim—leaving nose and mouth clear to breathe. After this, supplemental help may be to apply additional cold wet cloths to the base of the back of the head and to the back of the neck. This is an emergency time-buying procedure to delay brain death by triggering the Diving Reflex. The Diving Reflex is a natural oxygen-conserving reflex which can delay the irreversible brain damage thought to occur within four minutes of oxygen deprivation. Works on conscious and unconscious victims; may be applied by child or self-administered; technique may be described over the phone. Works in under 30 seconds. Works in victims of suffocation, SIDS, drownings, drug overdose, choking, electrocution, and other victims of respiratory failure or deprivation of oxygen for any reason.

Endnotes

1. *Scientific American*, August 1977, 57.
2. S. Wolf, R.A. Schneider, and M.E. Groover, "Further Studies on the Circulatory and Metabolic Alterations of the Oxygen-Conserving (Diving) Reflex in Man," (paper presented before the American Clinical and Climatological Association, Colorado Springs, Colo., 21 October 1964).
3. P.K. Hunt, "Effect and Treatment of the Diving Reflex," *Canadian Medical Association Journal* (21 December 1974).
4. J. Atkins, S. Leshin, C. Skelton, and K. Widenthal, "The Diving Reflex Used to Treat Paroxysmal Atrial Tachycardia," *Lancet* (4 January 1975): 12.
5. Wolf et al., "Further Studies."
6. Ibid.
7. Ibid.
8. *Newsweek*, 22 August 1977, 79.
9. *New York Times*, 7 August 1977, 20.
10. *Scientific American*, August 1977, 57.
11. Atkins et al., "Diving Reflex," 12.
12. *Newsweek*, 13 January 1975, 50.
13. P.G. Landsberg, "Bradycardia During Human Diving," *South African Medical Journal* (5 April 1975): 626-630.
14. M.A. Wayne, "Conversion of Paroxysmal Atrial Tachycardia by Facial Immersion in Ice Water," *Journal of the American College of Emergency Physicians* (6 May 1976).

15. V. Whitman, "The Diving Reflex in Termination of Supraventricular Tachycardia in Childhood," *Journal of the American College of Emergency Physicians*, letter to the editor (December 1976).

16. Letter to Jeffrey Dobkin from Dr. Linus Pauling, dated September 2, 1992.

Thanks...

> *And we hope you have enjoyed this book. Please see more of Jeffrey Dobkin's work at www.dobkin.com. Other books, audio and video products by Jeff Dobkin are shown after the reference section.*

> *If you liked this book and found it of good value, read it again. There's a good bit of information in here and we've found that a second reading is a great rocommendation. If you really liked it, recommend it to a friend. Thanks.*

> *As always, your comments—both good and bad—get read at the top, and we try to respond to all correspondence.*

> *The Book Marketing Team at*
> *The Danielle Adams Publishing Company*

The following pages...
are dedicated to Bacon's Magazine Directory
and to their "Directory of Marketing Classifications"
which are found in the front of their Magazine Directory.

   When marketing any product, this is where you find
your prospects and customers—all grouped together in
"market segments" or "market niches." Each magazine
directory (from any of the different publishers - whether
in print or online) has a list similar to this to help you find
the targeted group that you are searching for.
   Bacon's market classification listing is one of the best,
and is incredibly useful as a marketing tool and a wonderful education in marketing just by itself.
   This list of market classifications is instrumental to the
One Evening Marketing Plan featured earlier in this book.
You can order this list from Bacon's Informational Services for FREE. It appears on just two pages in the front
of their directory but since this book is in a smaller format, it runs longer. Hope you find this of good value in
your marketing.

The Danielle Adams Publishing Company
Box 100, Merion Station PA 19066

Bacon's Magazine Directory, Market Classifications

Reprinted with permission from Bacon's Information, Inc.

The Danielle Adams Publishing Company
Box 100, Merion Station PA 19066

Bacon's Magazine Directory, Market Classifications

Group / Count	Market Classification	Page
27 - (16)	**Export/Import & International Trade**	1008
27A - (16)	Export/Import & International Trade	1008
28 - (502)	**Farming**	1011
28A - (29)	General Farm Journals	1011
28B - (157)	Farming - Regional	1015
28C - (9)	Farm Chemicals & Fertilizers	1038
28D - (40)	Fruit, Nut & Vegetable	1039
28E - (67)	Horses & Horse Breeding	1045
28F - (131)	Livestock	1055
28G - (12)	Poultry	1073
28I - (6)	Specialized Farming	1074
28J - (6)	Meat Packing & Merchandising	1075
28K - (6)	Farm Equipment	1076
28M - (12)	Milling, Feed & Grain	1077
28N - (27)	Field Crops	1079
29 - (378)	**Fitness & Personal Health**	1084
29A - (94)	Fitness & Personal Health	1084
29B - (89)	Alternative Health & Spirituality	1108
29C - (15)	Health Clubs/Fitness Professionals	1122
29D - (31)	Disabled/Physically Challenged	1125
29E - (149)	Consumer Healthcare	1129
30 - (129)	**Florist, Landscaping & Gardening**	1152
30A - (72)	Florist, Landscape & Nursery Trade	1152
30B - (57)	Gardening	1164
31 - (190)	**Food**	1176
31A - (47)	Food Industry & Processing	1176
31B - (4)	Confectionery	1184
31C - (19)	Nutrition Trade	1185
31D - (120)	Food & Nutrition Consumer	1188
32 - (39)	**Furniture & Interiors**	1215
32A - (39)	Furniture & Interiors	1215
33 - (58)	**Fraternal & Club**	1224
33A - (58)	Fraternal & Club	1224
34 - (1166)	**General Interest Consumer**	1231
34A - (133)	General Editorial	1231
34B - (876)	General Editorial-Metro	1268
34C - (20)	News Magazines	1432
34D - (137)	Political & Social Opinion	1458
35 - (75)	**Gifts, Antiques & Collectibles**	1482
35A - (75)	Gifts, Antiques & Collectibles	1482
36 - (57)	**Grocery & Food Marketing**	1493
36A - (39)	Grocery & Food Marketing	1493
36B - (18)	Grocery – Regional	1500
37 - (283)	**Home**	1504
37A - (190)	Home	1504
37B - (93)	Home Building, Buying & Remodeling	1552
38 - (37)	**Home Audio/Video & Personal Electronics**	1569
38A - (13)	Home Audio/Video & Electronics Trade	1569
38B - (24)	Consumer Interest Audio/Video	1572
39 - (312)	**Hospitals & Healthcare**	1578
39A - (73)	Hospital & Healthcare Administration	1578
39B - (144)	Healthcare Trade	1590

Reprinted with permission from Bacon's Information, Inc.

The Danielle Adams Publishing Company
Box 100, Merion Station PA 19066

Group / Count	Market Classification	Page
39C - (67)	Medical & Diagnostic Equipment	1613
39D - (28)	E M S/Emergency Medical Services	1624
40 - (25)	**Hotels, Motels & Resorts**	1630
40A - (25)	Hotels, Motels & Resorts	1630
41 - (210)	**Industrial**	1635
41A - (131)	Industrial	1635
41B - (26)	Design & Product Engineering	1657
41C - (22)	Security	1662
41D - (31)	Occupational Health & Safety	1667
42 - (17)	**Instrumentation & Controls**	1672
42A - (17)	Instrumentation & Controls	1672
43 - (84)	**Insurance**	1676
43A - (84)	Insurance	1676
44 - (27)	**Jewelry**	1691
44A - (27)	Jewelry	1691
45 - (331)	**Legal**	1696
45A - (178)	Legal	1696
45B - (153)	Legal - Regional	1722
46 - (51)	**Lumber & Forestry**	1748
46A - (27)	Lumber	1748
46B - (24)	Forestry	1751
48 - (136)	**Marine**	1756
48A - (29)	Marine & Boat Trade	1756
48B - (95)	Pleasure Craft	1760
48C - (12)	Commercial Fishing	1778
49 - (57)	**Men's**	1781
49A - (41)	Men's General Interest	1781
49B - (16)	Adult Publications	1796
50 - (1178)	**Medical**	1801
50A - (120)	General Medical	1801
50B - (296)	Specialized Medicine	1822
50C - (10)	Chiropractic	1870
50D - (32)	Obstetrics/Gynecology	1871
50E - (30)	Veterinary	1876
50F - (78)	Medical - Regional	1881
50G - (54)	Surgery	1894
50H - (57)	Medical Laboratory/Research	1902
50I - (38)	Cardiology	1912
50J - (50)	Orthopedics/Physical Therapy	1918
50K - (93)	Psychiatry/Psychology	1926
50L - (37)	Pediatrics	1941
50M - (27)	Radiology	1947
50N - (160)	Nursing	1951
50P - (54)	Oncology/Cancer	1978
50Q - (21)	Diabetes	1986
50R - (8)	Anesthesiology	1990
50S - (13)	Cosmetic & Reconstructive Surgery	1991
51 - (70)	**Metalworking & Machinery**	1994
51A - (65)	Metalworking & Machinery	1994
51B - (5)	Welding	2005
52 - (173)	**Military & History**	2007
52A - (89)	Military	2007

The Danielle Adams Publishing Company
Box 100, Merion Station PA 19066

Bacon's Magazine Directory, Market Classifications

Reprinted with permission from Bacon's Information, Inc.

The Danielle Adams Publishing Company
Box 100, Merion Station PA 19066

The Danielle Adams Publishing Company
Box 100, Merion Station PA 19066

Bacon's Magazine Directory, Market Classifications

Group / Count	Market Classification	Page
84A - (20)	Toys, Crafts, Arts & Hobbies Trade	2715
84B - (168)	Toys, Crafts & Hobbies	2718
84C - (90)	Art	2742
84D - (9)	Ceramics, Glass & Pottery	2754
84E - (23)	Collecting Cards, Comics & Memorabilia	2755
85 - (59)	**Traffic, Shipping & Warehousing**	2760
85A - (59)	Traffic, Shipping & Warehousing	2760
86 - (427)	**Travel & Tourism**	2770
86A - (51)	Travel Trade	2770
86B - (49)	Auto Club Publications	2780
86C - (32)	Airline Inflight	2790
86D - (184)	Visitor's Guide	2797
86E - (101)	Travel	2827
86F - (10)	Business & Corporate Travel	2848
87 - (147)	**Waste Management/Pollution Control**	2851
87A - (60)	Pollution Control/Recycling	2851
87B - (37)	Waste Management	2860
87C - (50)	Water & Sanitation	2866
88 - (41)	**Wearing Apparel Industry**	2874
88A - (33)	Wearing Apparel	2874
88B - (8)	Shoes & Leather Goods	2887
89 - (348)	**Women's**	2890
89A - (186)	Women's General Interest	2890
89B - (88)	Weddings	2947
89C - (62)	Beauty & Fashion	2964
89D - (12)	Romance	2987
90 - (29)	**Woodworking**	2990
90A - (29)	Woodworking	2990

Reprinted with permission from Bacon's Information, Inc.

The Danielle Adams Publishing Company
Box 100, Merion Station PA 19066

~ References ~

Directories, Magazines, Newsletters, Services, and Reference Manuals - Other Tools of the Trade.

Public Relations Specific:

Public Relations Quarterly
Penn Hill Publications
738 Main Street · Suite 447
Waltham, MA 02451
Phone: 800/572-3451; 781/647-3200 • Fax 781/647-3214
www.Hudsonsdirectory.com
Each journal is about 50 pages of industry-authored articles on PR. If you are serious about studying PR, this publication makes great reading. All authors are independent, so all articles are fresh and new.

Also published by Penn Hill Publications:

Hudson's Washington News Media Contacts Directory
Focused in the Washington area, over 350 pages of news media contacts - newspapers (D.C. & foreign), radio, T.V. magazines, writers and photographers, newsletters (by subject) in an easy-to-use marketing tool. Information is clear and presented concisely: referenced, cross-referenced, and indexed to make using this book a pleasure. $289.00 in printed version or same price for on-line; both for $329.00. Always ask if a promotion is running as the price may be cheaper at that time.

Publishing Newsletters. If you've ever thought about publishing a newsletter, don't. That's right: don't. Call me and ask for the no-holds-barred article I've written about why not to publish a newsletter. But... some folks do anyhow. So, if you must, I recommend this book. *Publishing Newsletters* shows you in excellent scope and depth exactly how to design and manage your newsletter property. This is real meat and potatoes stuff about design, writing, content, editorial style, production and printing, marketing, finding and keeping subscribers, and management. Definitely worth the $39.95 + $4 shipping. Best book I've ever read on this subject. Recommended.

Public Relations Tactics

Public Relations Society of America
33 Maiden Lane, 11th Floor
New York, NY 10038-5150
Phone: 212/460-1400 • Fax 212/995-0757
www.prsa.org
Newspaper devoted to public relations. Stuffed with short, data-packed articles, *Tactics* provides news, trends, and how-to information for PR professionals in an easy-to-read format. Stories are in-depth, and the editors take you behind the news, and show you how the news is manufactured and controlled. They must be doing something right; their subscription list is over 25,000 strong. Call for a sample copy.

Bulldog Reporter

Infocom Group
5900 Hollis Street, Suite L
Emeryville, CA 94608
Phone: 800/959-1059 • Fax 510/596-9331
www.infocomgroup.com
Lifestyle Media, $649, Twice-monthly (includes on line service)
Business Media, $649, Twice-monthly (includes on-line service)
Inside Health - on-line only, $1995 annual subscription
Inside tips on how to increase your publicity and work more successfully with the media. Included are: who's receiving what story at which show or magazine; who moved where; and a short segment on which PR groups have landed which accounts.

PR Newswire
Newswire

810 Seventh Avenue, 35th Floor
New York, NY 10019
Phone: 800/832-5522; 212/282-1929 • Fax 212/541-6414
www.prnewswire.com
Press release distribution service to newspapers and the financial community. Wire news-release distribution service that will transmit your release to selected area newspapers and newsrooms, depending on the coverage you purchase. Local, regional, national, and international distribution of press releases is offered. National distribution starts at $550 for transmission of up to 400 words. Regional, state and local newslines, photo transmission, E-Wire, fax, and video broadcast services. National headquarters are in New York, local offices in about 28 cities. Call for a complete listing of all their services; get a copy of their 130-page distribution directory.

Editor and Publisher   ***Newspaper Trade Publications***

VNU Publishing
770 Broadway
New York, NY 10003
Editorial: 800/336-4380
Subscriptions: 800/562-2706; 818/487-4582
www.mediainfo.com
Monthly, $99/year
A NEWSPAPER SPECIFIC magazine for the newspaper trade. Newspaper media only, but very strong. Each weekly issue is full of stories and articles about issues facing newspaper journalists. One of the best newspaper/PR industry trade publications. Big help wanted section for writers and editors. A good look at the inside of the newspaper business and how it relates to PR. This is the trade journal pulse of the industry. Their biggest help with press release campaigns to newspapers comes from their yearbook:

Editor and Publisher International Year Book

Editorial - Contact 646/654-5209
Subscriptions: 800/562-2706; 818/487-4582
Comes in three parts: <u>Part One</u> shows the top 100 newspapers, the top advertising networks, and the bulk of the U.S. and Canadian newspapers including address, phone and fax numbers, email and Web site, key personnel, circulation, subscription rates, and mechanical specifications for inserting ads. It also has a section for special service dailies, like college and university newspapers, tabloid newspapers, and special newspaper groups.

    <u>Part One</u> also contains a foreign newspaper section; a news picture and syndicated services section; an equipment and supplies section; various membership directories; associations and clubs; representative; and a list of other organizations in the industry such as clipping bureaus, unions, and press correspondents. It's pretty thorough. Cost is $140.

    <u>Part Two</u> offers U.S. and Canadian weeklies and special newspapers—such as Hispanic newspapers, gay newspapers, religious newspapers and so forth along with their circulation, subscription rates, publishers and editors. Cost is $125.

    <u>Part Three</u> is a "Who's Where" volume—filled with personal phone numbers of all the major players. Cost is $60. All three volumes are group-priced at $230 .

The Danielle Adams Publishing Company
Box 100, Merion Station PA 19066

Bradley Communications Corp.

135 East Plumstead Avenue • P.O. Box 1206
Lansdowne, PA 19050-8206
Phone: 800/989-1400; 610/259-0707 • Fax 610/284-3704
www.FreePublicity.com

Bradley Communications Corp. offers several products and services to help you get national radio, TV, newspaper and magazine publicity. Their clients have been booked or featured by such media outlets as Oprah, Larry King Live, Good Morning America, Los Angeles Times, New York Times, Dateline NBC, Associated Press, Glamour and more.

Radio-TV Interview Report is a twice-monthly trade publication, sent to over 4,000 radio/TV producers nationwide who look for interesting guests available for interviews. The publication consists completely of ads from authors and other experts seeking radio/TV publicity. Ad costs start at $877 and RTIR's staff will write your ad at no extra charge. RTIR has launched such best sellers as Chicken Soup for the Soul and Embraced by the Light. For full info, call 1-800-989-1400 ext. 408 or go to their website at www.rtir.com

Harrison's Guide to the Top National TV Talk Shows contains detailed profiles and contact info for the nation's top 235 national news and talk broadcast programs. For each show, up to twelve individual contacts are listed, along with the topic(s) they cover. In addition to a printed directory, you also get all the names as a database file so you can quickly create mailing lists. Cost is $347 for a single-copy with no updates, $697 for a one-year subscription with monthly updates. Info at www.AppearOnTopTVShows.com

National Publicity Summit is a twice-yearly conference limited to 100 attendees who get to personally meet 70-80 top journalists from top media outlets like ABC's The View, Today Show, Good Morning America, Time, Newsweek, Entrepreneur, MSNBC, Fox News, CNN, Live with Regis & Kelly, Parents, Family Circle, Parade and other publications and radio/TV shows. Info at www.NationalPublicitySummit.com

Trade Shows

Most trade shows sell their lists of exhibitors and their lists of attendees. Both of these lists make a fine targeted audience mailing list. Lists are tightly focused to industry personnel. In addition, going to a trade show is an excellent way to get industry information, find resources, receive productfeedback, generally explore new ways of marketing face-to-face with both exhibitors and attendees, and poke around and find out information— and have fun, too.

Tradeshow Week® Data Book   *Trade Show Directory*
Reed Business Information
360 Park Avenue South, 18th floor
New York, NY 10010
Phone: 800/375-4212 · 646-746-7885 Fax: 646-746-6814
$439 includes shipping
www.tradeshowweek.com
This 1,800 plus-page directory of U.S. and Canadian trade shows and public shows has a main industrial classification section, and sections for trade show associations; breaks out show listings alphabetically, by new shows, and by size; and has a geographic index, chronological index, and show management index. Whew!

Each show listing includes a show management statement of what the show is about, who the show management is, the show sponsor, registration fees, booth or space cost, profile of exhibitors, profile of attendees, and show statistics such as attendance, number of exhibiting companies, square footage, show history, and the year of the first show. This is a good, in-depth reference tool, published every October.

Besides this huge data book, Reed also publishes a *weekly* magazine: *Tradeshow Week*—$439/year. Published every Monday, this contains up-to-the-second, accurate information on the trade show industry. The *Tradeshow Week Data Book* has the distinction of being the single largest and heaviest book on our reference shelf! www.tradeshowweek.com.

TSNN.com   *Reference Website*
The largest tradeshow website, data on over 15,000 tradeshows. An excellent resource on the web..

The Danielle Adams Publishing Company
Box 100, Merion Station PA 19066

~ Great References ~
and Trusted Resources

Sandoval Printing   *Printing*

Gil, Joyce, Chris, & Tony Sandoval
9 Minnetonka Road
Hi-Nella, NJ 08083
Phone: 856/435-7320 · Fax 856/435-7507
www.printing.sandoval.com • e-mail: printing@sandoval.com
Minnetonka Road? Hi-Nella? Yes! Quit laughing, I'm serious. Short to medium runs (1,000 to 100,000 pieces; one- to five-color work). While not the cheapest, excellent work from an honest crew. I have known and trusted Gil and his family for over 30 years as my own first choice of printers—and I can be pretty demanding. As his customer and friend, I will personally guarantee his craftsmanship, pride, and the good old-fashioned honest value of any printing he does for you. Quality work shipped promptly, time after time.

National Mail Order Association   *Organization*

NMOA
2807 Polk Street NE
Minneapolis, MN 55418
Phone: 612/788-1673 · Fax 612/788-1147
www.nmoa.org
An association designed to assist entrepreneurs and small business owners who have an interest in mail order. Offers helpful literature and booklets on increasing effectiveness when marketing through the mail. Also offers product marketing and development for its members through its Web site. Good folks, and if you're lucky enough to speak with John Schulte—the chairman—personally (he answers the phone sometimes), you'll find a wealth of information right at your fingertips. Initial membership for entrepreneurs is $199, renewal is $99 annually

Mail Order Marketing News $35.95/year   *Newsletter*

TJT Publications
P.O. Box 55685
Valencia, CA 91385
Phone 661/291-2353 · Fax: 661/291-2354
www.tjtmarketing.com · e-mail: TJTPUB@aol.com
An insider's view of some of the many programs offered to home-office mail order marketers. Good guy and editor Terry Thomas writes about what's working, and bashes the scams you should stay away from. He tells it like it is in this monthly publication. My only regret about this newsletter—I wish it were longer. Fun reading, and filled with tips about direct mail and direct marketing; even my articles show up here—in many cases <u>before</u> they are published anywhere else. Ask for a sample copy. Very recommended. Terry is a great guy and right on the money with his writing. One of the best mailing lists for homebased businesses available, too.

National Directory of Catalogs   *Directory*

$795 Print, $1095 CD Rom, Both $1695 (single user)
Oxbridge Communications
186 Fifth Avenue, 6th Floor
New York, NY 10010
Phone: 800/955-0231; 212/741-0231 • Fax 212/633-2938
www.mediafinder.com
Over 11,000 U.S. and Canadian catalogs. Each listing includes catalog and company names, website and email, physical address, phone number, products carried, personnel, and list rental data for direct marketers. Also press runs and paper specifications. This is thorough, accurate, and nicely put together, this is the read deal and the gold standard of the industry. If you only have one reference tool for catalogs, Oxbridge Communications National Directory of Catalogs is absolutely your best choice.

New online services now also available from Oxbridge. For $50 per month you can access their huge database, create lists, and print pages. The interface is simple to use. While you can't download information for this small fee, (you can only print it out) this is the only place in the world you can get access to this huge amount of specific data at so low of an initial cost. A tremendous resource. Call Oxbridge for further information.

The Directory of Mail Order Catalogs   *Directory*

21st Edition—2007 - $350
Grey House Publishing
185 Millerton Road
Millerton, NY 12546
Phone: 800/562-2139; 518/789-8700 • Fax 518/789-0556
www.greyhouse.com • e-mail: books@greyhouse.com
Lists over 10,000 consumer catalog companies. Contains catalog names, addresses, phone numbers, Web site URLs, content, specialty products offered; also names of presidents, marketing managers, buyers, list managers, you name it—this directory is great. The bulk of the catalog is subdivided into 44 product-oriented sections such as "Baby Products," or "Hunting and Fishing." Also, all the listings are indexed several ways—by company and catalog name, by an "online" index, and by a product index. This is an awesome directory and we use this here in our office, too.

Grey House also publishes the ***Directory of Business to Business Catalogs*** ($165) containing over 6,000 entries of business to business product catalogs. Indexed by company and catalog name, geographic index, and "online" index.

The ***Directory of Business Information Resources*** ($195) lists each industry's associations, newsletters, magazines and journals, and trade shows and conventions, with 21,000 entries divided into 98 business areas.

Also available from Grey House Publishing: The new

Food and Beverage Marketplace · New Three Volume Set

This is the pulse of the food industry, and if you do any food marketing, this is the reference set you need. The new 3 volume food and beverage marketplace contains over 40,000 food and beverage manfacturers, suppliers transportation specialists, wearhouses, wholesalers, importers, exporters, distributors and brokers.

Contains over references to products, brand names, key executives of food manufacturing companies and food mail order companies, plus associations, publications, and directories and trade shows in the food industry.

Multichannel Merchant • Direct Magazine   *Magazine*
Prism Business Media
11 River Bend Drive South
P.O. Box 4949
Stamford, CT 06907-0949
Phone: 203/358-9900 • Fax 203/358-5811
www.prismb2b.com • www.directmag.com,
www.multichannelmerchant.com
Excellent tabloid-size magazines that have their hands on the pulse of the direct marketing, catalog and internet industries. Most articles feature larger mailers and catalogers with supplemental articles on online, web, retail and B-to-B merchants. Filled with great ideas.

Target Marketing Magazine   *Magazine*
Catalog Success Magazine
North American Publishing Company
1500 Spring Garden Street Suite 1200
Philadelphia, PA 19130
Phone: 215/238-5300 • Fax 215/238-5270
www.targetonline.com
One year, 12 issues, $65
Excellent resource for direct mail and direct marketing information. How-to, and information-rich!

DM News   *Newspaper*
100 Avenue of the Americas
New York, NY 10013
Phone: 212/295-7300 • Fax 212/925-8752
www.dmnews.com
Weekly newsprint tabloid,
Direct marketing and industry news-oriented. Excellent resource.

Direct Marketing   *Online*
Hoke Communications
224 Seventh Street
Garden City, NY 11503
516/746-6700 • Fax 516/294-8141
This magazine set the industry standard for years, and is still pretty darn good. Now offered on line with archives to all their articles. Heck, they even published lots of my articles.

The Danielle Adams Publishing Company
Box 100, Merion Station PA 19066

List Resources

Two of the best resources on lists on the planet, used by list brokers and industry personnel are the following two reference books. Each is a huge directory, showing thousands and thousands of lists along with their owner, size, rates, list broker, age, cost, hotline buyers, and other pertinent data. Use these directories at the library, photocopy the pages, then call the list vendors for additional information on each list. Dig deep—it'll pay off in the long run. For an excellent short course in purchasing mailing lists, see the chapter entitled "How to Buy a Great Mailing List" in the book *Uncommon Marketing Techniques,* by Jeffrey Dobkin. Or check out the many articles about lists in my newest book, *Inside Secrets of Direct Marketing.*

SRDS Direct Marketing List Source™   *Directory*
SRDS
1700 Higgins Road
Des Plaines, IL 60018   Visa/MC, AMEX
Phone: 800/851-SRDS (7737); 847/375-5000 • Fax 847/375-5001
www.SRDS.com
One year, 3 issues is $646 & <u>includes online access</u>. SRDS publishes a huge reference book on mailing lists, just like it does in the magazine industry for periodicals. The *SRDS Direct Marketing List Source*™ shows more than 50,000 business, consumer, and agri-market lists and list sources. Like the SRDS directory of magazines, this book is a complete reference manual in itself. One of the two most comprehensive resources available for the list industry, and a standard in the industry. 90-Day online access: $310. See the addtional write up of other SRDS directories later in the reference section. We use this at our own office.

National Directory of Media Mailing Lists
Oxbridge Communications
150 Fifth Avenue
New York, NY 10011
Phone: 800/955-0231; 212/741-0231 • Fax 212/633-2938
www.mediafinder.com
No longer in a print version, but offered as CD-ROM - $1095.
A comprehensive resource of catalog, magazine and newsletter lists available for rent or purchase. Now you can get a keyword search of the hugh database at Oxbridge Communications for just $50/month, including their mailing lists data. While you can't download the result, you can print it out. Call Oxbridge Communications for particulars.

Association Directories

Associations are an unusually excellent source of mailing lists. Better associations always list the industry's major players. Local associations like the chamber of commerce in your area are usually good for local business names. Here are two great sources for associations:

National Trade and Professional Associations of the United States
Columbia Books, Inc.
8120Woodmont Ave., Suite 110
Bethesda, MD 20814
Phone: 888/265-0600
www.columbiabooks.com
$199, Over 1,000 pages in this reference book lists over 8,000 associations. It's published annually along with its companion book, ***The State and Regional Associations of the U.S. Directory*** ($179). The state and regional association guide is particularly useful if you are targeting specific geographic areas and want access to top local association contacts not included in the national book. *The State and Regional Associations of the U.S. Directory* also has a higher percentage of association managers who, while managing multiple associations, cross many industry lines when sourcing vendors or affinity marketers.

Available online for the annual subscription of $699, a free 5-day demo trial is available on their site: www.associationexecs.com. All of the data is also available on disk - handy if you are a frequent mailer.

The Encyclopedia of Associations   *Directory*
The Gale Group
27500 Drake Road
Farmington Hills, MI 48331
Phone: 800-877-GALE • 248/699-4253 • Fax 248/699-8075
This hardbound, three-volume set ($715) is the mother lode of associations— showing detailed information on more than 23,000 local, state, national, and international associations.

Referenced and cross-referenced every which way possible, this set lets you reach the 30,000 members of Retinitis Pigmentosa International, the 200 members of the 1954 Buick Skylark Club, the 20 members of the Vacuum Cleaner Manufacturers Association (VCMA), or the 10 members of the Holy Innocents Reparation Committee with equal ease. Also available on disk, CD, and online through Lexis-Nexis.

The Danielle Adams Publishing Company
Box 100, Merion Station PA 19066

The association directories I wrote about are wonderful resources for marketing to the association's members. Virtually all of the larger associations send their own newsletter or magazine to their members. These often-overlooked publications are usually grateful for the opportunity to run your press release, and most are certainly happy to receive some ad revenue if you place an ad. If the publication is a newsletter or thin magazine, your chance of having your ad seen and getting noticed at the top of the field is even greater. Also, association publications are usually nonprofit, so rates are generally favorable when compared with more traditional industry magazines. A big plus: house publications are regarded as a more credible "insider" source—so your ad will appear more credible, too.

List Vendors

Most of the larger list companies offer a booklet or catalog of all the lists they sell—many of which number in the thousands. In addition, some of these booklets contain excellent information on specifying lists. All of them are free, and I recommend you call a few companies and get their catalogs, if for no reason other than to see what's out there and check out the thousands of lists that are available.

I wrote the following article for another book I've written, and since it has such a funny opening paragraph—not to mention the relevance of the content to this reference section—its reprint follows.

Free Catalogs of Compiled Mailing Lists

I wanted to know what's available in compiled lists, so I dredged out a few of my direct marketing trade journals from under the mass of papers, old pizza boxes and the few remains of previous lunches on my desk and called all the list vendors in each. Here's what I found out: Pizza is good only for three, maybe four days without refrigeration, but the pepperoni still remains tasty for up to a week. Also:

Edith Roman (800/223-2194; www.edithroman.com) publishes an excellent glossy, 95-page catalog of both consumer and business response and compiled lists. Lists are arranged alphabetically, and by SIC code and geographic breakouts, counts are included for each list. You can easily find lists for almost any industry—27,827 stone, clay, glass, and concrete products manufacturers—or any niche—2,822 ophthalmic goods wholesalers, 2,711 ventilating systems-cleaners, 3,086 tattoo parlors. Their catalog is easy to use for both the experienced and others, with a logical layout and explanation of how to use it. Perfect bound.

Dunhill International List Company (800-DUNHILL; www.dunhills.com) publishes an easy-to-use 77-page 8 1/2" x 11" catalog on bleached newsprint. Dunhill offers specialty lists shown in alphabetized sequence, such as 25,921

foundations with officers, 811,000 health insurance agents, and 2,825 single-parent organizations; as well as master files of, for example, 2,225,214 women investors, or 588,482 lawyers. They also break out lists by alpha and SIC. As expected, you can get businesses or business executives by state, income, title, or type of firm, and attorneys or medical doctors by specialty.

American Business Information (800/555-5335, 402/592-9000; www.infoUSA.com), the firm that went about buying up almost every list company that would sell just a few years ago, offers 11 million businesses by Yellow Pages heading, number of employees, SIC code, sales volume, phone number, and credit rating code. They also offer 195 million consumers by age, estimated income, home value, and other selects. Their 72-page, 81/2" x 11" catalog is easy to use and like some of the other catalogs, offers a few specialty lists, like 12 million executives by ethnic surname, 3 million fax numbers, 663,000 work-at-home businesses, and 3 million businesses in affluent neighborhoods, to name a few. They also offer lists by SIC code, and some are pretty darn esoteric, like 1,068 beverage dispensing equipment wholesalers and 403 bronze-table manufacturers. They offer free counts if you call them. When I called and gave them my phone number, they gave me my mailing address and asked if it was still correct.

Direct Media (203/532-1000) Now online at www.mailinglist.com. You can get counts and find information on line.

American List Council (800/403-1870; www.amlist.com) sent a 60-page catalog broken down into segments containing consumer lists, business lists, lists by SIC codes and their proprietary response lists—which includes some weird ones such as a master file of ailment sufferers, a few of which I wouldn't want over at my house: 537,458 gastritis sufferers, 404,990 bladder control/incontinence sufferers, and 790,470 ladies with yeast infections, ouch—that's just gotta hurt. As most of the other major list vendors do, they also handle lists for some of the larger mail order houses: 1,337,167 L.L. Bean Mail Order Buyers (M.O.B.), 2,695,137 Spiegel M.O.B., and 4,856,781 Victoria's Secret M.O.B.; and some of the larger magazine subscription lists, such as 925,243 *PC Magazine* subscribers. The 8l/2" x 11" catalog is easy to use.

Hugo Dunhill Mailing Lists, Inc. (888/274-5735; www.hdml.com) puts together a well-designed and extremely information-intense catalog of lots and lots of lists. Arranged alphabetically and then referenced in SIC code order, the Hugo Dunhill catalog goes deep into some wells that are dry in other list houses' catalogs. Along with the traditional—108,472 accounting firms—you can get tax preparers broken down by specialty: 144 associations, 4,305 attorneys, 558 bankers, 25,478 CPAs, and so forth. You can also get some esoteric lists: 129 Daughters of the Nile, or a selection of church societies (women's) selected by denomination: Methodist Women's Church, Lutheran Church Women's Clubs, or even 84,092 churches with video equipment. If you can name it, you can get a list of all the people in it. If you can't name it, call Hugo and speak to him, like I did. He's a lot of help in a short amount of time.

The Danielle Adams Publishing Company
Box 100, Merion Station PA 19066

Dun and Bradstreet (973/605-6457; www.dnb.com) is one of the granddaddies of the list industry, and they warehouse a master file of almost everything and on everybody. They have a full resource file on your credit, even if you don't want them to have it. That credit information is available in a list, even if you don't want your competitors to get it. You can also get a CD-ROM with 11 million businesses on it—so you can analyze and manipulate your own data, then pay for only the list of names or businesses you use. Their 48-page catalog is organized by SIC code.

List Resources, continued...

MKTG Services

140 Terry Drive, Suite 103, Newtown, PA 18940
Phone 800-936-6210.

A marketing services company and data provider. Offers information services and lists that help companies and organizations with lead generation and customer retention programs. Includes direct mail, email marketing, online lead generation, telemarketing, and brokerage services. Sandi Baker is my contact and she's great: smart, bright and cheerful, with an excellent depth of knowledge. Website: www.mktgservices.com
email info@mktgservices.com

Standard Trade Practice List Rental Agreement

THIS CONTRACT IS WRITTEN WITH THE SOLE INTENT TO PREVENT THE ABUSE OF THIS LIST IN AN ACTIVITY OTHER THAN ITS ORIGINAL SALE AGREEMENT.

LIST RENTAL AGREEMENT FOR THE LIST OF PURCHASERS FROM _____ HEREINAFTER CALLED COMPANY, AND PERSONS OR OTHER COMPANIES HEREINAFTER CALLED USER, WISHING TO USE OUR LIST. OUR LIST IS A PROPRIETARY PRODUCT, AND THIS IS A NARROW LICENSE FOR ITS USE. USER AGREES TO THE TERMS AND CONDITIONS SET FORTH IN THIS AGREEMENT, BY SIGNATURE AND BY USE OF THIS LIST. THIS CONTRACT APPLIES TO COMPANY'S LIST WHETHER SUPPLIED IN TAPE, DISK, LABEL, OR ANY OTHER FORMAT. USER HAS NO RIGHTS TO LIST OTHER THAN THOSE SPECIFICALLY STATED IN THIS CONTRACT.

COMPANY'S LIST IS THE SOLE PROPERTY OF COMPANY. ITS ORIGINATION IS FROM BONA FIDE ORDERS FOR COMPANY'S PRODUCTS. IT IS COMPRISED OF DIRECT MAIL ORIGIN ORDERS WITH APPROXIMATELY _____ PERCENT OF ITS ORDERS ORIGINATING THROUGH SPACE ADVERTISING.

THIS LIST IS SOLD ON A ONE TIME BASIS, THE LIST MAY BE MAILED ONE TIME, AT ONCE. USER HAS NO RIGHTS TO THE LIST OR THE LIST INFORMATION EXCEPT THOSE EXPLICITLY GIVEN HIM IN THIS AGREEMENT. USER IS PROHIBITED FROM TRANSFERRING, DUPLICATING, COPYING OR MODIFYING THE LIST OR PROCESSING THE LIST AGAINST OTHER LISTS, WITHOUT THE EXPRESS WRITTEN PERMISSION OF COMPANY. THIS RESTRICTION IS TO INCLUDE USE OF COMPANY'S LIST TO REVEAL DUPLICATES FROM OTHER LISTS, WHICH IS CONSIDERED USE.

MATERIALS TO BE MAILED MUST FIRST BE SUBMITTED TO COMPANY FOR IDENTIFICATION AND APPROVAL. RESTRICTIONS OF THE USE OF THIS LIST ARE TO THE IDENTIFIED AND APPROVED MATERIAL, AND THE SPECIFIC MAIL DATES OR USE PERIOD. THE NUMBER OF TIMES USER IS PERMITTED TO CONTACT, USE, SCAN, READ, OR IN ANY WAY MANIPULATE THE DATA ON THE LIST BY ANY METHOD IS ONCE. IN THE EVENT USER WISHES TO MAIL AGAIN TO ANY PART OF THIS LIST, SUCH AS THOSE NAMES FOUND ON ANOTHER LIST SOURCE AND BY THEIR DUPLICATION HAVE ADDITIONAL VALUE, USER MUST RECEIVE WRITTEN PERMISSION BEFORE USE FROM COMPANY FOR USE OF THOSE NAMES FOR ADDITIONAL MAILINGS, AND PAY A PREMIUM AS SET FORTH BY COMPANY FOR SUCH USE. IN THE EVENT OF A BREACH OF THIS CLAUSE, COMPANY WILL CHARGE USER AND USER WILL PAY FULL PRICE OF THE USE OF THE ENTIRE LIST FOR THE USE OF THESE NAMES, EVEN THOUGH THESE NAMES DO NOT COMPRISE THE ENTIRE LIST. THIS CLAUSE AND THE CHARGES OF USAGE OF THE ENTIRE LIST WILL APPLY FOR ANY PARTIAL USE OF LIST UNLESS OTHERWISE STATED IN WRITING BY COMPANY. THE COMPANY LIST, HEREINAFTER CALLED LIST, AND THE INFORMATION CONTAINED IN IT REGARDLESS OF FORM OR FORMAT ARE THE PROPERTY OF THE COMPANY AND CONSTITUTE TRADE SECRETS, AND USER HAS THE RESPONSIBILITY TO TREAT THE INFORMATION AS CONFIDENTIAL, AND NOT PERMIT ITS UNAUTHORIZED USE OR DISCLOSURE. USER IS PROHIBITED FROM TRANSFERRING, DUPLICATING, COPYING OR MODIFYING THE LIST, OR PROCESSING IT AGAINST OTHER LISTS TO ENHANCE, TAG, VERIFY OR ADD TO THOSE OTHER LISTS OR COMPANY'S LIST, UNLESS USER HAS RECEIVED COMPANY'S EXPRESS WRITTEN CONSENT TO DO SO. USER IS FURTHER PROHIBITED FROM EMPLOYING ANY METHOD TO ADD, DETECT, ALTER OR ELIMINATE DECOYS.

WE RECOGNIZE THE NEED FOR SOME INFORMATION TO BE RETAINED BY USER, AND WE PERMIT A NON-MAILABLE MATCHCODE TO BE KEPT BY USER FOR THE SOLE PURPOSE OF RESPONSE ANALYSIS AND TO SUPPRESS NAMES AND ADDRESSES IN LATER MAILINGS OF THE SAME OFFER BY SAME USER IN SUBSEQUENT PURCHASES OF OUR LIST FOR ADDITIONAL MAILINGS.

THERE ARE NO NET NAME, QUALIFYING, OR COMPETITION PROTECTION ARRANGEMENTS. USER IS EXPRESSLY RESPONSIBLE FOR ALL MATERIALS AND THE RETURN OF SUCH MATERIAL IF THEY ARE TO BE RETURNED, ONCE THEY ARE RECEIVED BY USER. IT IS AGREED COMPANY IS NOT RESPONSIBLE AND SHALL BE HELD HARMLESS IN THE EVENT USER OR A CONSTITUENT THROUGH USER'S ACTIONS SEEKS DAMAGES WHETHER REAL OR IMAGINARY FROM THE LIST OR ITS USE. FURTHER IT IS AGREED COMPANY WILL BE HELD HARMLESS WHETHER AT FAULT OR NOT BECAUSE OF THE DELAY OR FAILURE TO DELIVER LIST AS SET FORTH.

BREACH: IN THE EVENT OF BREACH OF THIS CONTRACT, PARTICULARLY A BREACH OF THE PROVISIONS THAT DEAL WITH THE INTEGRITY OF THIS LIST, COMPANY IS EXPRESSLY GIVEN THE RIGHT TO OBTAIN AN INJUNCTION AGAINST THE ABUSED ACTIVITIES, AS WELL AS BUT NOT LIMITED TO ENFORCE THE AGREEMENT AND COLLECT FULL LIST RENTAL FOR EACH BREACHED PART, COLLECT FULL LIST RENTAL FOR ALL LIST OR SECTION THEREOF USED, AND FOR EACH INJURY. IN ADDITION, COMPANY IS ENTITLED TO RECOVER AND COLLECT IN ADDITION BUT NOT LIMITED TO DAMAGES AND THE ABOVE, LEGAL FEES AND EXPENSES INVOLVED IN TRAVEL, FOOD, ACCOMMODATIONS, LODGING, IF PURSUIT IS OUTSIDE COMPANY'S LOCAL JURISDICTION OR STATE, AS WELL AS LEGAL, ATTORNEYS, AND COURT FEES AND EXPENSES.

IT IS THE EXPRESS INTEREST IN THIS CONTRACT THAT COMPANY WILL NOT HAVE TO EMPLOY ANY OF THIS ABOVE, AND THAT THIS USE OF THIS LIST WILL BE OF VALUE, AND PROFITABLE FOR USER. THE SEVERITY OF THIS CONTRACT IS WRITTEN WITH THE SOLE INTENT TO PREVENT THE ABUSE OF THIS LIST IN AN ACTIVITY OTHER THAN ITS ORIGINAL SALE AGREEMENT. IT IS OUR DESIRE TO BE A VALUED VENDOR TO USER ON A LONG TERM BASIS.

Accepted by_____

Print Name_____ Company_____

Position_____ Date_____

The Danielle Adams Publishing Company
Box 100, Merion Station PA 19066

My Very Own List Rental Agreement

I wrote this list rental agreement to protect our own mailing list. I actually drafted this whole contract for the small part of the contract that has the most meaning: when signed, buyers agree to pay for court costs and attorney fees if they abuse the list by mailing to it more than once. All the rest is actually interference so the contract is longer and this clause won't stick out like a sore thumb. Without this provision in the contract, if a company mails to your list more than once (which is outside of its contract, as a list is always rented for a one time use), and you take the company to court and win, you merely win the money they should have paid you in the first place, the cost of renting the list. So a deceptive mailer who buys your list with that intent has little incentive to abide by your contract. With this clause in your contract, they will have to pay for your attorney and court costs—which may be substantial—and thus it's a better deterrent to keep them from abusing your list in the first place. Of course, no sheet of paper stops a crook. And just to be safe, check with your attorney first: I'm a writer, not a lawyer. Then, feel free to use this contract.*

By the way, I didn't necessarily want anyone to read it, I just wanted them to sign it. So I designed it so no one would read it: Helvetica, intercharacter spacing set tight, all caps, with the leading set solid 8/8. To the best of my knowledge, no one ever has read it when presented in this final contract form, because of its difficult-to-read style. Go on - see if you can read it. I'll wait...

If you ever need a document like this to protect the sale of your own list, go ahead and use it. Tell the person using your list it's a standard agreement that you got it out of a book. You did, didn't you? Hope it's helpful. And I hope you are enjoying my book and finding it of great value. This contract is also available as a download in an electronic format for $24.95 - so you can modify it without retyping it. *This is copyrighted material. You must be the original purchaser of this book to use this contract, or have paid for the download. Thanks. This supports our micro publishing house. PS: I charge this amount because I have to dig this contract out through all the crap in my computer, get your email address, put your charge through manually, and then send. It's not automatic and it takes me at least 20 minutes. If I had to charge ten bucks or fifteen bucks it's not worth it to me. So at $25, you buy me dinner if you need this contract. Fair enough? Thanks.

Magazine and Media Directories

Bacon's Media Directories   *Directories*
332 South Michigan Avenue
Chicago, IL 60604   Visa/MC, AMEX
Phone: 800/621-0561; 312/922-2400 • Fax:: 312/922-3126
www.bacons.com
Since I've written about Bacon's directories extensively throughout this book, I'll just list the many directories they publish. All of Bacon's media directories are extremely great products, and I recommend them without hesitation. We use most of their printed directories in our own office for our own and our clients' marketing campaigns. Printed Directories:
Bacon's Newspaper Directory and Bacon's Magazine Directory
     (2 volumes) - $450
Bacon's Radio/TV/Cable Directory (broadcast media; 2 volumes) - $450
Internet Media Directory - $450 (Online news content websites)

Online: MediaSource Research Module -   **Online**
Online database access to all directory data - $2,695, North America

The following two printed directories include all Newspapers, Magazines, TV, Radio, and Internet Data from these states:
Bacon's New York Publicity Outlets Directory $400
Bacon's California Media Directory $400
These are are two top-notch marketing reference tools—probably the most comprehensive books for the specific areas they serve. Both publications are strategic for marketing and PR campaigns in the electronic and news media. They offer the most telephone numbers for specific individuals of any resource, anywhere. If you're good on the phone or market in New York or California, these are a must.

Bacon's Media Distribution Services   **Press Release Distribution**
www.bacons.com
The folks at Bacon's will help you in selecting your target publications and then will make copies of your release and photo, stuff into your envelops, and distribute your release for you. See the extensive write-up of Bacon's press release distribution service in the Marketing chapter. Exceptionally strong in magazines, but also great for newspaper press releases. Reasonably priced and recommended.

The Danielle Adams Publishing Company
Box 100, Merion Station PA 19066

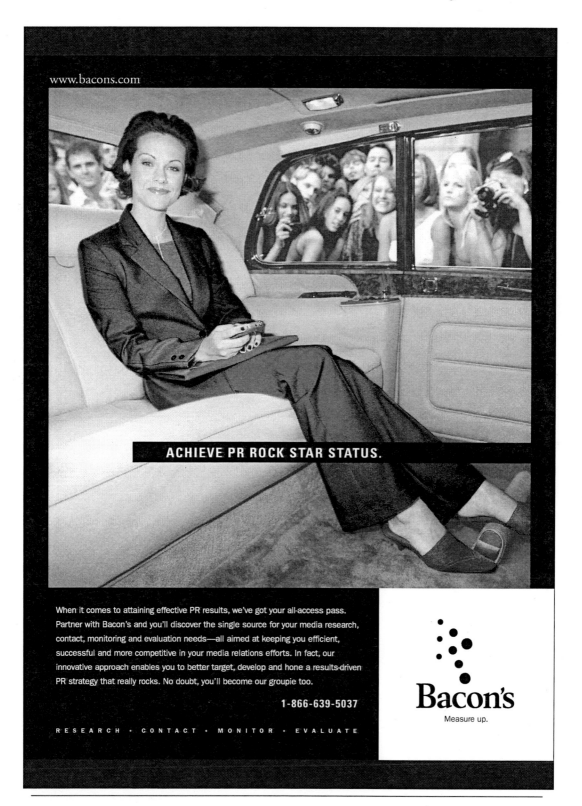

www.bacons.com

ACHIEVE PR ROCK STAR STATUS.

When it comes to attaining effective PR results, we've got your all-access pass. Partner with Bacon's and you'll discover the single source for your media research, contact, monitoring and evaluation needs—all aimed at keeping you efficient, successful and more competitive in your media relations efforts. In fact, our innovative approach enables you to better target, develop and hone a results-driven PR strategy that really rocks. No doubt, you'll become our groupie too.

1-866-639-5037

Bacon's
Measure up.

RESEARCH • CONTACT • MONITOR • EVALUATE

Oxbridge Communications

Directories & Online

186 Fifth Avenue, 6th floor.
New York, NY 10010
Phone: 800/955-0231; 212/741-0231 • Fax 212/633-2938
www.mediafinder.com & www.Oxbridge.com

Oxbridge Communications' *Standard Periodical Directory* - $1595. CD-ROM, $1,995 (both print and CD, $2995) One of the largest—if not <u>the</u> largest—reference directories published. I don't know of any finer reference of magazines and newsletters. If you can only get one reference tool, this is the one. Hardcover; more than 2,000 pages. Circulation, advertising, and list rental data for more than 75,000 periodicals. This is the combination of Oxbridge's magazine and newsletter listing directories. It is the ultimate resource in the industry.

Oxbridge Communications' *Directory of Newsletters* - $745. CD-ROM, $795; both printed directory and CD-ROM, $1,120. Most marketers miss the boat by not purchasing ads or sending news releases to newsletter publishers. One of the most valuable marketing tools around, this directory—with over 20,000 entries—is the most comprehensive directory of newsletters ever. Incredible and recommended.

Oxbridge Communications' *National Directory of Magazines* - $695. CD-ROM, $795; both, $1,120. Same great directory depth, but just magazines—over 22,000 of them. We use this in our own office and it's awesome! One of the most valuable reference tools for marketers and PR agents.

Oxbridge Communications' *National Directory of Catalogs* - $795. The most exhaustive directory of catalogs in the U.S. Over 11,000 catalogs, over 1,250 pages. On CD-ROM, $1095. Contains product lines, personnel, frequency, circulation, press run, signature size, page count, target audience, list availability. Ever wish your product was in a few great catalogs? Want to find out what's out there? Need to see competitors' products? Whew - this is a product marketer's dream.

Directory of Magazine & Newsletter Mailing Lists - CD-ROM, $1095. Lists and list rental information for all magazines, newsletters and catalogs in the huge Oxbridge Communications database.

The Danielle Adams Publishing Company
Box 100, Merion Station PA 19066

Standard Periodical Directory (2006 Edition) *New Edition Every January*

- ☐ **$1,595 Print Version**
- ☐ **$1,995 Single User CD-ROM**
- ☐ **$2,995 Print & CD-ROM**

Vital circulation, advertising, production, and list rental data for more than 56,000 North American Periodicals. Includes magazines, newsletters, newspapers, journals, and directories.

National Directory of Magazines (2006 Edition) *New Edition Every September*

- ☐ **$995 Print Version**
- ☐ **$1,195 Single User CD-ROM (Jan. 2006)**
- ☐ **$1,995 Print & CD-ROM (Jan. 2006)**

Provides information for over 18,000 U.S. and Canadian publications, including magazines, journals, and tabloids. Contains staff, advertising rates, circulation, mailing list information, and production details.

Oxbridge Directory of Newsletters (2006 Edition) *New Edition Every June*

- ☐ **$995 Print Version**
- ☐ **$1,195 Single User CD-ROM (Jan. 2006)**
- ☐ **$1,995 Print & CD-ROM (Jan. 2006)**

Includes over 13,000 newsletters, loose-leaf publications, bulletins, and fax letters making this the largest source of information on this growing, influential medium.

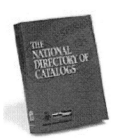

National Directory of Catalogs (2006 Edition) *New Edition Every April*

- ☐ **$795 Print Version**
- ☐ **$1,095 Single User CD-ROM (Jan. 2006)**
- ☐ **$1,695 Print & CD-ROM (Jan. 2006)**

More than 11,000 North American catalogs. Listing includes the catalog name, address, phone number, products carried, personnel, list rental data for direct marketers, and production information for vendors.

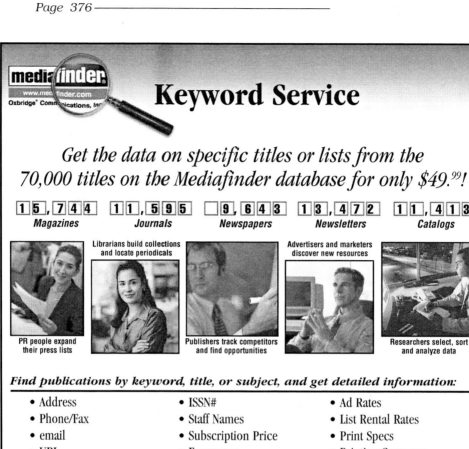

Keyword Service

Get the data on specific titles or lists from the 70,000 titles on the Mediafinder database for only $49.⁹⁹!

1 5 , 7 4 4	1 1 , 5 9 5	9 , 6 4 3	1 3 , 4 7 2	1 1 , 4 1 3
Magazines	*Journals*	*Newspapers*	*Newsletters*	*Catalogs*

Librarians build collections and locate periodicals

Advertisers and marketers discover new resources

PR people expand their press lists

Publishers track competitors and find opportunities

Researchers select, sort and analyze data

Find publications by keyword, title, or subject, and get detailed information:

- Address
- Phone/Fax
- email
- URL
- Editorial Description

- ISSN#
- Staff Names
- Subscription Price
- Frequency
- Circulation

- Ad Rates
- List Rental Rates
- Print Specs
- Printing Company
- List Management Company

Queries:

1. Enter keyword(s) and get count of titles, publication type, and editorial description. Click on the first title to see the information you get . . . .   [Gardening] [GO]

2. Key in a title and see if we have it . . . .   [Lawn & Garden] [GO]

3. Get list of titles for any of our 263 categories . . . .   [Select A Category]
   Furniture
   Gambling
   Games & Toys
   Garden & Horticulture

Keyword Service:

1 Month $49.99
1 Year $495.00

Oxbridge® Communications, Inc.

(212)741-0231 • *Toll-Free:* 800-955-0231 • *E-mail us:* custserv@mediafinderweb.com

Visit:

www.mediafinder.com

Oxbridge Communications   *Online*
MediaFinder® — Instant Online Access to the 70,000 titles.

Gain immediate access to the largest database of U.S and Canadian periodicals and catalogs available anywhere in the world. By subscribing to the MediaFinder, You get full use of this entire database. Information is always fresh and current up to the second, as it's updated daily.

Online access to all the Oxbridge Media Databases and Directories: $795 for 6 months, and $1295 full year for a full subscription that can be searched, sorted, and downloaded. Includes all publications—both magazines and newsletters, and includes the National Directory of Catalogs in an easy to use, intuitive Internet interface.

Now available on CD: The North American data base of all Oxbridge Publications, $2295. If you need the deepest marketing campaign you can possibly get, these exhaustive works from Oxbridge are the best tools in the industry. They are the most comprehensive, and the ultimate resource in marketing. Oxbridge Communications are world-class in all their directories, and they get my highest recommendations.

NEW - from Oxbridge Communications
Access all their data for only $50/Month!

You can now subscribe to MediaFinder® Keyword Search service that gives contact information, ad and list rental information, circulation, staff names, and a description of content for all fo the 70,000 titles in Media Finder. The information can be searched by keyword or subject category, and can be printed out, just not downloaded. This is a real bargain and the lowest cost in the industry for access to such a huge amount of data. It's a great service for compiling your own mailing list for press releases or your own list of publications to advertise in (including many newsletters that now take advertising and are often economical to advertise in.) You can also compile a list of publications that rent their lists in your specialty field or find catalogs that will sell your merchandise or rent their own customer lists. All for only $50. Well, actually $49.99. Call Oxbridge Communications for additional information. This is an incredible value.

SRDS   *Directories*

1700 Higgins Road · Des Plaines, IL 60018
Phone: 800/851-SRDS (7737); 847/375-5000 • Fax 847/375-5001
www.SRDS.com

***Business Publication Advertising Source*™** One year, 4 issues, $821. This price includes online access. Contains over 9,700 domestic and international business publications broken into more than 186 market classifications. One of the major magazine directories. To test out their online service, you can get a trial of 90-day online access for $399.

***Consumer Magazine Advertising Source*™** One year, 4 issues, $805. Includes online access. Detailed descriptions of over 3,200 domestic consumer magazines arranged into 75 market classifications. Over 300 farm publications. 90-Day online access (only): $398.

***Newspaper Advertising Source*™** One year, 4 issues, $809. Comprehensive information listing over 3,200 newspapers organized by city and state. Subscription includes online access. 90-Day online access: $399.

***TV & Cable Source*™** One year, 4 issues, $596. Over 4,700 listings of commercial stations, broadcast networks, cable systems, cable networks, syndicators, and sales rep firms. Includes programming, personnel, format, and positioning statement. 90-Day online access: $284.

***Radio Advertising Source*™** One year, 4 issues, $607. Resource contains detailed listings of over 10,000 stations. Information includes format, audience profile, personnel, special and syndicator programming—over 1,300 pages. Subscription includes online access. 90-Day online access: $284.

***Interactive Advertising Source*™** One year, 2 issues, $644. Explore the advertising possibilities on the Internet, online services, and Web sites. Learn about interactive kiosks and displays, banner ads and their costs, and more. 90-Day online access: $310

***Direct Marketing List Source*™** One year, 3 issues, $646. Includes online access. Over 50,000 lists in 212 market classifications. Over 600 package-insert programs. This comprehensive book of lists is a standard in the industry. 90-Day online access: $310.

***Out-of-Home Advertising Source*™** Annual, $380. An introduction to going beyond traditional media such as magazines and newspapers (that are delivered to your home). Over 2,000 out-of-home marketing vehicles such as aerials/inflatables, bus bench, outdoor, taxi, transit, airport, hotel, movie theater, sports events, shopping malls, in-flight, in-store, event, and mobile advertising, to name but a few of the 19 media categories. Includes on-line access.

The Danielle Adams Publishing Company
Box 100, Merion Station PA 19066

The National PR Pitch Book
Infocom Group
5900 Hollis Street, Suite R2, Emeryville, CA 94608-2008
Phone: 800/959-1059 • Fax 510/596-9331
www.infocomgroup.com
Business & Consumer Edition - $550
With 10 tabbed sections like "Wire Services," "Media Organization Index," "Regional TV," "Personnel Index," and "Syndicated Columnists," you almost forget there are more traditional marketing sections on magazines, national TV and cable shows, and radio and newspapers. But the real beauty of this 800-plus-page book is that most of the 24,000 top journalists covering business and consumer topics were interviewed on how they like to be pitched, and on what topics—included in each listing are the editors' own recommendations for your best approach to reach them favorably, along with their personal interests in editorial coverage.

Many write-ups tell the best time of day to call, what to send, and their editorial mission. This book excels at supplying the contact dossiers and assignment beats of individual editors, writers, and producers; it also gives their direct-dial phone numbers, fax numbers, and email addresses. Prices for the *National PR Pitch Book* series are: *The Business & Consumer Edition*, $550; *Issues, Policy & Politics*, $550; *Computers & Technology*, $500; *Health, Fitness & Medicine*, $500; *Food, Hospitality & Travel*, $500; and *Investment Banking & Financial Services*, $500. Nice insider stuff.

Also available from Infocom: *The Insider's Guide to Pitching* The Wall Street Journal ($99), *Power Packed Press Releases* ($40), *30 Insider's Techniques for Scoring Media Coverage* ($29), and the *Bulldog Reporter* PR newsletter ($649) and at press time two editions were available.

All-in-One Directory   **Directory**
Gebbie Press
P.O. Box 1000, New Paltz, NY 12561 $155.00
www.gebbiepress.com
PR Pro - on CD, $565: Emails, runs reports and creates mailing lables.
Raw Data File (for import into your own database) $415.00
Phone: 845/255-7560 • Fax 845/256-1239
Published in a single 6" x 9", spiral-bound, 550-page directory. Over 24,000 entries encompassing daily and weekly newspapers, broadcast radio stations,broadcast television stations, and leading magazines in over 100 editorial catagories. A handy reference directory that's easy to use and less costly than some of the bigger directories. We use this in our office, too.

___YES! I'D LIKE TO ORDER THE FOLLOWING PRODUCTS FROM JEFFREY DOBKIN

"SUCCESSFUL LOW COST DIRECT MARKETING METHODS" *JUST $24.95*

"DIRECT MARKETING STRATEGIES"

"DIRECT MARKETING STRATEGIES" JUST $14.95 Dobkin's articles have been published in over 200 magazines. This book is a collection of Jeffrey's best on marketing and direct marketing - plus a few funny pieces just to keep you smiling. Over 200 pages of enjoyable reading in a fast-paced, jump-in-anywhere style.

"THE INTELLIGENT TESTING SYSTEM"

For using classified ads and direct mail. How to buy classifieds at huge discounts for entire states with a single phone call. Ten audio cassettes specifically written and narrated by Jeffrey Dobkin for this program, plus 2 huge binders with over 50 of Dobkin's articles and a complete reference section. ©2002. $299.95

AUDIO PRESENTATIONS, JEFFREY DOBKIN   *JUST $24.95*

60 Minute Audio of one of Jeff's Presentations on CD. **FAST PACED AND FUN.**
Audio #2 Jeff Dobkin interviewed by Markus Allen on Mailing lists.
Audio #3 Radio Interview, highlighting the article Ten Ways to Thank Customers. (This Audio is just $9.95.)

VIDEO PRESENTATIONS, JEFFREY DOBKIN   *JUST $34.95*

60 Minute Video of one of Jeff's Presentations on VHS Tape. Boy, if you thought his audio presentations were bad, wait till you see this. Homemade, awful lighting, Jeff looks discheveled, but oh well... the information is there!
Also available: Inventor's Presentation on 2 DVDs - Home brewed & more of the same. *Just $34.95*

THE PEN CAMPAIGN - LETTER SERIES

Get all 14 Letters of this amazing Campaign Just $49.95
Send a pen to your best prospects each month to stay in their mind all year long.

Check, List or Circle items, Send Check, Money Order, or charge to Visa/MC, or AMEX.
Pleased add just $4 Shipping for any size order. See more products at www.dobkin.com

PRINT Name_____

Address_____

City, St_____Zip_____
UPS needs a STREET address

Telephone_____Signature_____
_____Please keep me on your mailing list!

Charge/Credit Card Number_____Expires_____

Thank you for your order! For additional orders, photocopy this form or just use a sheet of paper.

RUSH ORDER FORM

Quantity	Product	Price Each	Total
		Shipping Just $4	
		Total	

PUBLISHED BY -
~ THE DANIELLE ADAMS PUBLISHING CO. ~
BOX 100 ☆ MERION STATION, PA 19066
FAX 610/642-6832 ☆ VOICE 610/642-1000

©2007

"A FUN FLIP-BOOK OF CHANGABLE SIGNS FOR CAR, HOME AND OFFICE"

NEW —

"VITAL SIGNS"
~ Over 100 Priceless Sayings ~
Ready to Hang 'Most Anywhere: Car · Office · Home
Printed One Per Page - Ready to Display!

For Information or to order Ca[
866-AWESOME
(866-293-7663)

~ Pop-Out Easel ~
Stands book on desk or counter!
Display any sign - at any time!
Included FREE! Built right into each book!

Hang in Car Window!
Spiral Bound w/Hanger
Suction cup included, too!

Vital Signs - *a bumper-sticker flip book of over 100 funny signs!*
A FUN BOOK OF SIGNS YOU CAN DISPLAY ON A DESK, OR HANG 'MOST ANYWHERE

I didn't say it way your fault, I said I was going to blame you · I married Mr. Right, Mr. Always Right · Next time, wave ALL your fingers at me · Ring Bell and run, the dog needs the exercise · Keep honking while I reload · Don't worry, I forgot your name, too! · I was just looking for your name tag, really... · Squirrels, nature's little speed bumps... plus 92 more! Just $12.95

PUBLISHED BY -
~ THE DANIELLE ADAMS PUBLISHING CO. ~
BOX 100 ☆ MERION STATION, PA 19066
FAX 610/642-6832 ☆ VOICE 610/642-1000
©2007

BOOKS
THEY'RE EVERYTHING
YOU'VE EVER IMAGINED...
AND MORE!

DANIELLE ADAMS
PUBLISHING COMPANY

Men have feelings, too.
Just kidding!

**If you don't like
the way I'm driving,**
YOU come get these handcuffs off!

~ Squirrels ~
Nature's little speed bumps

**Honk if you love
peace and quiet.**

Let me show you how
the guards used to do it...

**Hell yes I'm drunk!
What do you think I am,
a stunt driver?**

I didn't say it was **your fault...**
I said I was going to blame you.

The trouble with life is...
there's no background music.

Suction Cup Included
Book hangs in car
window!

If life was fair...
Elvis would be alive, and all
the impersonators would be dead.

**Helen Waite is now in charge of all
RUSH ORDERS.
If you are in a hurry, please go to
Helen Waite.**

~ New Flip Book ~
Wire Binding w/ Hanger- Displays
ANY Page, Any Sign, Anytime!

**Keep Honking
While I Reload...**

Real men
don't read instructions.

~ New: Pop-Out Easel ~
Stands book on desk or counter
Display any sign - at any time!
Included FREE with each book!

Of course I don't look busy...
I did it right the first time!

**Would you like to Speak
with the Man in Charge...**
Or the woman who knows what's going on.

The Danielle Adams Publishing Company
Box 100, Merion Station PA 19066

The Danielle Adams Publishing Company
Box 100, Merion Station PA 19066